KADDISH
FOR KOVNO

LIFE AND DEATH IN A
LITHUANIAN GHETTO
1941–1945

William W. Mishell

Chicago Review Press

Library of Congress Cataloging-in-Publication Data

Mishell, William W., 1918–1994
    Kaddish for Kovno.
      1. Jews—Lithuania—Kaunas—Persecutions.
2. Holocaust, Jewish (1939–1945)—Lithuania—Kaunas—
Personal narratives.   3. Mishell, William W., 1918–1994.
4. Kaunas (Lithuania)—Ethnic relations.   5. Dachau
(Germany : Concentration camp)   I. Title.
DS135.K93K286   1998   947'.5   88-2587
ISBN 1-55652-340-8

Published by Chicago Review Press, Incorporated
814 North Franklin Street
Chicago, Illinois 60610
ISBN 1-55652-340-8
5 4 3 2 1

Printed in the United States of America

Photos 4–18 are reprinted with the kind permission of the Association of
Lithuanian Jews in Israel.

To my dear wife,
the mother of our children
and herself a survivor of ghetto Siauliai
and concentration camp Stutthof

CONTENTS

BOOK THREE: DACHAU

BOOK FOUR: THE BALANCE SHEET

THE SUMMONS

Since the end of World War II, I was constantly haunted by the urge to sit down and write a book depicting the most horrible events in the history of Lithuania and, indeed, in the annals of the world: the persecution and extermination of the Jews by the Nazis and their willing, world-wide collaborators. This conspiracy against humanity, decency, and morality had thrown men into the deepest abyss of degradation. The question which festered in the back of my mind and which demanded an answer was: why did I survive when six million of my people did not? Didn't this place a heavy moral responsibility on my shoulders to do something about their deaths? Didn't this demand of me, at the very least, to put the events on paper for my own family and possibly for generations to come? It did, yet it was way beyond my physical and emotional strength to sit down and relive that horror all over again. Consequently, I delayed this decision for years, only to have my conscience pressure and harass me even harder. For years, I spent many sleepless nights thinking about my responsibility. It always came back to me: six million did not live to tell their tale, and it was my duty to relate their torment, their pain, their suffering to an indifferent, callous, impassive world which permitted these events to occur and to go unpunished.

So how did I finally get over my inhibitions and self-restraint? How was it that I finally decided to sit down and write?

Many events in the last years have broken the ice, the most important of which was the resurgence of anti-Semitism, portending the possibility of a new, even bloodier holocaust which ultimately might consume the entire world. In addition, pseudo-scientific literature had surfaced, claiming that there was never a holocaust. In the face of the most devastating, detailed documentation in film, photos, official documents, speeches, exhumed bodies, exposed mass graves, people have the audacity to deny all the events that the Germans themselves, with their natural, painstaking love for detail and accuracy, have unashamedly recorded. But worse yet,

millions of people support these theories and allegations knowing full
well that they are lies. In many cases, this literature is justified on the basis
of freedom of speech. But both the writers and their supporters know the
truth. They simply choose to hide behind locked doors lest the world
discover the skeletons inside. And there indeed are skeletons of millions
of people massacred, shot, gassed, tortured to death with insane medical
experiments, and starved through inhuman slave labor in concentration
camps.

Unfortunately, however, these pseudo-scientists are not alone. Many
history books ignore these brutal events and don't mention them at all, as
if they did not happen. I have checked countless history books and have
found in some of them the most irrelevant events of the Nazi era described in great detail, but not one single word about the most ghastly
persecution of the Jewish people in history. Not one word about gas vans,
gas chambers, crematoria, and hundreds of concentration camps which
mushroomed all over Europe. It is as if this were just a figment of the
imagination. This attempt to ignore the horrors of the biggest crime in
history, Nazism, is more than unforgiveable. It is criminal, since ignoring
the crime does not make it go away, it only perpetuates it.

Stirred by this literature, I decided to record an eyewitness account for
posterity. I tried to portray the events in the book as I recall them to the
best of my ability. Where my memory was sketchy, I researched books
and checked with survivors. I tried to give as accurate a picture as
possible. My goal was to show the Christian world a picture of itself in
the hope that these memoirs will, if not eliminate, at least to some extent
mitigate anti-Semitism as we know it today.

Finally, if this publication with all its horror will open the eyes of at
least a few people, my survival and my efforts, as well as my agony while
writing this book, will not have been in vain.

If international-finance Jewry . . . would succeed once more in plunging nations into a world war, the consequences will be . . . the annihilation of the Jewish race in Europe.

—Adolf Hitler

Anyone who gets rid of the Jew, regenerates and moves towards an era of bloom, greatness and beauty. . . . Anyone who fights, destroys and radically gets rid of him lives on and will never die.

—Dr. Robert Ley, Cologne Party Boss

It took from three to fifteen minutes to kill the people in the death chamber. . . . We knew when the people were dead because their screaming stopped.

—Rudolf Hoess, Camp Commandant of Auschwitz

A thousand years will pass and the guilt of Germany will not be erased.

—Hans Frank, Governor General of Poland

The things I saw beggar description. . . . The visual evidence and the verbal testimony of starvation, cruelty, and bestiality were so overpowering as to leave me a bit sick. In one room, where there were piled up twenty or thirty naked men, killed by starvation, George Patton would not even enter. He said he would get sick if he did so. I made the visit deliberately, in order to be in a position to give first-hand evidence of these things if ever, in the future, there develops a tendency to charge these allegations merely to "propaganda."

—General Dwight D. Eisenhower

The smell of death overwhelmed us even before we passed through the stockade. More than 3200 naked, emaciated bodies had been flung into shallow graves. Others lay in the streets where they had fallen. . . . Eisenhower's face whitened into a mask. Patton walked over to a corner and sickened. I was too revolted to speak. For here death had been so fouled by degradation that it both stunned and numbed us. . . .

—Omar N. Bradley, *A Soldier's Story*

BOOK ONE

THIS TALE MUST BE TOLD

We do not know whether any one of us will survive this Gehenna, but if only one of us should make it, this tale must be told, and despite the enormous strain talking about it, I will tell you all. Brace yourselves, you may need tranquilizers too.

—Mr. Joffe, attorney at law

A Note to the Reader

The word *Action* must be explained from the very beginning, since it will be repeated throughout the text many times.

In the process of exterminating the Jews of Europe, the Germans and their collaborators carried out mass shootings, deportations, confiscation of property, and rounding up of Jews who were scattered over wide areas into one central gathering place, called the ghetto. These Jews were later executed. All these operations, carefully planned in advance and carried out with typical German thoroughness, were referred to by one word, *Action* (*Aktion* in German). Thus the ghetto went through numerous Actions, specifically designated as the Big Action, the Small Ghetto Action, the Children's Action, and so on. Most of these Actions ended in the destruction and annihilation of thousands of Jews by the most barbaric methods imaginable.

As to names, *Mishell* is the Americanized Mishelski, the author's original name. *Kovno, Vilna,* and *Ponar* are Jewish vernacular names for the Lithuanian towns of Kaunas, Vilnius, and Paneriai.

1

THE BETTER DAYS

My childhood in Lithuania was a happy and rather sheltered one. My earliest recollections were of trips I took with my mother to Germany and Latvia. My parents, being well-off and educated, did not spare their children anything. At first we had a Russian-speaking nanny, from whom I learned to speak fluent Russian. Later on, my parents imported a German governess from East Prussia, who was a typical "Prussian general." From her I learned to speak fluent German and a sense of duty and responsibility. I was dressed immaculately, behaved correctly, almost too precisely for a young child. She also taught me to play the piano. Thus, by the time I was ready for school, I already spoke fluent Russian and German and played the piano fairly nicely.

My parents at first wanted me to go to the German gymnasium in Kovno, which was fashionable at that time. My grandmother fiercely objected to it. After the first anti-Semitic incident at school, I was promptly transferred to a private Hebrew gymnasium, where all the children and teachers were Jewish.

My mother was a real lady, very pretty and always dressed in the latest styles. At a very early age, I was taken to concerts and to the Lithuanian National Opera and Ballet. My father was a gifted businessman and the apartment building we lived in belonged to him. He also was a big sports fan and on weekends he would take me to the soccer game. In the evening, my father spent time with me discussing the events of the day. We delved into politics, current events, and we even talked about the early history of the Jews in Lithuania.

It was from him that I first learned that Jews had lived in Lithuania as far back as the twelfth century. Historians had traced down a small Jewish community in Grodno (Gardinas) in the year 1128 and in Kovno, our hometown, as far back as 1280. From 1316 to 1341 Lithuania was ruled by the grand duke Gediminas, who was very tolerant of religious and national minorities. He greatly increased the territory of Lithuania and converted it into a major power. His sons Algirdas and Kestutis conquered even more land, all the way to the Black Sea. The Lithuanians were still pagans and were the last in Europe to be converted to Christianity. Being pagans they did not care about the Jewish religion and there was no religious anti-Semitism in the country. While in Europe, entire Jewish communities perished during the Crusades and later during the Bubonic Plague, the Jews in Lithuania were spared. After Algirdas and Kestutis, the next was the grand duke Vytautas the Great. He ruled from 1386 to 1430 and his rule was considered the high point of Lithuanian power. He was even more tolerant than his grandfather and gave the Jews many privileges.

In the meantime Lithuania converted to Christianity and became Catholic. The attitude towards the Jews, however, remained under the influence of the spirit of Vytautas the Great. But as the power of the church in Lithuania grew, the position of the Jews got weaker and in 1495 Lithuania expelled its Jews. Eight years later, in 1503, though, the rulers of Lithuania realized that they had done more harm to Lithuania than to the Jews and they invited them back. Later, during the pogroms in Russia in the years 1648–1649, the Jews in Lithuania did not suffer; it remained a peaceful island in a hostile Europe. Unfortunately, however, eventually Russia occupied Lithuania and converted it into a Russian province. Not only did the situation of the Jews become much worse, but the Lithuanians themselves were now oppressed by the Russians.

But much more fascinating than the early history of the Jews in Lithuania were my father's stories about World War One and the early years of Lithuanian independence. When the war started, the Czarist government decided that the Jews were pro-German and therefore not reliable. In 1915 a decree was issued that the Jews of Lithuania had to be evacuated deep into the Ukraine. This was a terrible edict. The Jews lost everything and could take along only the bare necessities. When the revolution came in 1917 and the Czarist government fell, the situation of the Jews became even worse. They were caught between the warring factions of the Bolsheviks and the White Guard. The goal of every Jew was to return home. With Russia out of the war, the Jews grabbed the very first opportunity, dropped everything and returned to Lithuania. Large numbers of Jewish youths organized and joined the Lithuanian volunteers in their fight for independence. In September and later, December of 1917, the Lithuanian leadership met in Vilna and set up a national council, the so-called Taryba, which declared the independence of Lithuania on 16 February 1918. The Lithuanians, being inexperienced in international relations, invited the Jews to join the Taryba. The Jews were offered full autonomy and a golden era began for the Lithuanian Jews. The Jewish members of the Taryba accepted assignments to the peace conference in Versailles and the peace negotiations with Moscow. Through the international connections of the Jews, they helped the Lithuanian delegation to make valuable contacts. Through their efforts, Vilna was assigned to Lithuania and not to Poland, which also had a claim to it. A rather significant role was also played by the American Jews of Lithuanian origin in the de jure recognition of Lithuania. With the assistance of substantial sums of money from relatives in America, the Lithuanian Jews started to develop major industries in the larger cities of Lithuania. The years 1919–1922 were the best for Lithuanian Jews.

This honeymoon, however, did not last long. The Lithuanian people, who, under the Russian occupation, were deprived of many rights, had no intelligentsia to speak of when independence was proclaimed. In a short three years, however, the Lithuanian people had made substantial strides and started to exert heavy pressure on the positions the Jews had occupied. The fiercely nationalistic Lithuanian government felt obliged to help the Lithuanians. They started to give their own people privileges and put all kinds of hurdles in the paths of the Jews. Anti-Semitic incidences began to occur. Particularly painful was a night in February of 1923, when all Jewish language signs were marred with black tar.

The progressive Lithuanians were deeply hurt by this act of tyranny and Dr. J. Basanavicius, one of the most illustrious leaders for freedom of Lithuania, found it necessary to write a letter of protest. But this did not stop the reactionary government from rapidly moving in the direction of liquidating the entire Jewish autonomy structure. By 1926 all that was left of the Jewish autonomy was a wide network of Hebrew schools and a network of Jewish Folk Banks. In December 1926, a group of military officers and members of the nationalist party, under the leadership of Antanas Smetona, engineered a rebellion and wrested power from the legitimately elected government. The Jews were now vigorously expelled from all positions. The government ordered that all tradesmen must pass qualifying examinations, a method by which many Jews lost the right to pursue their trade. Another order was passed that any jurist had to have court experience before he could pass the bar. Since the courts belonged to the government, no Jew was given a chance to be admitted to the court and all the Jewish law students were suddenly deprived of a chance to become lawyers.

The situation in the school of medicine was not much different. Here, a strict numerus clausus limited the number of Jewish applicants, and even those who succeeded in entering were harassed by some anti-Semitic professors. The Jewish students at the engineering school did not have it much easier, either. There were several professors who made our lives hard. The Lithuanian merchants created an organization called Verslininkai, or Traders. This organization's goal was to push the Jews out of commerce and industry. All these developments created a lot of animosity and fed the anti-Semitic fires.

By the time I was ready to enter the university, there were almost no Jews in any branch of government. With the exception of one world-famous jurist, there was not a single professor or assistant at the university, there were no Jews in the army, police, banking, cooperatives, or Jewish teachers in the Lithuanian school network. Finally, the Verslininkai started to push the Jews out of their last foothold—the business world. The Jews were now left with petty trade, which was not attractive to the Lithuanians, with manual trades, and with factory work, if the plant was Jewish-owned.

In the university, we were isolated. Most of the professors were either openly anti-Semitic or generally unfriendly, although there were some exceptions. The student body, particularly after Hitler's ascent to power, became more hostile. We were assaulted when we spoke Yiddish on the premises among ourselves and ridiculed when we tried to speak Lithuanian, but with an accent. It was a no-win situation.

Around 1938 or 1939, elections to a student council were called. We had very little interest in the council. But when some of our friends came to the university to vote, they were beaten up and denied admission. We were outraged. Every Jewish student got on the phone and urged our colleagues to meet at one of the fraternities and to go to vote en masse. When we showed up in front of the university numbering in the hundreds, the hooligans moved aside and we entered the booths. As a result we elected a substantially larger number of representatives than had there been no anti-Semitic outburst. The pressure against the Jews and the political situation in Nazi Germany instigated many Jews to leave the country and to emigrate to wherever they were admitted.

The majority of the Jews in Lithuania lived in small towns and villages and there was virtually no assimilation. The local population was on one hand anti-Semitic towards the Jewish people as a whole, yet got along very well with the Jew with whom they had contact. The Lithuanians grew up with a heavy anti-Semitic background. The clergyman Valancius, a prominent writer, was anti-Jewish in his writings and influenced the Christian-oriented youth against the Jews; so was the national poet

Kudirka, who wrote the national anthem and whose pen was dripping with hate towards the Jews. Yet, despite the hate, the Jews remained patriotic. We were thankful for the school system Lithuania let us have and for the protection we had from the government against hooligans.

The largest community in the country was in Kovno. It was almost unbelievable, how a small Jewish community of about thirty-five thousand Jews was able to support three full-time Hebrew and one Yiddish gymnasium. This same community also supported five Jewish dailies, a folk theater, a Hebrew theatrical studio, and numerous youth organizations.

After graduation from gymnasium I entered the engineering school and joined a fraternity. Then, in 1939, Germany attacked Poland and the war was on. In the spring of 1940, I got myself a part-time job with a Jewish contractor. I was directly responsible to the chief engineer, a Lithuanian by the name of Staskevicius. From the first day, I established an excellent rapport with him. I was with the company for scarcely a month when the Russians entered Lithuania. The Russian occupation changed our lives completely. By July 1940, Lithuania was proclaimed a Soviet Republic and nationalization of all property began. First, the company for which I worked was taken over by the army corps of engineers and the Jewish owner fired. The company was now run by an army colonel and a political commissar. As his first step the political commissar started to weed out all previous "capitalists." I, as a son of a known capitalist, was immediately put on the hit list. He then called in the chief engineer to review the entire personnel. When the commissar reached my name and suggested that I be laid off, Staskevicius took a very strong stand in favor of me. It was a very courageous stand on behalf of a "capitalist." After a fairly heated discussion, he managed to persuade the commissar and I was retained on the staff. Once on the staff, the commissar got to know me closer and his attitude towards me changed. In the meantime, it became outright dangerous not to have a job. My father, who had never worked for somebody else, started to look for a job. Despite the fact that he was a former capitalist, his enormous connections were a valuable asset to any company, and he had no trouble getting a job with a major government outfit.

Dr. Max Solc, my brother-in-law, in the meantime took advantage of the fact that Jewish doctors could get jobs in government institutions and got himself a job in the military hospital. Even my sister, Vera, decided to take a job and became a secretary in a major industrial firm. The only one not working remained my mother, who was taking care of the home. We even kept our maid, Verute, which was a bourgeois luxury.

When our turn to be nationalized came, all of us were working. Under normal circumstances, the previous home owners were evicted from their houses to remove them from their former property, which now became the possession of "all the people." In most cases the previous landlords were deported to smaller outlying communities and left to rot. When the nationalizing committee came to our house, they had all the papers ordering our eviction ready. When they asked me what I was doing, they were completely dumbfounded when I told them that I was working for the headquarters of the army engineers. One of the interrogators went straight to the phone and called our office. He requested to talk to the political commissar and got him on the line. Five minutes later he apologized, packed up all the documents dealing with our expulsion, and left our home. As a result, we remained in our home, in our luxurious apartment, up to the end of the Russian occupation.

But the occupation of Lithuania by communist Russia was an extremely severe blow to most Lithuanian Jews. The Russians nationalized all private property, including our apartment building and all businesses. The Jews were totally destroyed economically. The large number of small shopkeepers lost their stores and were left without income. Almost all Jewish organizations and student fraternities were liquidated. The Jewish leadership was arrested because it was Zionist-oriented. Most synagogues were closed. The entire Hebrew school system and all the world-famous rabbinical seminaries, the pride of Lithuanian Jewry, were dissolved. The Jewish bank system was nationalized. The few rich Jews lost their businesses and many landlords were forced to leave the big cities and move to small villages. With one mighty blow by the Russian bear, all the achievements of Lithuanian Jewry in the twenty-two years of Lithuanian independence were destroyed. The mood among the majority of the Jews was one of deep depression. There was, however, one redeeming feature: with war raging in Europe, Lithuania could not remain independent for much longer. If asked, we certainly would have opted to remain in a free Lithuania, but between Russia and Germany, we as Jews had no choice: under Germany we were doomed, under Russia we were free. The Lithuanians, however, preferred the Germans.

The other important fact was that as citizens with equal rights, many jobs previously closed to the Jews suddenly opened up to them. Jews suddenly could serve in the government, teach at the universities, work in the government cooperatives and other institutions. With their economic base totally destroyed, the Jews reached out to whatever was offered to them. This contributed further to the strained relations between the two nations. And although there were relatively few Jews who got those new jobs, to the Lithuanians it looked like an invasion. In the communist party central committee, there were approximately forty to fifty Lithuanians and only two Jews. Equally, there were about twenty Lithuanian commissars and about forty assistants, but only one Jew among them. All the top positions from the president down were occupied by Lithuanians. It was true that some Jews did obtain some higher positions, but their number was small. But when one thought of the fact that there was not a single Jew before in these places, every Jew looked unreasonably conspicuous.

At my job, I progressed very nicely and my prospects for the future were extremely bright. After a specified time working there, I would be awarded the title of military engineer and a rank of lieutenant in the corps of engineers. From there, I would automatically progress to a higher rank and more prestigious work.

Dr. Solc's position was also connected with the military system and his prospects were just as bright. Vera in the meantime gave birth to Ruthie, and we could not be happier. But in 1941, when the Russians realized that there may be war between Russia and Germany, they decided to deport all the unreliable elements to deep Russia. The deportations were initiated by the Lithuanian chief of police, were later followed up by the commissar for internal affairs, and the last instructions were signed by a Russian. None of the above was a Jew! Based on Lithuanian sources 0.9% of the Lithuanian population and 1.5% of the Jewish were deported. Yet the Lithuanians saw only their own and pointed the finger at the Jews, who really suffered more than the Lithuanians.

On 15 June 1941 the deportations started. It was a terrible day. Hundreds of friends of mine were among the deportees, since all of them were either Zionists or from well-to-do families. Without wasting much time, our family went into hiding. For several nights we slept in Williampole at the house of my uncle. After several days, the deportations stopped and all the people were moved out of Lithuania in echelons towards Siberia. We returned home, but could not get over a mysterious feeling that maybe the deportees unwittingly were at the receiving end of a major lucky strike. They were being taken to the depths of Russia, away from the war and away from the border with murderous Nazi Germany, while we remained in Lithuania close to the powder keg. The mood in the country was as before an explosion. During the day and at night the Russians conducted air raid exercises. My father commented that, God knows, soon this might be real.

Saturday evening, 21 June, I went to see my best friend Nahum Shoham to discuss the political situation. If not for the deportations, things looked very bright. The war in Europe was somewhere far away, German planes were bombing Britain and Nazi troops were in North Africa, but we were spared. The evening was beautiful. It was nice and cool, the sky was full of stars and we decided to take a walk to one of the city parks. At the end of the park, there was a high masonry tower with a clock on top of it. As we were sitting and chatting, the clock struck twelve, a tune followed, inaugurating 22 June 1941. We just did not feel like going home yet. Our conversation inevitably turned to the deportations. It worried us, because these deportations had suddenly created enormous strains on the Lithuanian society and increased very perceptibly the anti-Semitic feelings. While the deportations were primarily arranged by Russians and Lithuanians, there were also some Jews in the police. There was no doubt in our mind that even if there were only one Jew in the entire police force, the Lithuanians would accuse all the Jews of it. We chatted till late at night and it must have been one in the morning when I came home.

I went promptly to bed and fell asleep. At around 3:30 in the morning, I was suddenly awakened by several bursts of a peculiar nature coming from the direction of the military airport. More bursts followed in rapid succession. The second volley awakened the rest of the family. We looked through the window towards the noise and saw smoke coming from the hill where the military airport was. The family did not seem to be worried about it, but when one more round of blasts came from the same direction and a cloud of dust rose high above the horizon, I started to shake. I remembered well that the first German targets were always the airfields and the bursts sounded frightfully like bombs.

"Dad," I said instinctively, "I am afraid these may be bombs, we may be at war."

"Nonsense," said my father, "go to bed and have a good night's sleep. You must be tired," and with these words he went back to bed.

But I was not so easily pacified. I went to the radio and switched it on. I scanned the entire scale, but found only static. I could not sleep any more. After a while I decided to go back to the radio and check again. Something was telling me that I was right. I turned on the radio again and it struck me like a bomb. The German radio was playing martial music and an announcement was made that the war was on! It was 22 June, the exact same day Napoleon had crossed the Nemunas (Niemen) in his attack on Russia.

I immediately awakened the entire household and ran to arouse the neighbors. The reaction was total panic. We all gathered in our home. After some nervous discussion, the attorney Joffe and his wife and the family Vazbutski, with two small children, decided to run for the Russian border. In our household, we were deeply divided. Max and I wanted to run, but my father was against it. He stressed that during World War One he was a refugee in Russia and had no desire to live through it again.

Besides, he stressed, Lithuania was his home, his country, and if anything was to happen, he wanted it to be on Lithuanian and not foreign soil. He surmised that the German occupation would be rough, with brutal persecution, humiliation, arrests, and beatings. Some people might even end up in concentration camps. But, after all, bad as they were, the Germans were a highly cultured people and not mass murderers.

I ran to my friend Nahum to see what they were planning to do. Their house was on a major highway and the road was already jammed with vehicles of all sorts: cars, buses, trucks, motorcycles, bicycles, horse and buggies, and people on foot. Most of the traffic was heading north, away from Germany. There were also Russian military trucks, but not too many. I rang the doorbell and waited. Nahum opened the door and let me in. They were just as confused as we. They had also considered running, but decided to stay. Nahum had a big map, which he opened as casually as he might have during the Polish and French campaigns. It had not sunk in yet, that this time we were not outside observers, but participants.

"At first we considered packing up and running," Nahum commented, "but we have absolutely no chance. The German army is motorized and if Poland and France are any guide, they will be moving at first very quickly and they will overtake everybody. Under these circumstances, we decided to stay. What do you intend to do?"

"Well, my father is categorically opposed to running. Max and Vera have a three-week-old baby and are hardly in a position to run. That leaves me alone. It is a very agonizing decision. It is difficult to run and even more difficult to stay. I guess I better be going home to see what else is new. Maybe my father has changed his mind."

When I walked out to the street, the highway was packed. The next corner was the main street of Kovno, which was unusually crowded. There were never so many people on the street as now. A casual look at the faces could tell you who was a Lithuanian and who was a Jew. The Lithuanians were in a jovial mood, laughing, joking, and greeting each other. The Jews, on the other hand, had deeply worried looks on their faces.

I went back home where Max and Vera were on the phone calling their colleagues and sampling their opinions. Most of their friends were cautious and decided to wait at least one day to see how effective a response the Red Army would provide. My father left home and went into the street to see whether he could decipher what the mood was.

When my father came home, he was quite disturbed. "We have no government," he said. "I remember when the last war started, there were dozens of orders issued the very first day—what to do, how to behave, where to report and so on. This time around there is not a single order."

"And how about the front?" I asked.

"No doubt we are retreating in haste," he said.

Meanwhile, Dvora Solc, Max's mother, came to our home and told us that her son Hayim and his wife Nehama had decided to run towards the Russian border and that they had already left. The other sons had decided to remain.

Late in the afternoon, a Lithuanian friend, Paplavski, came to our home and advised us to seriously consider running away. He knew from Lithuanian sources that once the Russians were gone, our security could not be guaranteed. This was a rather grim prediction, particularly since it came from a Lithuanian friend.

The evening was approaching and we had lost a most valuable day. At night, a lot of shooting could be heard and bombs were dropped, shaking our house. We and our tenants scurried to the basement, where we spent a sleepless night. When dawn came, we all went back to our apartments. Early in the morning, I decided to go to the office to find out what they were planning to do. As I entered the door, I immediately saw that we had committed a fatal blunder. The office had been completely evacuated. All the Russians were gone and with them almost all the Jewish personnel. The Lithuanians, however, were all there! Not a single one was missing. Not only were they all there, but the mood was one of complete exhilaration. Nobody was working, everybody was laughing and joking, and everybody looked at me as if I were a ghost from another planet. There was a hate in their eyes that I had never noticed before.

"Your buddies are gone," one quipped. "They packed up yesterday and left town and even did not leave a forwarding address. Where were you? Why didn't you come to join the fun?"

Our chief engineer, Staskevicius, called me aside and said, "You are a very fine engineer, but if I were you, I would try to escape; you are not safe here any more. I wish I could help you. You should have been here yesterday, they cleaned out all the papers. They burned everything they could not take along. Everyone who wanted to leave with them was given a place on the truck. I understand there are still trains leaving the station this morning. Try to get there, it may not be too late. I sincerely wish you luck, you may need it."

I even did not bother to say good bye to the rest of the team. They seemed to have turned their coats already, and were anxiously awaiting the entry of the Germans.

I ran out to the street in a hurry to rush home. The street was crowded with hundreds of people streaming in the direction of the railroad station. I hastened to run home to tell my family what I had just experienced in the office.

"Let us not waste time. There is still a train at the station, we may still catch it," I said, "things look very bad indeed. When Paplavski warned us yesterday, I was not concerned, but today in the office, seeing the hate in the faces of my Lithuanian colleagues, who were still sweet and friendly only yesterday, I am really scared. Come on, hurry, before it is too late, we have lost too much time already!"

My story apparently shook up everybody, including my father. Under the pressure of the rest of the family, he finally agreed to come along. We grabbed whatever we could, Vera wrapped Ruthie in a blanket, we slammed the door behind us and moved as quickly as we could in the direction of the railroad station. By now, the streets had emptied and an ominous silence permeated the air. We managed to run just about halfway to the station when we heard church bells ringing and from open windows we heard the Verdi march from *Aida* with announcements in Lithuanian that the radio station was in the hands of the Lithuanian partisans and the country was at last free from the hated bolsheviks.

We were now caught halfway between home and the station, not knowing which way to turn. A quick decision had to be made. The decision was to rush home. It was reasonable to assume that at home we would be safer than on the street, particularly if the train had already left and the partisans were in control of the city. The streets were now completely empty and the population was expecting the entry of either the Germans or the Lithuanian partisans.

We reached our home without incident. We put on the radio. The station was indeed under the control of the Lithuanian partisans, who for some reason chose to play the same march over and over again. In between they made announcements to the Lithuanian population telling them that Lithuania was free at last. After each statement the march came on. This march suddenly became to me synonymous with this fateful day in the history of the Jews in Lithuania and with the fate of my family. The chapter of the Russian occupation was closing and a new, bitter chapter was now to begin.

2

ARRESTS AND POGROM

Once back home, my mother fainted from excitement. Verute, our maid, who had remained in our home, helped mother to her bed and put water on the stove to make tea. Vera gave mother a tranquilizer and mother quickly regained her composure. We all gathered in the living room and listened to the radio. What we could not get over was the fact that while the Germans had not yet entered the city and thousands of straggling Russians were still in town, the Lithuanian partisans apparently were sufficiently armed and organized to pull off that trick. It suddenly dawned on us that all that past year, while we were trying to reshape our lives, the Lithuanians were clandestinely busy arming themselves. They, apparently, even knew the date of the invasion! It suddenly became totally incomprehensible, how we had not noticed anything. Not only were we fooled by the Lithuanians, but the entire Russian secret police had missed this organized, heavily-armed military force. This force was now not only in control of the radio station, but of most of the country's roads and villages. The rest of the day just did not want to end. The discussion was on edge and every sentence began with the words "we should have . . ."

"We should have run on Sunday."

"I should have been in my office Sunday morning to check the situation."

My father was very annoyed by all this talk. For better or worse, life would go on, he figured. In fact, the worst was until the German army entered the city, since until such a time the town belonged to hooligans.

With respect to action by Lithuanian hoodlums, we seemed to be safer than others, since our house was just one block from the presidential palace and the area was mixed. This fact suddenly assumed major importance, since if any excesses against Jews could be expected, they most likely would occur in purely Jewish areas.

The city of Kovno and the suburbs, although not by law, were in practice fairly rigidly segregated and Jewish areas were quite easily identified. Kovno with its suburbs was not a big city and its total population at the outbreak of the war was about 120,000, of which about thirty-five thousand were Jews. We never paid any particular attention to the segregated patterns of the city. In fact, many Jews liked to live in a close, Jewish society where they were better able to observe their customs and follow their traditions. We always knew that the Lithuanian population to a great extent was anti-Semitic. The only reason that our situation in Lithuania was comparatively better than in neighboring countries, was that the Lithuanian government had large sums of money in America and was eager to maintain peace and tranquility in the country. The outbreak of the war, however, removed all shackles and restraints from the population and anti-Semitic outbreaks could now be expected. How bad these outbreaks would be, where and when they would occur, was anybody's guess. We had no illusion that bad times were upon us. It was also clear that the more segregated an area was, the more subject it was to a possible pogrom.

The most segregated of all areas in the city was the suburb of Slobotke. This suburb was divided into two areas. The area right across the bridge over the Neris, was 100% Jewish. This was the home of the famous Slobotker Yeshiva, the rabbinical school, and numerous synagogues connected with the Yeshiva. Around it lived all the famous rabbis, the rabbinical students, and the Jews connected with this religious center. But, besides the religious center, it was also a cultural center with many Jewish institutions. Many Jewish leaders and writers were born here and got their deep Jewish roots in these uniquely Jewish surroundings. The people were mostly poor, but of extremely high moral values. Crime was nonexistent in Slobotke among the Jews. Divorce or intermarriage was unheard-of. It was a world in itself, immersed in tradition and study.

By contrast, the area northeast of it was 100% Lithuanian. Here the workers of the factories had their little houses, which they built with their own hands. Here were also low-rent big block buildings which were built by the Russians for the factory workers who could not afford anything better.

We were all assembled in our living room in complete disbelief. Only two days prior we were free and equal citizens in our hometown and now, suddenly, we were totally devoid of any rights, prey for any hooligan. It almost seemed ludicrous: we were suddenly more afraid of our yesterday's neighbors, people with whom we had lived for generations, than of the Germans. Now we waited for the Germans to protect us from the mob. Our only hope was that our fears would prove to be exaggerated.

We turned on the radio to hear the latest news and were astounded by what we heard. The same radio at which we listened for music and news was suddenly spewing venom against Jews. Its content was a clear incitement to a pogrom. Lies and distortions were hurled indiscriminately against the Jews over the air. If we had any remaining illusions, this radio outburst quickly confirmed our worst fears.

It was Monday night and we decided to lock ourselves up in the basement as a precaution against a pogrom. Nobody could close their eyes. Fear and alarm was written on everybody's face. We thought that the morning would never come. When the night finally did pass and nothing happened we were a little relieved.

In this frame of mind we went back upstairs. It didn't enter anybody's mind that this was the beginning of a total, complete, and uncompromising planned destruction of the entire Jewry of Europe, and with it, of Lithuania. If we had a premonition of even 1% of what was later to come, not a single Jew would have remained in all of Lithuania.

We sat down at the table, but nobody could eat. The conversation was edgy and the mood dejected and dispirited. Only my father seemed to be able to maintain his composure.

A little later in the day we turned on the radio again and there were two important announcements. One was regarding doctors. It stated that in view of the fact that there were many wounded and some doctors did not report to their clinics, all doctors were advised to wear a piece of cloth bearing a red cross on their arm and report to their respective clinics in the morning. Safe passage would be guaranteed. This was important for Max, as he would have to report to his clinic. The second announcement dealt with private property. There was a declaration that the Soviet occupation was over and all nationalized property was to revert back to its original owners. This affected my father. Before nationalization, the apartment building belonged to him and thus he, theoretically, was again its legitimate owner. But this was not the end of the announcement, more followed. Among them was a vicious anti-Semitic statement by the commander of the Lithuanian forces of the city, a well-known colonel. He reported that it had been established that Jews were shooting at German troops in areas where they had already entered Lithuania and that Kovno was imminently expecting the entry of the victorious German troops. It made clear that if Jews shoot at the Germans, one hundred Jews would be shot for every German soldier killed. This was a clear invitation to a pogrom. Obviously, if one hundred Jewish lives were that cheap, then Jews were now fair game. This announcement, issued on the sole initiative of the Lithuanian forces (the Germans had not even entered town as yet), clearly showed us that the local anti-Semites did not intend to wait for German directives regarding Jews and were ready to move on their own. This was frightening.

A little later in the day, an instruction was added to this notification which ordered all owners of buildings to lock the gates to the yard, to prevent shooting at the German army and eliminating any chance of somebody suspicious hiding in the yard. It now seemed that my father was responsible for the gate. My father listened to the announcement, got up, and headed towards the door. When five minutes passed and he had not returned, we started to wonder what was keeping him. When he was not back in fifteen minutes, we knew that something must have happened. The police station was only four blocks away and people there knew him very well. In better days he had wined and dined the head of the police on many occasions and had given gifts to the foot patrol who served our area. I decided to call the police and explain the problem. We were still naive at that point and the true situation had not yet sunk in. The policeman listened to me and promised to check. Tuesday night was spent without father, but we still hoped. Late that night, the Germans entered the city.

Wednesday morning, Max got up and started to get ready to go to his clinic. Vera was frantic and tried to persuade him not to go. After father was hauled away without a trace, we thought that staying away from the street was the only policy that made sense. Max, however, disagreed. He felt that it was his duty as a physician to respond to a call, and besides, he might be safer in the clinic than at home. The discussion with Max was heated but finally he prevailed and left the house. Nervous anxiety hung heavy in our home that day. He was due back around three o'clock. Would he return?

In the meantime, things for the Jews kept getting worse by the minute. From our window we could see that the streets were filling up with hundreds of uniformed Lithuanian soldiers and civilians with white arm-bands, bearing arms. There were very few Germans on the streets and the control seemed to be in the hands of these armed Lithuanians.

Time was moving along at a snail's pace and our thoughts were with Max and father. We decided to place a second call to the police, but this was equally nonproductive. Around three o'clock, Max finally did return, but his face was tense and he looked distressed.

"Vera," he said, "things are very bad. Jews are being rounded up and dragged out of their homes by partisans and are being badly beaten with rifle butts."

"Do you think we should consider leaving Kovno and going back to Daugai? There you were the doctor of the entire area and all the peasants knew and respected you. I don't think they would harm you and your family."

"It is hard to say. Daugai seems to have some advantages, but Kovno has thirty-five thousand Jews and they cannot arrest all of them. We have to wait and see."

Max was exhausted both physically and mentally. He had just witnessed a cruel spectacle which he would never forget.

Suddenly there was a knock on the door. A shudder went through our bones. But before we had a chance to respond, we heard the voice of our janitor from the hall. "The radio has just announced that all Jewish men have to report to the municipal building on the plaza immediately. Anybody who does not comply will be shot."

He did not wait for an answer, but hurried to tell the news to the other Jewish tenants in the house. He was laughing and whistling when he ran down the stairs.

We had barely gotten used to the shock of the news that Max just brought from the street, and now this. We put on the radio, and indeed here it was. The order was repeated in clear and simple language.

"I am not going. They will have to drag me out of here," I said.

"Let us call the police and find out," said Max.

We called the police and were told to stay home, the order had been withdrawn. We drew a breath of relief, but the bad taste was already in our mouths.

Thursday morning, Max again left for the clinic and we remained at home. I got up with a splitting headache. I checked my temperature and found that I had a high fever. I did not know whether I had contracted a cold or if it was from tension. I took a few aspirins, but they did not help. My head was pounding and swirling. I took a handkerchief, wetted it, and put it to my head. Suddenly, around ten o'clock in the morning, we heard a terrible noise outside of our house—voices yelling and screaming, the pounding of heavy boots on the sidewalk, and knocks with rifle butts on a door downstairs. We rushed to the window: our house was surrounded by Lithuanian partisans, several dozen of them, all heavily armed. Before we had a chance to catch our breath, they were at our door. They rapped on the door as if trying to knock it down. Verute rushed to the door and opened it. Six men charged into our apartment, guns drawn, and screamed, "Somebody was shooting from this window, who was it?"

We never had a gun in the house. The whole thing was just pure fabrication.

"We did not shoot," said mother, stuttering, "we don't even have a gun in the house, you can search, if you like."

"Shut up," one Lithuanian, who seemed to be the ringleader, screamed at the top of his voice, "I heard it myself. Who was it? You?" and he pointed at me.

"He did not do it, sir," said Verute, "he didn't."

"Who are you? You are Lithuanian, aren't you? What are you doing here with Jews? You have no business living together with Jews. We don't serve Jews anymore."

He turned around, punched me in the face, and with rifle pointing at my back led me out of the room. My mother fell to his feet and begged him to let me stay, but to no avail. He kicked her in the stomach and led me out. It was clear. He had accused me of shooting, an accusation they made at every Jewish house. Obviously, I was now a hostage needed to round up a hundred Jews as threatened in the radio announcement. As I walked out the door, I heard my mother say to Vera, "They are going to shoot him. I will not survive this. God, oh God, what have we done wrong, where have we sinned to deserve such a fate?"

The partisans led me out of the door onto the street and directed me towards the center of town. Other partisans in the meantime had arrested all the other men in the house.

Under constant verbal and physical abuse, I was led at gunpoint along the middle of the street and brought to the yard of the security police. A heavy iron gate opened up, I was pushed in, and the gate closed behind me.

The yard presented a terrifying view. Hundreds of Jews already there, most of them unshaven and many bloodied beyond recognition. Not having enough facilities for so many people, the yard smelled awful. The partisans were screaming and ranting and threatening to slaughter all the Jews. One young bandit in the upper teens was bragging, "We will slaughter all you Jews, you hear me. We will slaughter all of you."

I sat down somewhere, wherever I could find a place. My headache was bothering me fiercely, but that was now the least of my worries. As I looked around the yard, I saw a guard at one end with a telephone near him. I still did not realize what was happening to me and how serious it was. I still refused to believe that they would slaughter us. Without much thought, I got up and walked over to the guard and asked his permission to use the telephone. I must have been insane even to try it. But the guard was sure I was a Lithuanian, particularly since I was blond and blue-eyed and spoke perfect Lithuanian. Besides, he never would have expected a Jew to have the nerve to come up to a guard and ask for a phone. He did not think much of it and gave me the receiver. I called home immediately and asked for Verute, not my mother, since her Lithuanian was not good enough. I told Verute that I was at the headquarters of the security police and asked her to relay that to my mother. Perhaps some of our Lithuanian friends could do something for me. I thanked the guard and went straight back to the place where I had been sitting.

In the meantime, more and more Jews were brought in, many of them in terrible shape and severe pain. Meanwhile, a security officer came out and delivered a stinging attack to the group around me. As he spoke, I realized that I was sitting in a separate corner of the yard where only Lithuanians were gathered. Looking like a native, nobody had noticed me. My problem suddenly became whether to move over to the Jewish side or continue faking being Lithuanian. My head was spinning and my brain was working feverishly. I was certainly safer here. I decided to wait and see. After the verbal attack by the security officer, he started to call the Lithuanians into his office, calling each one by his name. Obviously, these were people who had been arrested on specific charges and their identities were known. Thus, my chances of getting away with my charade were nil. I decided inconspicuously to join the Jewish group. Slowly, I moved over and found myself sitting next to a Jewish man whom I did not recognize.

"Mishelski," I suddenly heard him say, "don't you recognize me?"

I was surprised to hear my name. Who was that fellow who seemed to know me?

"I am Lakin, remember me?"

I could not believe my eyes. I looked closer and, indeed, it was him, the son of a teacher of mine. Lakin was my age, but had suddenly aged ten years. His face was drawn, his eyes sunk in their sockets, his hair was grey and his hands shaking.

"Lakin, of course I know you."

"Mishelski, I don't know whether you are aware of it," he whispered, "but yesterday evening, there was a murderous pogrom in Slobotke and the entire family Mishelski, your cousins, were murdered."

He stopped, he was choking.

"Oh, no," I said with voice breaking, "how do you know?"

"Last night, a large band of partisans and some college students descended on Slobotke with rifles, guns, knives, and axes and carried out a vicious pogrom. As soon as it got dark, they rushed the area and systematically killed every Jew from Jurbarko Street all the way to our house. The screams could be heard for miles."

"God Almighty. How did you escape?" I asked.

"Well, by the time they got to our house, it was already daylight and too bright to continue their bloody work. We were all hidden in the basement, but it would not have helped, as they searched every room."

"And how did you get here?"

"Well, about an hour or so later a group of policemen came back and chased all the Jews out into the street. We were then sent to the houses of the Jews who were killed and had to remove the bodies. I removed the bodies of your family. But this is not all. They also killed Rabbi Osowski, whose body was badly mutilated. I found him near a blood-stained Bible on the floor. We took all the bodies and buried them in one mass grave at the shores of the river Neris."

"How did they let you remain alive after everything you have witnessed?"

"Indeed, they shot one group like ours after they completed their work and it seemed that they had intended to shoot us too. But after we were done, a higher officer came and told them to take us here. Apparently there is more work like this to be done here. I wish I were dead," he finished.

This was an incredible story. The area he described where the pogrom took place encompassed the major Jewish center, including the rabbinical school and the student quarters. From his description it seemed that at least one thousand or more Jews might have been massacred in this pogrom.

The pogrom in Slobotke was monstrous. It was infinitely worse than the pogrom in Kishineff, which had stirred the conscience of the entire civilized world and brought about the condemnation of the czarist regime by all decent people. This pogrom cost the Jewish people forty-five dead, eighty-six seriously and five hundred lightly wounded. It was like a Sunday school picnic compared to the pogrom in Slobotke. Yet history will never record this pogrom, since in comparison with things to come it became completely insignificant.

"Lakin, and what happened to the rabbinical students?" I asked.

"Not a single one survived. They were all killed. All the Torah scrolls were burned."

While we were talking, more and more Jews were being brought in. With every group of Jews that came in, the horror stories of incredible savagery mounted.

Meanwhile the stench in the yard became unbearable. The single toilet was clogged and human feces were floating in urine about a foot deep in the room. A young bandit got very upset over the condition in the toilet and grabbed several Jews and ordered them to clean out the toilet with their bare hands. When one Jew was not fast enough, he grabbed him and dunked him in the stool.

Late towards afternoon, a group of partisans came in and demanded Jewish volunteers for work. Among the partisans, I immediately recognized the one who had arrested me. When no volunteers were willing to step forward, he went into an anti-Semitic tirade. "You Jews are a lazy pack. You were always afraid of an honest day's work. You wanted us to do the dirty work for you. But those days are over. You all should be shot."

At that moment I had had enough. I don't know what prompted me to do it, but I got up, stepped forward, and volunteered for work. I knew what awaited me. But did it make any difference? We would not get out of this death pit alive anyway, so I might as well die with dignity. For a moment he was stunned. He stopped ranting and looked at me. He could not believe what he saw: a Jew volunteering for work under these circumstances. The Jews in the crowd looked with great apprehension at me, but nobody followed my example. When nobody else was ready to volunteer, the partisan picked the number he needed at random and sent us on to the job. The job was to dig a huge ditch and to bury dozens of mutilated bodies. All the bodies were naked and all of them were Jewish. We could not be mistaken about it: all the men were circumcized and in Lithuania only the Jews used to circumcize their male children. The women, most likely, were also Jewish, since all of them had dark hair, whereas most Lithuanian girls were blonde. There were also detached parts of bodies like hands, legs, and heads, which were still fresh. Could they also have been victims of a pogrom? We did not know. Above the excavation pit stood partisans with their guns pointed at us, threatening to shoot if we did not hustle. The work was backbreaking, but we completed it before the sun had set. We now expected the worst. But to our amazement we were told to line up and to start marching. How surprised were the other Jews in the compound, when we were led back into the yard.

When we were seated, a youngster of sixteen picked me out of the crowd. He had recognized me as the Jew who had volunteered for work.

"Hey, you there," he pointed at me, "you are an expert at volunteering, why don't you volunteer to sing me a few communist songs?"

I scrambled to my feet, although I was dead tired, and hustled towards him.

"Well, how about a song, you Jew swine."

I was now braced for a good thrashing. Apparently my volunteering was a mistake after all. In the meantime, another group of Jews was brought in and he found it more amusing to intimidate them. He let me go and I was happy to be rid of him.

That night was spent under the open sky. Fortunately, the weather was still nice. The air was a little better, since the toilet was now clean and functioning, but the poor fellow who had cleaned the toilet now was smelling terribly.

Little by little the sun started to come up and a beautiful summer morning was about to set in. It was Friday, only the sixth day of the war. In the morning, the procession of Jews chased out of their homes started over again. By now, we had no more room at all and people were piled on top of one another. They were all hungry, not shaven, unwashed, and many covered with bloodstains. Late in the morning, a group of Jews was brought in, accompanied by the same partisan who had arrested me. He chased the Jews in, walked into the yard and stopped. He looked around and suddenly spotted me. "You," he said, "get up and follow me."

My knees buckled. What did he want from me? Why did he pick me out of the entire multitude of humanity? Of course, I was the only one recognizable in the crowd: I was the one who had volunteered yesterday. This was now the second time that I was picked out of the crowd because the partisans could recognize me. How silly it seemed now, that I had acted so spontaneously yesterday. But it was done and could not be taken back. I looked at him and followed wherever he was leading me. He took me into an office where a group of partisans were gathered. One of them, apparently some chief, began an interrogation of me. After a lengthy anti-Semitic outburst he said, "You Jews are all communists. You probably were one too, weren't you?"

"No, sir," I replied, "I was never a communist. We had an apartment building which was nationalized by the communists, not exactly a friendly act."

"Oh, so that is it, you were a Jewish capitalist pig."

This was a no-win situation, I thought to myself. If I was a communist that was bad, but if I was a capitalist that was wrong again. For all it was worth, I could be the pope, but as long as I was a Jew, it was the wrong thing to be.

"No," I replied, "we were not capitalists, but hard-working people who saved enough money to buy a piece of property."

"You speak Lithuanian very well," he suddenly changed the conversation, "rather unusual for a Jew; you also volunteered for work yesterday, didn't you?"

Here we go again, I thought to myself, you damn fool! "Yes, I did," I replied.

"You Jews are parasites, you know, none of you want to work, but you seem to be different. You are free, you can go home."

I barely managed to pronounce just one word. "Thanks." I was choking.

The same partisan who arrested me yesterday led me out of the office and towards the gate. At the gate he gave an order to the sentry to let me out and he went back. I could hardly believe it. Here, I was suddenly free! But how would I get home without being rearrested? My head began to churn. Which way should I turn—towards the main street or towards the side street? On the main street there were many people, among them many partisans. I could be easily recognized. On the side streets, however, were very few people, but I would also be more conspicuous. Instinctively, I chose the main street. The street was jam-packed. There were literally thousands of people enjoying a beautiful afternoon. Everybody was happy and jovial and nobody seemed to pay attention to me. I walked leisurely, not to arouse any attention.

All the way home, I thought about that partisan. What really made him do this? He, who already had hundreds of Jewish lives on his conscience, just saved one from certain death. Did he know who I was? Did he know my father? Was he really impressed by my act of volunteering? I could not figure this one out and most likely will never know, and at that juncture it was irrelevant. I was out of the death trap.

When I approached our home, I quickly got off the main street and ducked into the house as fast as I could. I knocked on the door very gently to avoid alarming anyone and waited. There was no answer. I immediately started to worry. Could the partisans also have arrested the other members of the family? But certainly Verute should have been home. I knocked a little louder. This time Verute came to the door.

"Who is it?" she asked.

"That's me, Vulia," I answered.

The door sprang open and my mother came running hysterically towards me. I looked like a ghost to her. She just could not believe her eyes.

"You are home, you are home. I cannot believe it. I never thought I would see you alive again. You don't know what is going on in town. There was a murderous pogrom in Slobotke, almost a thousand Jews have been killed. You don't know anything. Come, I will give you something to eat, you probably have not eaten all day."

She was so excited that she could not stop talking.

"Relax, mom," I said, "I am home and well and everything will be all right. How do you know about the pogrom?"

"My sister-in-law, Hayale, called us to let us know that their house was spared. They saw the entire slaughter from their attic."

Meanwhile I had a chance to wash up and to have a bite. Little by little, I told her all I knew about the pogrom and all that I had been through. I also told her that the entire family Mishelski was wiped out. Again, the tears started to roll down her cheeks.

Max was not home yet and we were anxiously awaiting his return from the clinic. When Max arrived, we could see by his expression that he was immensely upset. He rushed to me and embraced me. "I am glad to see you home. You don't know what is going on in town!"

I thought to myself that I had just heard these words from mother when I entered the house. Vera served Max a bowl of soup and Max started to relate his tale.

"You know the Lietukis garage across from our clinic. I just saw a massacre of Jews which is beyond description. A group of Jews were brought in from the street and forced to clean the garage floor of horse manure with their bare hands. These Jews were treated very harshly. A whole group of civilians stood outside the garage and were observing the spectacle. When the men completed their work, they were led to the water hoses and, apparently, instructed to wash up. Suddenly, a group of partisans decided to have some fun and a massacre began. With spades, sticks, rifle butts, crowbars, and other tools from the garage they started assaulting the Jews. There must have been at least fifty or more Jews, all of them severely wounded, lying on the pavement crying and moaning. The partisans then grabbed many Jews by their hair and dragged them across the lot to the amusement of the bystanders. When the Jews collapsed, they turned the hoses on them and revived them. Once revived, they again beat them until they died. Then, later, another group of Jews was brought in to wash up the pavement and to remove the bodies."

"I wonder whether we should not consider suicide, you have poison in the medicine cabinet," Vera suddenly said in total desperation.

"Not on your life, I am not going to make their job easy. I am ready for the worst."

In the evening when the sun went down, the holy Sabbath set in over Kovno. The Sabbath in Kovno was very special. Before the Bolsheviks occupied Lithuania, Jews would go to the synagogue. Most Jewish shops were closed and the holiday was felt in the street. Even the Lithuanians knew it was Sabbath. The Jews did not care that they were losing business. Sabbath was Sabbath, and the Sabbath was much more important! The Lithuanians believed that the Jews were money hungry, but nothing was further from the truth and the Sabbath was proof of it. Yes, many Jews were shopkeepers, small and large, but even the poorest, who needed the few extra Lit to eke out his meager existence, did not care. He closed his shop and went to the synagogue. In the synagogue the mood was festive, the greeting was, a good Sabbath, and all daily worries were put aside.

At home the Sabbath was also felt. It was different from the daily routine. My grandmother would light and bless the candles and bake white bread, prepare fish and chicken for the Friday evening meal, and the entire family, children, parents, and grandchildren, would eat together. Father would make a blessing over the wine and introduce the Sabbath with an appropriate prayer. There was warmth and love at home. With the entrance of the Russians into Lithuania, this all changed. Outwardly, the Sabbath was not felt as much as before. Most of the stores were nationalized and were now open on the Sabbath. But at home we kept the Sabbath as before. The Lithuanians always accused the Jews as being communists. The Sabbath alone proved them wrong, except they did not want proof to the contrary.

It was Sabbath now in Kovno. The sun was down, but so also was our entire life. Father was not home and who knew what suffering he was now subjected to. Thousands of Jews were already under arrest and thousands more already killed and tortured to death in Kovno and in the small towns of Lithuania. The collaborators in the small towns did not wait for orders from the Germans, either. Just as in Kovno, the mob took the initiative and moved against the Jews. The better people among the Lithuanians were outnumbered and did not dare to speak out.

Surely it could have been even worse, eerie as it may sound. I could have been in the courtyard of the security police and our family could have shared the fate of the Jews who were killed in the pogrom in Slobotke.

We were exhausted, mentally and physically. And more was still to come. This was just a beginning, not even one week! We all went to bed, not to sleep, but to bed, since who could now sleep?

This was our first Sabbath eve under the new order. And what a Sabbath eve it was.

3

LOST HOPES

On Saturday the excesses against the Jewish population continued. Again the same ploy was used: the Jews were shooting from the windows at the German troops. This accusation was utterly ridiculous: first of all, the Jews never had arms in Lithuania; and secondly, no German soldiers were present where most of the Jews were being arrested, beaten up, and manhandled. Saturday, the Jewish Sabbath, only made the partisans' zeal higher. Groups of Jews were made to dance in front of jeering crowds and then were beaten in full view of the population, including Germans, but nobody intervened. Jews who were accustomed to going to synagogue stayed at home and went into hiding.

It was futile to hope that the entry of the German army would provide a semblance of order. Under every international convention, an occupying army was responsible for maintaining law and order. But the Germans did not seem to bother. They observed the slaughter heartlessly and some of them even took pictures of the bloodbath.

The day passed in anxious anticipation of whether the pogrom-bound partisans were going to return to our house and arrest us. Nobody could eat, everybody was sitting gloomily and counting the hours that were barely moving. Off and on, we would go to the radio to hear the news from the front. We still believed that the Russians were ten feet tall and that the German advance would be speedily repelled. This would have cooled the rage of the hooligans. But that was not to be. The news from the front was bad and getting worse. With disgust we would turn the radio off. By the end of Saturday, just in Kovno over a thousand Jews had been killed and thousands more arrested.

On Sunday morning Verute, as usual, went to church. Our hopes hinged on what the priests in the churches were going to say. Verute, our live-in maid, was a devout, deeply religious Catholic. She never married and belonged to some Catholic order. She never failed to go to church on Sunday. To her the priest was a holy man whose instructions she carried out faithfully. She was a devoted servant and loved us sincerely. To us, she almost was like a member of the family. We never checked up on her and never cared when she went to church. This was her personal life. Being a nun, she did not have any boyfriends and was not involved in any politics. But this Sunday we were restless. We were eager for her to return from church to hear what the priest had to say.

The Lithuanian population was almost entirely Catholic, deeply religious, and the influence of the clergy was pronounced. On Sunday all the churches were full and even the one year of communist rule failed to put a dent in the religious behaviour. The priests were highly-educated people and were revered by the population. Many clergymen were successful authors and writers and their influence went far beyond the four corners of the church. It was for this reason that we were so anxious to hear what they had to say in church on this first Sunday without the communist regime checking up on every statement. There was absolutely no doubt that if the priests said just one word to discourage the population from committing crimes against the Jews, it would have a profound effect. What the partisans were committing was pure murder. It was not an act in defense of the country, no battle was raging. It was an act against defenseless people who, deep in their hearts, loved Lithuania but happened to be Jewish.

I did not need any better example than my own father. His feelings for Lithuania were so profound that he refused to run when the war started. And there were thousands of Jews who felt as he did. These were the people whom the partisans were now murdering indiscriminately. They were volunteering for the job! A strong government could have stopped this bloodbath. But nobody intervened, which only heightened the mob fervor. The liberal Lithuanians were too small a minority to help us. Our only salvation now was the church. Anyone believing in God and Judeo-Christian ethics had to be revulsed at the goings-on in town. The sixth commandment stated: Thou shall not kill, and it was the duty of the clergy to stop the pogroms and the indiscriminate killing of Jews. This Sunday was the acid test. What would the priest say?

After mass Verute came home and walked straight into the kitchen. My mother and I followed her. Verute was surprised to see us.

"Verute, I will be very blunt with you," mother said, "we are very eager to know what the priest had to say. Did he mention the Jews?"

"Verute hesitated for a minute, then said, "Yes, he did, my lady."

"Did he admonish the partisans not to proceed against the Jews?"

"No, on the contrary, he praised them for their patriotism, for their devotion to Lithuania, and for their courage in fighting the communists. He praised the Nazis and Hitler as the liberators of Lithuania and urged the people to cooperate with the Germans. He even mentioned that some clergy is planning to send a telegram to Hitler promising to fight along-side the Germans against the Bolsheviks."

"But how about the Jews?" asked mother.

"Yes, he did mention the Jews. He mentioned that the Jews had cooperated with the communists against the interests of Lithuania."

"Did he talk about what was going on in town with regard to the Jews?"

"No, he only stressed that the true enemy were the Bolsheviks and it was important for the Lithuanian population to cooperate with the victorious German army."

An ominous quiet set in. We had nothing more to ask. The news was far worse than we had expected. Our last hope was now dashed. It seemed that a part of the clergy was ready to cooperate with Hitler. Of course, we did not know whether this was the attitude of all the clergymen, but for us what really counted was that the priests had not acted to stop the pogrom. After we returned to the living room, we sat down to digest what Verute had just told us.

"Did you hear," I said to Vera, "That the priests are urging the Lithuanians to cooperate with the Germans? Not a word to stop the massacre."

All the cards were now stacked against us and in the absence of any restraining force, not even the church, we could now expect just about anything.

Since it was Sunday Max was home early. The question about the provincial town of Daugai, where Max had served as a doctor, came up again.

"It seems to me," Vera said, "that in Daugai we should be fairly safe. After all, you were their doctor for years and the population liked you. It's worth checking."

"I think I have an idea. You surely remember the Jewish pharmacist in Daugai. He used to buy merchandise from a Lithuanian pharmacist in Kovno; he was a very fine Christian, very liberal. Since I have a Red Cross badge and can move around, I could look him up on my way from the clinic and ask him what he knows about our mutual friend from Daugai."

Of course the prospect of moving to Daugai was far from exciting. We would be returning to a primitive life without running water, indoor facilities, electricity, or sidewalks. But if our lives depended on it, we would have moved back to the caves to escape the wrath of the so-called civilized world.

The rest of the day passed in nearly total silence. From the moment we realized that the church was not willing to intercede on our behalf, we spent every night in fear.

On Monday morning the arrests still continued but with diminished intensity. We heard nothing from our Lithuanian friends. Nobody came to visit us and nobody called, not even Paplavski, whom we considered a close friend. We were suddenly lepers.

On Tuesday, around noontime, after Max had left to go to the clinic, there was a knock on our door. When we did not open the door fast enough, a voice screamed in German, "Aufmachen, Polizei!" Open up, the police.

Everybody began to shake. As if the Lithuanian mob weren't enough, we now had to deal with the German police. We opened the door and two German policemen came in. Both seemed to be drunk and smelled of vodka.

"We are from the German police," one instructed us, "and we have orders to confiscate your radio and all gold rings and jewelry."

As long as they did not pull any guns and did not threaten to shoot anybody, we were willing to concede. But Vera was not intimidated. She walked up to the policemen and calmly asked for identification and a written order.

"You Jewish bitch," one screamed, "you have a hell of a nerve questioning a German officer," and he slapped her in the face.

Vera wiped her nose, which was bleeding slightly, and walked straight to the phone and asked the operator for the German police headquarters. Before we knew what had happened, the two Germans were gone. We were all still in shock.

"What made you do this?" mother asked her.

"I don't know," Vera answered, "I am so full of anger from all the events of these last days that I just did not care. I sort of had a feeling that Germans don't simply come without orders from above, they are too disciplined for that, and if they had orders they would have displayed them without argument."

Wednesday was the day Max was supposed to go to the Lithuanian pharmacist. We were now anxiously awaiting his return from town. Would he have the opportunity to meet the man, and would he have some information about Daugai and our friend the Jewish pharmacist?

Finally Max came home. From his looks we knew that the news was bad. For several minutes he just could not find the right words to open up.

"Well, did you see him?" Vera asked finally, as Max was still not talking.

"Yes, I did," came the answer. "It is horrible, completely beyond belief. I met the Christian pharmacist. He told me that in fact he had just returned from Daugai. 'Doctor,' he told me, 'I am so ashamed, these are my people who did this. How could they? The local collaborators with the help of some outside partisans took most of the Jewish men and some women away and shot them all in the nearby forest. I just cannot believe it.' When I asked him what happened to the Jewish pharmacist and his family, he said that he was in the pharmacy and found it ransacked. He spoke to some of his friends in the village, but most refused to discuss the matter with him. One friend of his, however, told him the entire gruesome story of the massacre. He was awfully bitter about the whole thing and his voice was trembling as he was talking. 'Doctor,' he continued, 'not all the Lithuanians are participating in this. Believe me if I say, there are still many, many fine Lithuanians who feel very bad about it but they are outnumbered and their voices are not heard!' When I asked him whether the massacre was only in Daugai, he said that from all appearances it was not local."

We were stunned. Max and Vera knew almost every Jew in the village. And now most of them were gone, shot by anti-Semitic hoodlums just because they were Jews.

Our last hope was gone. Daugai was out! The provincial towns were even less safe than Kovno. For better or worse, our fate was sealed with the Jews in Kovno. And to top it off, we had not heard from Max's mother and his two younger brothers during this entire time.

Dvora and her two younger sons Benjamin and Manny lived quite far from us and, like so many people in Lithuania, had no telephone. Thus, we were in the same town, engulfed by danger, and with no way to get in touch with them. As we were sitting in the living room and brooding, we had the impression that somebody was lightly scratching at the entrance door. Verute also became aware of this strange noise and asked us whether she should open the door. Mother agreed. Verute went to the door, unlocked the bolt and opened it. Vera instinctively walked over to the crib and took Ruthie into her arms. Max put on his Red Cross badge to be able to identify himself as a doctor and I and Mother just sat there with our eyes glued to the door. To our complete surprise, Dvora Solc walked into the house. Everybody uttered a sigh of relief. But Dvora did not look good at all. Her cheek was swollen and her eye was blue and black.

"Mother," Max exclaimed, "how did you dare to walk all this way from your house here? You could have been arrested, you look so typically Jewish."

Indeed, Dvora was a typical Jewish woman, dark skinned and with black hair. Her eyes were deep black and in them you could see the image of all the grief of Jewish suffering. Her facial expression was always serious and sad. But she was an extremely proud and courageous woman. Shortly after her youngest son, Manny, was born, her husband became ill and for years she had to take care of him and her five sons. Yet she never complained and always trusted that this was God's will, which made it easier for her to bear the yoke. When Benjamin entered rabbinical school in Slobotke, she decided to move from Daugai to Kovno, where she, Benjamin and Manny were now living.

Her appearance shook us all up. Dvora patted Max on his back, looked around, turned to my mother, and asked in a quiet voice, "Luba, where is Boruch Hirsh? I don't see him."

Boruch Hirsh was the full name of my father.

"He was taken away by the partisans," answered my mother, "we have not heard from him since he was arrested a week ago Tuesday. And where are Benjamin and Manny?"

"They were dragged out of the house two days ago, on Monday."

Max became pale. "Tell me, how did it happen?" he asked.

"A whole gang of armed partisans broke into our house, broke the door and commanded Manny and Benjamin to come out and follow them. I tried to talk them out of it, but to no avail. One of them punched me in the face and screamed: 'Don't worry, you Jewish bitch, we are only taking them to work, they will come back,' and with this they left."

Max was terribly shaken.

"Don't worry," said Dvora, "God is not going to forsake them, they are pious and God-fearing boys and they will come back."

And Dvora really believed it. She refused to accept reality. She trusted in God and His judgement, and He could not be wrong and punish her boys.

Dvora stayed with us that night. Max would not let her go home. Any other mother would have been hysterical and difficult to console, losing two sons in one shot, but not Dvora. Her trust in God was not shaken and she was calmer and more collected than any of us. In fact, she was comforting Max, who was visibly distraught by the event. We also did not tell her the news about Daugai. After all, Daugai was her hometown. The news of Daugai would have been too much for her to bear.

The next morning Dvora got ready and wanted to go home, but here Max intervened very forcefully that she should not go.

"What if the boys come home and don't find me. What will they think?

They will be worried that something happened to me," Dvora insisted.

But Max knew too much about what was going on in town to let her go. He could not tell her that only a miracle could bring them back. Extremely few, if any, were so fortunate to be released, as I was.

"No, mother, you are not going," he insisted, "and this is final. How about me, did you think of me, how worried I would be not knowing whether you came safely home?"

The discussion ended with Dvora staying.

Meanwhile, our attention turned to her son Wolf, from whom she had not heard anything since the outbreak of the hostilities. Wolf was about twenty-eight years old, and after graduating from high school, he went to Vienna to study business administration. Wolf was athletically built and did not look Jewish at all. He also spoke perfect Lithuanian and could easily pass as a native. During his senior year in Vienna the Anschluss took place, and only because he did not look Jewish he was not molested. But after graduation, when he returned to Lithuania, he told us sickening stories of how the Jews were mistreated by the Austrian Nazis. He had no illusions. He had seen the Nazis in action and was determined to leave Europe. The first thing he did upon return was to apply for emigration to the United States. He received affidavits from some relatives and was waiting for a quota. But the quota never came. Finally, it was too late. The war in Europe was already on, the Russians in the meantime had occupied Lithuania, and emigration became impossible. During the Russian occupation he got a job which often took him to other cities in the country. And it just so happened that during one of those trips he was stranded when the war broke out.

Dvora, the perennial optimist, refused to accept the idea that he may have been hurt or killed. She was sure that whatever he had decided to do at the time, he was safe. He was young, strong, and energetic and most important, he did not look Jewish, a trait which suddenly became of utmost importance.

The situation of Hayim, her third son, was also unclear. When the war started he had no trouble making up his mind: he was determined to run. He came to Dvora to say goodbye and did not even take the time to come to say farewell to us. He felt that there was no time to be wasted and since he had decided to run, the sooner he started, the better it was. He and Nehama left on Sunday morning, before anybody had even thought about evacuating.

Now here she was in our house with only Max around her. But she did not allow any doubt to enter her mind. God is almighty and merciful and everything would still turn out all right.

4

THE SEVENTH FORT

It was once again Sunday, the beginning of the third week of the war. Dvora was still with us. Verute, as usual, went to church, but we did not care anymore. We had heard everything there was to be heard. Even if the church issued a condemnation now, too much damage had already been done.

Max was home, since the worst emergency was over. Suddenly the telephone rang. A ring of the telephone at this time could only bring bad tidings. Everybody was startled. Max went to the phone and asked who it was. At the other end was attorney Joffe, our neighbor from downstairs.

Attorney Joffe and his wife had lived in our house for years and their apartment was directly below ours. In his early forties, he was a big man with wide shoulders, a very successful lawyer. In 1918, during the war of liberation, he had volunteered for the fledgling Lithuanian army to fight for Lithuanian independence. He even earned some kind of distinction for bravery. In the army, he had made some valuable contacts and after earning his law degree, when he opened his own practice, he enjoyed a rather impressive Lithuanian clientele. He and Mrs. Joffe had no children and were very active in the community. When the war started, I ran down to his apartment and woke him up. I will never forget his facial expression, the shock, the disbelief, the horror on his face. I was still young and simply did not realize the seriousness of the moment. During the meeting of all the tenants in our apartment building he forcefully argued for escaping as soon as possible. He and Mrs. Joffe left on Sunday afternoon and we had not heard from them until this phone call. Where had he been all this time? We were now extremely eager to know what he had been through. Particularly I wanted to find out what happened, since I was the one who had never made peace with the idea that I did not run.

"How are you, Mr. Joffe," Max said, "how come you are in town?"

Max listened to a few statements by Mr. Joffe and said, "Yes, Mr. Joffe, we will be in your home in a few minutes."

Max turned to us and said, "Mr. Joffe wants us to come down to his apartment, he said he could not talk over the phone, but emphasized that he wanted to see us all."

An air of anxious anticipation suddenly gripped us. What had he to say? Why couldn't he talk over the phone? There certainly was something wrong. We all decided to go down, including Vera, who left Ruthie with Verute. We made ourselves presentable and walked down the one flight to his apartment.

Attorney Joffe himself opened the door. His appearance was shocking. This was not the attorney Joffe we knew. This man had aged. He looked fearful, grey, emaciated. His large chest had sunk, his hands were trembling, and his eyes resembled those of a person from an insane asylum. He had lost as much as twenty pounds and had to hold on to the wall to avoid collapsing. He immediately noticed our shock.

"Come in," he said, "don't worry, I look fine now. You should have seen me yesterday evening when I came home. This is pretty good in comparison."

We noticed that his voice had changed, too. He had a booming baritone with a lot of authority. But now he was talking in a whisper and his voice was shaking. He even had to stop to complete a simple sentence. What had happened to him in those two weeks? My God, how could a person change like this in so short a time! If this was how the people looked who had attempted escape, maybe it was better after all that we did not. The maid, who had stayed in the apartment during these two weeks, made tea for everybody and we settled down in his study to hear his tale. And a tale it was.

"You certainly are anxious to know why I asked you to come down," he opened, "I really don't know how to begin."

"Well, if anybody should know how to talk it is you, you are one of the best attorneys in town," Max replied.

"Unfortunately, my law practice did not prepare me for this. I guess I will simply come right out with it, rather than prolong the suspense and the agony."

The air was electrified. What shock did he have for us, that he referred to as "suspense and agony"?

"Be prepared, I have news for you from Mr. Mishelski!" he said.

These words exploded like a bombshell. We had not heard from father for almost two weeks, since he had been abducted on that fateful Tuesday. For a second, an air of hope entered the room. At least he was alive!

"Where did you see him?" asked mother.

"He is at the Seventh Fort with thousands of Jews who were arrested during these last two weeks."

"How is he? Tell us all about it," we all exclaimed almost in unison.

"Don't ask how he is. Ask what can be done for him. Things are bad, very bad."

Another moment of silence set in. Attorney Joffe was still groping for words. Max decided to rephrase the question.

"How did you get together with Mr. Mishelski? We thought you were in Russia by now."

"I wish I were," came the answer. "Running might have been the biggest mistake I ever made."

Everybody was caught by surprise by this statement.

"Sunday morning when the war started, and you, Vulia, came to tell us the news, I was shocked. The fear of the Nazis and possible pogroms was so big that I did not weigh the possibilities of being able to reach the Russian border. It seemed much easier than it actually was. We packed some valuables into our bags and left around three o'clock. We hurried to the railroad station where we encountered the first of many panic-laden scenes. Huge crowds were trying to enter the train and the people were clawing at each other like animals. Tougher men just simply removed people from the train and pushed their way in. When we arrived, the crowd was huge and growing by the minute. We were still early enough to be able to get into one of the wagons. The wagon was full, standing room only. We were like sardines in a can and the day was hot and one could suffocate. The people started to break the windows in order to let air in, but nobody would budge. Being in the train meant a lease on life.

But the train did not move. Rumor had it that the rails were damaged by German bombs and there was no free passage. We sat on the tracks for hours and when the train finally left, it was almost dawn. The train moved slowly and we were concerned about its lack of speed. We were on the road for barely half an hour when German bombers appeared in the air and started dropping bombs. Several bombs hit the locomotive and the journey came to an end. People in the front cars were screaming and crying. The bombs had ripped the front car open and dozens of people were killed or severely injured. People spattered with blood were looking for help, others had parts of their bodies torn off or ripped open. It was a horror scene! We were fortunate not to have been hurt. The wounded and dying were lying on the ground, but nobody stopped to give a helping hand. We decided to press on and to try to continue on foot despite the time loss. After a short while, we encountered a small group of Jews coming towards us. We were surprised. When the group approached us, they warned us not to proceed, because there were some very heavy battles in the area and they were returning home."

Joffe stopped again. We waited patiently for him to continue.

"We turned around and decided to circumvent the area and to press on. The main force could not yet have advanced this far. Well, to make the story short, we struggled for another day, but the advance of the German forces was so swift that we had no more chance to get through. We then turned around and started on our way home."

"Were many Jews turning around and returning to their homes?" asked Max, "did you see my brother Hayim by any chance?"

"No, I did not."

Max breathed a little easier, maybe Hayim was lucky after all. The story of attorney Joffe was getting to be like something in the movies, we almost forgot for a second that he was relating to us his own experiences.

"The way back home was rough. Most roads were already controlled by Lithuanian partisans and we had to avoid them. And sure enough, before we had a chance to get to the city, we were caught and arrested. Mrs. Joffe was immediately taken away somewhere else. I have not heard from her since and I was taken to one of the prisons under their control. Here, to my complete surprise I met Mr. Mishelski."

He now stopped; it became difficult for him to continue.

"Doctor," he continued after a while, "I need a tranquilizer. I probably should not be talking about what happened now, but I feel you and the whole world ought to know it. We do not know whether any one of us will survive this Gehenna, but if only one of us should make it, this tale must be told and despite the enormous strain talking about it, I will tell you all. Brace yourselves, you may need tranquilizers too."

This was one hell of an introduction. For a while everybody was quiet. Max went upstairs and brought a few very potent tranquilizers and gave them to the attorney. Mr. Joffe's eyes had assumed an expression of complete insanity, his hands were trembling, and his hair seemed to stand up. His appearance was like somebody obsessed.

"I want to stress again that normally I would not have told you all this, but the world has to know about it. I want to tell it as long as everything is still fresh in my mind. I hope we all will survive this, but I am sure that if not all, somebody will. After several days of torture, abuse and mistreatment, the entire group of Jews from this prison was taken to the Seventh Fort."

The Seventh Fort was one of the fortifications built by the Russians before World War One. At the time the fort was built, it was far outside the city, but during Lithuanian independence the area was developed to the limits of the fort. The fort as a fortification was now useless under modern warfare conditions and was only used by the army for storage and other purposes. The fort itself was surrounded by heavy masonry walls, topped with barbed wire and observation towers. The military barracks were located partly underground with several feet of soil on top of the roof. One sidewall was exposed, with low windows located close to the ground and a door near a slope which rose steeply until it covered the building. These slopes surrounded the entire compound, so that the center of the compound was sort of in an artificial valley. The barracks were unheated and damp, but since nobody used them, it really did not matter. At one end was an arch with a heavy steel door which was guarded by a sentry. At the other end of the fort was an artesian well which supplied water to the compound, and in the rear was a pedestrian path from which the inside of the fort could be seen.

Mr. Joffe coughed a little to clear his throat, and continued.

"Here we found the Jews that had been arrested before, all of them lying on the ground. Under heavy blows with the butts of the rifles, we were chased down the slopes into the large hole. The entire area was full of humanity. The women and small children, we found out, were locked up in the underground barracks. Here we were now kept for days without even a piece of bread or a drink of water. On top of the slopes were hundreds of Lithuanian partisans with machine guns. Escape was totally impossible. We received strict orders to sit on the ground and not to talk. When somebody moved or was caught talking, the partisans would open automatic fire into the crowd. Not everyone was lucky enough to be killed outright. Most of the people hit were severely injured and were crying and sobbing in pain. Many of the wounded were twisting in agony and asking the bandits to kill them, but the bastards would laugh and say, 'you were told to be quiet,' but would not shoot, and instead let them die in pain. The living and the dead were lying side by side and the camp administration would not let them be buried."

Mr. Joffe stopped again for a little while.

"The mid-July sun was hot and merciless and the people were fainting for a drop of water. No food or water was brought for days. The nights were not much better. Under the open sky, without food or decent clothing, the people were shivering from cold or fever. But as if this weren't enough, we could hear water from the artesian well, but were not allowed to get even a drop of it. The thirst was just as bad as the shooting. At least the ones who were shot instantly were forever rid of this hell. People finally started to rebel, clamoring for water. At first they were shot at, but when the clamor did not stop an order came from the supervisors to take a group to the well. They were permitted to drink some water and were then shot on the spot. The stronger ones were then forced to bury the dead ones and then they, too, were killed. But the clamoring did not stop and the people kept screaming. When the demand for water increased, the partisans opened a murderous fire into the mass of people. The next day, water was brought in. People started to fight and push to get to the water. The distribution of water stopped."

By now Vera and mother started to cry and Max gave them tranquilizers.

"Should I continue?" asked Joffe.

"Yes, you should, you yourself said that the story must be told and you are right," Max replied, "no matter how gruesome the following details are going to be."

"Next we received some half-baked bread, from which many people got cramps. Again, when people started to wince, they were shot. Every day more and more people were brought in from the outside and chased into the valley. Next, a new ploy was used to shoot people. The partisans demanded intelligent people for work. Some people responded to the call; they were taken away and again the shots from automatic rifles could be heard. Only the guards returned. Finally the people could take no more and a group got up and tried to attack the guards. But without guns, weakened by hunger and thirst, they were no match and were mercilessly gunned down by the bandits. When the stench of the dead became too much to bear even for the guards and their overlords, an order was given to take the bodies to the area behind the artesian well. None of the Jews who took the bodies from the grounds came back. The living ones buried the dead and then were killed by the guards, sometimes by beating rather than by shooting.

"Two days ago, early Friday morning, we saw how the women and children were led out from the underground barracks and taken to the iron gate. They looked terrible: bloody, torn clothes, pale, shaky, barely walking. The gates opened and they disappeared behind them. Immediately after the gates closed, without any warning the guards suddenly opened a murderous fire into the valley completely at random, just blanketing the area with bullets, covering the site with dead and injured.

"Suddenly, the shooting stopped. Some high Lithuanian officers came in; one was at least a colonel and ordered a ceasefire. A lower officer then declared that all men who fought as volunteers in the Lithuanian army during the war of liberation were to assemble at the gate. I was scared to report, since anybody who ever reported previously never returned. But Mr. Mishelski persuaded me to go. I had nothing to lose, particularly after this last murderous fire. I got up and walked out of the hole to the gate. There were approximately seventy of us. At first we were ridiculed to the amusement of the bystanders, but then we were told to line up in formation, the gate opened, and we were led outside."

Mr. Joffe stopped again. It was hard for him to relive all the horror.

"We were then taken to the central prison where we were interrogated and checked whether we were really volunteers. Yesterday afternoon, that is Saturday, they let us out and told us to go home. Our maid did not recognize me at all when she opened the door. The way you see me now, I look great. You should have seen me yesterday!"

A long silence set in. By the time he ended we were all sick to our stomachs.

"What about the civilian population? The fort is in the midst of a dense local population. Isn't there any reaction to the atrocities?" Vera asked.

"I do not know. The shooting is done outdoors and the shots reverberate through the entire area. People were watching from the open end where you can see the fort inside. Apparently everybody knows what is going on there."

"And what do you think will happen to the rest of the people who are still alive?" asked mother, in the hope that father was still alive.

"That is the reason why I chose to tell you everything. There is no doubt in my mind that nobody will get out of that hell alive. This is why I ask you, do what you can. Contact any Lithuanian friend you think can help. Try to bribe someone. But do your utmost to get Mr. Mishelski out of there. Now!"

With this he asked us to let him go to bed, he just could not take it any more. When we said goodbye to him, he stressed one more time, "Don't delay it even one minute, his rescue may hinge on minutes . . ."

With this we departed, leaving Mr. Joffe exhausted and sick.

When we came home all of us needed another dose of tranquilizers. We were shattered by the facts we had just heard. We immediately went to the phone and called Paplavski, asking him to come to us early in the morning, since it was an emergency.

All night one thought just would not let me sleep. It kept coming back over and over again: that was the place where my father was! That was the place where I would have been, if not for the freak incident in the security police yard. What a terrible thought! What terrible agony I was spared!

On Monday 7 July, early in the morning, Paplavski was in our home. We told him what we had heard from Mr. Joffe. Paplavski knew about the shootings, since he himself lived close by, but he did not know that father was there, too.

"What do you suggest we do?" I asked him, "do you have anybody who can help?"

"Yes, I do know some Lithuanian military men, but whether they can be helpful I cannot tell. I think I should go straight to the fort to see who the officers are who are in charge," said Paplavski.

"I am coming along with you," said Vera.

"No way," yelled Max, who had not yet left for the clinic, "you are not going."

"Max, I am going and this is final, this is my father!" said Vera.

Max knew this tone of voice. When she spoke like this there was no arguing.

"I don't look Jewish at all," she emphasized, "I am blonde, blue-eyed, with Paplavski at my side no one in his right mind would suspect that I am Jewish."

"If you want to come along," Paplavski added, "take some gold coins with you, we may need them. Maybe somehow somebody can be bribed."

Vera went to the drawer where father used to keep gold coins, took as many as she could comfortably fit into her purse, and turned to Paplavski. "Where are we going first?"

"We are going straight to the Seventh Fort," was Paplavski's answer. "No guessing, let us see who are the officers coming and going."

With this they left the house. Max was scared but he knew he could not change her mind. He, too, left the house on the way to the clinic.

For an agonizing several hours we waited. Around twelve noon they were both back.

"Thank God," exclaimed mother, when they entered the house, "you are back. What have you achieved?"

Instead of an answer Vera broke down in terrible pain. "It is too late, mother. They were all shot yesterday on Sunday, the Christian Sabbath, when they should have been in church. They were all buried in one mass grave."

That's how my father was killed.

We all burst into a heartbreaking outcry. The tears were coming down in buckets. It was all over. Father could not be saved and neither could three thousand other innocent Jews. We were just one day too late. But the tale of the Seventh Fort was not yet complete. Late in the afternoon, when Max returned from the clinic, he first ran to Ruthie's room to see whether Vera was home. He breathed a sigh of relief when he saw her.

"I see bad news in your face," Max said. "Do you have any news from the fort?"

"It is all over, Max, it is all over," Vera cried. "Father has been shot in a mass execution that completely defies imagination."

"What do you mean?" Max asked.

"These bandits killed everybody on Sunday, thousands of innocent Jewish men, and father among them."

"This is impossible, it cannot be, this is murder, plain murder," screamed Max in pain, "I cannot believe it!"

"You can," said Vera, "I was just there, they are all dead and buried. The place is as quiet as a cemetery. The shooting was going on all night and all day. The estimate is three thousand Jews."

Max had to take Ruthie out of her hands and put her into the crib. Vera lay down on the sofa and buried her head in the pillow, when somebody knocked on the rear door of our apartment. Again everybody curled up. At the door was the maid of Mr. Joffe.

"Doctor," she said, "Mr. Joffe wants you to come immediately. It is an emergency."

We were not surprised. After what he had been through, it was a miracle he even could talk. Hell was too weak a description for what he had experienced in the last few weeks. He never should have spoken about it so soon after coming from the fort.

We did not come along with Max. When Max did not return after twenty minutes we started to wonder what was he doing there so long. We realized that it must have been serious, or the maid would not have said it was an emergency. He surely was not dying?

After a little more than half an hour Max was back. We looked at his facial expression, trying to anticipate what had happened.

"What is it, Max?" asked Vera, "is he alive?"

"No, no!" and he shook his head. "It is not him," said Max, "it is Mrs. Joffe. She was in the Seventh Fort too, among the women who were taken out on Friday, remember? She was released, she is back home, you should see how she looks, don't even ask. Better looking people are being buried every day. I don't know whether she will make it. Fortunately she is responding to medication. In a few hours I will go again to check. When I was through with her, he needed a tranquilizer too. The poor man, funny as it may sound, he really is lucky, he himself is home and he has his wife back too. You have to be lucky even in adversity, even amidst such a catastrophe. Our father and three thousand Jews will never return. Their families will never see them again."

It was late in the evening when Max went down again. This time he returned fast.

"The medicine has performed well, it is a real miracle. She is aware and already talking and I hope that tomorrow she will feel a lot better."

With that we all retired to bed. We were all exhausted. The day's events were too much to bear even for a person with iron nerves.

On Tuesday morning before going to the clinic, Max went to the Joffes to check on their condition and came back very pleased. The improvement was remarkable. The care and warmth at home had untied her nerves and she was now resembling a normal human being.

On Tuesday evening Mr. Joffe came up to our apartment and asked for Max. She needed some medication again, he also wanted us to come down. He felt that talking to people would do her good, it would act as therapy after these weeks of torture.

"Are you sure we should come down, too?" Vera asked. "Doesn't she need a rest?"

"Well, she slept all night and almost all day today," answered Joffe, "and she feels that she has the urge to talk, to get it off her chest. She feels that sharing would lighten her burden."

We agreed. On the way down to their apartment, Joffe stopped and said to Max, "Doctor, I should not be saying it, but I have a premonition that I will not survive this, I have a funny feeling and I am glad that my wife is willing to talk. As I said, somebody must remain alive to tell the tale of how people turned into animals."

"Don't talk like this," answered Max, "nobody knows who will survive and who not. If your fortune was not to remain alive you would not have come out of the Seventh Fort."

With this, we reached the door and entered the apartment. Mrs. Joffe could hardly be recognized. We were wondering, did she always have so many grey hairs? or did they just turn white? She was lying in bed, propped up to a sitting position.

"I am so glad to see nice, friendly faces again after such an ordeal," she said.

"We are glad to see you home. We realize what you must have been through."

"Don't say that until you have heard it all, the most twisted mind could not imagine the torture we were put through."

This introduction reminded me of the first words Joffe had said to us before he initiated us into his horror tale.

"You apparently know everything until we got to the city and were arrested. Well, the women were immediately taken to the underground barracks, where we all lay down on the bare concrete, one on top of the other. For several days we had no food and no water. They would not even let us out. The children were crying and sobbing and were asking their mothers why they were not taking them back home. The weaker women fainted from the thirst and the horrible air. But the nights were even worse than the days. Partisans with flashlights would come in and rob the women of their jewelry. Then others would come and beat up the women because they had nothing to give any more. A favorite sort of entertainment was to order the women to take off their clothes and dance. When they got sufficiently excited they picked out the more beautiful ones and took them out by force and raped them. Remember Frieda Perlman and her friend Miss Berkowitz, both were interns in the Jewish Community Hospital?"

"Of course I remember them," I said, "they lived one floor above us, in fact, they were arrested together with me."

"One night they were both taken out, raped, and then shot. We heard their struggle and their screams and then the shots. When one mother would not let the bandits take her daughter out, they both were dragged out, raped, and shot. The girls then started to smear their faces with dirt to look ugly."

Mrs. Joffe stopped for a while, she needed a moment to regain her composure.

"A few days later they let us out to have some fresh air. Some food was also distributed. Last week, on Friday, without any explanation we were told to go outside. We were lined up and told to march. We were marched from the Seventh Fort to the Ninth Fort, an extremely long walk even for a healthy man. We struggled with our last resources not to fall behind. Somehow we survived those few days and were released."

She stopped. "I don't know why we deserve this kind of treatment," she finished.

We talked for a short while and then went back upstairs, completely devastated by the facts we had heard from this unlucky couple.

A few months later, when we were already in the ghetto, we heard the epilogue of this tragedy. A colleague of Max had met a Lithuanian doctor from whom he found out all the gruesome details of the final hours of the massacre. This Lithuanian doctor was treating a partisan who had gone berserk and tried to commit suicide. When the doctor tried to establish the reason for his attempted suicide, he found out that the man was a member of the troops that shot the Jews at the Seventh Forth. He described how that last Sunday they were given alcoholic beverages until most of them were totally drunk. They were then given automatic weapons and taken to the fort to supplement the number of guards who were assigned to shoot. On Sunday, a murderous fire was opened into the valley. The Jews were crying and screaming, trying to get out and run, but there was no escape from it. Hundreds were only wounded and moaning in agony. But the guards just kept shooting. A few managed to come close, he could even see very clearly the agony on their faces, but he just let them have it. After hours of massive fire by hundreds of partisans, everything became quiet, almost eerie after all that shooting. Everybody was dead with only a few here and there still turning in pain. The guard let them die in severe distress. He would not even honor their wish to be killed.

Weeks after the massacre this partisan could not sleep, he was haunted and tormented by the faces he saw in the valley of the Seventh Fort. Trying to put an end to his mental torture, he slit his wrists, but was brought in time to the hospital and saved.

The Final Solution had begun, and millions more of innocent Jews were unaware and unsuspecting of what was in the cards for them and for us in the ghetto of Kovno.

5

LAST DAYS IN THE CITY

When we returned to our apartment, we could hardly talk. Everybody had a lump in his throat. We went to bed without saying a word, everyone immersed in his own thoughts. This was simply unbelievable. How could people who were only yesterday peaceful neighbors turn on their fellow citizens with such ferocity just because they were Jews? How could officers issue such orders and guards open fire on helpless people and murder thousands of them without blinking an eye? How did Hitler succeed in turning a civilized world into barbarians? And finally, who knew how many friends and relatives had perished among these three thousand victims? All these thoughts were torturing us and would not let us sleep.

Suddenly a noise in the apartment of the family Vazbutski, across the hall, brought us all back to reality. How could it be? The Vazbutskis had left Sunday, the first day of the war, with their children, trying to escape to Russia. The apartment was locked and vacant. All this time we never heard anybody inside. Could it be German soldiers, Lithuanian partisans, or maybe our janitor? He knew that the Vazbutskis were gone. Everybody got up from bed and tiptoed to the door to listen. There was no doubt. Somebody was roaming around inside. After ten or fifteen minutes the mysterious noise stopped. We stayed at the door for a little while, but when the noise did not come back, we returned to bed.

It was another restless night. Max left for the clinic, but he had been notified already that as of next week he did not have to report to work anymore, the emergency was over and they did not need any Jews. He had barely left, when the noise in the apartment could be heard again.

46

Suddenly the door opened and somebody walked out of there. We were scared. The events of the last few weeks had ruined our nerves. Barely had the door across the hall closed as our doorbell rang. We were startled: the unknown ghost was at our door! When Verute opened the door, we just could not believe our eyes. In the door stood Mrs. Vazbutski.

"Mrs. Vazbutski," we all exclaimed, "how come you are here, what happened?"

Mrs. Vazbutski said that she would talk to us a little later. In the meantime, she was wondering whether we had something to eat. She and her children had not eaten for the last three days. We did not ask any more questions. Mother gave her bread, milk, and eggs and asked her what else we could do for her.

"If you have aspirin, I would appreciate it, the children are sick and running a high fever," she said.

Mother gave her some aspirin and asked her whether Mr. Vazbutski was home too.

"No," answered Mrs. Vazbutski, "he was arrested by partisans about eight or nine days ago and I have not heard from him since. But please excuse me, I want to rush."

We could not get over it. The Vazbutskis had not made it either and were forced to return. But this at least could have been expected with small children. Mother did not waste much time and in about half an hour had a quick warm meal for them. Mrs. Vazbutski was glad to see us. Her children looked terrible. Their faces expressed fear and shock and they were afraid of us, whom they had known since their birth. We tried to engage in a conversation with Mrs. Vazbutski, but unlike the Joffes, she was very reserved and not willing to talk. But from the short conversation we were able to piece the whole story together. Basically they had tried the same thing as the Joffes. Their first destination was the train, but they were too late. They then decided to continue on foot. The older child was walking but the younger had to be carried. The roads were jam-packed with refugees and, with two children, they were constantly falling behind. The roads were also under constant barrage by air. Eventually, they were overtaken by advance German units and forced to turn around and go back. The road back home was even worse than earlier on, full of partisans. They were stopped and her husband arrested and taken away to an unknown destination. On the road they had to stop and beg for food from Lithuanian farmers, who more often than not threatened them if they did not keep on moving. The children were now sick and crying. For the last few days they had had no food at all. Only God knew how she managed to make it all the way home.

When Max came home we told him all about it, but since she did not ask Max to come in to check the children, he decided not to offer his services. The arrest of Mr. Vazbutski only heightened Max's anxiety about his brothers Hayim and Wolf.

Thursday afternoon, 10 July, there was a lot of news concerning the Jews of Kovno. First of all a number of edicts were issued, among them the following:

1. The Jews who had fled Kovno at the beginning of the war had no right to return to their apartments. Returning Jews would be shot and people sheltering such Jews would be severely punished.

2. All Jews must wear a yellow star of David on both front and back of the left chest about eight centimeters in size. Jews without signs would be shot.

3. Jews were not allowed to walk on the sidewalks and were permitted to walk in the gutter only.

4. A ghetto was going to be established in Slobotke and the Jews were to relocate to the ghetto by 15 August.

5. Jews were prohibited to sell their property.

6. Jews were not allowed to go to any public places or use any public transportation facilities.

7. Jews were not allowed to have radios and had to turn their radios in.

But even more important than the above edicts was the news that a Jewish delegation had seen the chief of the Gestapo. These Jews were picked up by German agents and brought to their office. Needless to say, these so-called representatives were petrified. They were not sure whether they were under arrest or were being taken for a bloody interrogation to some Gestapo cellar. Instead, they were led into an office where, without being permitted to sit down, they were informed of the following:

a. Since all Jews were communists and the Lithuanian population could not tolerate Bolsheviks among them, the Jews would be resettled in a ghetto in Slobotke.

b. The exact boundaries of the ghetto would be announced shortly.

c. The deadline to complete the move to Slobotke was set as 15 August 1941.

d. The Jews were to select among themselves a group of prominent members of their community to act as a council through which all orders would be issued.

e. Among the functions of the council would be to assure a speedy and orderly transition from the city to the ghetto.

f. The Gestapo assures the representatives that there would be no more excesses against the Jews.

With this they were released and told to be ready for further orders.

The news about the meeting and the proposed creation of a ghetto in Slobotke spread like wildfire through the Jewish community. But particularly reassuring was the news that there would be no more excesses against the Jewish population.

Jews started to appear on the streets, initially in very small numbers and in the beginning primarily only women. But as the days wore on, the number of Jews on the streets slowly started to increase. This was of major importance to the Jews who had fled in the beginning of the war and were trying to return to the city, and for the Jews from the provincial towns, who were fleeing these towns and the massacres there. All of them were trying to reach Kovno, which they believed to be safer. Within several days hundreds of Jews were back in the city and despite the edict that they would be shot, risked their lives to get back into their apartments. But in most cases the apartments had already been grabbed by Lithuanians. These Jews were now looking up relatives and friends in the hope of finding shelter.

It was around that time that Rivka Gluck suddenly showed up at the door to our apartment. Rivka, her sisters Sonja and Ester, and their brother Moshe were the children of a first cousin of my father. A gorgeous girl, Rivka was full of life. Somewhat unpolished, her language rough, she was a tough character. Slightly taller than average, she had pitch-black hair, light brown eyes and a figure as if carved out of marble. Her breasts were round and stiff and more often than not she did not even wear a brassiere. She always wore short skirts and tight blouses to show off her figure. Not intellectually inclined, she graduated from a public school in Mariampole, where she was born and raised. She got herself a job where she stayed till the outbreak of the war.

Rivka's appearance at our door startled us. She looked well, as if the events of the past few weeks might have passed her by. It did not take Rivka long to notice that father was not home.

"Where is your father?" she asked Vera.

"We don't have good news about father, I am afraid," said Vera. "I don't know how much you have heard about the events here in Kovno, but an estimated three thousand Jews were shot a few days ago at the Seventh Fort. Father was among them."

"Oh, no!" exclaimed Rivka. "I knew about trouble in Kovno, but I did not know that so many Jews had been shot."

"Where were you these few weeks?" asked Max.

"I was hidden in the house of a Lithuanian girlfriend of mine, in a village near Mariampole, rather close to the German border. Sunday morning, before we were even aware that the war was on, the Germans were already in town. The Lithuanian population ran out to the street and greeted the Germans with flowers and applause, but the Jews stayed in their homes, completely shocked by the event. But what followed was far worse than we ever imagined. Within a few days the events unfolded with mind-boggling speed. First the synagogue was burned down, then all the prominent Jews, including the rabbi and the Jewish doctor, were rounded up. When they were released they could hardly be recognized. And that was only the beginning," Rivka continued.

Rivka proceeded to describe the events that followed. It was a story that we would hear for some weeks to come, from survivors and refugees from dozens of villages and dozens of massacres that had been carried out by the partisans with the assistance of local collaborators. It was a story of abuse, humiliation, beatings, and bludgeoning of indescribable brutality, with the Jews being driven from their homes, locked up in barns, synagogues, and various other locations in town, and kept there for days without food or water, while the local population descended on the empty homes, plundering and ransacking. Subsequently the Jews were led in groups, men, women, and children, to the nearby forest and executed in front of prepared trenches, or occasionally even ones which they themselves were forced to dig. The executions were carried out by shooting with machine guns. Night was the preferred time for the executions, but quite often they were committed in broad daylight with sightseers watching the gruesome procedure. When possible, these murders were carried out on a Saturday, the Jewish Sabbath, to "reward" the Jews on their holy day. After the executions, which lasted to the early hours on Sunday, the partisans would join the villagers in church for early mass, where the murderers were praised by the local crowd. All these proceedings were carried out in full view of the local population, and not a single individual tried to stop them, or even to admonish the perpetrators.

Again and again, while narrating her gruesome tale, Rivka had to stop and catch her breath. It was obviously too much for her, while we were shocked into total disbelief at the depth to which our erstwhile neighbors had descended in their hate of the Jews.

"And what happened after the massacre?" mother asked.

"In about a week or so, when things were quieting down, I first wanted to go back to Mariampole to my parents' house, but my girlfriend found out that there had been mass executions in Mariampole too, that my brother had decided to run towards Russia, and my parents had been led away somewhere with other prominent Jews of the town and shot. The apartment had been ransacked and I had no place to go. So I decided to try to reach Kovno and my sister Sonja."

"Yes, what about Sonja?" asked mother.

"When I came to Sonja's apartment, I found that Lithuanians were already living there. Apparently they ran to the Russian border. I then tried Ester's home, but she was gone too. So here I am."

"Don't worry, Rivka, our home is your home. We ought to stand by our kin in times of trouble like these."

In the meantime Vera left the house to go to the street, where the Jewish committee was forming. When she returned she had a lot of news to report. She was pleased to find out that at the head of the council would be Dr. Elkes, a close friend of ours. She also found out that the limits of the ghetto had been set and the move to Slobotke could start immediately. Furthermore, she saw hundreds of families who had returned to Kovno and now had no place to go since their apartments had been taken over by Lithuanians. She also found out that the estimate of the Jews, including returnees, refugees, and people who were still in their homes, was about thirty thousand, and the number of Lithuanians who lived in the area to be turned over to the Jews was barely four thousand! This meant squeezing more than seven Jews for every Lithuanian, into quarters which were not too spacious to begin with. Another newsworthy item was that committees were now being formed to assist the council, and among the committees was a medical group to help establish a hospital in the ghetto. Max decided to join this committee.

Meanwhile more Jews were drifting into the city. Our biggest surprise was when Rivka's sister Sonja, with her daughter Eetke but without her husband, also appeared at our home. Rivka and Sonja were both hysterical. Neither one had expected to find the other in our home.

We were now treated to yet another tale of horror. When the war started Sonja and Eddie, her husband, decided to run towards the Russian border. The road was crowded with thousands of people and besides, the Russians used that same highway to retreat. The trucks carrying the soldiers of the Red Army picked up no one, not even their own stragglers. That's how panicky the retreat was. The Germans constantly strafed the road, sowing death and destruction.

As Sonja and her husband proceeded, the road got more and more crowded as people from nearby villages, consumed by panic, also decided to run. Tired and hungry, they pressed on in hopes of getting ahead of the fast-advancing Germans. On the second day their feet got blisters and started to swell and the child could not continue any longer. Eddie had to carry her from now on. Despite the difficulties they managed to reach the Russian border, but the Russians had strict orders not to let any civilians in and all the people had to turn around and go back. Suddenly, a flash brought the news that the Russians had opened the border and let everybody pass, but it was too late, the Germans had already overtaken them.

The only thing left to do was to try to reach Dvinsk and from there back home. But in Dvinsk all Jewish men were arrested and sent to the local prison. Sonja decided to stay in the vicinity of the prison in case the men would be released. But on Wednesday 9 July all the men were taken out of the prison and led in small groups under heavy German guard to an area outside the prison gates, where they were shot. Outside the prison walls people were standing and watching the gruesome spectacle, which could be clearly observed from the highway. Sonja was just outside the prison. She could hear the shots and the screams. To witness the actual massacre, all she had to do was to join the crowd.

After it was all over the crowd dispersed and Sonja and Eetke brokenheartedly set upon the road to return home. Luckily she managed to reach Kovno, but found her apartment taken by some Lithuanians. And when she discovered that Ester's apartment was also occupied, she came to us.

When she had finished, she turned to Rivka. "Rivkale, did you hear from our parents and our brother?"

Rivka hesitated, but when Sonja insisted she told her everything. Sonja, who had calmed down for a while, broke down again. A day or so later an aunt of theirs got in touch with us. When she found out that Rivka and Sonja were here, she begged them to come to sleep with her. She was all alone and was scared. Sonja and Rivka agreed, but asked us to keep them in mind, and if at all possible, to live with us in the ghetto.

But the final chapter of this "calm" period came the next day. We were all home when the doorbell rang. When we opened the door, we were stunned: in the door stood Wolf, Max's brother. Now it was the turn of Max and Vera to cry over each other's shoulders. The only one who did not cry was Dvora. In her almost superhuman aplomb she remained calm and collected. All she had to say was, "I knew you will be safe, God has watched over you and he will bring back to me also Benjamin and Manny. And about Hayim I don't even doubt. He will reach Russia."

Wolf's story was almost a duplicate of Sonja's. He too was in Dvinsk, but with his typical Lithuanian looks he had no trouble disappearing and coming back to Kovno. After reaching Kovno he first went to Dvora's apartment, and when he did not find her home, he rushed to us. Fortunately Dvora's apartment had not yet been confiscated and Wolf and Dvora went home the next day.

This was our "calm" period. Hadn't the Gestapo promised that there would be no more excesses against the Jews?

Once it became official that a ghetto would be established in Slobotke and that the Jews would have to resettle there, ours and everyone else's major worry became finding a home, or even one room to provide a roof over our heads. The first outline of the future ghetto included all the Jewish areas in Slobotke. This meant that Aunt Hayale, my mother's sister-in-law, with her old mother, would remain in their own home, which could easily accommodate our family. We contacted her and she was happy to have us rather than strangers forced upon her. We were happy too, since we were now assured of a decent place to live. But the Lithuanian officials were very displeased with the boundaries set for the ghetto. They insisted that the area assigned to the Jews was too big. Under the pressure of those Lithuanians a few major areas previously assigned to the ghetto limits were now excluded, among them the area where Hayale's house was located. This was catastrophic. We now had to start all over again looking for shelter.

The new boundaries of the ghetto were finally set in an area about 70% of the size originally planned. In its final form, it was divided into two ghettos: one called the Small Ghetto and the other the Big Ghetto. The dividing line between the two was Paneriu Street, which was outside the limits of both ghettos. Both ghettos were surrounded by high barbed wire, running along both sides of Paneriu Street, completely separating the two. The only link between them was a wooden bridge, built by the Jews during the last week of July. The Germans could separate both ghettos completely and break any contact between the two by simply blocking the bridge. The Small Ghetto was comprised of several blocks in each direction, into which four thousand Jews were to be crammed. This was one of the most congested areas in the ghetto. Six or seven families to one kitchen was the rule rather than an exception.

The Big Ghetto also had several easily identifiable areas. One area was the old Jewish quarters of Slobotke, which extended to a cemetery. The cemetery was several blocks long, surrounded by a high wire fence. Along Krisciukaicio Street in this stretch, there were only few houses, and none on the side of the cemetery. Krisciukaicio was the last street before reaching the river Neris. Thus, this stretch along the cemetery was like a thin neck, and was called the corridor. Again, this area could be easily severed from the balance of the Big Ghetto by blocking the corridor.

The rest of the Big Ghetto was one large area with its biggest street called Varniu. Varniu Street extended in an east-west direction, running slightly on a skew along the entire ghetto. At its northern end were located big block buildings, called Blocks A, B, and C. These were blocks built by the Russians for low-income workers employed in the numerous factories in Slobotke. These blocks had not yet been completed when the war started. The Jews moved into the unfinished apartments, which they then completed while living in them. On the south side of Varniu, not far from the blocks, was the Jewish council, and kitty-corner from the council was our house, which overlooked a large plaza. The gates to the ghetto were situated at the end of Krisciukaicio and Varniu Streets. At the other end of Varniu, near the river, was a big lumberyard, and at the end of Krisciukaicio Street were former factories, now abandoned.

On 10 July 1941, when the order to move into the ghetto was issued and the boundaries finally defined, a mad scramble ensued to secure living quarters. Jews with money were offering their luxury apartments in exchange for the miserable huts of the Lithuanians, who had to clear the area. A bidding war started to see who could pay more to the Lithuanians. People who had nothing to offer, among them Sonja, Rivka, all the refugees and returnees, were left out in the cold. At first we tried to get an apartment in the blocks, but these were quickly grabbed up by people working in the Jewish council and their immediate relatives. Obviously the Jews were at a tremendous disadvantage: the Lithuanians had a choice of over eight thousand apartments for four thousand people, and the Jews had to fit thirty thousand people into about one thousand units, very small ones on top of it. The scramble for space was furious. We contacted our former janitor and offered him our luxury apartment with part of the furniture, for his farmhouse. He agreed. We were happy, at least we had a space. But when we got ready to move, we found out that a very close friend of ours, Orchik, who knew about our deal, had subsequently contacted this same janitor and outbid us for his house. The janitor closed the deal with Orchik and refused to talk to us. We were frantic. We had lost all that valuable time, knowing that we had a place, only to find out that we were double-crossed by one of our best friends. I immediately contacted a Lithuanian by the name of Stasys Kairys, whom I knew for years.

Kairys came the same day to inspect his deal, to see whether or not it was good enough for him. He was very excited and accepted it. Our apartment was not only luxurious, but was located half a block away from the mansion of the president of Lithuania. We left Kairys our piano, a full bedroom set, everything we had in the kitchen, some furniture in the dining room, and lots of other smaller items which we could not take along with us since they would not fit into the small house of his. We closed the deal and started to move immediately. We were anxious to be assured of this place, especially after our experience with Orchik.

During the moving period the city of Kovno was completely disheveled. Hundreds of Lithuanians found out about the decree and came with their horses and wagons to move the Jews. The prices they charged were atrocious, but we had no choice. Not paying the price meant leaving all the belongings in town and moving into the ghetto empty-handed.

One day when we returned from Slobotke after moving some of our belongings, somebody knocked on our door. When we opened it we were totally surprised, for at the door was Rivka with her sister Ester. Ester, after Sonja, was the second eldest in the family. She lived in Kovno with her husband and their one-year-old son Willie, or Wolfinke, as she used to call him. We already knew from Sonja that Ester had also tried to escape, so her appearance at our door was quite a surprise.

"Ester, how come you are in Kovno?" mother exclaimed in astonishment, "we thought you were on the road running."

Instead of answering the question, Ester rushed to my mother and embraced her. "Yes, we did run, but we did not make it either," she finally opened up.

"We also had planned to run," mother said, "actually we were already on our way, but we were too late and we returned home right away."

"Good for you," replied Ester, "you are really lucky. You have no idea how much grief, pain, and suffering you were spared. I cannot even begin to describe it to you."

"Don't think we had a picnic here," I got into the act, "you at least tried!"

"Be quiet, you should have been on the road, then you would not talk like this. All I saw was people being killed by attacks from the air, being killed by the partisans, people wounded and dying, shot in mass executions, and the ones who survived were returning in the thousands, again falling into the hands of the bandits."

"It is no use to discuss this issue. But where are Willie and your husband?" I asked. Ester started to cry.

"Don't talk about it," Rivka mixed in. "I will tell you about it a little later."

Mother and Vera took her to the living room and Max, Rivka, and I went to Max's study.

"When the war started," Rivka began, "Ester and her husband decided to run. Ester's mother-in-law tried to dissuade them with every possible argument, but was not successful. She even suggested that they leave the child with her, because it seemed impossible to make this hazardous trip with a one-year-old baby. But Ester would hear none of it. So they said goodbye to her and left."

"How far did they get and where is her husband?" I asked.

"You would not believe it," Rivka continued. "They picked the exact same road as Sonja and Eddie and made it to Dvinsk. They never met each other; that is how many people were on the road. Here they too were overtaken by the advancing Germans and eventually all men, several thousand of them, were arrested. After a few days they were all shot. So here you are. Both my brothers-in-law, without having seen each other, were shot at the same time and both were buried in the same mass grave."

Rivka's voice was breaking as she narrated this tale of horror.

"But she was still lucky when she returned home with her baby. At least her mother-in-law still had her apartment and she was not left out in the cold."

"It sounds macabre when you say she was lucky," Max interjected.

"I am sorry," said Rivka, "I did not mean it that way. But at least she has a place, whereas Sonja has lost her husband and did not even have a dress into which to change."

While we were talking to Rivka, Ester had relaxed and we joined them. Mother selected some dresses and some shoes and gave them to Rivka for her and for Sonja. After staying with us for a little while, they left our house.

In the meantime, there was hardly a day when no new edicts were issued against the Jews. The latest among these were the following:

1. All main streets were now off-limits to Jews and the Jews were allowed on side streets between six AM and eight PM only.

2. Jews were not allowed to have photo cameras, typewriters, bicycles, and some other specified items and had to turn them in.

3. Jews who were not in the ghetto by 15 August would be arrested and shot.

4. Jews were not allowed to employ non-Jewish help. This included domestic help.

5. Jews were forbidden to go to the market to shop for food.

Following the above edicts, Verute now had to leave our home. Since we could no longer go to the market, we still took advantage of her to buy as much food as we could accommodate in our cold storage. When the time came to leave, Verute was very upset, particularly since she had been with us for so many years. Due to the very limited quarters we were to move into, we could take along only the most essential items and the rest we had to leave. Mother decided to select some clothes to give to Verute. We stuffed about four valises with clothing and told Verute she should keep it for us, should we ever need it.

"My lady, you don't have to worry even for one minute," said Verute, "any time you will need something, just let me know, I am going to be in touch with you," and Verute crossed her heart as proof of her sincerity.

Verute made several trips to take the valises, which were big and heavy. At the last moment she went to Ruthie's crib, gave her a kiss, and left for good. When Verute was gone, I could not resist asking mother why she gave her so many pieces of clothing. "Mother," I said, "what made you do this? You might as well have left these clothes here with Kairys. What difference does this make? We probably will not survive the war anyway."

"It makes a big difference," mother replied. "First of all, I trust Verute like myself. She has served us well and was always honest and reliable. On the other hand, what do I know about Kairys? He could as well be a hooligan and never return to us even an iota. Besides, we already left him a fortune. Just our antique dining room set alone, with all this carved wood, is more than he could ever have afforded on the salary from his job, even if he saved every penny he earned. And how about the bedroom, the desk, and the piano! And how about all the other things? My God, we left him a fortune for his lousy hut!"

The more she talked, the more upset she got about the injustice which we were forced to accept, just to secure a roof over our heads. She loved our home and our furniture, which she had acquired with so much care. And now all this was being left behind.

"No, Vulia, I wish I could have left part of what I left to this guy Kairys to Verute, but what can you do."

Mother was right. The deal we had concluded with this fellow Kairys was a ruthless rip-off, yet we still had to be thankful. Thousands of Jews had no place to go at all.

For us, Verute's departure was a problem, since without her, our shopping for food became difficult. But this was only temporary, since in a few days we were to move anyway. This particular decree, however, was more serious for people who had no space to store food, as we had. When some people became desperate for food, they tried to go to the farms directly. The occupation force found out about it and decided to put a stop to it. One day they staked out the roads and arrested twenty-six Jews. The Gestapo then took them to the Ninth Fort where they were forced to dig graves for themselves. When the graves were ready, they were shot. A second group of Jews was then caught from the streets and brought to the fort, where they were told to cover the mass grave with dirt. Upon release they were told to return to their homes and make sure they told everybody what they had seen and why the people were shot. This was a warning that anyone caught even near a farm would share the same fate. The warning was effective and the trips to the farms stopped. But there were twenty-six Jews who were no longer scared—they were dead! They died because they wanted to bring some food to their hungry children, and somewhere twenty-six families were mourning the loss of beloved husbands and fathers.

The moving process was exhausting. With thirty thousand Jews on the move, vehicles were at a premium and, thus, many of our belongings were carried in bags on our backs during the heat of the summer days for a distance of about four to five miles. For the rest of the heavy things, we hired a Lithuanian with a horse and buggy at an exorbitant price. In the first days of August, we were already in the ghetto.

One day shortly before the ghetto was supposed to be sealed off from the outside world, Kairys suddenly showed up in the ghetto. We were flabbergasted. What else did he want from us? In the course of the conversation he explained to us that the Germans were confiscating Jewish property which the Lithuanians could not prove was theirs. He demanded that we sign an agreement, which he had already drawn up, stating that we had sold him our piano in exchange for the vegetables in his garden. If we refused he would go to the German authorities and tell them that we were communists. This was quite some threat. The Germans shot Jews with the slightest provocation and his word against ours was not even needed. We were Jews and he a Lithuanian and that was enough. I was shocked. I knew him from before the war and never expected this from him.

"Mr. Kairys," I said, "I never expected to hear such a statement from you. You know me from before the war, besides, I think we have treated you rather fairly in our exchange of properties. You cannot complain."

"But as I explained to you, things for us Lithuanians are not exactly easy either."

"Of course, I would not argue this point," I replied, "I only wish I could trade my troubles for yours."

"But troubles are troubles, you know, and your own troubles always loom larger to you than those of your neighbors," Kairys replied. "In any case, I need the signature on this paper or the piano will be confiscated."

He handed the paper to mother, who signed it and handed it back to him. It did not make any difference how good the agreement was. Anybody with half a brain could see that the agreement was phony. His vegetables were worth at most twenty dollars. Our piano, imported from abroad, was probably worth a hundred times that, or more. But Kairys was satisfied. He now had "proof" that the piano was his. To us, it did not matter. It did not look as if we would ever survive this hell, and if we did, we were sure that we would have no problem getting it back from him. This was our last worry. We could only wish that we should ever have to face this problem. Kairys still stayed with us for a few minutes, then put the paper into his pocket and left. No sooner had he left than my mother turned to me and said, "Do you still believe we should have left the clothes to Kairys?"

In the meantime the news from the fronts was very bad. The Germans were advancing almost nonstop deep into the interior of Russia. Equally discouraging were the reports from the provincial towns. Every day, new refugees showed up at the council with more and more horror stories about massacres of thousands of Jews in the small towns.

Although the resettlement of the Jews was proceeding at full speed, thousands of Jews were still stranded in town. Some still had no place to go and others were still in the process of transferring their belongings to the ghetto.

On 7 August, totally unexpectedly, Lithuanian partisans started arresting Jews on the streets. The original impression was that the Jews were being gathered for work, which had become more or less common during the construction of the bridge and the barbed wire fence. But the arrests were exceptionally haphazard and men of all ages were being rounded up, many of them older people who were unable to work. Within a few hours they had arrested over a thousand Jews. These people were crowded into trucks and hauled away. A panic gripped the Jewish community and men disappeared from the streets almost instantaneously. The next day these Jews were taken to the Fourth Fort, where they were massacred. This massacre became known as the "Black Thursday Massacre." Among those shot was a classmate of mine, Boris Aronowitsch, a soft-spoken boy, a genius in mathematics, and a sincere and devoted friend.

This mass execution shook all the Jews who were still in town, and everybody, whether they had a place to go or not, rushed to the ghetto. The ones who were lucky joined friends or family, and the rest were moved to the abandoned factories at the end of Krisciukaicio Street. Several thousand Jews were dumped into this "reservation" with all of them sleeping on the floor, practically one on top of the other. Their meager belongings were dropped in a big heap with almost no way to get to them. This place became known as Krisciukaicio 107, the address of the abandoned factories.

By 15 August the ghetto was enclosed and there were no more Jews in Kovno or its suburbs. The ghetto was put under the supervision of the German civilian administration, with S. A. Sturmfuehrer Jordan in charge. A former Lithuanian mayor of Vilna was assigned as his assistant. The Jewish council, which the Jews now called the Komitet, or the committee, settled in a two-story house across Varniu Street and began to organize the ghetto. We were getting ready to be shut off from the outside world, getting used to living behind barbed wires. A new life was about to begin.

BOOK TWO

A PAGE OF GLORY

Most of you know what it means when a hundred corpses are lying side by side, or five hundred, or a thousand. To have stuck it out and at the same time—apart from exceptions caused by human weakness—to have remained decent fellows, that is what has made us hard. This is a page of glory in our history, which has never been written and is never to be written. . . . We had the moral right, we had the duty to our people to destroy this people. . . .

—*Heinrich Himmler, 1943*

MAP OF GHETTO KOVNO

first reduction 8•15•41

barbed wire fence

small ghetto, cleared 10•4•41

area cleared 1•11•42

area cleared 10•43

area cleared 12•22•43

1   ghetto bridge
2   ghetto gates
3   Jewish council
4   graphics shop
5   small ghetto hospital
6   slobotker yeshiva
7   ghetto workshops
8   author's house
9   big ghetto hospital
10 blocks A,B,C
11 corridor

VIENOZINSKIO STREET

DEMOKRATU STREET

DEMOKRATU PLAZA

C
10
A   B

VARNIU STREET

PANERIU STREET

VYTENIO STREET

2
3
4
8

7

9
11

SAJUNGOS PLAZA

CEMETERY

5

LINKUVOS STREET

KRISCIUKAICIO STREET

River Neris (Vilija)

TILZES STREET

6

2

JURBARKO STREET

RAUDONDVARIO STREET

concrete bridge

0   100 M   500 M

6

THE FIRST ACTIONS

The house into which we had moved was a typical Lithuanian farm-house. It had electricity, but no running water. Water had to be carried in from a well in the yard, where the water froze in the winter and formed icy patches where one could slip and get seriously hurt. A wooden outhouse at the end of the yard served as the toilet facility all year round. The house itself was a two-story wooden frame structure with a full second story on the street side and a mansard-type back. We lived on the second floor of this house. The mansard-type back room was assigned to Max, Vera, and Ruthie. My mother, Rivka, Sonja with her six-year-old daughter Eetke, an elderly aunt, and I lived in the small dining room just ahead of Vera's room. Dvora Solc lived in a small corridor which was converted into a room, and the Chazans, a middle-aged couple, lived in the front room facing the street, with their fourteen-year-old daughter. All in all, a total of thirteen people shared a space which was previously occupied by a Lithuanian couple and their child. The kitchen was tiny. A wood-burning stove with high side walls penetrating the dining and mansard-type rooms was located in one corner. The high walls were designed to heat the entire rear half of the apartment during the winter. In the kitchen, the Lithuanian couple had a sheet metal cabinet which had a compartment for water on top, a sink about table high, and a space for a bucket in a cabinet at the bottom. This was the running water.

Since our home in Kovno was modern, with running water, the Lithua-nians didn't need this cabinet any more and they "sold" it to us. Vera's room had a crib for Ruthie, a sofa for Max and Vera, and a small cabinet. Behind the exterior wall there was a shallow sloping roof. This space was used for storage. A small plywood door leading to this space was unobstructed for access. The roof space was very shallow and a person could not stand upright in it, since the rafters were too low. There was enough room in this space, however, for a few people crouching, or lying down on the unfinished floor. In moving the furniture back and forth, I discovered that the sheet-metal cabinet, our so-called indoor plumbing, could fit in front of the access door and could hide the rafter space behind. We rearranged the room in such a way that the cabinet was moved in front of the access and, to the non-observing eye, this was a perfect hide-out. One had to know the layout of the second floor to even suspect that there was a space behind it. Being sheet metal, the cabinet was very light and could easily be moved.

"Max," I said, "you stand outside and I will move the cabinet into position. You tell me when the cabinet is in the right place, so that nothing can be suspected."

I crawled in and started maneuvering from inside.

"Hold it," said Max, "that way it is fine, don't move it."

We made marks on the outside and on the inside, where the cabinet was supposed to stand, and I crawled out. The first primitive hide-out was born. We did not know whether or not we would ever need it, but it was comforting to know that in an emergency we had a place to hide. Rivka and Sonja were also apprised of the hide-out. We hoped that it would never be needed.

In the meantime barbed wire fences were being installed all around the ghetto so that we would be completely isolated from the outside world. By Thursday, 14 August, the fence was not yet completed and the ghetto administration was threatened with grim consequences should the fence be unfinished by the deadline. Almost every able-bodied man was recruited by the ghetto police to help complete our own incarceration.

It was a typically hot August day and the work was backbreaking. Posts had to be buried deep into the ground and the barbed wires had to be securely attached to them. Hardly anybody on the job avoided scratches or lacerated hands and fingers. We worked for an entire day without food until the job was done. Outside the ghetto, Lithuanians were standing and watching us work. "They finally put you to work," said one, jeering and laughing.

"Yeah, at last you will learn to earn your bread in an honest way," said another.

At the same time we were busy installing the fence, a representative of the German administration was at the Jewish council. He ordered the council to recruit five hundred professionals—doctors, lawyers, engineers, and other college graduates—for work on Monday, 18 August. He explained that the people had to be intelligent and conversant in Russian and German since the work consisted of sorting and straightening out the records in the City Hall of Kovno, which were left in complete disarray by the retreating Russians. The work would be indoors and three meals would be provided. He assured the council that the treatment would be proper, in order to give the men an opportunity to do a decent job. Under the starvation conditions of the ghetto, the lure of three meals a day was not to be underestimated.

The news about this new job offer quickly circulated around the ghetto. The ghetto police informed as many of the Jewish intelligentsia as possible in the hope of helping people to an easier office job.

With our job at the fence finally done, I scrambled home. My mother was shocked. Here I stood, my clothes torn, my face covered with dust and sweat, my fingers bleeding, and I myself so exhausted I could hardly speak. My mother took a towel, wiped my face, and gave me a glass of water. When I had relaxed a bit, she said to me, "Vulik, I have good news for you. The ghetto administration had just announced that the Germans have asked for five hundred intelligent men for clean office work in the city to bring archives in order. You are supposed to get three meals a day. What do you say?"

I listened carefully without saying a word. When my answer did not come immediately, my mother said again, "I think you should consider it. Is what you have been through today any better?"

"No, of course not, but why do they need Jews for such a job? There might be secret papers there, too. Why can't they use Lithuanians?"

"Well, I guess the Lithuanians have to be paid high wages and here they are getting an intelligent force for virtually nothing, just three meals a day."

"Your logic sounds good, but my intuition says something else. Just think, it is already two months after the start of the war and you mean to say that in those two months nobody bothered to take care of the documents?"

"I guess they have more important things to think about. After all, they are involved in a war, which takes precedence. These papers can wait, the war cannot."

"You are giving me a good argument, but it just sounds unreal. They just don't go around thinking up how to please a few Jewish intellectuals."

"They are not trying to please you. They are trying to get a job done. I still believe that the offer is on the level. Just look at you, is that what you want to be doing?"

My mother was obviously trying everything to persuade me to go. She wanted to protect me from another day like this. After a short pause I said to her, "Mom, we still have a few days till Monday. The decision doesn't have to be made until the eighteenth and today is only the fourteenth. Let's sleep on it."

The next few days were restless ones for me. I was torn between the choice of a seemingly half-way decent job indoors or a life at backbreaking slave labor. Max, fortunately, was not involved in this decision. He was helping to set up the ghetto hospital and was exempt. My choice was between reporting to work or hiding in the hide-out. Hiding was a dangerous thing. If caught, the person could be shot.

In the morning of 18 August I got up and made myself ready to go to work. I had reached my decision. My mother was happy. She felt it was her influence that made me decide to go. She was pleased that her son would not have to perform difficult manual labor, he would be in an office under tolerable conditions. Before leaving, I looked through the window and saw people moving towards the gate. In the crowd I noticed quite a few friends of mine: several engineers, a few doctors, friends of Max's. This put me somewhat at ease. All of them could not be crazy. Apparently they, too, had reached the same decision. I walked out and started towards the gate. As I proceeded in that direction, I overheard a few people talking. There were only about four hundred people at the gate and the Jewish police and even worse, the Lithuanian partisans, were forcibly dragging people out of their homes to fill the quota. Also, the size of the guard seemed rather large.

This struck me as odd. This was supposed to be a job where we were to be treated in a civilized manner; was this the treatment awaiting us? Oh, no, I would not be caught in this mess! Without hesitation, I turned around and rushed back home.

My mother was astounded. "What happened, why are you back?" she asked.

"Don't ask questions," I said, "move the cabinet, I am going into hiding."

The cabinet was pushed aside and I quickly crawled into the roof space. Mother helped me close the space, still dumbfounded about what had happened. The police and the Lithuanians continued the search.

That morning a group of five hundred thirty-four intellectuals left the ghetto, presumably for City Hall for office work. All day I stayed in the roof space. The day in the hot chamber was unbearable. The sun was beating down on the roof and the air inside was like a furnace, but I stuck it out. In the evening, when the men were supposed to return, members of their families assembled at the gate. The clock struck six, seven, eight, but nobody showed up. Finally a messenger from the authorities came and tried to calm everybody down. The amount of work was so overwhelming that they decided to keep the men overnight. But next day came and went, without a sign of the workers. Once again, assurances were made that they had completed their work, but were sent away for two weeks to help with work on farms and would be back soon.

My mother was in a strange mood. On the one hand, she was relieved that I was safe, but on the other, she felt terrible for the people who didn't return, among them so many friends of mine and Max's.

The weeks passed, but no news came from the workers. Daily the families besieged the council, but nothing authoritative could be obtained. Meanwhile some Lithuanians came to the ghetto fence and told the people who lived there that all five hundred thirty-four Jews had been shot the same day, 18 August, at the Fourth Fort in Panemune. Nobody paid much attention to them: their information was dismissed as vicious rumors by anti-Semitic Lithuanians who only wanted to aggravate the Jews. But the Jewish administration started to suspect foul play. Through outside contacts they discovered that the information was true. That same day the men had been led away in several smaller groups to an area containing deeply excavated holes in the ground. Then the Lithuanian guard, also known as the Third Operational Group, shot them all. Several men who tried to escape were killed on the run. Almost the entire intelligentsia of Jewish Kovno had thus been liquidated in one mass execution. All of us—the ghetto council, the police, the doctors, the lawyers, the engineers—all of us were fooled by the promise of three meals a day. I was spared this time. Our hide-out had saved my life.

The mood in the ghetto was one of total desperation. But we were not given any respite for even one moment. For about two weeks, starting the morning of 19 August, the ghetto was to experience brutal house searches. On Tuesday morning, under the command of police chief Tornbaum, a mass of German soldiers and trucks descended. In a typical systematic German way, they went from house to house and confiscated anything of value, from gold and silver to furniture and electric appliances. They cleaned out all drawers and closets, searching every nook and corner, and left the rooms in complete disarray. The Jews were not even allowed to complain. Any wrong move would provoke a severe beating. These were trained bullies, experienced in Gestapo tactics and only too willing to apply their bloody skills. Any gold or silver pieces were taken away immediately. Even wedding rings had to be taken off fingers and turned in. When my mother could not take the ring off fast enough, a ring she had had on her hand for close to thirty years, the soldier threatened to cut off the finger together with the ring. Whenever a soldier noticed a nice piece of furniture, he ordered it taken out and loaded onto the waiting truck. Electric appliances were confiscated to the very last piece. Any decent suit or coat was taken out of the closet and piled into the trucks. Pockets had to be turned upside down and all the money was taken away. We did not lose any furniture, since all the best pieces we had left with Kairys. But more than anything else they were after gold, silver, and jewelry, which they did not find in our home. We had hidden it when we moved into the ghetto. We knew already from the past two months that both the Lithuanians and the Germans were roaming free in the city and helping themselves to Jewish loot. The only things not hidden were minor items, which were left out deliberately to pacify the intruders.

The inspections proceeded systematically from house to house until the entire ghetto had been thoroughly combed. But this was not all. Once the first stage was completed, another wave of searches started. This wave was accompanied by severe beatings, particularly of the men. My mother was very concerned about my presence.

"Vulia," she said, "you have to get out of the house during the house searches. Why don't you go to the committee, which is right across the street, and try to get yourself some temporary work. We have so many close friends in there, you should have no problem."

"I guess you are right, Mom," I said, "but it may not be as easy as you say. Just look out the window, look at the crowd in front of the committee."

"It does not mean that these people want to get involved with the committee. Most of them are still looking for a roof over their heads," mother replied.

"This is true, but . . . " I started.

"No buts," mother interrupted me, "just go and try, you have nothing to lose."

With that I left the house and walked over to the committee. How lucky we were that our house was so close. To get into the inside of the building was almost impossible. The pushing and shoving, the screaming and crying was completely out of control. And indeed, as mother had suspected, the majority of the people were without lodging and were looking to be placed with some other families. When I managed to fight my way in, I discovered, to my surprise, that a former classmate of mine was in charge of the employment board. He was genuinely glad to see me.

"Labl," I said, "I am surprised to see you here!"

"It is really nice to see you, too," said Labl. "Do you have a place to live?"

"Yes, our home is right across the street from the committee," I answered.

"That is great! How about joining us here in the committee?"

This was more than I expected. Instead of me begging for a job, here I had an offer!

"Gladly," I replied, "I will do anything you will let me have."

"Wonderful," said Labl, "get into the back room and wait, I will be right with you."

Labl did not let me wait long. He came right in and gave me some papers to go through and told me to report to work every day at the committee.

When I came home mother just could not believe it. This was like manna from heaven. I had put in my foot into the door of the committee. Little did I know what the consequences of this event would be in our existence later on.

In the meantime the first wave of searches was completed and the Germans moved straight into phase two. If phase one was bad, phase two was far worse. The Actions were accompanied not only by beatings, but also by shooting. Wherever they found something that should have been cleaned out earlier, they charged that the item was deliberately hidden and they shot the man in the house on the spot. In every quarter of the ghetto they found reason to shoot somebody, to intimidate and disseminate panic. Wherever they did not find men in the house, they made the women undress completely and even went as far as to perform gynecological investigations under the pretext that they may be hiding gold.

The next day rumors were spread that the search parties would come with dogs which can sniff rare metals. And indeed the next day the soldiers had German shepherds with them which attacked the helpless people upon the slightest command from their handlers. Again people were shot and rumors were spread that the dogs indeed had some capacity to sniff out gold. The panic was escalating with every new Jew killed. Many people started to reconsider whether it was not better to get rid of the gold.

During this phase of the Gold Action, close friends of ours, Nathan and Simon, came to our home. They told us that they had a safe place where they had hidden all their gold and the gold of their father-in-law, Itzik, and offered to take our gold and hide it, too. The offer looked very attractive, but mother declined.

Meanwhile the second phase of the Action was completed. But the Germans saw that there was by no means enough gold in the loot. Obviously a lot of it must have been hidden. In the evening, Sturmfuehrer Jordan came to the committee and announced that the searches would continue and that the German command was aware that a lot of gold and valuables were hidden by the Jews. Consequently the committee was ordered to announce to the ghetto that tomorrow the Jews must voluntarily remit all the hidden gold and valuables. Two days were given for the voluntary operation. After that new searches would begin and wherever gold was found, one hundred Jews in the area would be shot.

This was a very severe threat indeed, and we knew that they would not hesitate to do it. It struck the ghetto like thunder. Responsible Jews were worried that this meant a new massacre and extraordinary pressure was now applied to the population to get rid of the gold and to save lives. I was ordered by Labl to go with a few other men from house to house to talk to people and to collect the gold. In these two days, I saw more gold, diamonds, and jewelry than the biggest wholesale house will ever have. The estimate was tens of millions of dollars worth of jewelry.

The paranoia in the ghetto was raised to such a pitch that people who had their gold hidden in presumably safe places dug it out and brought it to the collection centers. When we checked with Nathan and Simon as to what they intended to do, they told us that the gold was safe and they intended to keep it. But mother was not moved.

In the meantime I had collected jewelry of such value and beauty that I could not resist going home first to show it to mother and Vera before returning it to the center. Vera looked them over piece by piece and put some of them on her neck and fingers. There were rubies, sapphires, emeralds, all of them fixed in hand-crafted settings, made to order by skillful, superb artists. Vera changing the jewelry and looking into the mirror reminded me of the scene from the opera *Faust*, where Marguerite admires her new jewelry and sings her famous Jewel aria. For an instant, ever so short, Vera was in a dream world, totally removed from the real setting around her. For a moment, she was oblivious of the fact that this was a macabre dream, that in reality she was not getting jewelry, but was being robbed of it, robbed blind by a murderous band of Nazi henchmen. Not only were we being deprived of our legitimate property, but life was in jeopardy. Any minute we could be shot just for possessing some of these gems with which Vera was now toying. But for this one moment of forgetfulness, she was far from it all in a fantasy world of her own.

Mother, on the other hand, did not touch the jewelry. She had had enough jewelry, and the threat of shooting hundreds of Jews for one piece of jewelry was too big a responsibility. Nobody wanted it!

Upon mother's prodding, I took most of our jewelry, worth a fortune, to the gathering place. The only thing mother was not ready to part with was an extraordinary set of gold flatware. I took the rest of the jewelry out of the house as ostentatiously as possible, so that all our neighbors could see that we were getting rid of our gold. The more people turned in their valuables, the more pressure came to bear on the people who were still hanging on to their treasures. In many cases these treasures had been in the family for generations and it was more for sentimental reasons that the people were desperately hanging on to them despite all threats. But when it came down to the threat of shooting one hundred Jews for every piece of gold, things started to change.

In the meantime my assignment took me and my party to the Small Ghetto. Here I accidentally ran into a home where Mrs. Joffe, the wife of the attorney, happened to open the door. When she noticed me, she became hysterical. We went into the house and tried to comfort her. At the moment, I did not understand what had brought this about. When she had calmed down, I found out, to my complete astonishment, that attorney Joffe was one of the victims who was shot and killed during the second phase of the Action. When I walked out of her house, I could not get over it. The words he had spoken to Max kept coming back to me over and over again: "Doctor, I should not be saying this, but I have a premonition that I will not survive this . . . ." I never thought that his premonition would come true so soon. This was incredible, here was a man who had just survived one of the worst massacres of the time, the Seventh Fort. By all rights, he was destined by some superior power to survive. I was speechless. I could not continue with my co-workers and asked them to go on without me. I ran home to tell my family the horrible news. Everyone reacted as I did. Somehow, everybody simultaneously recalled his premonition. When the shock had worn off, mother went to the hiding place, removed the flatware, gave it to me, and said, "I don't need it, life is too precious, bring it to the gathering center. If God has willed that we survive, we will have other jewelry and flatware. I want my conscience to be clean that nobody got shot because of me."

It must have been terribly hard for mother to part with it. I saw it in her eyes. This was father's gift on one of her anniversaries and tremendous nostalgia was connected with it, but circumstances were much too serious. People at the gathering place could not get over the beauty of this unique set. It was passed from hand to hand with everybody commenting on the gold crown adorning the flatware.

"Anyone wants to take a chance on hiding it, you can have it," I said, but nobody was willing, the panic and responsibility were just too great.

In the evening the Germans came and picked up the loot. The robbers had a field day. The next morning the Germans were back again and proceeded with random spot checks. They did not find anything. Overnight the ghetto was turned into a bunch of paupers, locked behind barbed wire at the will of the teutonic barbarians.

Yet Max, without telling anybody, decided to hide his gold watch. He made sure that nobody knew about it. His logic was that once somebody knew, a careless remark could be fatal. Thus the complete secrecy was warranted. Not even Vera was apprised of it. This was a major gamble, but it paid dividends about three years later, during Vera's illness, when we needed gold desperately for medicine and could not get any.

But Max was not the only one. All over the ghetto people who were not easily intimidated secretly refused to surrender their gold.

7

GIZA

On Friday, 5 September, the Germans were back in the ghetto for some spot checking, but when they did not find any more valuables, they left. The weekend was unusually quiet, but the tension in the ghetto did not subside.

In the meantime Max went to the Small Ghetto every morning where a hospital was being set up. This work meant seven days a week without rest. The job consisted of rounding up instruments and equipment which the doctors had managed to hide during the Gold Action, contacting colleagues and pharmacists, and putting the hospital into operation. In the course of this assignment he met a former colleague of his, Dr. Gerber, who was involved in the same task. Dr. Gerber was about the same age as Max, and Max was very pleased to be working alongside him. Occasionally they would walk home together from the hospital. Dr. Gerber's home was on the way to ours and was located inside the Big Ghetto, just beyond the so-called corridor.

With the Gold Action now completed, I was concerned about what my next assignment would be. During the weekend I had a lot of time to contemplate, and I came up with an interesting idea. The ghetto was now in the stage of being organized, but nobody had a map of it: not the committee, not the police, not the office in charge of dwellings. Yet the need for a map was there, particularly since so many Jews were still without a roof over their heads. I felt that I could fill this need. I had just graduated from engineering school and had a good knowledge of surveying, mapping, and graphics. This would be ideal for me. Monday morning when I came to the committee, I suggested it to Labl. He was ecstatic

73

and could not get over how such a basic thought had not occurred to anybody. I was immediately given a certificate indicating that I was an employee of the committee and in charge of surveying the ghetto. This certificate was useful in case I should be stopped by the Jewish police and dragged off to some other job. I grabbed the opportunity with both hands and thrust myself into my new assignment. The job was not exactly easy, since I had no instruments whatsoever. But this became a challenge to me. At least it took my mind off our distressing situation, and I was doing something I was trained to do. But there was a side benefit to this assignment. The job took me to every corner of the ghetto, since I had to make sure that no house was missed.

One morning while surveying the Small Ghetto I accidentally ran into Giza, the girl I had dated for almost a year just before the Russians occupied Lithuania in 1940. Giza's family was among the most respected and prominent in town and she reflected it in her behaviour. During my college years I was never short of nice girlfriends and the young people in our circle were all very refined. But this girl had class. Prior to this encounter, I had not seen her for almost a year. I was busy with my job in the army corps of engineers and had no time for dating. Besides, the Russian occupation had changed our lives fundamentally and I found myself in a brand-new circle of friends. Although I had not forgotten her, I was just too busy to keep up our friendship.

Running into her so suddenly opened up old feelings and my heart started pounding rapidly. I looked at her and she at me and suddenly we were in each other's arms. In this one year, she had matured and developed. Whereas she was then a young kid, she was now a mature woman. I felt her warm body in my embrace. Her breasts were fuller and shapelier than I had remembered from our last date. I could feel her heart pounding too.

"Giza," I finally opened up, "what pleasure to hold you in my arms again."

"The pleasure is mutual," she replied. "I often thought of you in this past year. Our short courtship was probably one of my fondest memories."

"I did not forget you either," I replied, "but this Russian occupation had everything turned upside down. Tell me about yourself, where were you during these terrible months since the beginning of the war, and where is your family?"

Giza's story was a familiar one. When the war started, her family had decided not to run and to hope for the best. During the arrests that followed, her father and her grandfather were dragged out of the house by Lithuanian partisans and never came back. By all indications they were probably shot at the Seventh Fort together with my father. She was now living in one room with her mother and grandmother in the Small Ghetto. In the course of the conversation, I told her all about myself and we quickly switched to reminiscences about the good old days. In the meantime I was getting ready to leave. I told her where I lived and asked her to come and see me as soon as possible, which she promised. When I came home I told mother about it, who was very pleased at the prospect of seeing Giza. She really liked her. And why shouldn't she? Giza was sweet and likeable. All evening my mind was with her and I was excited over the prospect of having her visit me and maybe even reopening the old courtship, if times should ever get to be normal in the ghetto.

My work was proceeding nicely and by the end of the week I had covered a considerable part of the ghetto. On Monday, 15 September, when I came to the committee, I noticed a commotion there. People seemed to be very excited. The rumor was that Jordan, the Sturmfuehrer in charge of the ghetto, supposedly was locked up with the Jewish council. Needless to say, when Jordan was in the ghetto it meant trouble. I decided to wait and not to continue my survey work. When Jordan left the council refused to make any statement, but it was clear that something had happened. When no news was forthcoming I left on my usual assignment, but I could not work. I was nervous and tense. What was now brewing underneath the surface? I just had to know what the score was; life depended on it. I returned to the committee much earlier than usual. Labl called me aside, gave me two pieces of paper, and said, "Put them away, they may prove to be of major importance."

"What is it all about?" I asked, looking at the two scraps of paper, which had Jordan's signature.

"Remember when you came in this morning, Jordan was here? He locked himself up with the council and handed them five thousand of these certificates and ordered them to be distributed to artisans and various trade specialists," Labl continued.

"Did he elaborate on it?"

"No, he did not explain what it was for, but stressed that these certificates be distributed as soon as possible, and my logic tells me that no matter what their significance, it is much better to have one of them. I have a hunch that they divide the useful from the non-useful Jews, or Jordan would not have specifically singled out tradesmen."

"By the way, how did you get those?" I asked.

"We were called into the council and given certificates for key employees and I managed to get two for you," Labl answered.

"Could you get me two more for my sister and her husband?" I asked.

"No, these passes are treated like gold."

"Then there is even more reason to suspect that there is much more behind it than meets the eye," I said, and with this I left the committee and ran home. The rumor about the passes in the meantime was spreading through the ghetto and people got apprehensive and started to congregate on the plaza outside the committee. When I entered our house, my family already had heard about the passes. When I showed mother my two passes and relayed my fears to her, mother decided to rush to the committee and to talk to Mr. Goldberg, another member of the council and a very close friend of ours. As an employee of the committee, I managed to get my mother past the Jewish police at the door of the council. She requested to see Mr. Goldberg and was allowed to enter. After much pleading and begging, Mr. Goldberg ordered the secretary to issue two certificates to mother. Thus our entire family had a certificate each.

In the meantime the anxiety in the ghetto was growing.

On Tuesday the sixteenth some certificates were distributed, but not knowing how many artisans there were in the ghetto and where they were living slowed the distribution down. Now the committee realized how important my map was, and I was ordered to complete it as fast as possible.

On Wednesday morning, when Max left to go to the Small Ghetto where the hospital was, he and the other people trying to enter the Small Ghetto were stopped at the bridge and not permitted to cross. The Small Ghetto was surrounded by a large contingent of Lithuanian partisans and Germans, who entered the Small Ghetto with guns drawn. The Lithuanians started to chase all the people out of their homes. The Jews were chased under a hail of beatings to a plaza, where a selection began. The Jews without passes were badly mistreated and ordered to the side. When the selection was completed, trucks entered the ghetto and the Jews from the bad side began to be loaded on to the trucks and were taken to the Ninth Fort. A panic gripped the entire ghetto. This was an Action! People were being transported to the extermination fort! Jews living near the fence across Paneriu Street abandoned their homes and started streaming towards the interior of the Large Ghetto, since nobody knew whether or not the soldiers would turn on the Large Ghetto, if they had to fulfill a quota. The people in the Small Ghetto, on the bad side, were crying and begging not to be loaded on to the trucks, but to no avail. Mothers were hugging children to their hearts and the children were petrified and numb.

While this was going on, a group of Germans with movie cameras were taking films of the entire proceedings. It could be clearly seen that the movies were concentrating on the Jews and the Lithuanians, but carefully avoiding covering any Germans. They were filming scenes where Lithuanians were mistreating Jews. In the meantime the Jews with the Jordan passes were not touched and seemed to be somehow under the protection of the Germans. The word that an Action was in progress and that the Jews with the Jordan passes were spared spread like wildfire through the ghetto. The importance of Jordan passes suddenly became apparent: Jews without the passes were being singled out for extermination, whereas Jews with passes were spared. But suddenly a few Germans on motorcycles appeared on the plaza and, waving some kind of paper, ordered the selection stopped and demanded that the Jews who were already on their way to the Ninth Fort be brought back. The Lithuanians were caught by complete surprise and retreated to a corner. The Jews were ordered to disperse and go home. The plaza emptied within minutes. The people could not get away fast enough from this nightmare, among them Giza, her mother and grandmother.

But the effect of this Action was profound. The fact that the people with Jordan passes were not touched created a panic among the people who did not have any. Late in the afternoon, when the special Lithuanian and German guard was withdrawn and it had become clear that the Action was over, a mob descended on the committee demanding Jordan passes, which suddenly became life passes. The scene outside the committee resembled a revolution. The Jewish police were trying to hold the mob back, but to no avail. Life was now at stake and no statements by anyone from the committee and no police force could contain the crowd. A speaker from the committee who tried to explain that the committee did not have enough certificates was screamed down and attacked and had to be rescued by the Jewish police through a back door. The mob finally broke through the totally inadequate police and forced its way into the building. Here the mob ransacked the house, overturned tables, broke into cabinets, pulled out all drawers, but no certificates were found. Finally the mob, not having found any certificates, dispersed and went home.

The big riddle in the ghetto was, what was the purpose of this latest Action? Was it a test Action, to see how the Jews would behave under the real thing? Or was it to incite one Jew against the other by distributing an insufficient number of life certificates? Or was it to prove that all the excesses against the Jews were being perpetrated by the local population and not the Germans? It was, of course, also possible that the intent was to exterminate all except the artisans who could be useful temporarily for the German war effort. There was no satisfactory answer to any of these hypotheses. But one thing was clear: the Jordan passes were indeed life passes, and the controversy would not die down so soon.

In the evening I ran over to the Small Ghetto to see Giza. I found the family terribly worried. Here were three helpless women, without a man in the family, without hope to get a life pass for any of them. What would become of them in case of another Action?

The next day when I returned to the committee, everybody was busy cleaning up the mess. Late in the afternoon, when order was restored, some beautiful signs were put up on the doors marking the department in that room. The signs were in German. They were all made in tempera paint with nice, clean letters, neatly arranged borders, precisely centered, with a star of David in the background. The signs were real masterpieces. I myself was very good in drafting in school, but this was absolutely tops. I could not stop admiring them. When I got into the office where Labl was working, I asked him who it was who had made those signs.

"The work was done by a German Jew from Berlin, a graduate of a well-known graphics institute there, by the name of Peter, and he works for our department out of his house."

"I sure would like to meet him," I said, "the man is a superb artist."

"He lives in the ghetto not too far from here. Come to think of it, you should get together with him. You are now about ready to start drawing the plan of the ghetto, and he could help you make a nice presentation."

"Sounds very interesting."

"No problem," said Labl, "here is his address. Tell him I sent you to him. Explain to him what you are doing and see how you could join forces."

This was an intriguing proposition. The next morning I took all my papers with me and was ready to discuss with him the suggestion made by Labl. I had no difficulty finding his house.

I knocked on the door and Peter let me in. I explained to him briefly the purpose of my visit and he led me into a room where in a corner he had set up a little atelier. He showed me his work, which I found absolutely superb, and he looked at my sketches and was very pleased with them. From the very first moment we hit it off right. We talked for a little while and discussed how the plan should be presented, what I would do and where his work would come in. We both agreed that I should come to him again as soon as I finished my part of the plan. This was the beginning of an association that lasted throughout all the years of the war.

When I returned to the committee I told Labl about our agreement, and he suggested that I get my tools and set up a little workshop in one corner of the room. We immediately cleared out one area in one of the rooms. I brought in my drafting board, a few drafting sheets, some of my tools, and started my work. In about two days I had my plan completed and went to Peter to add his part to it. Peter complimented me on my presentation. I explained to Peter that I had a corner in the committee assigned to me and suggested that he join me there rather than work from his home. He did not show too much enthusiasm for my idea, he wanted to be on his own and maintain his artistic freedom. But I tried to convince him that these were not normal times, where he was trying to develop a business of his own. In our situation, it was better to be close to where the action was, to get to know the Jewish leaders and to be apprised of the daily situation right at the source. Some of the information thus received could be decisive and life itself could depend on it. Just the Jordan passes alone were a case in point. After a short discussion he came around to see my point and said that he would join me.

The next day he had the job completed and met me in the committee. He opened the plan and showed it to me. The work was superb. Labl took the plan right away to the council and showed it to them. Before we knew what had happened, we had orders for about half a dozen more plans: for the council, for the ghetto police, for the department of dwellings, and for a few others. Peter, in the meantime, had worked out a deal whereby his department would be independent and not attached to any other, so as not to have a boss dictating to him what to do and how to do it. This was the beginning of the Mal-und Zeichenwerkstatt, or the graphics department of the ghetto.

No sooner had we started the department than new orders started to come in. The first one was from the ghetto police, who wanted us to make armbands with the inscription Jewish Ghetto Police, so they could be easily identified. Peter prepared several designs and after one of them was accepted, he cut a template and showed me the technique of using it. We had just barely started and we already needed help. The first to join us was Nolik, a very gifted young artist, whose paintings and sketches had surprised even Peter. When the police armbands hit the street, the other departments decided that for their identification they, too, needed armbands. This increased our workload even more. Within one week Nucia and Bobbie joined our shop. The die was cast. Our shop was a reality and our entire life in the ghetto from now on would rotate around the Mal-und Zeichenwerkstatt.

The closing of the ghetto brought with it extermination for the unlucky, and for the survivors hunger, a ruthless routine of slave labor, and a ceaseless barrage of rumors originated by the Gestapo. The food ration per week for every Jew was minuscule and the supplement for workers was just as small. There were no provisions for milk, cheese, butter, potatoes, fruits, vegetables, or sugar. What poor rations we had were not always delivered to the ghetto. With no access to any other source of food, people soon were on the brink of starvation.

The second curse of the ghetto was the forced labor. The Germans discovered that they had a free work force in the ghetto and they did not hesitate to exploit it. Most of the jobs were in the open field with no shelter from rain or snow, cold or heat. Severe beatings were as common as flies in the summer and verbal abuse was so usual that nobody even paid any attention any more. The only ones who had it somewhat better were the various specialists, who generally worked under sheltered conditions and occasionally even got food on the job. Besides the problems at the various working places, one was never sure whether or not the Germans would one day pick up the entire brigade and take it away, never to come back. After the intellectuals were taken out of the ghetto and shot, people were scared that they might leave in the morning and be dead by night. At first people were reluctant to leave the ghetto and tried to avoid the outside brigades. But the Germans demanded that the ghetto procure the necessary number of laborers for the various working places and the Jewish ghetto police was saddled with the task of rounding up Jews and forcibly sending them to work. Faced with this problem, the ghetto administration carried out a registration of all able-bodied men and women. Work duty applied to men from fourteen to sixty and for women from fifteen to fifty-five. Only women with children under four years of age were released, but even this changed later. The work week was set to six or seven days for men and five days for women.

The worst of these jobs was at the aerodrome, the military airport, which the German high command had decided to build in Kovno. The work consisted of twelve hours day and night, no food, terrible German supervisors, hard work, and on top of it no opportunity to bring in food, since no civilians were admitted to the site. Needless to say, nobody wanted to work there. At first the German airforce asked for only several hundred men, but little by little they raised the demand to close to four thousand, which became a nightmare to procure.

Hunger has no restraints and transforms peaceful people into animals. When hunger in the ghetto grew to intolerable proportions, the work brigades became the only means of contacting farmers outside the ghetto from whom food could be obtained. This, more than anything else, forced the ghetto population to stop hiding and try to join the labor force. When a German officer came to claim a brigade for a relatively desirable site, workers got into fights to join it. The Jewish police and the ghetto guard had to intervene with bloody beatings, often injuring people seriously. But due to the severe hunger it was an almost insurmountable task to contain the people. The opposite was true when it came to pick workers for the aerodrome. No sooner was it announced that people for the aerodrome would be assembling, than everybody started scurrying for cover and streets had to be blocked off not to let the laborers get away.

To alleviate the plight of the aerodrome workers, the council was forced to institute a system of substitutes, whereby the workers of the ghetto institutions had to give one day to replace an aerodrome worker. This gave him a day off to rest or to join another brigade where he could bring in food for his starving family. Thus, every so often, Max and I would have to join the aerodrome work force.

On the aerodrome, at first, Russian prisoners of war also used to work. Endless columns of prisoners, as far as the eye could see, came to work every day. They were mistreated even worse than the Jews. Not only did they work the same long hours we did, but in the evening they were taken to their stockades, where they were kept under the open sky. Every day when they returned from work, dozens of them, youngsters barely eighteen years old, with sad, sorrowful faces, had to be supported on both sides by somewhat stronger p.o.w.'s, since they were already too weak to walk. The next morning they would be dead. Cruelty to the prisoners was beyond description. In a month or so, there were no more Russians. They either died of starvation or were massacred by the Germans. The Jews had to replace them now. When the ghetto could not procure enough men, women were forced to work on the aerodrome.

This was the situation in the ghetto when, on the evening of 25 September, totally unexpectedly, an officer of the ghetto guard dispatched a message to the Jewish council informing them that the day before a Jew fired a shot at the chief of the ghetto guard. He gave the council twenty-four hours to arrest the culprit and deliver him to the German police. Since the entire story was a fabrication, the council could not meet the demand and the entire ghetto was now anticipating the worst.

On the afternoon of Friday 26 September German police and Lithuanian partisans surrounded several square blocks of the ghetto where the attack had supposedly taken place. They chased the entire population of the area out into the street. Under severe beatings all of the Jews were hustled to a nearby plaza where a selection started. Anybody who had a Jordan pass was directed to one side and all the others, among them women, children, and elderly men, went to the other. All in all about one thousand people were selected and taken to the Ninth Fort, where they were shot the same day. The people with the certificates were not allowed to return to their homes for several days, since the Germans wanted to inspect the houses for hidden weapons. After a search that lasted a few

days, the displaced Jews were allowed to return to their homes, which
had been cleaned out of anything having any value at all. But more
important, in almost every household somebody was missing who would
never return.

But the ghetto was not given a chance to recuperate from this Action.
New rumors started to circulate. The Lithuanians near the Small Ghetto
informed the Jews that shortly they would have to vacate because their
houses were to be returned to the Lithuanian owners. In fact, the Lithuanians had requested the Germans to liquidate the Jews in the Small Ghetto
because they wanted their homes back. The rumors were spreading
rapidly. Where would they go if the Small Ghetto had to be evacuated?
There was no place in the Big Ghetto. Anxiety was escalating by the hour.

Late in the afternoon on Friday, totally unexpectedly, Giza showed up
at our house. I was surprised, but certainly glad to see her, and I gave her
a hug and a kiss. She looked worried, but even this could not conceal her
unusual beauty. After a short chat Giza confided that she was here to
consult with me about the rumors. They lived in the Small Ghetto and for
the last week none of the people there could sleep.

"Vulia," she said, "you certainly have heard those rumors about the
Small Ghetto."

"Yes, everybody has heard them," I replied.

"What do you think is going to happen to us?" she continued, "you
work in the committee and you surely know more than we do."

"Giza, darling, we are just as much in the dark as you are. I wish I
knew more and could advise you. In fact, I am not even sure I have the
right to advise. It would be too presumptuous on my part to play the role
of a prophet."

"I understand, but still, you are older and more mature."

"Giza, I am afraid we are facing an Action. I would advise hiding.
Giza, why don't you sleep here tonight," I said, "Max and I are scheduled to go to the aerodrome tomorrow to substitute for the airfield
workers and you could stay here all day without any problems. At night,
when we return, we will see what the situation will be."

"Vulia, it is very generous of you to make this offer, but I cannot accept
it. I cannot leave my mother in such a serious hour."

"But you cannot help her anyway. Don't be hasty in your reply, think
about it."

"No, Vulia, should anything happen, it would be on my conscience
always."

A silence suddenly permeated the room. A heavy cloud of inevitability
lingered around us. I looked at Giza and without consulting anybody else

in the household, I said, "Giza, let your mother come with you. We don't have much space, but we will manage."

Again a silence ensued. Giza was struggling. I had the impression that she wanted to accept the offer, but things were not so simple.

"Vulia," she said after a while of hesitation, "mother will not go without grandmother. I am sure of it."

I was ready to offer place for two, but three was a problem. Where would we put them? We were crowded as it was. Besides, how critical was the situation? Maybe nothing would happen after all.

"Giza, darling, I still believe that you should stay here at least for the night, you are here already. Tomorrow when I return from the airfield we will discuss this again."

"You are so wonderful, but mother will be worried if I don't return tonight."

"So why don't you talk it over with your mother tonight. Perhaps she won't mind you staying with us alone after all. Then tomorrow night take some of your most necessary belongings with you and come and stay with us until things calm down."

"I am not sure I can go through with it and leave mother and grand-mother alone, but I promise to talk to them. In any case I will let you know what we have decided."

The rest of the conversation was awfully subdued and all my attempts to cheer her up were fruitless. When she was ready to go, I embraced her and emphasized again, "Giza, I will see you tomorrow?"

"Yes, I promise," she said.

With these words she left our house. I went to bed thinking about tomorrow, when I would see her again. Tomorrow promised to be a long day: Max and I were due to go to the aerodrome and in the evening I expected Giza. Max made sure that he had a substitute in the hospital. In my case it was not needed.

It was a terribly restless night. The shooting at the Small Ghetto by the guards was louder than ever and I could not sleep. In the morning, Saturday 4 October, we got up and went to the gate. Here all the workers assembled to go to work. Our column was one of the first to leave, since this shift was the longest of all. At the aerodrome my thoughts drifted back to Giza. Would she come to stay with us tonight, as we had talked? The thoughts about Giza made my work a little easier.

Around six in the evening the foreman called it a day and we lined up to return. As we approached the ghetto, we suddenly saw a huge column of smoke. It seemed as if the entire ghetto was on fire. The black smoke and the flames could be seen for miles around. We started to hustle in fearful anticipation of what we might find, or worse, what we might not find any more!

While we were at the aerodrome the Small Ghetto was surrounded by large contingents of Lithuanian partisans and German police. Nobody was allowed in or out, not even the Jewish workers who had just returned from slave labor. Petrified, they remained on this side of the fence, looking anxiously into the area where their homes and families were left behind. Hungry and tired, they could not even go home to rest up and to have a hot bowl of soup.

But this was the least of their worries. As they were gathering around the bridge and near the fence, the murderers inside started chasing the terrified population of the Small Ghetto from their houses. They were driven under a hail of blows to a plaza, where the Jews with Jordan passes were sent to one side and all others to the opposite, exactly as before. The selection lasted several hours. When it was completed, columns of one hundred each were formed and marched through the gate to Paneriu Street in the direction of the Ninth Fort.

A terrible human drama was unfolding before the eyes of the Jews on both sides of the fence. It was clear: the people on the bad side were being taken to the Ninth Fort for a mass execution. Everybody on both sides of the street began to cry, and those on the Big Ghetto side tried desperately to catch a last glimpse of the loved ones who were being taken away right in front of their eyes, never to come back.

When the condemned Jews realized where they were heading, many tried to escape from the march, but were caught, mercilessly beaten, and driven back into the marching column. Only a few managed to break through and escape. The hospital where Max had worked for the last several weeks, as well as an orphanage and an old age home, were located in the Small Ghetto. The orphans, around two hundred of them, their teachers and nurses, and the elderly of the old age home with their personnel were loaded on to trucks and hauled away to the Ninth Fort for extermination. The cries of anguish on both sides of Paneriu Street could move the heart of the most hardened criminal, but not that of the Nazis and their collaborators.

When we reached the outskirts of the ghetto, we saw Jews standing at the first corner inside the ghetto fence, anticipating us.

"What has happened?" we screamed, "is the ghetto all right, what is burning?"

"Those murderers have carried out another Action in the Small Ghetto. They have liquidated it, taken out about two thousand Jews and led them to the Ninth Fort," they screamed.

"And the fire? What is going on?" we shouted back, "the fire?"

"The Nazis have nailed the doors and windows of the hospital shut and burned the patients alive, together with the doctors and nurses, those monsters!"

"My God!" I heard Max cry out, "I was supposed to be in the hospital today if I were not sent to the aerodrome. My God, what happened to the doctor that replaced me?"

But now, suddenly, my heart stopped. Giza, my Giza! What happened to her? Was she safe? No, I could not bear the thought. I started to shiver.

In the evening, when the Germans were finished, they chased the surviving Jews with the Jordan passes under a hail of blows across the bridge into the main ghetto. When I heard this, I rushed to the bridge to see, maybe, maybe . . . When I reached the bridge I saw those "lucky ones" running across it, trampling the people who fell. I searched in the crowd, but Giza was not there. I still hoped. I ran back home, maybe she was in our house? I ran upstairs, but Giza was not here. Giza the vivacious was gone forever. Not nineteen years old, she was shot and buried in a mass grave with two thousand Jews who were massacred that same day.

The following night was pure hell. I could not possibly sleep. I was tormented. Why didn't I insist that she stay? Why didn't I offer a place for all three of them? She would have been alive now. But this was water over the dam. She was now asleep forever. Asleep in a cold mass grave. And the murderer who pointed the gun at her was free, probably celebrating his heroism with his buddies in a tavern.

8

THE BIG ACTION

The mood in the ghetto after the latest Action was one of despair. Two thousand Jews were dead and more were homeless. Yet the Germans let us know that the work brigades were to arrive at their working places as usual. The Jewish police was summoned to go from house to house and urge the people to report for work or they would be chased out by force.

In the morning Max realized that he had no place to go, since there was no more hospital. The hospital, the patients, the nurses, the doctors—all were destroyed by the fire. It dawned on Max that his friend Dr. Gerber was also on the staff and he got worried. He decided to go to Dr. Gerber's home and check. We were all very apprehensive. When Max returned we all anticipated the worst.

"What did you find out?" asked Vera.

"He was also at the aerodrome," came the answer after a short, tense silence, "he is alive, but do you realize that it means that another doctor was burned to death!"

"God, when is this nightmare going to end?" sighed mother.

In the meantime, at the fronts, the Germans were advancing and reporting one victory after another. The only serious resistance the Germans had met was at Smolensk. But at least this was the first time that their invincibility had been challenged. Their armies were now moving towards Moscow. Leningrad was besieged and was expected to capitulate. In fact, one day the German High Command issued a standby alert for a most important announcement. Everyone expected that Leningrad had fallen. Late in the afternoon the radio broadcast that a huge tonnage of

British ships had been sunk in the Atlantic. It was obvious, however, that this announcement had been hastily concocted to make up for the anticipated news of the fall of Leningrad. Despite this, the resistance was crumbling and in many cities in the Ukraine, the German troops were greeted like liberators. With every German victory, our mood in the ghetto got more depressed. The critical issue was whether or not the Russians could hold out until winter.

Meanwhile the hunger in the ghetto continued to grow. Desperately people searched for ways to obtain additional food. Those of us who lived in peasant homes had little vegetable gardens, which others started to raid, uprooting the vegetables. These were not ready for picking yet, but nobody was willing to wait. Driven by hunger, a small carrot was better than no carrot. When this was noticed by the ghetto administration, an announcement was made that all vegetable gardens were ghetto property and nobody was to touch them. The administration was planning to gather the vegetables from all gardens and distribute them to the entire population. It suddenly dawned on me that I had a slip from Kairys certifying that I bought the vegetables from him for our piano. With that we went to the garden and started to remove whatever was in the ground. Before we had a chance, the Jewish police rushed to our site and forcibly chased us away. I did not give up, however, and took the slip of paper from Kairys and went to the headquarters of the Jewish police. Here I was told that I was not the only one with such a slip and that the order of the committee would stand.

The fact that the committee intended to appropriate all vegetable gardens had now become public knowledge. Nobody, however, was willing to entrust the committee with this task. Everybody figured that most of the vegetables would end up with the people having a hand in the pot and the population at large would remain with nothing. The next morning a mob descended on all gardens and people with bare hands dug up half-ripe potatoes, beets, carrots, and other vegetables. It looked like a locust plague descending on green fields. At first the Jewish ghetto police tried to stop the mob, but it was hopeless. Driven by hunger, people not only attacked the police, but also fought with each other for as little as one potato. When people living in houses which had no gardens saw what was going on, they, too, entered the melee. There were now people heaped on top of each other until every green spot was covered with humanity, fighting for a share of the crop. Within a couple of hours the entire landscape looked like a field which had been trampled on by a herd of elephants. Not a single green leaf was left in the ground. When there was nothing else to dig up the mob dispersed. The net effect of the stampede was a tremendous loss of food for the ghetto as a whole. Had the population waited for several weeks the vegetables would have been twice their size, but nobody was willing to wait.

The population barely had a chance to recover from the Action in the Small Ghetto when new rumors again started to circulate. They concerned ditches that were being dug at the Ninth Fort. The Lithuanians had some very detailed information about the work that was going on there and they seemed authentic enough to drive the entire ghetto into panic. According to the rumors, the Russian prisoners of war had completed huge excavations. Ditches of such magnitude could swallow many thousands of people. Some people refused to believe that such atrocities could be possible. But the majority of us saw it as a very real threat. After all, five hundred thirty-four Jews were killed during the Intelligentsia Action. On 26 September, they killed one thousand people; during the last Action they killed two thousand. Was it possible that they had now perfected their mass extermination methods and were ready for even larger numbers? The steady progression of numbers indicated that their team was ready and that the ditches were for us!

On 26 October, the bubble burst. Rauca, the member of the Security Police and the S.D. in Kovno who had carried out the Intelligentsia Action, showed up at the council. He announced that since the ghetto had so many people who were unable to work, the German administration had decided to establish two ghettos: one for all who were employable and one for all who could not work. According to him, it was only fair that working people should be getting higher food rations than the non-working people, and this arrangement would accommodate the food distribution more effectively. (What a sudden concern for the poor working Jews!) Tuesday 28 October was assigned as the day to carry out this plan and, therefore, nobody would be allowed to go to work. All the inhabitants of the ghetto were to assemble at six o'clock in the morning on the Democratu Plaza, the largest open area in the ghetto. An inspection of the entire population would then take place. Rauca also warned that all doors to all houses were to remain open and thorough inspections would be carried out to make sure nobody was hiding. Anyone found hiding would be shot on the spot. Fliers were to be posted to let the people know about this decree. With this he departed.

The council was stunned. What did this decree mean? Were Rauca's assurances legitimate? Was this only some kind of a census, or was this a new Action? Nobody could know for sure, but coupled with the rumors that ditches had been prepared at the Ninth Fort, the announcement looked very ominous, indeed. For several hours the council deliberated and finally came to the conclusion that there was no alternative but to comply.

Rauca's appearance at the committee heightened the tension in the ghetto. Everyone conjectured what Rauca had discussed with the committee, but nobody knew for sure. They waited for some kind of an announcement from the council.

Monday 27 October Peter was summoned to the council. We in the workshop waited. When Peter returned, his face was drawn. He looked very worried. He entered the shop, sat down in his chair, called us over, and announced, "I have been instructed to prepare a dozen posters to inform the ghetto about a census of the entire ghetto tomorrow. Everyone, old and young, male and female, healthy or sick, is to appear on the Democratu Plaza. The doors of the houses are to remain open for inspection and anyone found at home will be shot. Get out drafting paper and tools and get ready to prepare these announcements as quickly as possible. Here is the text."

We were stunned. What did it mean? Was it an Action? We tried to discuss the matter with Peter but he refused to talk. Time was short and the people had to be notified of the situation. Even Peter did not know that the ghetto was to be divided into working and non-working inmates. We got down to business and produced the posters as fast as we could. Once ready, special runners were dispatched throughout the ghetto to put them up.

The publication of the posters heightened the already feverish tension. Thousands of people gathered in front of the committee in hopes of getting more information. In the meantime, a German from the aerodrome came to the committee bearing certificates which he demanded be distributed among the aerodrome workers as proof that they were employed at the airfield. Apparently this was intended to be an Action. Why else would the airport personnel be concerned about proof of working status? A mob now descended on the committee and the people demanded certificates. Even people who did not work at the airfield were suddenly eager to have them. Everybody knew that Jews with Jordan passes were spared and it was reasonable to assume that these new certificates would play a similar role tomorrow. The mob could not be controlled. The people broke through the police cordon and invaded the committee building. As during the Jordan pass distribution, the building was ransacked and many people trampled on in the melee. However, they remained without certificates.

Around five in the afternoon Peter was again summoned to Dr. Elkes. When he returned he had new instructions. According to the council, all the people would have to assemble in specific locations according to the working place to which they belonged. Thus the police would line up in formation, the workers of the committee would stand apart, and every brigade would also have its own spot. Peter's instructions were to prepare signs painted on boards naming the individual groups, so they could be identified. Every one of us was given several wooden plaques. We grabbed paint and brushes and started feverishly to prepare the signs. By nine in the evening we had completed all of them. The tension was so oppressive that we were all exhausted.

My return home was eagerly awaited by the family. Maybe I had some more news. We gathered around the table and discussed the expectations of tomorrow. The most important problem that had to be resolved was where to stand. We had two choices: either join the members of the committee with me, or stand with the workers of the aerodrome where Max was now working. Max figured that it was safer to assemble with the aerodrome workers. If this was indeed an Action, the Germans would place the most value on those people working for them in war-related places. I insisted, however, that if the Germans intended to keep a ghetto, even for a short time, they needed an administration to carry out the orders for them. The argument lasted late into the night. After all, this was not a minor decision. Life could depend on it. We even considered splitting up, or hiding in our hide-out. But this was much too risky. During the Intellectuals Action I could afford to do it, because most of the people remained in their homes. There was enough noise in the house and in the streets that an unintentional noise in the hide-out could be missed. But with everybody on the plaza and nobody around, this was dangerous. By nightfall the decision was made. We would stand together with the committee workers. Rivka, Sonja, her daughter, and their aunt would join the aerodrome workers.

Another sleepless night passed. We didn't even undress. The tension was far too great. Around five o'clock in the morning doors started to open and people began to flock into the streets. The morning was very chilly, a typical autumn day with a thin layer of snow covering the ground. It was still dark and the air was extremely damp. The last visible stars gradually disappeared as the crowd started to swell. One could see mothers with children in their arms, old people who could barely walk, small children holding the hands of their mothers, grown-ups supporting their elderly parents or grandparents, and even invalids supported by canes. Some people who were unable to walk were carried out on stretchers. Everybody tried to make it out of the house to avoid being shot. Approximately twenty-eight thousand people were thus moved in the direction of Democratu Plaza.

When we reached the plaza, we joined the committee workers. At approximately eight o'clock the people who worked the last shift at the airfield were directed by the police to the plaza. They had worked a straight twenty-four hours, two shifts, because the ghetto was no longer allowed to let people out for work and the German airfield authority refused to let the people go home without replacement. These people were not even given a chance to clean up. They were sent directly to the plaza with dirty clothes and shoes and faces grey from the cement they had just mixed by hand. Scared stiff, they ran through the plaza looking for their loved ones, to join them in this momentous hour.

A little later a group of German police followed by an unusually heavy contingent of Lithuanian partisans, heavily armed and mostly inebriated, entered the plaza. Nobody spoke. Suddenly Rauca appeared on the plaza and an air of doom overcame everybody. All the columns were now instructed to file past Rauca. With an unusual calmness he directed people to the right or to the left, totally ignoring family composition. At will and with obvious delight, he separated parents from children, husbands from wives, and children from mothers. Gruesome scenes could be observed all over the plaza: parents crying, children screaming, partisans chasing people who tried to be reunited with their families and beating them murderously. When our turn came to pass Rauca, I needed all the strength I could muster not to collapse. Mother, who had fixed herself up, looked young and healthy and had no trouble being sent with me to the right side. But when Max, Vera, and Ruthie reached him, he sent them to the left. He apparently had no use for a family with a small child. We were stunned. Mother was about ready to scream when a Jewish policeman ran over and stopped her. "Don't scream, you will only be conspicuous," he said, "let me take care of it." Before we had a chance, while the column was proceeding past Rauca, he ran over to Max and shoved them quietly to the right, saving their lives.

The selection continued relentlessly and thousands of people were directed to the left. At first these were mostly the elderly, the sick, and families with many children. But when Rauca noticed that his count was too low, the selection took on an indiscriminate character. All certificates were disregarded, even Jordan passes. Many workers sent to the left side tried to explain to Rauca that they were specialists in war-related trades, but everything was ignored. As the selection gained momentum, more and more people were dispatched to the left side. So many healthy people were sent there that we almost started to wonder whether or not we were on the good side. The selected people were chased by the partisans to the now vacant Small Ghetto. The day wore on indefinitely. Frozen from the cold, wintery day, hungry and nervous, it seemed that the day would never end. Suddenly Max took me aside and pointed into the distance. There, outside the ghetto limits, thousands of Lithuanians were gathered, observing the eerie spectacle.

On the plaza, meanwhile, many older people succumbed and died. Others were severely wounded and left lying on the ground. While the selection was proceeding on the plaza, the houses were checked and ransacked. Anybody found at home, primarily the sick, were piled up in trucks and shipped directly to the Ninth Fort.

Late in the evening the selection ended and we were instructed to return home. The walk across the plaza was like crossing a battlefield with wounded and dead strewn all along the site. We had no idea how many were directed to the left side, but from all indications it was about ten thousand people.

When we came home, we simply broke down from tension and exhaustion. Little by little the members of our household returned home. We were lucky. Except for Rivka's aunt, everybody was spared. Dvora managed to get by Rauca without him noticing her age, and so did the Chazans with their teenage daughter. The families downstairs weren't so lucky. Here one family had lost a mother, another a woman and her daughter. Rivka and Sonja were crying and we tried to console them. We were not sure yet what the fate of the ten thousand people would be.

In the Small Ghetto the people were also left guessing. Many assumed that there were to be two ghettos again, and most people tried to grab a better home or corner, occasionally even fighting over a place.

In the morning I was awakened by a strange noise from the street. One of our windows faced the highway leading to the Ninth Fort. When I realized that the noise was coming from that direction, I ran to the window. Through the window I could see long columns of people moving in the direction of the Ninth Fort. I could hear the cries of hundreds of people being led to their execution. I swiftly got dressed and ran straight to the house of Jacob Goldberg, who lived nearby. I woke him up and told him the terrible news. He, too, was appalled, got dressed as fast as he could, and hurried to Dr. Elkes. Something had to be done. Maybe somebody could still be saved. Dr. Elkes rushed to the bridge leading to the Small Ghetto and requested permission to talk to the German officer in charge of the operation. He was given permission to present his request. He crossed the bridge and tried to explain to the German that among these people were some of the best craftsmen in war-related trades and he wanted them singled out and returned to the ghetto. But when the people in the Small Ghetto noticed Dr. Elkes, desperate pushing and shoving ensued. Everybody tried to get his attention. The partisans tried to contain the mob and began using their rifle butts indiscriminately over the heads of the people. One partisan got so excited that he hit Dr. Elkes over the head, severely wounding him. Dr. Elkes, bleeding profusely, had to be taken to his home, where several doctors tried to contain the flow of blood. As a result, the attempt to save some of the craftsmen failed. Meanwhile the entire ghetto was alarmed and everybody left their houses to see the tragedy unfold. It was a scene from Dante's *Inferno*, thousands of people driven to the Ninth Fort to be massacred and another eighteen thousand wailing over the fate of the convicted.

The Ninth Fort was considered an impregnable fortress during World War One and was built by the Czarist regime against a possible onslaught by the troops of the Kaiser. Located on top of the hill, it overlooked the city of Kovno and was only four miles northwest of the center of town. The army barracks were dug deep into the ground, were terribly damp and cold, and had small windows on one side protected by iron guards of substantial size, so as to render them escape-proof. These iron guards were installed later when the fortress was converted to a jail for political prisoners. All doors inside the barracks leading to the outside were made of heavy steel with secure locks or padlocks. The entire complex had interconnecting underground tunnels for communication between the individual barracks. Deep trenches surrounded all fortifications. The entire complex was enclosed by high concrete walls about three feet wide, extending about twenty feet above the bottom of the trench on top of which were rows of barbed wire. High guard towers overlooked the compound.

This fort was now converted into a death factory by the German master race. Here "sub-humans" and "low-race" people were to be eliminated. In 1941, when the Germans expected to win the war, they did not try to hide their activities, which could be easily seen over the concrete wall from the surrounding two story buildings. However, not only could the shootings and horror scenes be seen from those houses, but the cries of the unlucky victims were carried by the wind far beyond the limits of the fort.

The people from the Small Ghetto were now led in columns of one hundred each to this Ninth Fort. Condemned to be massacred, they were first brought to the barracks. Here huge trucks were placed in front of the windows, whose motors were run without mufflers for the duration of the execution, to drown out any noise from the ditches outside. Through the heavy walls of the underground barracks and the noise of the motors, the people could not hear the crying, screaming, and shooting going on outside. Then, one hundred at a time, people were selected and told that they were going to wash up. They were told to undress and were promised new clothes after the bath. But when they reached the trenches the guards fell upon them, beating and chasing them until they fell over each other and were immediately shot by the Lithuanian partisans. The cries from the children and the mothers were deafening, but the murderers calmly proceeded with their work. This gruesome spectacle paralyzed the will of the victims to resist. Numerous people were killed instantly, but large numbers of Jews were still alive when the next group was brought in, told to undress, and chased on top of the dead and wounded already in the ditch. Some people whom the bullets had missed tried to extricate themselves from the mass of dead and sighing humanity around them and, drenched in blood, they tried to escape, but were murderously beaten by the henchmen. This procedure lasted the entire day. The victims were not even covered with earth, there just was no time. Finally, when the job was done, the Germans took the discarded clothing and any belongings to the Gestapo Headquarters as war booty.

During one of these shootings, a major disturbance ensued when some people refused to obey orders. During this melee a young teenager managed to escape. Hiding in some bushes, he witnessed the entire bloodbath, including the shooting of his parents. Several days later he managed to escape and reach the ghetto, where he related the entire horror story to a numb Aeltestenrat. The details were kept in strict secrecy, not to sow panic in the ghetto. The Lithuanians, however, knew all about the events of the day and many of them told the Jews living near the fence whatever they had seen with their own eyes. There was no doubt left: all ten thousand Jews met their death at the fort. Later these horror stories and the gruesome details were written down by some members of the council and incorporated into a secret document which our graphics department was to prepare during the first winter in the ghetto, for posterity.

This massacre dispelled all illusions that the Germans might let us live because they needed manpower. Too many young, healthy men and women had been destroyed. We had reached the end of our road. We were being massacred by the most brutal methods, with total disregard of age, sex, or state of health. We were now on death row and we knew it. It was only a matter of time when our turn would come. The world did not care. Our former neighbors rejoiced or at best were passive, not willing to get involved.

A few days later the Jewish brigade working in the Gestapo yard returned from work numb with shock. They had just been given the job of sorting out the clothing of the Jews shot at the Ninth Fort.

The full brunt of the catastrophe did not sink in until a week or two after the Action, when little by little we started to realize who of our relatives or friends were missing. In my case the list was almost endless.

In our immediate family we had lost mother's sister-in-law with her mother, an aunt on my father's side, her two daughters, and a few second cousins. Of my former high-school instructors, all were gone, as if the murderers had known who the teachers were. Among them were several nationally known experts who had written textbooks that were used not only in Lithuania, but in all neighboring countries. There were my Latin, Math, Hebrew, German, geography, and natural science teachers, my grade school teachers, and many more. The majority of my college friends were gone. Of my closest friends, only Nahum Shoham and Labl escaped unharmed. Of family friends, Mrs. Joffe, the wife of the attorney, Mrs. Vazbutski and her two children, and scores of others were gone. What was true for us was true for everybody in the ghetto. Everyone could make a list of dozens of names of relatives and friends who were missing.

Hopelessness was the mood in the ghetto as the month of November approached. Even if we were given grace for a few months, winter and deprivation would end what bullets failed to do. The biggest question was whether it was still worth living.

We were overwhelmed by the fact that all the shooting was done in full daylight with absolutely no attempt to hide or conceal the crime. The Ninth Fort, during World War One far outside the city limits, was now completely surrounded by houses and the shots could be heard for dozens of blocks around. Not only could they hear the goings-on in the fort, but everything could be observed from many of these buildings and even from some streets. Everyone knew what was going on. The Germans and their local collaborators were so sure that the war had already been won that they even did not worry about someday being accountable for their deeds. Little wonder the mood in the ghetto was full of gloom and despair.

9

THE FIRST WINTER

On 29 October, as the Germans and their local collaborators were busy shooting the Jews at the Ninth Fort, the Jewish slave labor brigades did not leave for work. All the brigades that had been organized in the past months were in total disarray, since in each brigade dozens and even hundreds of people were at that moment being shot at the fort. The population at large was also disorganized and disheartened. There was almost no home where somebody had not been taken away. The people no longer gave a damn about work or food. They were apathetic, waiting for the final chapter to be played out and the curtain to fall over six hundred years of Jewish history in Kovno. It no longer made sense to fight. What for, to suffer for another month of hunger, slave labor, beatings, frost, humiliation, and mistreatment, only to be shot anyway? The living almost envied the dead. They at least had been relieved of all the misery, pain, and humiliation.

The next morning, again, hardly anybody showed up at the gate. The Germans immediately issued an order that everybody was to report for work, or the ghetto would suffer severe consequences. Previously this threat was able to scare the ghetto and force it to obedience. This time the German order was met with total apathy.

This was the first time that the Germans had met with noncompliance. The Big Action had given the ghetto a rude awakening. The generally accepted philosophy in the ghetto had been that the Germans needed a work force and as long as the Jews were able to provide it, they would be spared. But the Big Action destroyed this myth. During the previous Actions, certificates proving that one was working were honored and thus

96

there was hope for the able-bodied people. But once these passes had lost their value, all hopes for survival were dashed.

It did not take long for the Germans to realize what the mood in the ghetto was. But since they were not yet ready to liquidate the ghetto, they were interested in utilizing the free Jewish labor as long as it was available. It was for this reason that S. A. Sturmfuehrer Jordan, the head of the ghetto, and SS Hauptscharfuehrer Rauca came to the council to provide assurances in the name of the German authorities that the Big Action was the last one and no more Actions would take place. The ghetto would enter a period of calm during which the Jews were expected to fulfill their work obligation faithfully. These assurances were met with understandable skepticism. We had heard such pronouncements before and there was no reason to believe that this time would be any different. But what the German assurances could not achieve, hunger did. And it was severe. Despair and apathy don't put food on the table. There were only two ways of bringing food into the ghetto, both potentially life-threatening. One was to join the brigades outside and the other was to trade through the fence. Of these, trading across the fence was far more dangerous. The ghetto guard had instructions to shoot to kill anyone dealing at the fence. The way to trade across the barbed wire involved bribing the guards. But even after accepting the bribe, one was never sure that the sentry would comply. After an incident of killing a Jew, the trading would stop for a few days, only to resume again under the pressure of hunger.

Bringing in food from a brigade was safer, but the quantities one could carry for miles after a hard day's work were limited. Even here apprehension was punishable by beating, confiscation of the food and, occasionally, by death. People who worked inside the ghetto or had a brigade where food could not be procured, sold merchandise to the traders who, in turn, made a profit. This enabled them to earn enough to keep some of the provisions for themselves. Rivka and Sonja were among the people who were left almost penniless and it was imperative to get them a brigade where they could earn a living. Fortunately my connections in the ghetto administration enabled me to get reasonable jobs for both as well as for Max. With these jobs our food supply started to improve slightly. With no Actions throughout November and December, our daily routine started to take shape. In the evening we would bring up several pails of water from the outside well. Water would spill and freeze, creating hazardous conditions. Washing up was done in the kitchen in a basin. The water was cold, since firewood was very scarce and was kept for cooking.

The first to arise in the morning was Sonja. Her brigade was among the first to leave and she had to be at the gate before the rest of us. Sonja and her daughter Eetke slept together in one of our double beds, which was located kitty-corner from mine. My bed was situated so that I could look straight into theirs. When I turned to my right I faced the door to the kitchen. There was a sliding door which could not be closed tightly, leaving a narrow gap between the door and the jamb. Early in the morning, as soon as the sun rose on the horizon, she would slip out of bed and quietly tiptoe across the room to the kitchen. She was still in her nightgown, which was sufficiently transparent to reveal her breasts and even the outline of her pubic hair. She would slowly close the door and disappear behind it. I could hear the water being poured out of the pail into the basin, the sound of washing up, drying herself, and then spilling the water into a pail reserved for dirty water. Once completed, she would return to the room, pick up her panties, and slip into them. Still turned with her face to me she would slip off her nightgown, exposing her breasts, totally disregarding my presence. She would then continue dressing and donned her attire appropriate for her job. At first I did not pay any attention to her. Hunger dominated my thoughts and drives totally. But as our food situation started to improve, natural inclinations started to manifest themselves. I suddenly became aware of this peculiar morning routine and would lie quietly in bed and inconspicuously observe her. I started to wonder: was she unaware of me, or was she sending signals to me?

Once Sonja was done it was Rivka's turn. Rivka was much more exciting to watch than Sonja. She was much younger and exceptionally beautiful. She too had to pass my bed in the morning. Her shape, as expressed through the nightgown, was just as perfect as they come. While it was fun to observe Sonja, she never excited me sexually. But with Rivka it was different. Her breasts were so stiff that they barely moved when she slipped by my bed. After washing up she would return to her bed and face the corner of the room rather than me. She would let the nightgown slip down and for a few precious seconds she would expose her superb back. When turning to pick up her clothes I could see one breast projecting behind her arm. Her skin was alabaster white and the locks of her pitch black hair accentuated the contrast. She was exciting. And while at first I used to think of her as a cousin of mine, this cousin business quickly started to disappear.

But even more exciting than the morning interlude was every so often an exciting evening, when the girls were taking a bath. Both were now completely undressed and were helping each other to wash up. The bath was taken in a large basin standing on the floor. With my bed facing the door to the kitchen and with the light in the kitchen burning while my room was dark, I could clearly see them through the gap in the sliding door. I could not help feeling that the girls knew that I was watching them, but they did not make any effort to hide or cover the door. I had the impression that they had fun in showing off, particularly Rivka, who was always in full view.

The rest of the morning was routine. Mother would get up next and prepare some food for Max, who had to leave shortly. Then, it was my turn, since all I had to do to get to work was to cross the street. Once we were out, mother and Vera would get ready.

Every week the number of people going to work increased and the food situation improved, which was welcome news for the starved ghetto. However, with the advent of winter, a new dimension was added to our woes—firewood!

All of the Lithuanian huts had ovens and a stove which were fired by wood. But the Germans did not provide any firewood for the ghetto and we were now quite severely feeling the cold. There was not even enough wood to warm up food and since the Germans had confiscated all our electrical appliances, the ghetto faced serious troubles. And, to add insult to injury, the winter of 1941–42 was the severest one in memory. Temperatures of minus 40 degrees Fahrenheit were common for weeks. People used to return from work with serious frostbite injuries and required medical attention which was practically non-existent. But with all this hardship, we were glad to see the winter come and wished it would be as severe as possible. We still hoped that a hard winter would break the Nazi war machine and what the allied troops failed to do on the fronts, the winter would accomplish. But this was just wishful thinking.

Eating cold food, washing with cold water, and sleeping in unheated quarters took a toll on the population. In desperation people looked for a solution to the problem. Our house, like so many others, was neatly surrounded by a wooden fence, and at night we would go out and rip off a plank or two and sneak it into the house. However, we were not the only ones to notice this unexpected good fortune. Suddenly planks all over were disappearing overnight and people started noticing it. One morning, spontaneously, there was a rush to the fences. The scene was reminiscent of the vegetable garden raid. Thousands of people, men, women, and even children, descended on the fences with picks, hammers, or any tool that was handy and, yelling and screaming, began fighting each other over every plank or piece of wood. The crowd was just as desperate and ferocious as during the previous raid. My entire family was on the street. Even Dvora, an elderly lady, joined in. The Jewish police was summoned by the committee to stop the chaos, but to no avail. As before, they were no match for a desperate mob. Obviously this orgy was dangerous. The houses and the fences were not ours and the Germans could impose severe penalties for this destruction of property, but nobody cared. We were on the verge of freezing to death and could not be concerned with potential sanctions. Within a couple of hours the entire complexion of the ghetto had changed. Suddenly it was one huge site with houses located here and there in the open. One could walk clear across the entire ghetto in any direction without having to walk around fences. When there was absolutely nothing to confiscate, people dispersed. For a little while the firewood situation had been solved. Surprisingly the Germans did not seem to care, since no retribution followed the affair.

A big problem continued to be providing the ghetto with work. Since all working people received a supplementary food ration, the pressure from the people who had no place to go and needed work to add to their food supply grew daily. This extra ration, although meager, was extremely important, considering our dire circumstances. For every additional ounce of bread received on the ration card, less food from an outside source had to be brought in or traded for. This pressure on the committee had to be resolved and the Aeltestenrat was contemplating all kinds of solutions. After lengthy deliberations, somebody in the committee came up with the idea of setting up workshops inside the ghetto. This would be ideal for people who were too weak to march five or six miles to and from work and still be able to stand the rigors of hard manual labor. If the Germans allowed such workshops to be created, they would increase the work force of the ghetto substantially. Moreover, if the local German officials could enrich themselves through these workshops, they would be interested in preserving the Jewish work force for their own benefit. The next time Jordan came to the council, the people in charge explained the idea to the best of their ability. They particularly stressed that the ghetto had many first-class tailors, shoemakers, and hatmakers and they could mend, fix, and repair torn uniforms, boots, and hats for the army. Jordan showed interest in the presentation and promised to have an answer the next time around.

The answer came sooner than anticipated. Apparently the German rulers of the ghetto quickly realized the potential bonanza and gave the committee the green light. The committee started preparations immediately. Krisciukaicio Street 107, the place where thousands of homeless Jews were housed before the Big Action, was assigned as the place for the workshops. The people who were still living there were moved to other places, which after the massacre of ten thousand Jews could now be found. In the middle of November the premises were cleaned and renovated. By the end of December and the beginning of January the workshops started, with a tailor, a shoemaker, a milliner, and a furrier. Their first assignment was to fix thousands of pieces of clothes, suits, coats, and other apparel robbed from the Jews during the early house searches and later from the victims of the various massacres. As soon as the workshops got into full swing, the Germans indeed started to use them for mending uniforms for the army.

The success of the first venture emboldened the committee to think about other workshops in which they could interest the Germans. Before long there was a carpentry shop, a tinsmith, a locksmith shop, and several others.

One morning a group of middle-aged women came to the council and showed them samples of stuffed animals which they had made by hand and tried to interest the committee in setting up shop for them. The Germans might be interested in these as gifts. The committee did not take them seriously and dismissed them. But these women were not easily discouraged and tried again. Dr. Elkes, who had very keen perceptions, felt that the idea might have some merit. On the surface it looked absurd: stuffed animals manufactured in the ghetto. The council would look like a bunch of fools. Yet, on the spur of the moment, he decided to discuss the matter with Peter, a gifted artist, who may have some ideas of his own.

When Peter was called to see Dr. Elkes, our first thought was, of course, the worst. There was enough reason to be worried. Rumors had been circulating for some time, the worst of which was that the Germans were planning to sterilize the entire male population of the ghetto. Our hearts were beating furiously as Peter walked in through the door.

"I see that you are all worried, so let me first put your minds at ease," he said. "No new Action is being contemplated. You all know that the ghetto has started workshops for various specialists and tradesmen. Guess what? A group of women wants to produce stuffed animals for the Germans . . ."

We did not let him finish the sentence. Loud laughter greeted this statement. How silly could one get? Here was a war in Russia and all the Germans had to worry about were stuffed animals made by old Jewish women.

"Hold it," Peter interrupted us, "don't dismiss the idea so easily. You will be surprised, but this could be a beginning of a toy workshop. You see, the Germans have wives and children at home and if we can succeed in producing decent toys, it would remind them of home and their kids. They would be glad to take those toys and send them home, particularly since they would not cost them any money, and we could gain some goodwill. In short, we have the assignment to prepare in the shortest possible time a graphic presentation of what we intend to do and to make it as attractive as possible."

"Exciting, really exciting!" We suddenly came to realize the potential of it.

"Yes, it is," agreed Peter, "I don't know how long the Nazis are going to let us live, but for the time being we will be involved in some exciting things. You, Nolik, and you, Nucia, are gifted artists. I will give you a few ideas to sketch. Vulia, you can make the diagrams and the overall presentation. In fact, as I see it, this can become a big operation. We could use one more good artist. Do you know any?"

"Yes," said Nolik, "I know an artist from Prague. His name is Pipsi."

"Good, ask him to come here tomorrow if he is interested."

The rest of the evening was spent exchanging ideas. Peter was making sketches and laying out the presentation and we were listening as he churned out one idea after another. For the first time in months I had a good night's sleep. Here was something to look forward to, not always Actions.

In the morning we got acquainted with Pipsi, a handsome, friendly chap, blond, blue-eyed, full of life and a wonderful sense of humor. He, too, liked Peter's idea and a feverish job started in preparing the presentation. Sketches were drawn and discarded and new sketches made. In two days a complete album was ready for the council. The album included about two dozen toys and among them stuffed animals, but these bore little or no resemblance to the ones proposed by the ladies.

Peter took the album to the council. The job was a masterpiece. With this presentation they did not have to be worried. The worst that could happen would be a refusal and the shop would not be created.

Usually Jordan's appearance in the ghetto filled us with fear. For the first time in our lives we were actually awaiting his arrival. The next afternoon Peter was called to the council to make the presentation. Jordan was there. Hardly scared of the hangman Jordan, Peter proceeded to present the sketches one by one. All the members of the council watched Jordan's face for a clue. For the first time in his dealings with Jews, Jordan listened instead of issuing orders for new decrees. When the presentation was finished, Jordan got up and said, "You have my permission to establish the shop." With this he left the room.

"Well, Peter," said Dr. Elkes, "you've got an assignment. Start immediately."

Peter came back to the shop excited. "We have Jordan's permission to proceed. It is upon us now to make this venture a success. We need hard work and lots of luck. The ghetto has absolutely nothing to work with, no tools, no materials, and no craftsmen."

"Hold it, Peter," I said, "you are from Germany, where Jews were businessmen and professionals. Here in Lithuania, we have the finest specialists in just about every trade."

"Very well," said Peter, "I will be at the committee tomorrow to secure a place for our workshop. I will also talk to our labor department regarding specialists."

The next few days were busy ones. The committee provided us with space and asked for a list of tools we might need. It was assumed that, now that Jordan had shown interest in the project, such a list could be presented to him. Things developed much faster than expected. We got tools, even a few machines, paint, and some raw materials. Although the quantities were small, they were sufficient for a successful beginning. We found quite a few specialists, amongst them the brothers Kahn, who were superb craftsmen in wood. We also set up a finishing department, where toys were sanded, assembled, and painted. A group of about half a dozen girls were accepted to the department, since the job was not physically demanding. It required instead a great deal of patience. Among the girls who joined us was a girl by the name of Minnie Percikowitsch.

Meanwhile our workload in the graphics department had grown and the space in the committee building became too crowded. Peter, now enjoying complete trust of the council, went before the ghetto administration and requested additional space. The council immediately ordered the evacuation of the second floor of the adjacent building. Within a few days we moved into our new quarters, from which we could see the administration building and its yard through one of the windows, and the room where the Chazans lived from another. We now had ample space and the rooms were arranged in a practical and convenient manner. At first all the design work for the toy shop was done in our department. But when the toy workshop got into full swing, Pipsi and Nolik went to the toy factory, where space was prepared for them.

Peter now shuffled between the two shops. Half a day he spent in the toy factory and half in our place. In his absence Pipsi was in charge in the toy department and I ran the graphics shop. But three people were no longer sufficient for the volume of work we had on hand, and my best friend Nahum Shoham and Nolik's friend Larry joined us.

Feverish activity now started in both shops and our lives suddenly took on a new complexion; we were now, probably, the luckiest group in the entire ghetto. Although we worked inside the ghetto and had no contact to bring in food from a brigade, we were absorbed in our work to such an extent that we were able to ignore the troubles around us. A new chapter started for all of us, and for me in particular.

While we were absorbed in this little domain of ours, the world around us did not stop. The German offensive was finally grinding to a halt. They had not succeeded in any of their goals: the Red Army had not collapsed and they had failed to take Moscow and Leningrad. The German press was still writing about big victories; one day the German newspaper in

Kovno even boasted that the Red Army no longer existed and the German troops were merely cleaning up isolated pockets of resistance. In reality, however, the Russians unexpectedly brought in reserves from the Far East, of whose existence the Germans were not even aware, and commenced a counteroffensive. They managed to retake Rshev in the Moscow theater and Rostow near the Black Sea. This gave the ghetto a new lease on life. Perhaps Hitler would end up like Napoleon in the vast spaces of Russia after all. But the Russians had suffered too many casualties and did not have enough strength to pursue their advantage. The Russian offensive stalled and a stalemate ensued. However, they forced the Germans into an unexpected winter campaign.

While the German campaign was now fully stopped, the news hit the ghetto that Japan had attacked the United States of America with grave losses to the Americans, and that Germany had declared war on the U.S. However, the significance of this event was entirely lost on us, particularly since no fast salvation could come of it. For us and for the Germans the most important factor was the gruelling Russian winter. Our delivery could come only from a collapse of the Germans at the Eastern Front.

One day in December Peter was once again called to the council. Usually this meant a new announcement which our graphics department would have to prepare and which never spelled anything good. When Peter returned, he said, "We have to quickly prepare posters for the ghetto. The Germans have ordered the Jews to gather tomorrow on the Democratu Plaza and deliver all the fur coats in our possession."

An ominous silence followed. I turned to Peter. "Peter, this sounds again like an Action and the fur coats are only a pretext."

"Most people in the committee are also suspicious, but the posters have to be made, nevertheless," said Peter.

Reluctantly we sat down and prepared the posters.

When the posters hit the streets, the ghetto got into an uproar. Everybody was sure that the furs were only a pretext and behind the camouflage of furs the real thing was another Action. Everything pointed to this. First, the Germans were terribly on edge due to their reverses on the fronts and they were looking for a scapegoat. Secondly, every time there was an Action they used a gimmick to make us as unsuspecting as possible. During the Action against the intelligentsia, it was sorting documents; during the Big Action, it was a census. Now the gimmick was furs! No, nobody would be fooled this time. The more the tension grew, the more the people were determined not to heed the order. Everybody preferred to be shot in his house rather than to be taken to the Ninth Fort and be massacred and buried in a mass grave. The night was as nerve-wracking as before the Big Action.

The next day the ghetto was shut off from the outside world and no commandoes were allowed to leave for work, which only reinforced the belief that we were facing an Action. The ghetto administration was also nervous when it realized that the people were balking, and it requested to meet with the Germans to explain the situation. After some lengthy explanations, the Germans finally conceded that they would allow the ghetto to designate a few collection centers, would not insist on gathering on the Democratu Plaza, and would allow the ghetto police to carry out the Action. The furs would have to be delivered before the end of the day, or house searches would follow. Our shop again had to produce posters quickly. The posters with the German concessions were greeted with a great deal of relief; it would cost us our furs, but not lives. The people delivered everything they had, even old dirty furs, just to avoid possible death if the fur was later discovered. Tens of thousands of dollars worth of furs were delivered that day to the Germans, and we were destined to freeze even more than before.

With the Fur Action behind us, the ghetto again started to calm down. Meanwhile a new German administration was assigned to the ghetto, which insisted on strict obedience of all previous edicts, particularly the curfew. Nobody was allowed on the street between 10 P.M. and 5 A.M. Also, the edict that every Jew had to take off his hat from afar when noticing a German or Lithuanian guard was to be enforced. They emphasized that they would shoot without warning for disobeying these regulations. To prove their seriousness, a few Jews were shot to death the very first days they had taken over the supervision of the guard, just for bringing food in through the gate on the way from town.

Under this strained situation a fateful day was approaching for Dr. Gerber. He now worked in a brigade where he could bring in some food. His brigade, however, was very strenuous and he had to work beyond his physical strength. One bitter cold evening in January, he was marching with his brigade back from town to the ghetto. It had been a particularly hard day for him: he had been beaten repeatedly and barraged with obscene language. Dr. Gerber was mentally and physically exhausted. His hands and feet were frozen stiff. His thoughts were with his young wife and the better times they had together before this nightmare befell the Jews of Kovno. The only thing that kept him moving were his dreams. He was barely able to move his frozen feet, which felt like two pieces of ice. As he was creeping along, he did not notice that he had approached the corridor. Suddenly, a shot pierced the quiet of the night. A pain in the left shoulder awoke him from his dreams. The pain was excruciating and his shirt felt warm and wet. Unconscious, he fell to the ground.

Dr. Gerber had committed a crime. In his eagerness to get home, he had forgotten to tip his hat when passing the Lithuanian guard. The guard did not hesitate. In front of him he saw a Jew, a subhuman creature. The guard's gun was loaded all day long, just waiting for the finger to pull the trigger. And what better opportunity could have presented itself to this illiterate partisan? Not only would he not be punished, he would be praised for so faithfully obeying the law! Upon hearing the shot, the Jews in the corridor scattered for cover. Fateful seconds were ticking away for Dr. Gerber. The guard calmly reloaded his gun and yelled to the fear-stricken Jews, "That will teach you a lesson to properly honor a guard. Get the swine away."

A few men rushed to Dr. Gerber, picked him up, and carried him to the new hospital, but it was too late. Dr. Gerber died in the hospital in which he had worked and helped to save lives. Dr. Gerber had to pay the price. He had committed two crimes: first, he was born a Jew, and second, he forgot to tip his hat. The partisan had made his point. He had taught the Jews a lesson nobody would ever forget. But for Dr. Gerber it was too late.

Life, however, had to go on despite all our troubles and we were by no means at the end of our travail. Barely a week after this incident, a new bombshell racked the ghetto: The German administration let it be known that by 6 February the ghetto would have to produce five hundred workers to be sent to Riga, Latvia. As in the past, nobody believed them. It sounded too much like the five hundred intelligent people for work in the city. Nobody was ready to volunteer, and nobody wanted to be caught. The Germans knew that they would meet with stubborn resistance and they decided to let the committee and the Jewish police do the dirty job for them. The entire operation was to be carried out in full secrecy so as to disturb the ghetto as little as possible. The principle by which the committee decided to select the workers was based primarily on inflicting as little hardship as possible upon families: in other words, single people, men or women. The committee prepared such lists and the police were notified to stand by. When I found out about the list, I ran home and warned Rivka. She was the right age, healthy, and single and therefore could very likely be on the list. Rivka immediately packed up and went into hiding. But the secret about the lists could not be kept for long. Many people in the ghetto got wind of it and most prospective candidates disappeared. At night the Jewish police descended on the ghetto with the list in their hands, but fewer than two hundred people were apprehended. The people who were selected to be shipped to Riga were desperate and their friends and relatives were crying and cursing the Jewish police and the committee. Everybody was positive that they would be shot.

When the Germans realized that the ghetto administration was in no position to carry out the orders, they released the two hundred people, who immediately went into hiding. The next day the Germans carried out the Action themselves with their usual brutality, totally disregarding family composition. Dozens of people from the workshops and even the committee were among the victims thus rounded up. When the number was still short of five hundred, they started house-to-house searches. Vera touched up mother so that even Dvora didn't recognize her. Facial powder was used on her hair to provide a touch of gray, shadows were put beneath the eyes to look like sacks. Mother also removed the partial she had and by the time Vera was through with her, she looked at least seventy years old. How different it was from last time around, during the Big Action, when mother was made up to look youthful. That time, coal was used to touch up any gray hair and rouge was used to provide some color to the cheeks. What a transformation! A difference of forty years in appearance just by a good make-up job. I in the meantime decided to hide in our hide-out. When the German team came to check our house Vera carried Ruthie in her arms and mother was faking an old grandmother. The Germans looked around, did not find anybody, and left.

Finally, after a great deal of difficulty, necessitating forced apprehension of some people from the returning brigades, they had their five hundred and left the ghetto. Under heavy guard, these people were taken to the train station of Kovno.

After the way the people were selected and rounded up, nobody believed that they were really being sent to Riga for work. However as it turned out, a short while later we started to get letters from Riga, through underground channels which could be authenticated, and the fear for their fate subsided. The day after the transport had left, the Germans demanded their regular workers back at their jobs and the ghetto returned to normal.

Barely had the ghetto returned to its routine than new troubles erupted. This time it was a Book Action, followed by the clearing of one more area in the midst of a severe winter. Throughout this entire ordeal, we in our two shops were trying to keep our minds on our work.

10

MINNIE

In the graphics department we had now much more room than before.
We did not have to share any space with the various departments of the
administration and were not subjected to the noise and disorder created
by the mob that was constantly besieging the committee. The layout of
our shop by ghetto standards was luxurious. Turning left from the entrance, there was a corridor which led to the interior of the shop. In this
corridor we had a rack for coats and a long buffet in which we kept our
supplies. This hall then led to a drafting room, with several drafting
boards and a few chairs. This room was open to the right of the corridor
where Peter set up his atelier. In this atelier he had a desk, several chairs, a
drafting board, a sofa, and a cabinet for his tools. The walls were deco-
rated with a big map of the ghetto and a board with a display of all the
armbands we had done up to that date. We already had quite an impressive array of samples. We also had several diagrams showing the
growth of the labor pool supplied to the German authorities. We tried to
set up our shop as neatly as possible for two reasons: first, we were now
marked to spend almost all our waking hours in the shop, six and often
even seven days a week, and secondly, we were expecting that Germans
would visit our shop and it had to be presentable. It was indeed a cozy
place by ghetto standards: it was clean, quiet, and had a lot of light.

In the meantime the Germans had noticed our work and became
interested in it. At first all the German institutions connected with the
ghetto requested ghetto plans, which they had seen before. Once we were
done with those, the request came for diagrams of the contribution by the

ghetto to the work force outside the ghetto. These diagrams now became very important. Two things had happened since we had entered the ghetto: first, the war was at a stalemate and the Germans now needed every able-bodied man for the war effort; and secondly, the Germans started to draft Lithuanians into so-called labor brigades. But the Lithuanians balked and had to be recruited by force. Here the Germans stumbled against resistance which could not be broken by the same means they used against the Jews, and their quotas were never met. Thus the available work force was only the Jews. It is for this reason that when the Germans requested from us diagrams of the Jewish labor force, we were interested in making them as impressive as possible. We were still hoping that maybe the need for our work would stop the massacres. No matter how foolish this hypothesis was, we wanted to believe it.

One day Peter was called in to the council. When he returned, we saw right away that he had something interesting for us.

"Children," he started, "I have some extremely interesting news. We have an assignment from the Aeltestenrat to do some secret work, but you have to commit yourself to total secrecy. The Aeltestenrat wants us to prepare an album for posterity. They will provide us with material which to a great extent is not common knowledge, and we will arrange it. Once ready, it will be given to some Lithuanian for safe-keeping until the war ends. If any of the council survives, they will retrieve it and show it to the world. If nobody survives, the Lithuanian will give it to some Jewish organization."

"What a superb idea! At least one day the entire world will know what we went through during those years."

"I have decided to transfer Nolik and Pipsi temporarily back to the graphics department to give the project an artistic touch. This will indeed be a historic document, if it only survives the war and gets into the right hands."

The rest of the day was spent in discussing the format and information that would appear in the album. The secretary of the Aeltestenrat was already feverishly preparing documents to be used in the project.

The next day Nolik and Pipsi were in our shop and Peter went to the council to get some of the documents. While waiting, we engaged in some light chat.

"Pipsi, how do you like your work in the toy shop?" I asked Pipsi.

"I love it," he answered, "we have a lot of freedom to develop our ideas. You should visit us, you would like it, and more than anything else you would like the girls. Our finishing department is like a beauty contest. The kids are adorable. Why don't you come tonight? You have a pass to enter the shops and do not need any permission from anybody."

"I think it is a great idea. I have not been in the shop since the finishing department started, and it might be interesting to see the new toys and also the girls."

In the meantime, Peter returned with some material from the committee and started to sort the papers and to throw out some ideas. Nolik was assigned the title sheet, which was a figure of Justice with blindfolds over her eyes and a scale in her hand. But the figure was broken, an indication of the cruel world in which we were living. I got to do several diagrams depicting the destruction of the ghetto. Pipsi and Nucia got the assignment of drawing up to small scale all the armbands we had done so far. Peter himself was sketching and supervising the work. In the evening we had to hide all the material to make sure it did not fall into hands that had no business with it.

In the evening I accepted Pipsi's invitation and we went to the toy shop. Pipsi, with a great deal of pride, showed me around. Indeed it was very impressive. When I entered the room where the girls were working, I was amazed. Pipsi and Nolik had not exaggerated when they said that this could have been a beauty contest: each girl was more lovely than the other. Pipsi introduced me by pointing out that I was in a position in the graphics shop similar to his in the toy factory. We chatted a little with the girls, I made a few compliments which came sincerely from my heart, and the gang responded with some laughter and giggling.

The next morning, when everybody was back in our graphics shop, I came up with an idea. "Pipsi," I said, "you have a gorgeous team of girls in your shop and I have a great team of fellows here. How about getting together and having a party? We have enough troubles, let's live it up. We may not be around tomorrow to enjoy it!"

"It's a great idea," said Pipsi, "I am all for it! How about you fellows?"

The fellows did not need much coaxing either, and we decided to move expeditiously to set up the party.

"Where can we have it?" asked Nolik. "Any ideas?"

Several ideas were advanced, but under the enormous congestion in the ghetto no place could accommodate a group of fifteen youngsters and the party almost fell through before it even started. Suddenly I had a bright idea. We did not have to have the party in one of our homes. The party could be arranged at some friend's house who was not part of our shops. The name of Lazik at once came to my mind. Lazik was by ghetto standards a wealthy man. He was the biggest trader through the fence and through bribery managed to live in one of the blocks in a big room all by himself. This was the ideal place for it.

"Pipsi, I think I have a solution to the problem," I said. "We do not have to make the party in one of our homes, where there is no place for a larger group. We could make it in the home of a friend of mine. Is there any objection to involve an outsider?"

"Not at all," said Pipsi, "do you have somebody specific in mind?"

"Yes! I don't know whether any of you know him; his name is Lazik."

"Lazik? Who does not know Lazik," said Nucia, "everybody knows him in the ghetto."

"Sure, I know him too," said Pipsi, "does he have a big enough place?"

"Yes, it should accommodate all of us, although it will be somewhat crowded."

"Crowded is fine," said Nolik, "it will be more fun."

"Fine, so it is a deal. I will talk to him today, don't spread the word yet."

In the evening I went to see Lazik. He was glad to see me. Lazik was a very talkative fellow and before I had a chance to say a word he was already relating to me his latest deals at the fence. His deals were really impressive and his contribution indirectly to the ghetto was important in the sense that he was able to trade all kinds of merchandise for food. But not only was he talkative, he was also self-confident.

"Vulka, if there will be only one survivor after this catastrophe, that survivor will be me. I am going to live no matter what the Nazis pull on us. They will never get me."

"It is wonderful to be so confident," I said, "I envy you. I am not as sure as you are. In fact, I believe just the opposite; that no matter what the outcome of the war, they will still have enough time to kill us all."

"Don't be a pessimist. They will break their necks long before that," he replied.

After chatting for a little while I came out with my proposition about a party.

"A party!" he exclaimed, "great! We will have one hell of a party and you can rely on Lazik! When do you want it? Is this coming Sunday fine with you, Vulka?"

"Is it enough time for you?" I asked.

"I can make a party tomorrow, if you wish, I never have problems."

"So it is this coming Sunday," I said, "say seven o'clock?"

"Great! You fellows better be ready, we are going to have a whale of a party."

With this we parted.

Next morning I told everybody that we would have a party next Sunday at Lazik's. Everybody was elated. What an escape from our drab existence! We almost felt as if we had won a victory over Nazism. They could not snuff out our spirit. We were alive and were defying them. Everyone was now waiting for Sunday. We were all wondering how Lazik could set up a party in a ghetto without a record player, without a radio, without liquor, and without food. But we did not care: a party is a party, no matter how poorly stocked and provided.

The week passed quickly and Sunday came. In the evening we all dressed up a little better, although we hardly had any good clothes left after the house searches. When I came in most of the gang was already there. Although the room was quite big, it was indeed crowded. In addition to our own crowd, there was also a friend of Lazik's, a guy by the name of Moses Rabinowitsch. Moses was about our age, full of life, and fit into the group perfectly.

At first we were chatting, getting acquainted with the rest of the gang. After a little while, when everybody had a chance to get to know everyone else, Lazik pulled his first surprise.

"Children, a few days ago, Vulka asked me to prepare a little party for the gang, and since I promised him that it would be a great party, I have seen to it that it should not be dull. Consequently I have come up with a few surprises for you, so just relax," and Lazik went to a cabinet and pulled out a small bottle of vodka.

"Vodka!" everybody exclaimed, "bravo, Lazik, bravo! We knew we could expect you to pull something out of your hat!"

Vodka was totally non-existent in the ghetto. Nobody cared about booze. Our biggest worry was to have food on the table and even that was scarce. But Lazik was a big trader and with his connections he managed to get a small bottle for the party. For fifteen or sixteen people, there was just enough for one shot for everyone.

"Lechayim! For the destruction of the Nazis and their helpers," he proposed a toast, "but don't drink it all at once, this has to last you the entire evening."

"Lechayim," we answered, "for victory by the Allies."

Everybody took a sip, leaving some for later.

"Heck," said Pipsi suddenly, "why should we wait for later? Let us drink it all. If we wait too long a good part of this sweet nectar will evaporate. Let everyone propose a toast and let us clean the glasses!"

"Right, let us clean the glasses! Here is a toast: Hitler should break his neck!"

"Amen! Let him take Himmler and Goering along."

Toasts were coming from all sides and we finished the bottle to the last drop. Not used to alcohol, one toast was enough for all of us. We were now in the right mood.

"What is next, Lazik?" I asked.

"Don't worry, the evening is still young." Before we knew it, he dragged Sarah Starovolski out from the crowd.

"It is your turn now," he said.

Sarah was a dark-haired girl, with black eyes, round face, and extremely charming, with lots of personality. She had a wonderful voice and was a gifted entertainer. Sarah got into the center of the room and gave us a rendition of French songs from movies by Danielle Darieux which were absolutely fabulous.

"Je chante, je chante soir et matin, je chante . . ." She charmed us like a real pro. We just would not let her stop. When she got good and tired, Lazik gave her a kiss and told her to rest up. We all applauded and waited for Lazik to come up with his next surprise.

"I think we will let her rest for a while," he said, "we have a big program today, let us not take advantage of one poor kid."

"Right, Lazik, let us keep going."

"I have now prepared a few party games for you, get ready to kiss and be kissed, don't be shy." And Lazik pulled out of his sleeve an assortment of games we had never seen before. Every game ended with some boy kissing some girl. I embraced the girls that happened to be my partners so I could feel their warm bodies near me, without even caring which one I had in my arms. They were all cute and I could not go wrong no matter whom I kissed. With the effect of the booze still in our veins, these games provided endless fun. When we finally had enough of it, Lazik pulled his next surprise. Moses had brought a record player with records, which was a rarity in the ghetto, and we all sat down to relax and listen to music. Moses had selected various hit songs by Rosita Serano, as well as music by Boulanger. He also brought with him some Russian romances. Most of the music was in a minor key, dreamy tunes which changed our mood to nostalgia. Everybody was quiet and listened.

Throughout this concert, I could not get rid of the feeling that I was being observed by one girl. I had seen her in the toy workshop in the finishing department. When I looked up to see who was watching me, she would lower her eyes to avoid my view. For a while we all relaxed to the sound of these romantic tunes and imagined that we were in Kovno in our warm prewar homes among our old friends, the majority of whom were no longer with us, despite their very tender age.

"Wake up!" we suddenly were awakened by Lazik, "we are not through yet. Moses, you take over now."

Moses took away the record player and the records and started his art. He was a superb storyteller and was great at telling jokes. The mood suddenly changed and laughter was heard again in the room. Pipsi, Peter, and I were also top-notch story and joke tellers and soon we got into the act too. Again, while I was telling my jokes and I was aroused and in good form, I could not help but feel that stare by this girl, but I did not pay any attention, I was having too much fun.

But now it was getting late and Lazik suggested that we do some community singing before departing. We picked zionist tunes which we had learned in our youth organizations before the war and with a soft voice we carried our beloved melodies till late in the evening. Finally the party was drawing to a close. We all praised Lazik for a job well done. As everybody filed out, each of us got to accompany one girl home. Before I had a chance to select the girl I wanted, I found myself with the girl who was constantly observing me before. She was terribly sweet, petite, black hair, deep dreamy black eyes, a captivating smile, a contagious giggle, and a very slight accent which I thought had a touch of French. Her figure was like that of a little doll, small stiff breasts, rounded hips, and beautiful legs. But God Almighty, she was barely seventeen and looked even younger. I was a little disappointed. I wanted to get hold of one of the older girls with whom I hoped to have some fun. This kid, however, was too young for me, she was still so innocent and most important, she positively was still a virgin. She was so naive and inexperienced that I could not be mistaken. She promised to be wonderful company, but I could not even get to first base with her, let alone to bed.

But I did not let her feel my disappointment. On the contrary, I made a few compliments which in her naivete she took very seriously. I put my arm around her shoulders and accompanied her slowly to her house. The evening was beautiful, lit by an almost full moon, the air was crisp, and we both were very young. We spent quite a while at her door. Before saying good-bye I embraced her, pulled her to my chest and planted a big juicy kiss on her lips. I felt her body quiver in my arms. This was probably the first time she had ever been kissed by a boy. I felt warmth under my skin, but did not intend to follow it up by a more aggressive move. I said good-bye to her and expressed my wish to see her again tomorrow, which I did purely to be polite. But she was delighted and accepted right away. We parted and she ran up the stairs, floating like a little butterfly on a cloud of air. She looked delightful as she disappeared on the third floor.

On my way home I was wondering. I felt funny. Her vision kept coming back to me over and over again. Had she conquered me with her innocence? No, she was charming, but she was still only a child, way too young for me. When I came home my thoughts kept coming back to the party and to the good time I had, and invariably she was in the picture.

This night I was restless, but it was different than usual: was it the booze I had drunk for the first time in six months, was it the romantic music, or was it Minnie, the girl I had accompanied home that night?

Next morning when we all met in our graphics shop, everybody was still buzzing about the party.

"How did you like the girl you accompanied home?" asked Nolik.

"I don't know how I got stuck with her, she is still so childish."

"Didn't you notice that she was observing you all evening? You must be blind not to have seen it, she did not let her eyes off you."

"That is possible, but how did I get stuck with her?" I asked.

"Remember you were in the toy workshop a few days ago?"

"Sure, how can I forget it, that's where the idea for the party was born."

"All right, after you left she asked who you were. You made quite an impression on her. So after the party we all arranged it that you should get stuck with her."

"Aha! A conspiracy of sorts. Not very fair, fellows. She is still a virgin, what am I going to do with her? I finally feel again like a man, but I could not touch her, she is so innocent, that would be taking advantage of an unsuspecting, lovely kid."

There was not much time for conversation. Everyone of us had an assignment to do and time was short. We all sat down at our respective desks and continued where we had left off. I had difficulty concentrating on my work. My thoughts kept coming back to the party and to Minnie. I tried to reconstruct the events from the time we left Lazik's place till the time we parted. At first I was angry with myself for not noticing my friends' conspiracy and permitting them to frame me. I had noticed in the crowd quite a few girls which at first glance appealed to me more than Minnie.

But the more I thought of Minnie, the more she grew on me. If not for her age, she definitely was the most beautiful of all the girls, there was no doubt in my mind about it. My question was now: should I meet her today, or break the date? Obviously if she were just a little older and not so naive, the question would have been academic. I would have been delighted to be matched up with her. But deep down I had sex on my mind, and this requirement had to be shelved with her. But I had promised to see her tonight and no matter how I felt about it, I was not about to disappoint her by snubbing her and not showing up. And besides, why shouldn't I meet her? Did I have something better, something more interesting for the evening? She was cute, she was pretty, just to look at her would complete my evening, just to listen to her giggle would cheer me up. That was it, I resolved to see her this evening.

"Vulia, you are awfully quiet today," suddenly Nolik interrupted my thoughts.

"It seems to me that you guys are rather quiet yourselves. Did the party get under your skin?"

"I don't know whether it was the party, I think it is more the girls than the party," said Pipsi.

"How do you like your girl?" I asked him. "What was her name again?"

"Her name is Sarah Segal and I promised to see her today," answered Pipsi.

"So did I," I replied. "I, too, promised to pick Minnie up from the toy shop. How about joining me?"

"Suits me fine," Pipsi said, "anybody else wants to join us?"

"I will come along," said Nolik.

"Wonderful, let's try to keep the spirit that was kindled yesterday at the party alive," I said.

The other fellows did not choose to join in.

When we were through with work, the three of us put on our coats and hats and left for the toy shop. The girls were already waiting for us. In fact, a third girl by the name of Reeva was also with them and Nolik asked her to join him.

"What is the plan," asked Pipsi.

"Let's take a walk on Varniu Street, the evening is cold but really very beautiful," I suggested.

The evening was indeed beautiful. Although it was very cold, it was still, and the moon was shining, making Varniu Street all the more striking. Our goal was to put our troubles aside and make believe that the times were normal—a very difficult assignment indeed. Besides, none of us had a home which could accommodate three couples. There would have been standing room only under our present congested conditions. Everybody agreed, and we turned right towards Varniu. The topic of our discussion was the party. Everybody was absolutely elated. We had such a good time that we wished the party had lasted forever. I had my arm around Minnie's shoulder and she had hers around my waist. Pipsi and Sarah also embraced each other.

After a little while we got cold, and we decided to go up to our graphics department. I had a key to the shop and there was no reason to believe that Peter would object to it. We opened the curtains and let the moon shine into the room and left the lights off. Here, under the dim light of the moon, I had a chance to observe Minnie. She was indeed beautiful. Her features were like out of a fairy tale and her voice was like music. I felt a peculiar warmth as I was watching her. She, too, was observing me, but every time our eyes met she would let hers down, displaying her beautiful eyelashes. From the party, our conversation turned to art and music. To my amazement, despite her young age, I found her to be quite knowledgeable in both fields, which impressed me deeply. So she was not only gorgeous but also very intelligent. For the moment sex was completely forgotten. The discussion was so pleasant and lively that we even did not notice how late it had gotten.

We left the shop, said goodbye to each other, and everyone took his girl home. From the shop to Minnie's home was a walk of maybe six minutes. Despite the late hour, we remained in her hallway for quite a while and continued to chat. Before parting I took her in my arms and gave her a kiss which left her speechless. She reciprocated gladly and I promised to see her again tomorrow. On the way home I had a wonderful feeling which was completely different from what I had ever experienced with any of my other girls. I was happy, there was something to look forward to the next day and the next. I only hoped that a new Action would not destroy this happiness. When I came home, everybody was already asleep except mother. She was waiting for me.

"Mother, why aren't you asleep?" I asked her.

"I was waiting for you. Where were you? You know you have not eaten anything. Come, I will give you something to eat."

"I guess I mentioned to you about the party. I met a girl there who seems to be very nice, so we met again today and I will pick her up from the toy shop tomorrow, too."

"You seem to like that girl, I can hear it in your voice. You know you cannot fool a mother."

"I am really not sure yet. But she is pretty and quite intelligent."

"I am glad for you. You need some diversion with all the troubles we are having and who knows how much more there is still in store for us."

"Don't talk like that, you are spoiling my mood. That is exactly what I am trying to get away from."

Mother gave me something to eat and we both went to bed.

The next day in the shop was a very busy one. We were racing to complete the secret assignment for the council. I was deeply involved in my work, but deep down my thoughts were with Minnie. I was constantly whistling some of the tunes we had heard at the party.

"You seem to be still under the spell of the party, you are whistling all the tunes we heard from the records," said Nucia.

"Yes, I am. The party was the greatest thing to come our way since we have been in the ghetto," I replied.

"No argument about it," was Nucia's reaction.

The day in the office passed very quickly and at the end of the day I went to the toy shop to pick up Minnie. She was waiting for me at the gate.

"Hi, Minnie," I said, and gave her a kiss. "How are you? How was your day today?"

"Wonderful! Couldn't have been better," came the reply.

"I would like to invite you to a restaurant for a fancy dinner," I kidded.

"It's a deal, I am all set," she replied.

"Which restaurant would you like to go to?" All the cafes were now not only off limits to us, but we could not get out of the ghetto to get near them.

"Versailles," she joked, "I like the band there."

"The band at Conrad's is just as good, you know, but unfortunately, both bands are now in the ghetto, since all the musicians are Jewish."

"Yes, indeed, I forgot. So we may have to give up the idea."

"No, we don't. We might as well choose a menu. What difference does it make, right?"

And we proceeded to fantasize about the fanciest dishes. She was giggling. She liked the light conversation. Generally talk about food in the ghetto was very common. The less food we had the more we talked about it, and the more we let our imaginations run wild. We finally reached Varniu Street.

"Minnie," I switched the conversation, "do I hear a slight accent in your speech?"

"Yes, I do have a very slight French accent, since I have lived in Paris."

"In Paris?" I was surprised.

"Yes. I was born in Kovno. But with the anti-Semitism in Lithuania on the rise, my father, who is a lawyer, could not get certification. And since we have family in Paris, they urged us to come to France where they hoped to help us. So we moved to France and then, when the war broke out and the Nazis occupied the city, we decided to move to the unoccupied zone of France."

"Go on," I urged her to continue her story.

"Life for Jews even in the unoccupied part of France under the Vichy regime was not exactly easy and my parents decided to return to Kovno."

"Did your parents ever try to go to America?"

"Yes, but we could not get any papers. The gates were simply closed to us Jews."

The more I spoke to her the more impressed I got.

"Do you also play an instrument?" I switched the conversation.

"Piano a little bit. You see, with all the moving, I really never had enough time to learn. Do you play?" she asked me.

"Yes, I do. And fairly well too. Too bad we have no piano here."

"Who is your favorite composer?" she asked.

"I am in love with Chopin, but technically I admire Liszt."

"Liszt, come to think of it, I have a record by Liszt, his Sixth Hungarian Rhapsody, as recorded by Alexander Brailovski."

"We can ask Moses to bring his record player and we could listen to it."

"We don't need Moses, I have a record player, too."

"Do you? This is wonderful. How about listening to some of your records?"

"No problem, I am all for it."

As we continued to chat and enjoy each other's company, it got late and I accompanied her to her house. As last night, we stayed in the hall for a while, we just did not feel like parting. She was in a talkative mood and kept telling me about her life in Paris and the unoccupied zone of France. I was observing her and the more I looked, the more enchanted I became. I noticed her beautiful long neck, her thin short straight nose, pointing slightly upward, her beautiful white skin with a touch of color in her cheeks. She was fascinating. Again we parted with a kiss and an embrace and agreed to meet every day.

The week passed quickly, the days just flew by. On Friday we stayed in our shop until late, since we wanted to complete the secret assignment. It was now my pleasure to accompany Peter home, since Peter suffered from night blindness.

"You know, Peter," I said, "the album really came out quite impressive. I hope it will get into the right hands one day."

"So do I," he replied, "this is a piece of history and if we don't document it now, nobody will ever believe that these things ever happened in the twentieth century."

"You are right, if we ourselves did not believe it until very recently, how could anybody who has not been through what we have, even begin to believe such barbaric events? But to change the subject, how did you enjoy the party?"

"It was far beyond what I had expected."

"You know, Peter, it occurred to me that we had not heard any music for more than six months until the party. In fact, Minnie told me that she, too, has a record player with a nice selection of records and we are thinking of getting together again without an elaborate party to hear just her records."

"Sounds interesting. Have you made any arrangements yet?"

"No, we are just thinking about it. We need a place for it."

In the back of my mind I hoped he would suggest meeting in the graphics department, but he instead surprised me with his next statement.

"Vulia, how many people would you consider for such a get-together? Five or six could be accommodated in my home," said Peter.

"Oh, I would love it! This can be a great follow-up to our party. Let us figure out: how about having Pipsi, Nolik, and Nucia, our old guard, and Minnie, of course."

"No objections, let us make it this coming Sunday."

Chatting like this, we reached his house. Peter stopped for a moment and said, "Why don't you come in with me. We will consult with Renee. She will have to have the house in order."

Renee had no objections and figured that three o'clock would be fine with her.

The next day I checked with the rest of the gang we had singled out. Everybody was delighted. We were now all looking forward to Sunday.

On Saturday we finished our work early and I had an entire afternoon to spend with Minnie. I suggested that we go to our house. When I entered with Minnie, mother was pleasantly surprised to see such a radiant, beautiful girl, and before the evening was over, mother was in love with her. When I returned after taking Minnie home, mother met me at the door. "Vulik, she is a doll. No wonder you are disappearing every evening."

On Sunday afternoon I picked Minnie up and we took the record player and the records and went to Peter's home. Here we met the rest of the gang. Reeva was also there, apparently Nolik had asked Peter whether she could join us. We chatted for a little while and then got down to the actual business we had really come for: to listen to music. Minnie had all the popular tunes from the *Nutcracker Suite* by Tschaikovsky. We listened to all the dances and finished with the Valse of the Flowers. I had never heard the *Nutcracker Suite* before and all the tunes were new to me, but particularly impressed I was by the Valse of the Flowers. After playing a few more records, Minnie gave me a sly look and pulled out one record.

"This one is for you," she said.

It was Liszt's Sixth Hungarian Rhapsody, as recorded by Alexander Brailovski. It was a marvelous recording, superbly performed by the artist, and everybody enjoyed it. We stayed for a little while longer and started to get ready to leave. Renee apologized for not serving anything, but who had anything to serve in the ghetto anyway. We did not mind it at all, in fact we were very thankful for letting us meet in their home. Pipsi and Nolik said good-bye to us, and I accompanied Minnie, Nucia, and Reeva home.

"It was a wonderful afternoon," Nucia said, "I enjoyed it immensely."

"I am only sorry that my selection of records is rather limited," added Minnie, "but I have some more at home, enough for several more evenings."

"How about it," I said, "let us keep the momentum going. We started with a project, so let us not stop it now, let me check whether we could work something out in my house. I will let you know."

By now we had dropped off Nucia and Reeva and we were on our way to Minnie's home. Minnie asked me to come up, which I accepted.

Minnie lived with her parents in one room in Block C on the third floor. Her parents were home and they greeted me very politely. Minnie looked very much like her mother, who also was not tall. Minnie's parents were very intelligent and they alternately used French, Russian, and Yiddish at home. After spending a little while with them, I left for home.

At home I asked mother and Vera whether they would mind if I used our small back room once in a while in the evening to get together with my friends. Nobody objected, and I decided to get together right away on Tuesday. Monday, I let Minnie, Nucia, and Reeva know about it and we were now all waiting for Tuesday evening.

Monday Peter handed in the album to the council and the pressure was off. Nolik and Pipsi returned to the toy workshop and we got back to our normal routine. Tuesday, after work, I picked up Minnie with the record player and the other records which we had not yet heard and went to our house. Nucia and Reeva were on time as planned and we all went into our back room. The room was really small and with four people it was crowded. We placed the record player on a chair and lay down on the sofa. The sofa was not particularly big and we had to lie practically on top of each other. I had Minnie's head resting on top of my chest and Nucia's on my hip. Reeva had her head on Nucia's stomach. We could barely move. I took advantage of my position to embrace Minnie and hold her tightly in my arms. The room was dark and the music was playing softly. At first we heard some Russian songs. Every time a record ended we had to unscramble and reset the machine, but every time I managed to get hold of Minnie and pull her over to me. We barely talked. We closed our eyes and let our dreams go wild.

It was late when we parted. Minnie decided to leave the record player in my house and we agreed to meet tomorrow to finish the rest of the records. As was our custom by now, I took Minnie home and enjoyed a few more precious moments in the hall with her. On the way home I thought about the evening. It was awfully romantic. I felt good. Despite the deep dark clouds constantly hanging over our heads, I was above the clouds; they did not bother me as badly as they did before I had met

Minnie. She had a peculiar ability to put me at peace with myself. Her entire being now dominated me. I had now only one thought: being with her again tomorrow.

As I was walking home and thinking, it occurred to me: why did I need Nucia and Reeva, why not have Minnie all to myself? I could embrace and kiss her unencumbered by witnesses. How much more enchanting it would be to lie on the sofa with her at my side and to listen to this wonderful music. I decided to let tomorrow's date pass as today, but not to set up another. I wanted it to be only me and her.

In the office the day was routine, and in the evening we again met in our back room. The setup was unique: the quiet around us, except for the soft music, the semi-dark room with only a glimmer of light coming from the outside, and we all young and impressionable. I could hear all three girls breathing heavily, I could almost hear their hearts beating. I had my head on Minnie's bosom and Nucia was trying to get my attention by cozying up to me and putting her head on my lap. I had difficulty not getting aroused. It might have been terribly embarrassing, since Nucia could have felt it. I was holding Minnie's hand in mine and stroking her gently. It was a fascinating evening. It was barely two weeks since the party and my life had turned around completely. When I accompanied Minnie home, I was terribly excited. Since we had now heard all of Minnie's records at least once, it was only natural not to set up another date with Nucia and Reeva. We were now free to meet alone the next time.

We were now even more eager to meet again. My family was cooperative. They felt that I was entitled to some enjoyment in this terrible hell and they let me have the room undisturbed. We would select some favorites among the records and have some music for our entertainment. Particularly, we liked the Valse of the Flowers. We both would lie down on the sofa, I would embrace her, caress her breasts, give her a kiss, but I was very careful to stay within limits of propriety. No matter how much I wanted her physically, I did not feel right to deprive her of her chastity. Generally our moral code in Lithuania was highly restrictive. Girls married early and were expected to be virgins. Parents kept a very tight reign on daughters. When a boy came to a house there was always somebody around and we had to control our emotions, or she would not be allowed to date the boy. Everything was kept within boundaries of decency. With this regime, Jewish boys had a hard time finding somebody just for a good time.

So here I was alone with a beautiful, sweet girl, in a half-dark room, with soothing music softening my resolve, but I forced myself to keep control. Occasionally I wondered whether I wasn't being silly. Why? For all it's worth, we might not even be alive tomorrow, but shot and buried in a mass grave. So what sense did it make to hold on to the old-fashioned virtues of virginity and chastity? Was it really so important in a vicious, immoral world? I tried to touch upon this subject in a roundabout way, without using so many words, but Minnie remained unconvinced. For her it was not the question of purity, but more of her self-respect, for her own dignity.

But we were young and overcome by love and emotion, and every evening we moved an inch closer to total involvement. At first I would put my hand innocently over her bosom. Next time I would dare to unbutton the blouse and put my hand under her bra. She would resist every new advance, but would ultimately yield. With every further advance the resistance would at first harden, but the temptation was too big for both of us. Finally I had her upper body stripped and her half-naked body in my embrace. That was as far as I wanted to go with her. She was embarrassed and I felt a nervous twitching of her body. I had the impression that she was concerned. Her breasts were small and she was probably self-conscious about it. But for her physique the size of her bust was just right. I was pleasantly surprised. When she noticed this, she relaxed. Further advance at present was more than I wanted to risk.

But ghetto life never let us really enjoy anything. Every so often there was news. One day it was a group of Jews caught trading with Lithuanians and all were arrested, taken to the Ninth Fort, and shot. Another time a Jew was shot for bringing in food. Such news weighed heavily on our hearts and spoiled our evenings. Then there was an order to close all synagogues under threat that anybody caught praying in a synagogue would be shot. Next, they forbade education for the children and all schools and kindergartens were to be abolished. Jewish children did not need any education since they would be shot anyway sooner or later, and the teachers could better serve the Reich by doing slave labor.

Just as bad were the rumors constantly disseminated by the Gestapo to keep the ghetto on edge. The latest rumor was that there had been a meeting at the highest level of the Nazi party where the decision had been reached to liquidate the entire European Jewry. This persistent rumor destroyed our last illusions. It was totally believable that such a monstrous decision could have been made. After all, in Lithuania about 80–85% of the Jewry had already been massacred, so why could not the Nazis do the same to the Jews all over Europe? It was mind-boggling, but after what we had seen in our country, anything was possible. This last piece of news had a devastating effect on everybody. As if to prove the rumors, an order was given to vacate another area of the ghetto because Jews from Western Europe were to be resettled in Kovno.

succumb to despair. Minnie and I met regularly, kept up our relationship, restraining our desires. We had reached another plateau: we were now petting and necking quite extensively, but never crossing the final line. One day the Lithuanians told the Jews living along Paneriu Street that deep ditches were being prepared at the Ninth Fort. That could mean nothing else than a new Action. From the description of these ditches, they could hold thousands of people. The ghetto was desperate: who would it be this time? The council, who by now had good outside connections, sent a Lithuanian to verify the rumors, who brought back the bad news that indeed there were large ditches being prepared at the fort. People again nervously besieged the committee to find out what they might know and be concealing. I picked up Minnie and we went to the committee. The latest news was even worse. The ghetto was surrounded by a substantially increased guard, just as before the Big Action. This was a clear indication that next morning something terrible would happen.

Minnie and I went across the street to my home. We did not talk. We just walked in a firm embrace, as if supporting each other. When we walked into our back room, we had nothing to say to each other. Would there still be a tomorrow for us? We were so young, we had not yet lived at all. We put on the record player, picked our favorite song, and lay down on the sofa. Minnie was sobbing. She did not want to die! Why? What had she done wrong? Why was the world so cruel? I embraced her. The record player was going as usual and dulled our senses. Slowly we started petting. I was very gentle, but she was much more receptive. Was there still sense to hold onto our moral code, when there would be no more world for us tomorrow? Before we knew it, we were grasped in a total embrace. When we awoke, the record player was still turning, but the record had long since been finished. We had both experienced full, complete, and uninhibited love for the first time.

When we came back to our senses we realized what had happened, but neither of us regretted it. It was bound to happen sooner or later, so it was today. I took Minnie home. We did not speak. In the doorway to Minnie's house I managed to say, "Minnie, I am sorry, I lost my control. I did not mean it to happen."

"Don't blame yourself, I am just as much to blame."

With this I went home, expecting tomorrow to be a terrible day.

The next morning when I got up I went to the kitchen window which faced the highway leading to the Ninth Fort and—God Almighty—there were columns of one hundred each slowly moving up the road.

"God, who are these people?" I thought to myself in awe.

When I entered the graphics department the columns were still moving.

We all got to the window, scared to our bones. I ran across to the committee. This was terrible! The committee knew all about it already. These were Austrian Jews taken to the East "for work". They were allowed to take with them some baggage to make the resettlement look more plausible. They were brought to the railroad station in Kovno, where they were led on foot at least eight miles to the Ninth Fort. On the way along Paneriu Street some of them even had a chance to say a few words to the Jews inside our ghetto. From Paneriu, they were led to the fort, where they were massacred.

The Ninth Fort had suddenly become an execution ground for European Jewry. The local anti-Semitic collaborators in the European countries helped the Nazis round up the Jews. The Germans then transported them to Lithuania, and our local collaborators, our peaceful neighbors of years past, did the final shooting. What a scenario! All of Europe was participating in our annihilation. This was the result of the anti-Semitism of the Christian population. God Almighty, was there ever a Jesus Christ who walked this earth of ours? Was this what He taught them?

As for the Jews of Kovno, we were spared this time at the expense of the innocent Jews of Austria, who went to their death not realizing it to the very last minute, until they stood staring into the bloody ditch to which they were being led.

When I came home I stumbled into Rivka, who stood in my way. I did not know whether she knew what happened yesterday between me and Minnie, but she must have suspected all long that we were deeply involved. She stopped me, gave me a rather dirty look, and made a statement which startled me.

"Since you have Minnie, you don't see anybody anymore, do you?"

She did not wait for my answer. There was acrimony in her statement. I suddenly realized that Rivka felt hurt and humiliated. She had tried everything to get her guy, and more. She was undressing in front of me, letting me see her beautiful body. She had done everything short of crawling into my bed, for which she was too proud, but I had paid no attention to her. It suddenly dawned on me that indeed it was no coincidence, she had been undressing so nonchalantly in the morning so I could see her. Then I realized that now only Sonja was dressing and undressing as before, baring her breasts to my view. Rivka was now extremely careful not to expose any parts of her body. In fact, I suddenly became aware that even the kitchen door could now be closed fully, leaving no slot for my observation. The whole puzzle started to fall into place: Sonja really did not care whether or not I was looking, but in the case of Rivka it had been deliberate. She must have felt rejected. Her charms had not worked on me. Here was Minnie, practically a child, and she had conquered me, something Rivka was unable to accomplish even with the tremendous advantage she had over Minnie, the fact that we lived in one room and she could try to use her charms on me in the morning and at night.

I felt bad for Rivka, for she was a good girl and extremely pretty on top of it, but she missed one thing that Minnie had in abundance: class! Rivka was too rough, too unpolished for my taste. I was instinctively afraid of her. With Minnie, however, it was different: I felt calm, relaxed, and happy around her. Every minute with her was precious. I did not want to hurt Rivka, but the harm was done. She probably would never forgive me, although she tried not to show her hurt feelings. She made only the one statement which she just could not restrain: "Since you have Minnie, you don't see anybody anymore, do you?" This statement kept coming back to me over and over again as I went to bed.

11

THE CONCERT

The extermination of the Austrian Jews had left a terrible impression on the Jews of Kovno. Was it our turn now? We had already paid a staggering price, with 80–85% of Lithuanian Jewry massacred. But was this really the price for letting us live, or was it only a suspended sentence until our time would come to be shot too?

A new theory was starting to surface now. Maybe, it went, if the Ninth Fort indeed was being transformed into a graveyard for European Jewry, the Nazi henchmen may have left us deliberately in the ghetto as a decoy. The foreign Jews were purposely led through Paneriu Street, so they could see that there indeed were ghettos in the East. Thus put at ease, they would not suspect that within an hour they all would be facing a ditch full of corpses and they themselves would be the next layer on top. This was a conceivable scenario. The Germans had no reason to rush to kill us. We were only half an hour away from the fort and they could always manage to get hold of us and chase us up the highway. In the meantime, they could take care of the Jews from faraway lands who had to be transported and thus were much more difficult to deal with.

Barely had the bodies of the Jews from Vienna a chance to cool when, one morning, a new transport of Jews was brought to Kovno for extermination. As before, they came to the railroad station, were forceably marched through town, past our ghetto to the highway, and ultimately to the fort. In the morning when we came to the shop, we were again greeted by the sight of columns of Jews, one hundred each, climbing the road up to the fort. Nobody was quite sure, but it seemed that this group was from France. It was mind-boggling: here the Germans were involved in a life and death struggle with Russia, trains and fuel were needed to supply the freezing troops at the front, yet transportation was available to ship Jews all the way from France across Europe to the Ninth Fort to be murdered.

In the evening when I met Minnie she was terribly upset. She had already heard the news and she and her parents were now worried about their family in France. Although she grieved for the Austrian Jews, when it hit closer to her own flesh and blood the wound was deeper and the pain more acute. But this transport was not yet the end of it. Several more transports came in short succession and then they stopped, for how long we did not know.

New orders continued from the Nazis. Suddenly, one day, a decree was issued ordering the termination of all pregnancies. Any woman caught pregnant would be shot! Jewish women were now forced to seek out medical help to check whether or not they were pregnant. Anyone found expecting a baby had to undergo an abortion. Abortion was an extremely risky procedure under the unsanitary conditions in the ghetto. Women in later stages of pregnancy were forced to induce early delivery at considerable risk to the mother. But carrying a baby was sure death. Women who were close to delivery were now hiding at home and praying that they would not be discovered until after the birth. Among those latter ones was Renee, who was expecting her first baby. Peter was very upset with this latest decree and was relieved when it was all over and Renee had given birth to a baby boy, named Raanan.

Another case was the family Davidowitsch. Mr. Davidowitsch was a Jew from Memel. He had been married for twelve years and they had no children. They had seen just about every doctor in town, but to no avail: Mrs. Davidowitsch was unable to conceive. In 1938, when the Nazis marched into Memel, the family came to Kovno. When the ghetto was being organized he began to work in the labor department of the committee, in the same room with us until our graphics department moved to its new quarters. I got to know him very well, particularly since he lived next door to us.

For the past few weeks, my mother commented that if she did not know that Mrs. D. could not conceive, she would have thought that she was pregnant. She was slightly heavier than when we first met her in the ghetto, which, hungry as we all were, seemed rather unusual. When the order about the mandatory abortion came Mr. D. was terribly upset and Mrs. D. was crying incessantly. We decided to go and see whether we could be of any help. It turned out that Mrs. D. was indeed pregnant! After twelve years of trying, suddenly, here under totally inhuman conditions, under the troubles and horrors of the ghetto, the couple was suddenly happy.

They had something to look forward to. They would be blessed with something that had eluded them for so long under normal conditions with good food and nourishment. Davidowitsch was now desperate. "You will not undergo an abortion, come what may," he told his wife.

And the Davidowitsches decided to take the chance and risk their lives. They would not be deprived of the only joy they could ever experience in the ghetto, that of having a child. For months Mrs. Davidowitsch would not show up on the street and the gamble finally paid off. Eventually she gave birth to a normal, healthy baby.

These two cases were not the only ones. There were dozens of women whose plight we did not know, who bore in silence their deep grief over a baby lost which they and their husbands were expecting with so much love. Did the Nazis ever think about it, how the world would have reacted had they imposed the same ban on French and Polish women after they had won the two campaigns? But obviously with Jews it was different. They were subhumans and dispensable.

It had now been quite a few months with no Actions in the ghetto and life began to seem normal. For us normal meant the absence of mass executions or deportations. It meant having just enough food to exist, although we had not seen butter, cheese, milk, or an egg for more than half a year. It meant survival of the community while individuals were shot. It meant life behind barbed wires, like criminals, like slave laborers without rest or relaxation. This was normal in the ghetto. The German master race had decided not to finish us off for the time being.

Under these conditons, the ghetto started to restructure its life. Small groups of youths organized underground activities and literary circles. One evening when I met Minnie, I told her that next weekend there would be a lecture on the national Jewish poet Bialik. These lectures were never publicized and were arranged for intimate groups only. Minnie was quite excited over the idea. Since she knew nothing about Bialik, she was eager to attend. The house where the meeting was arranged was a half-burned-out building, vacant and uninhabitable. The lecture was a refreshing and spiritually envigorating experience. On the way out we left the house in small groups, not to draw attention to ourselves. As we moved slowly out of the building, I peeked into one of the rooms and stopped suddenly. "Minnie," I said in disbelief, "look here into this room!"

Minnie stopped, looked into the room, and exclaimed in total surprise: "It's a piano!"

"Yes, I cannot believe it myself, a piano in the ghetto."

We waited until everybody was gone. I walked into the room and straight to the piano. The piano was decrepit and terribly dusty. One corner was slightly charred, apparently from the fire. I struck a chord and almost fainted. The piano was so out of tune that one could not even recognize the notes. Just as excited as I was when I first noticed the piano, so vivid was my disappointment when I realized that the piano was not playable. Where could one find a tuner in the ghetto? Minnie was sorry, too. She wanted to hear me play, but this was now out of the question.

When I came home I told Vera about it. Vera seemed to have the answer. There was in the ghetto a young pianist who had started a career as an entertainer. Somebody had once told Vera that he was also a piano tuner. I got his address and went to see him the next evening. He, too, was astounded that there was a piano in the ghetto and was happy, as he too was eager to play. He promised to tune it this weekend.

Sunday, late in the afternoon, I picked up Minnie and we went to that house. We carefully opened the door; nobody was there. I walked straight to the piano and what a difference! The piano was tuned and had a fairly good sound. We brought in two chairs from the assembly room and I sat down to play. After months of not having touched an instrument, my hands were stiff. After some scales my hands started to loosen up and I was able to get through a few pieces I had known so well. Minnie was visibly surprised. She did not expect me to play so well.

"Just wait a week or so, until I have regained the strength in my fingers. We will have lots of fun."

We spent the rest of the evening at the piano until my hands hurt.

"Tomorrow I will take some of my sheet music and I will start in earnest," I said.

I liked to play and loved music. Every day was now a pleasure. I refreshed my memory on some pieces by Chopin and Schubert and started to feel comfortable with the progress and execution. I also started to polish up on my jazz. I showed Minnie a few elementary exercises and told her to try it. It was fun. She would make mistakes and giggle and I played the role of the stern teacher. One day we decided to ask some of the gang to join us for an afternoon. They did not mind and one Sunday we all had a ball. None of the gang played the piano and I did all the entertaining.

The piano had now become sort of a companion of ours, like a friend with whom we shared our joys and our sorrows. One day we would play jazz and the other, some Chopin nocturnes. Often I would get so involved in my playing that I would forget where I was. Minnie for her part enjoyed it too. We almost could not imagine how we lived before without it. Month after month passed. Forgotten were the records and the record player. Our entertainment was now the piano. But nothing in the ghetto was forever. One day when we came to spend our customary evening at the piano, it was gone! This was a terrible blow. We almost felt as if we had lost a good friend. In fact we had lost more than that, since the piano had brought us so much closer together. There was no other entertainment in the ghetto to soothe our nerves, which were so often on edge. We walked through the rest of the building, but the piano, our companion, was gone. Our entire evening was ruined. I vowed to do my best to find it.

The most logical thing was to go the cultural department at the committee. The next day, to my surprise, I found out that indeed they had the piano. They had obtained from the Germans permission to form an orchestra in the ghetto. They were now in the midst of organizing it and needed the piano. The ghetto had very many talented musicians. In fact, most of the café bands were Jewish and all of them were in the ghetto.

The news about the orchestra was both good and bad: on one hand we were delighted that we would have an orchestra. On the other hand, however, we had lost our piano. I also found out that the orchestra would be in the building of the old Slobotker Yeshiva, where the big pogrom had taken place the first week of the war. The building was at the other end of the ghetto away from where we lived and where our shop was, and it was not practical to go through the entire ghetto, past the notorious corridor, just to play. We had to forget the piano for all practical purposes.

In the meantime the musicians started to organize and prepare for a concert. All the musicians were serving in the ghetto police and the police administration gave them time off to practice. It could be expected that the first concert would be soon.

The ghetto in general was not aware that an orchestra was being formed. It was a Jewish tradition that a mourner did not listen to music before a year was over, and the entire ghetto were mourners. We had lost just in Kovno alone over twenty thousand Jews. This consideration weighed heavily on the musicians and the organizers. There was a lot of reluctance to go through with the project, but finally the people in favor of an orchestra won out. The reasoning was that people who did not want to attend a concert did not have to. However, nobody could predict what the impact would be even on the people ready to listen to music.

During the summer of 1942 the orchestra was ready and a date was set for the concert. The program consisted of Russian, French, Jewish, and Italian music. The Germans had strictly forbidden to play works by German composers; the Jews could, God forbid, contaminate the pure German music. Thus there was no Beethoven, no Schubert, and many other well-known names. On the day of the concert I picked up Minnie and we went across the ghetto to the Slobotker Yeshiva. When we entered, the hall was already half full and people were still coming. It seemed that there would be a full house. I looked at the audience and memories of concerts I had attended in town came back to my mind. In the old days the crowd was dressed festively, the mood was joyous, the people relaxed and rested, all well-fed and in good humor. There was the scent of perfume and the glitter of jewelry. A concert in Kovno was more than just coming to listen to music, it was a social affair. But how different was the crowd today: the clothes were shabby, the faces drawn, no perfume or jewelry. Most of the people were hungry, tired from slave labor, and the mood was subdued. Everybody had the same feeling: was it really right to have a concert, when the blood of our murdered people was still warm? We were all just about to break the tradition of not listening to music before a year was gone. Some people bothered by this burden turned around and left the hall; they could not make peace with their conscience. In the entire crowd there was not a single smiling face, or a single person who had not lost family during one or another Action. We did not feel comfortable either, but we decided to stay.

The hall in the meantime was filling up and everybody sat down waiting for the concert to begin. The musicians started to assemble on the stage and we were waiting for the conductor, but instead of him, an officer from the cultural department of the ghetto entered the stage. He asked everybody to stand up and to honor our martyrs by a minute of silence. People got up and some quiet sobbing could be heard. When the minute was over, the man on the stage gave us an introduction explaining the strains and struggle the committee had been through before finally deciding to have the concert. His speech was very subdued and at the end he expressed hope that we would be forgiven for not waiting a year, since otherwise, under the circumstances in the ghetto, there never would be a concert. While the speech was well delivered and proper under the conditions, it probably would have been better if it had never been made. Too many wounds were touched by it and we were here not to aggravate but rather to soothe.

Finally the leader of one of the most prestigious bands took the podium. There was no applause. He started the concert with a piece by Mendelssohn, whom the Nazis had banned since he was of Jewish blood. The tune was melancholic and before he had a chance to get even half-way through, everybody in the audience had tears in their eyes. Not only the audience had succumbed to emotion, but one by one even the musicians had tears filling their eyes and could not go on. The conductor had to stop and ask the people and the musicians to relax. After a short while the piece was resumed from the beginning. People around us were sitting with handkerchiefs in their hands, but controlling themselves not to disturb the concert. When the piece was finished there was again no applause and some relief that we had managed to face the challenge. Next on the program was a singer. He selected a familiar Jewish folk song which described a bird, free and flying high in the sky, which was then caught and placed in a cage to die. The tune was a very sad one. Needless to say, everybody got the message and the sobbing started anew, but he was able to finish his song without interruption.

During the next number a commotion started and everybody was turning to the rear. Lo and behold! At the door were German officers! What were they doing here? Could the entire concert have been a trick by the Germans to get some young intelligent people assembled in the hall? Was this an Action? The Germans noticed the agitation and motioned to continue. Their job was to make sure that the orchestra did not break the rules. When they were convinced that no German works would be played, they left the hall. The concert then proceeded undisturbed. The last number played was *Scheherezade*, by Rimsky-Korsakov. Throughout the concert Minnie rested her head on my chest and was in a state where she was just about to start crying, but never really did. I held my arm around her waist and noticed that most of the people were in a partial embrace, as if trying to comfort each other. There was no applause even at the end of the program. On one hand we wanted to listen to more and more music, but on the other we were really glad it was over. The concert had taken a piece of life from each of us. The wounds were too fresh and still bleeding and a concert, which should have had the effect of a balm, actually only rubbed more salt into the raw flesh.

On the way home I could not get rid of the tune by Rimsky-Korsakov, just as I could never get rid of the tune from the march of *Aida* on the second day of the war.

As we were walking towards home, the clouds over our mood started to lift. "Minnie, the concert has really made a deep impression on you," I said.

"Yes, it did. I am glad I had enough fortitude not to break down and cry."

"Are you sorry you went?" I asked.

"No, I would go again. The next concert will be much easier to bear."

"Oh, I am sure of that. We were not yet prepared for this," I said, "next week they have again a concert, are you coming?"

"Of course I am!"

"So it is a date."

With this we parted. The first concert was now history.

The week passed quickly and we were approaching the date of the second concert. I picked up Minnie as usual. Most of the people were the same, but there were also many new faces in the crowd. The mood in the audience was loose and relaxed. The tension of last time was not there. It seemed that the ice had been broken. The people had made peace with the idea that the ghetto now had an orchestra and that we really had not committed any crime by listening to music before a year had passed after the last Action. Our conscience was clear and for the first time we expected to enjoy a concert rather than to be at odds with ourselves. The concert itself was also differently arranged. There was no speech by the official of the cultural department and no minute of silence. The program was slightly modified, eliminating some of the more melancholic tunes. There was even scattered applause when the soloist completed his number, *Gypsy Airs,* by Sarasate. It almost seemed as if the orchestra had won a victory of sorts over our tormentors. The concert again ended with the tune from *Scheherezade.*

After the concert we decided to take a walk. It was still early and the afternoon was perfect. On the way we passed the block buildings, where I noticed a group of youngsters kicking a football around. They had installed at one end of the area two goal posts and a crossbar and were passing the ball and shooting on goal. When we came closer I recognized a few friends of mine who for kicks passed the ball to me.

"Minnie," I said, "would you allow me to join the gang just for a few minutes to kick the ball around? I haven't played soccer for ages."

"No problem," she replied, "only don't get carried away and let me wait too long."

With this I ran into the field and joined the boys. It really felt good! Before long a few other guys joined in and we were having a great time. I did not know how long I had been playing, but when I looked up where Minnie was supposed to be, she was gone! I was suddenly awfully upset. I had committed a terrible blunder: I had given preference to the game over her. I dropped the game and ran to her home. I rushed up the stairs in one breath and knocked on the door. There was silence. Was she home and not answering? I waited a few seconds and knocked again. I thought that something had moved inside.

"Minnie, dear, I am sorry, it was all my fault, please open the door."

There was a ripple inside and I heard steps coming to the door. The door opened. It was her. She was terribly upset. I walked in, touched her hand, and said, "Minnie, darling, I did not mean to hurt you, I simply had the desire to play ball and did not notice how time passed. I thought it was just a few minutes."

"It was at least twenty minutes. You even did not turn around to look for me! I really wonder, do you indeed love me?"

"What a silly question, did you have any reason to doubt it during the past?"

"No, I cannot say that, you were always attentive and considerate."

"So why should you be jealous of a football?"

"I am not jealous of a football, I just felt neglected."

"Don't talk like this. You know better than that. I promise never to do it again."

She did not doubt my sincerity, but she had to drive the point home that I had been wrong in how I had handled the situation. After arguing a little more about it, we finally made up and I took her into my arms and pressed a hot kiss on her lips as a sign of reconciliation. She responded in kind and our first and only quarrel was settled.

12

MORE TROUBLE

The latest news from the fronts was extremely discouraging to the ghetto. The winter had passed without a German collapse and the spring brought new activity to the fronts. With the approaching summer the Germans started their second big drive into deep Russia. They were again celebrating one victory after another and the Russians were in full retreat on most fronts. In May 1942, after a siege of eight months, Sevastopol in the Crimea fell. The drive continued on to the Caucasus and on 8 August the Maikop oil fields fell to the Germans. The Russians were also in full retreat on the central front where they were falling back towards Stalingrad. By 23 August the German Sixth Army had reached the Volga.

While the Germans were celebrating their victories along the entire Russian front, Field Marshal Rommel swept his armies across the desert towards El-Alamein, which he reached by 31 August that year. In addition to all these victories, the German U-boats were now sinking seven hundred thousand tons of Allied shipping a month, more than could be replaced in all Allied shipyards, including those in America working full capacity and remote from any bombing. In a big speech, Hitler promised the German people that Stalingrad would be taken by the German troops in this offensive. These were not empty boasts. The war was going their way and with every victory, our situation became more precarious: should they win the war, our manpower would not be needed any more and all our efforts to buy time through hard work at the worst jobs were futile.

At the peak of the German successes, additional trouble came to rest at our doorsteps: the Lithuanian peasants in whose homes we were now living, encouraged by the German victories on the fronts, again decided to pressure the German administration to finish off the ghetto and demanded the return of their property. They did not care that this meant a massacre of about eighteen thousand Jews! The local German administration, however, was not interested in killing the rest of the Jews, at least not yet. For the time being they had the tremendous advantage of having the Jews around, who provided them with free labor. What would they have should the Lithuanians regain their homes? They would not even replace the Jews on these most undesirable jobs. Thus, with the Germans standing firm, nothing came out of this petition. It was the ultimate irony of fate that the Germans saved our lives under this extremely peculiar condition.

Although the mood in the ghetto was not exactly elated, as long as there were no extermination Actions an underground could be created. Their activities were secret and it was very difficult to penetrate them. These groups consisted of members of one or another Zionist party before the war, of students from fraternities, where people knew each other and there was no danger of somebody acting as an informant.

It was now September 1942, and although the Germans were still celebrating one victory after another, time to finish off the Russians during this offensive, before the winter, was running out, which only meant that we would be in it for a long time to come, provided they let us live. The only encouraging news was that since February there had been no Actions in the ghetto and even the last one—the deportation to Riga—was for slave labor, not extermination.

The month of September was slowly drawing to a close and October was ushered in with no major disasters on the fronts and no severe setbacks for us in the ghetto. We almost started to believe that this was the way it would be till the end of the war, when the bubble burst. The ghetto was presented with a new demand by the Germans: four hundred more Jews for Riga! And the Germans wanted the ghetto administration to do the entire job themselves. Tension started to mount throughout the ghetto. But there were two important differences this time: the ghetto was empowered to carry it out without German help, and secondly, we were sure that this was not an extermination Action. As to the first point, it meant that people who had good connections within the ghetto administration or the ghetto police had little to worry about, as long as German help would not be needed. This was good for people like me or Minnie. I had enough connections in the council and Minnie was a close relative of a man with enormous power in the administration by the name of Abraham. But this was bad for a girl like Rivka, who was single and had no connections at all. She was in danger and depended on me and my connections.

The most important point, however, was that letters reaching us from Riga described conditions there which were more or less comparable to those in our ghetto. Yet nobody wanted to get caught, except the people who now had family in Riga and wanted to be reunited with them. But when these volunteers saw the mood in the ghetto, many of them recalled their applications and went into hiding.

Meanwhile I had found out when the people would have to be handed over to the Germans. But what I did not know was that the night before, the ghetto police would spread out a dragnet throughout the ghetto and go from house to house, arresting the people on the list. Fortunately we noticed them in time and Rivka slipped into the hiding place. When the police knocked on the door, everybody played it cool. They searched the house, did not find her, and left. When we had the all-clear signal, we threw some clothing in to Rivka behind the wall and she remained there all day.

In the evening the balance of the people were caught upon return from work, at the gate. The usual crying and lamenting could be heard when the people were marched out of the ghetto. But at least they were not being marched to their deaths.

By the end of October we found out from the German press that General Montgomery had started a big offensive at El Alamein. We knew that heavy fighting was raging there, but from the German reports we had no way of knowing how it was going. However, we were vitally interested in the outcome of this battle since a victory by the Germans would have meant the destruction of all Jewish hopes in Palestine. We were now following that battle even with more anxiety than the battles on the Russian front, on which our fate hinged. At first the German reports were sketchy, but soon we found out that the Germans were in full retreat. Palestine was now finally safe!

Barely a few weeks later, rumors started to hit the ghetto that the Allies had successfully landed in North Africa. The news electrified us. Finally, in the west, the Germans were on the defensive for the first time! On 10 November 1942, in retaliation to the landing, Hitler ordered the occupation of Southern France, the so-called unoccupied area of the country. Minnie was terribly upset over it, because most of her relatives had fled there during the fall of Paris. I had difficulty consoling her.

The German defeats were now colossal and we were expecting retribution by the Germans.

On Sunday, 16 November 1942, they got the pretext they were looking for. On that day a Jew by the name of Mek and two of his friends had decided to escape from the ghetto to the Aryan side. They had bought Aryan papers and hoped for the best. After careful planning, Mek and his two friends were ready to attempt the escape through the barbed wire.

Mek, a man in his thirties, short and a little stocky, was not exactly a man capable of moving swiftly across barriers. After the first friend had successfully gotten across the fence, Mek tried to do the same, but was caught in the wires. Just at this time a ghetto guard noticed Mek dangling and ran to arrest him. The third Jew, seeing the guard, fled back into the ghetto, while the first one, who got across successfully, ducked into the bush. As if by design, it just so happened that a higher German officer was in the vicinity and saw the incident. When he approached the fence, so the accusation went, Mek allegedly pulled a gun and fired a shot. Somehow nobody was hurt, but the accusation spread like wildfire through the ghetto. Everybody remembered a similar accusation about one year before. One thousand innocent Jews were arrested because of it, and shot the same day! On everybody's mind was the same question: was this a prelude to another execution of one thousand Jews? An air of nervous anticipation gripped the ghetto. Within a few hours SS-police arrived in the ghetto and arrested the members of the council. At the same time the ghetto police was instructed to provide twenty hostages who would be shot if the Jew who managed to escape would not give himself up. Since no one knew who or where he was, this demand could hardly be met.

The ghetto leadership was faced with an awesome task: to select hostages for certain death. It was clear that if the hostages were not delivered in time, something worse would happen. At the predetermined time, a group of elderly, sick Jews and a few inmates from an insane asylum were selected and delivered. To heighten the anxiety in the ghetto, rumors were planted that mass graves were being dug at the notorious Ninth Fort. The tension grew by the minute. However, unknown to us, the SS wanted a major spectacle but not an Action. They thus announced that an investigation would be conducted. Late in the evening the investigation was completed and the findings were that Mek had acted on his own and not as part of a conspiracy and the ghetto was, therefore, not responsible. The decision was to hang Mek. The gallows would have to be built by the Jews and the executioner would also have to be a Jew from the ghetto. Everything had to be ready next morning. The members of the council as well as the hostages were released and sent back to the ghetto.

Tuesday 18 November was the date set for the execution. The place selected for the public hanging was the square right in front of the Jewish council, where most of the people had to pass during the day. This square also happened to be next to our home. Around noon a group of SS-men brought Mek to the ghetto. He could hardly be recognized for the torture he had endured the night before. The Germans had decided that just plain hanging was not enough. An order was issued that all the people in the ghetto, whoever was not working outside, were to be present. A group of German policemen made sure that nobody was home hiding.

Mek, despite the anguish and torture, summoned all the strength he could not to show any fear or weakness. Before he ascended the gallows he turned to one Jewish policeman and inquired about his mother and sister, with whom he had been living in one room. Were they safe? The policeman nodded, the Germans had not touched his family. What appeared to be a smile showed up on his face. "Please promise me that you will take care of them," he managed to say. The policeman promised. Little did either know that the night before the Germans had taken both his mother and sister to the Ninth Fort and had them shot.

Before the support from under his feet was pulled out, he faced his executioner and forgave him. "I know you are not guilty, you are forced to do it. I forgive you," he said. With this the support was pulled from underneath him, his body convulsed, and he remained hanging. An uncontrollable cry went out from the assembled people. Many women fainted, but the Germans were standing and laughing.

The body, by the order of the SS, was supposed to remain on the gallows for a full twenty-four hours, so that all could see it. This evening was cool, crisp, and lit by a bright moon and the body swayed in the wind like a tree. In our home we had trouble with Ruthie. She noticed the body outside the window and thought it was a toy. No matter how much we tried to keep her away from the window, she kept coming back and looking at it. Finally in the evening we got her to go to bed. But we in our home could not sleep. No matter where one looked were the gallows and the body. Even when one did not look, we could not get rid of the feeling that he was there. Like a ghost he pursued us.

Late in the night we heard steps on the stair, or were our nerves so strained that we were imagining things? But suddenly there was a knock on the door. We almost fainted. With a cold sweat on my forehead, I opened the door. In it stood a Jewish policeman from the ghetto. "Don't get alarmed," he said, "can you keep a secret?"

"Yes," I said, "what is it?"

"Remember," he said, "if anybody finds out about this, we both and all the members of our families will be in deep trouble."

I started to shiver. Through the window I saw the brightly lit body swaying on the gallows, and next to me, a ghost, a stranger with a mysterious threat.

Without answering my question, he took out a hidden camera from below his coat and snapped a few pictures through the window. Just possession of a camera was reason enough to be shot, let alone taking a picture of the gallows. But before I had a chance to say another word, he disappeared.

I remained petrified. What if someone found out about it? But then I relaxed. After all, what difference did it make? We would not survive the war anyway!

Although this Action cost the ghetto only three lives, it was a rude reminder that the Final Solution was still in full swing. Hanging was only one more way in the endless arsenal of torture and murder.

The SS victory over Mek, however, was a very meager one, for barely twelve hours later, on 19 November 1942, the Russian counteroffensive at Stalingrad had begun. The news from the front indicated big break-throughs by the Russians. Every day when the outside brigades returned home from town, the first question was about the Stalingrad front.

Minnie and I, meanwhile, were attending most of the concerts and reading books. One of the books was *The Forty Days of Musa Dagh*, by Franz Werfel, which made an indelible impression on us. The bloody, ruthless massacre of over a million Armenians by the Turks in 1915, in full view of an entire world, reminded us of our fate. The Armenians were starved to death, shot, drowned, tortured to exhaustion, and left in the desert to die of sunstroke and dehydration. We compared their fate with ours, the indifference of the world to their plight, and the complete abandonment of the poor people into the hands of a barbarous, tyrannical regime. Our analysis of the book indicated that if the world did not come to the rescue of the Armenians, who were Christians after all, how could we, Jews, expect help? No doubt Hitler knew all about those massacres and the criminal neglect by the free world, and was convinced that he could proceed with impunity against the helpless Jews. Our conclusion was that if we were ever to survive this war, it would not be because somebody came to our rescue, but because Hitler ran out of time.

One day when I returned from our shop, I found Mr. Bernstein, a neighbor of ours, waiting for me. I was surprised to see him.

"How are you, Mr. Mishelski," he greeted me when I came in, "you must be surprised to see me here, but I will make it very short. I know you are working in the graphics department across the street. You make all those armbands, don't you?"

"Yes, I do," I replied. I was wondering what he was driving at. What did he have to do with armbands and with our shop? He wasn't about to propose that I make armbands which he would sell to people in the ghetto illegally?

"I like your work, you know," he continued, "It is clean, clear and very sharp. Who in the shop does the coloring and the design, and who cuts the templates?"

"The design is done by me or my boss, the cutting of the templates by me."

"I am glad to hear it. As you know, the Lithuanian women on the farms wear kerchiefs. You, with your ability to paint on cloth and your skill in preparing designs, combined with my business experience, we could start to produce kerchiefs for the Lithuanian farm girls. I will supply to you the cloth needed for the kerchiefs, you will then apply a nice design, and I will sell them in town for foodstuff. With the food situation the way it is, none of us has enough to eat and a good contact with farmers could turn our lives around. What do you say?"

I looked at him in complete disbelief. Here we were in a ghetto, with no experience and no knowledge how to start something like this, thinking of producing hand-made kerchiefs and competing with well-established factories with modern facilities and distribution. It sounded like sheer nonsense to me. "Mr. Bernstein, your idea does not sound practical to me," I said. "Who will buy from us, and how do you intend to compete with factories producing these wares?"

"Don't worry, there are enough Lithuanian peasant women who will buy. Just have a nice design. Factories are not producing kerchiefs now. They are all set for war production and kerchiefs are not an item required for war."

"Nevertheless, the stores must have thousands of kerchiefs from before the war."

"I am sorry that I cannot get you excited over it. Think about it, I will be back, maybe you will change your mind. Talk it over at home."

With this he left our house. I decided to talk it over with Max and Vera. Both sided with me. They too, did not believe that this could be a viable deal. It just did not make sense, that we could compete on an open market with our hand-manufactured, second-rate merchandise against factory-made goods. But what I did not realize was that the stores in town were completely empty, with absolutely nothing to buy. Besides, I did not know the psychology of farm women. Unlike town folks, they did not like fashionable stores. They were used to the market. Most important, the merchandise from the Jews was bought for a piece of butter or bacon which they produced on their farms. The ghetto Jew was happy to sell just about anything for any price, only to get his hands on some food, which was so scarce in the ghetto. This did not escape the experienced business sense of Mr. Bernstein.

Next morning this whole episode was completely forgotten. But Mr. Bernstein, a skillful businessman, was not ready to give up so easily.

About a week later he showed up again at our house. He had a little package in his hand.

"Mr. Mishelski," he said, "I have something for you." He opened the package and took out a hand-painted kerchief. "I thought I would bring this to you. When you rejected my idea last time, I went to a friend, a house painter, and made the same suggestion to him. He grabbed the idea and this is his work."

I looked at the kerchief in front of me. The pattern was mediocre and the execution even worse. I had absolutely no doubt in my mind that if I had done it, the pattern would have been much nicer and the workmanship incomparably better.

"Have you sold any of these?" I asked Mr. Bernstein.

"Yes, without any difficulty."

"Do you like the pattern and workmanship?" I asked.

"As long as it sells, I really do not care. Obviously a better job can be done, that is why I came first to you, but you did not show any interest."

"So what do you want from me now?" I asked.

"I am not married to the other guy. If you come up with a decent kerchief, we could still do some business. I still believe that there is room not only for one, but a dozen more producers. The market is there."

With this Mr. Bernstein left. Was he right? Was there indeed a market? A successful venture could put food on our table. What was I risking? A piece of cloth? A few days of work? It was worth at least a try! I told Max and Vera that I had decided to have a shot at it and would prepare a pattern.

Next evening I sat down and sketched out several patterns and showed them later to Minnie. She herself was quite artistic. She looked at the various patterns, picked out one, gave me a few suggestions, and next evening the pattern was complete. I drew it up to scale on heavy drafting paper and carefully cut it out with a stylus, as if I were working in our graphics shop. When the pattern was finished, I asked mother to find a piece of cloth the size of a kerchief. I took out my drafting board, tacked the piece of cloth to the board, and completed my first kerchief. When it was done and dry I showed it to my family. Everyone was completely caught by surprise. Nobody expected the kerchief to come out so sharp and pretty. Max looked at the kerchief and said, "You know, I am taking it tomorrow with me into town and will try to sell it."

"Wonderful, I am really curious to see what will happen, but how will you carry it past the gate?" I asked.

"I will wrap it around my body underneath my belt. One kerchief will not show." With this he retired for the night. It was 3 December, my birthday!

Max left in the morning for work as usual. We anticipated his return with great interest. When Max came in that evening, we saw right away on his face that he had sold the kerchief.

"Well, Max, how did it go?" I asked.

"I feel like pulling your leg a little, but I guess it is too late for that. My face, I am sure, gave it away already," and with this he pulled out a piece of bacon from his soup dish, which had a double deck for hiding food. Since we had been in the ghetto we had not seen a piece of bacon that size.

"Not only did I sell it, but look at the piece of bacon I got for it! I just cannot believe it! This is the best deal I have made since I went to work in town, and what is better yet, I have an order for three more! Can you make three kerchiefs yet tonight?"

"What a question! Even if I have to sit up through the night, you will have them."

Before the war our house was kosher and we did not eat bacon. But under the ghetto conditions, food was food. Only the most religious people would rather starve than eat non-kosher food. We could not afford to be so particular. Bacon was the cheapest and most nutritious food available and not too many were lucky enough to be able to buy it. That night we were lucky, and we had our best meal in a long time.

After the meal mother took a white bed sheet and cut it up neatly into six pieces. I sat down to produce three more head scarves. In the morning Max wrapped himself in the cloths and left for work, and we were left wondering whether he could indeed sell as many as three kerchiefs. We were now awaiting his return from work even more anxiously than yesterday. In the evening, upon returning, Max was elated. He had sold all three kerchiefs and had even brought some butter and cheese. It had been almost a year and a half since we had seen such food. God had been good to us. We were still alive and finally we even had real food on the table. Ruthie, who was just eighteen months old and severely underweight, had her first bite of cheese in her life. Vera and mother had moist eyes from excitement. At last the poor starving child had something decent to eat.

"How about tomorrow, Max, do you need more kerchiefs?" I asked.

"As many as you can produce. The peasant women like your design and I have already more inquiries," came the reply.

Mother cut up another bed sheet and our factory was now in full swing. When Mr. Bernstein came to visit us again, we were already off and running with our own production. I showed him my first sample.

"I told you that I wanted to join forces with you, I knew that your work would be superb. Are you now interested in working with me?"

"Why not? I must admit, you were right. I totally underestimated this business."

After a short conversation we decided that Mr. Bernstein would supply the cloths and I would apply my design to them. He would then sell the final product. The profit would be shared equally. This arrangement would have no bearing on my own production, which would have the preference.

Our volume of work was now so big that I had to teach Vera, Max, and even mother how to use the pattern and how to apply the paint. Even Minnie occasionally helped me in my work. At times we let Rivka and Sonja take kerchiefs to their working places and earn additional income to alleviate their extremely difficult food situation.

Our kerchief factory was growing beyond our wildest dreams. I was developing new patterns and improving techniques, and for the first time in the ghetto we had enough to eat. My patterns were quite successful and more traders got in touch with us. After a little while we decided that Max should stop taking kerchiefs to town, the risk was too great. We would rather depend on various traders. Our life had taken a substantial turn for the better. The shop was now to be our companion and provider to the very end of the ghetto.

Meanwhile the news from the Russian front was very encouraging. The Russians had broken through northwest and south of Stalingrad and were about to open up big pincers, trying to cut off Stalingrad with the entire German Sixth Army, the glorious army which had defeated France and had marched through the Arc de Triomphe. About a week after the start of the attack, the two armies apparently had met and closed the ring. The German press was talking about a big counter-offensive led by Field Marshal von Manstein. We were praying for the success of the Russians, though we knew that a German defeat would be costly for the ghetto. But if we were ever to survive, it was only possible through a sudden collapse of the Germans.

By the middle of December all attempts to relieve the surrounded German troops at Stalingrad had failed and the Germans in the Caucasus were in a hasty retreat.

The defeats of the Germans were by now so staggering that even the German press could hardly conceal them. Our hardest problem was not to show our elation over the thrashing the Germans were now receiving. But no matter how we tried for fear of reprisals, it was totally impossible. We had suffered under those murderers for a year and a half, only to see the hour of their agony. Towards the end of January, when the final defeat was staring them in their eyes, the Nazi press started to publish letters from soldiers from surrounded Stalingrad to show their "spiritual strength" and to lift the morale of the nation. But, between the lines, we read those letters with an uncontrollable feeling of revenge. One letter was complaining about those "fanatical" Russian murderers, who were being defeated during the day only to return at night in even larger numbers absolutely not caring about life! Look who was talking about caring for life. Look who was now accusing the enemy of being murderers! The Nazis, who had elevated murder to its peak and glorified murderers, were now complaining about murder! But the shoe was on the other foot now. The bandits were now being destroyed. What a revenge! Just to have survived all our agony and tragedy to live to see this hour, was a gift from God.

Another letter complained about the soldiers suffering in Stalingrad, asking God why He let things like this happen to the brave German people. This letter was a classic. The godless barbarians who had forgotten the image of God in the hour of their victories, the murderers who were shooting tens of thousands of Jews and Russian prisoners of war without blinking an eye, suddenly now remembered that there was a God somewhere after all. Where was God when they were massacring innocent women and children in the forts of Lithuania, piling them one on top of the other in huge mass graves? Why didn't they look up to Him at that hour? But at that time they were playing God themselves, with the lives of millions of "subhumans." Oh, how good it felt to hear a German Nazi clamour for God! God! This was our revenge. God was now in Stalingrad. This was the Ninth Fort for the Germans.

The worse the situation of the Germans got, the less we tried to hide our joy, no matter what their bloody revenge would be. On the job sites, the Jews raised their heads and told the Lithuanians that the hour of reckoning for the murderers would come and the ones who participated in the massacres would one day be accountable for their deeds.

With every day, we could see the Germans mistreating the Jews worse and worse. The treatment on the job and at the gate was getting so rough, that people decided not to bring in any food for the time being. The pressure on the ghetto was growing, the beatings became murderous, and we were waiting for the final act in Stalingrad to be played out and with it, the final revenge over the ghetto.

On 2 February 1943, Paulus, now elevated to Field Marshal, finally surrendered and with him, twenty-four generals and tens of thousands of German troops. On 3 February the German radio finally acknowledged the surrender and issued a special communique praising the troops for their valiant fight.

The same day, the Gestapo moved against the ghetto. An order was issued to the German and Lithuanian police to arrest any Jew found away from the job site. The German and Lithuanian police proceeded immediately to pounce on the Jews like wounded animals. Jews caught were arrested and under a hail of blows taken to the Gestapo in the city, where they were tortured. The Gestapo demanded from them to reveal whether they had family in the ghetto. Some poor souls succumbed to the torture, whereupon the murderers called the ghetto guard instructing to arrest their families and take them to the ghetto prison.

The situation at the gate was not better. Here the most thorough search in the history of the ghetto was conducted, and everyone in possession of any food was immediately beaten and arrested. But not only the possession of food was a crime. Several Jews were arrested and tortured for bringing into the ghetto the local German newspaper! The Jews did not have to see their defeat in print and rejoice over it. The newspapers were confiscated, the Jews murderously manhandled, and their families arrested.

The next morning the infamous Gestapo truck drove by the ghetto with the Jews which were arrested in the city. The people could hardly be recognized from last night's torture. The truck was heading towards the Ninth Fort. Everybody in the ghetto, including the Jews in the truck, knew what their fate would be within the hour. About an hour later the same truck with blood-spattered soldiers returned to the ghetto. They did not even care to clean up their uniforms. The rest of the Jews and their families, arrested last night at the gate and in their homes, including children, were loaded onto the trucks and hauled away. Friends and relatives stood near the ghetto prison crying and weeping, trying to get a last glimpse of their loved ones who would be dead before the hour was over. The doomed Jews had a last look at the ghetto and their families before they were driven off in the death truck on the way to their own funeral.

All in all over fifty Jews were murdered. Their sin was that the Germans had lost the battle at Stalingrad.

While this massacre cast a deep shadow over the ghetto, it could not dampen our spirit, having lived to see the beginning of the Nazi demise.

13

SPRING 1943

Stalingrad was now history. The magnitude of the German defeat began to sink in for both the Nazis and their victims. Our mood was one of joy and fear, concern and anticipation, disquiet and delight. Whereas before we were afraid to ask about the news from the fronts, since the Germans were piling one victory on top of the other, now we anticipated the coming days, hoping and expecting new and greater victories by the Allies. With every victory the German mood became more anxious, more nervous, and more irritable. Beatings and arrests became more common, unprovoked executions of Jews became the order of the day.

The news from the home front was even worse. German towns and cities were now under constant bombardment, by night from the British and by day from the Americans. Hamburg, Berlin, Frankfurt became frequent targets and hundreds of thousands of Germans were rendered homeless. In the early days of the war, when the Luftwaffe was on the offensive at Warsaw, Rotterdam, London, and Coventry, the German people were exhilarated by reports of the devastation created by these bombings. Now, however, they began to feel the effects of air warfare in their own backyards. The German soldiers at the front received letters from home and knew the agony of their families, which only made them more bitter. The only outlet for their vengeance was the Jews, and they did not hesitate to demonstrate this.

They refused, however, to accept the fact that the war was lost. So unshaken was their confidence in the Fuehrer that they were still convinced that he in his infinite wisdom would still pull some rabbit out of his hat. But even stranger was the fact that while the entire world had no doubt that it was only a matter of time before the Third Reich collapsed, the Lithuanians rejected the thought that Germany's supremacy was slipping. While all over the occupied territories resistance grew and partisan groups began to form, in Lithuania there was almost no resistance activity. The hate of the Lithuanians towards Russia was so overwhelming that any thought of a Russian victory was totally unacceptable to them. Although in the long run the fate of Lithuania under a Nazi blueprint would have been far worse than any Russian design, the Lithuanians just could not see it. Hitler and Rosenberg had made it quite clear: Lithuania was to be annexed to the Reich, the intelligentsia deported, Germans in large numbers were to be settled on Lithuanian land with the ultimate goal of Germanizing the entire country. This was part of the famous "Drang nach Osten."

For us this was a big problem, since we could not expect any cooperation from the Lithuanians either in procuring weapons for the ghetto or in helping our youths to join partisan groups.

The picture in Poland and in Vilna was different in this respect. Although the Poles were just as anti-Semitic and anti-Russian as the Lithuanians, their hate of the German conqueror was boundless. And rightfully so. The German mistreatment of the Polish people was far beyond any limits of international law or civilized behavior. The Nazis arrested the cream of the Polish intelligentsia and many of them were sent to concentration camps. With the defeat of the Germans in the wind, the Poles started organizing an underground in hopes of rebuilding a Polish army and eventually of achieving freedom for Poland. With every German defeat at the Russian front, the underground grew stronger. The Jews of Poland, also emboldened by the prospect of a German defeat, started to arm themselves. Many of the youths were now escaping from the ghettos and joining the partisan ranks.

Vilna, the capital of Lithuania, was in a unique position. The population in the region was a mixture of Lithuanians, Poles, White Russians, and a large minority of Jews. Having been previously part of Poland, the partisan movement in the area was starting to form and Jewish youths had a chance of joining. In addition, as the front was approaching, a partisan movement started to form in Minsk, in White Russia. To reach the woods in Minsk was much easier from Vilna than from Kovno. Kovno was too far away, in totally hostile surroundings, and it was almost impossible to arrange a contact with the partisans.

The Nazis now turned their attention to the various smaller ghettos in the area of Vilna and decided to liquidate them. Before the war, the Vilna district including the town of Vilna had approximately one hundred fifty thousand Jews, of which seventy five thousand lived in the city proper.

During the murderous liquidation of the Jewish population from July to December 1941, most of the Jews of the area were brutally massacred. By the end of 1941, there were only fifteen thousand Jews left in Vilna and about five thousand in several smaller ghettos in the region. What the Ninth Fort was for Lithuanian Jewry in Kovno and its surroundings, Ponar (Ponary in Polish) was for the Jews of the region of Vilna. This was a particularly gruesome extermination site. Simple shooting of the Jews just was not good enough. Before they were finally relieved of all their suffering, they had to go through the most inhuman torture. Men, women, and children were beaten with sticks, clubs, leather belts, and truncheons and forced to run until they fell, whereupon they were even more severely beaten, often till death. Prettier girls were temporarily taken out of the death march, as if they were being spared, only to be raped and later shot. Occasionally, before the execution, Jews were forced to stand totally motionless until they collapsed, whereupon they were shot. Often the Jews were forced to undress, men and women together, and wait for hours until they were finally shot. It did not matter whether it was July or December, unbearably hot or freezing cold. The people were made to wait for hours for their execution, their murderers even making fun of them. Many executions were purposely carried out on Jewish holidays, like Yom Kippur or Passover. Just the mention of the name Ponar was enough to scare the daylights out of every Jew.

The Germans had decided to liquidate the few smaller ghettos in the Vilna region, but were at first not sure what to do with the people. Initially they decided to transfer these Jews to the ghetto in Kovno. Our council was informed about it and preparations were begun to accept the approximately five thousand Jews. At the last minute the Gestapo changed its mind and informed our leadership that the Jews would not be resettled in Kovno. They could not "inconvenience" the poor Jews in our ghetto, who were already cramped. The other Jews, however, were informed that they were still being transferred there. Resistance was minimal. When the train came to a halt, they discovered to their horror that they were in Ponar. But 1943 was not 1941 any more. In 1941 there was no point in struggling to survive. The war seemed to be lost. Hundreds of thousands of Jews had already been massacred and survival only meant suffering a few more months to be shot later. But in 1943 the situation was different: the Germans were losing the war, the captive nations had already started to rebel and organize an underground, and the Jews were eager to see the end of the beast. Some people managed to obtain firearms and many youngsters were already among the ranks of the partisans. The ones who were not armed were not as ready to obey the command of the executioners. This time around the Jews offered stubborn resistance, most of them with bare hands. Quite a few Germans and local collaborators were killed and a sizeable group of younger people managed to escape. Some of them made it to the partisans, while others managed to reach the ghettos in Vilna or Kovno. The majority, however, were killed in a merciless bloodbath.

As time went on more information trickled in about the extermination of Polish Jewry, but all the gruesome details had not reached us yet. The ghetto leadership knew far more, but was tight-lipped and trying not to spread the news. These latest events in the area of Vilna, however, demanded a re-evaluation of their philosophy. Was the ghetto really served by not letting the people know all the facts?

Meanwhile the news from the Vilna ghetto was not good. It was apparent that the ghetto was on the eve of being liquidated. All signs and all rumors pointed to it. It was also unclear what our fate would be. Something was bound to happen to us after the liquidation of Vilna, but what and when? True, we were much farther from the front than Vilna and the ghettoes around it. We were also in an area much more cooperative with the Nazis. But these factors could only postpone the final day of reckoning, not eliminate it.

Passover 1943 was approaching and we were apprehensive about whether the Germans would provide us with a surprise, as was very often their pattern on or before Jewish holidays. The surprise was not far away. In the beginning of spring, Russian airplanes started to visit Kovno more often and the city was even bombed once or twice. During the night flights, the Russians used to drop lights from the planes which descended very slowly and illuminated the entire town. While the Lithuanians and the Germans were scurrying for shelter, the Jews of the ghetto stood at the windows and greeted the planes with joy. These were like greetings to us from the free world, a reminder that our enemy was now in retreat. People would even go out into the street, despite the curfew. Here, outside, we had a better view of the planes. This was one of the few pleasures we had in the ghetto and we were not about to miss it for anything. The Germans were not unaware of this and decided to spoil the fun for us. Shortly before Passover, the Jewish council was informed that the Germans had evidence that the Jews were sending signals to the Russian aircraft and threatened severe punishment to the ghetto if it did not stop immediately. As proof they arrested some Jews in town who, according to their report, were apprehended with military parts used in such signaling devices. The whole accusation was manufactured, but we in the ghetto were worried. We expected a Stalingrad-type Action or even worse. The ghetto leadership was desperately trying to convince the Germans that none of the accusation were true, but how do you prove that the charges were false, when the people whom you had to convince of the fallacy of those charges were the ones who had manufactured them in the first place?

A few days before Passover something unexpected happened to me. Minnie told me that her parents had decided to celebrate this Passover with the usual Seder, the traditional festive meal during the first night of the holiday. They wanted to thank the Almighty for the turn of events which ultimately could lead also to our freedom, as it had in ancient times in Egypt. I was invited. Abraham, an influential member of the council, a relative of Minnie's family, and a friend of mine from the years of our fraternity, would be conducting the Seder and a few members of the family promised to attend.

I was elated and accepted the invitation by planting a passionate kiss on Minnie's lips. This was exciting. The preceding year in the ghetto hardly anybody had a Seder: there was nothing to celebrate, the effect of the past year extermination Actions was still hanging over the ghetto like a dark cloud. This Passover, however, was different: a glimmer of hope was kindled in our hearts by the recent events on the fronts. And despite all the vicious attempts by the Nazis to spoil our holiday, they were able to mar, but not to destroy it.

On Passover night I dressed in an outfit befitting a holiday. I pulled out my best suit, which the Germans had not taken away during the house searches, and I only hoped that the Germans would not decide on a last-minute night raid. Minnie's parents greeted me almost like family. They too were festively dressed. Minnie wore a dress which I had never seen before and looked like a doll. Abe was in top shape and warned us that the entire evening nobody should talk about Actions, exterminations, deportations etc. The evening was to be devoted to freedom, to reminiscences of past holidays, and to pleasant subjects. He himself was in good spirits and set an example for the rest of us. The table was arranged as if we were in Kovno before the war, although there was very little food on it. But Abe, with his wide connections, managed to have some wine on the table and even a little matzoh, the unleavened bread eaten at Passover. Abe conducted the Seder with exceptional ability and set the tone for the entire evening. Minnie, as the youngest at the table, asked the traditional four questions of Passover, and Minnie's mother, who had a very lovely voice, helped in singing the various holiday songs. When we came to the passage "Next year in Jerusalem," we stopped for a while. Everybody was overcome by emotion. Abe took advantage of the pause in the proceedings to tell a few stories about Jerusalem and the evening continued on. This Seder was one of the most unique I ever spent in my life— a Seder in the middle of a dark night, with hope as the leitmotif of the entire celebration. Nobody as much as mentioned our troubles the whole evening. We were in a dream world of our own, created by the holiday spirit and by our determination not to look back. Fortunately the evening was not spoiled by any German surprises. Apparently they were satisfied just with spreading rumors and scaring the daylights out of us.

I returned home shortly before ten o'clock, right before curfew. Mother was still up and was curious to know how it went. I chatted with her for a little while and then went to bed. The next morning, as I was getting ready to leave for work, mother approached me with a question which completely stunned me.

"Vulia, I know you love Minnie, I don't have to ask you that. Why don't you go with her to the civil marriage office and marry her?"

I was totally dumbfounded. I never expected mother to make this suggestion. She noticed that I was shocked.

"I hope you don't mind me telling you that," she continued, "but this seems to make good sense to me."

"It may make sense to you, but I don't see it the way you do. What is the sense of getting married? We cannot start a new life, we cannot start a family. We are now on the eve of possible liquidation of the ghetto, or at least fast approaching the day when there will be no more ghetto. Tomorrow, for all it is worth, we could be shot or deported. They may shoot men or women only, leaving the surviving spouse alone. We have seen too much of it recently."

"I do not agree with you," said mother, "but the time you are alive, why not be together?"

"Who knows how much time we have left, mother. They are in the process of liquidating Vilna now, how far behind can we be?"

"This is all true, but my intuition tells me you should think about it very seriously. Did Minnie ever raise this question?"

"No, this had never occurred to us. Besides, this is not a marriage, some clerk in the ghetto police entering your name in a book and telling you that you are now husband and wife. Even under normal circumstances I would not consider getting married yet. Mother, you don't seem to realize that I have hardly lived yet."

"I do not agree with any of your arguments, I still feel that I am right."

I was now ready to leave for work. I said goodbye and ran across the street to our shop. In our shop, the talk of the day was the latest underground information that Warsaw and Bialystok were arming and getting ready to offer resistance to any further extermination attempts. All the various groups in our ghetto were discussing this subject amongst themselves. The question on everybody's mind was which road we should take from now on: armed resistance at any price, or practical survival at a serious cost to our self-esteem. This was an awfully difficult problem. Never did we have such an acrimonious debate. No conclusion could be reached on a sensitive issue like this, and by the time curfew approached we had to leave with nerves on edge and our moods depressed at the hopelessness of our situation, in the midst of a hostile environment from which we could not expect any help at all.

The contrast between this evening and the Seder was striking. But this last meeting was in tune with our tense and helpless existence, while the Seder was a very rare exception in our ghetto reality.

During my academic years at the university I belonged to a student fraternity. Many members were successful lawyers, doctors, engineers, and other young professionals. When the Russians occupied Lithuania in 1940 the fraternity was dissolved, but we maintained our ties among ourselves without any formal meetings. After the occupation by the Nazis dozens of our members were shot during the Intelligentsia Action. Many others were destroyed later during the Big Action. The survivors were few, but among them was my best friend Nahum Shoham, with whom I had gone side by side through high school and the university. Another was Abraham, Minnie's relative, a superb attorney and, at the time, the secretary of the Jewish ghetto council. It was sometime late in June when, on a Sunday afternoon, Abraham called a meeting. It was supposed to be secret. Nobody outside our fraternity was supposed to know about it. He, like all the members of the ghetto council, had secret contacts with some important Lithuanians. Besides being privy to all the information the other council members had, Abraham also had some very important connections of his own among a few Lithuanian clergymen. It was understood that he would have some important news for us. All week we were curious about the meeting. Isolated from the outside world, we were completely cut off from any sources of information. Anything Abe would have to tell us was awaited with great anticipation.

Every surviving member of the fraterntiy was there. Just one look sufficed to see how few of us were left. Our emotions were mixed. On the one hand it was great to see all the old friends again, people with whom we had spent so many wonderful hours and who brought back all the fond memories of our college days. But we just could not rid ourselves of the sad feeling that so many had perished in so short a time, murdered at the hands of a criminal regime and bloodthirsty collaborators. In the past, before the war, we used to sing and to be mischievous. Today there were no songs in our hearts. Abe and some older members of the fraternity talked about the past and about the brothers who were no longer with us. After a short time devoted to socializing and chatting, Abe took the floor. A hush overcame the assembly. One could hear the pounding of his neighbor's heart. The air was full of anticipation. What did he know that we didn't? What was the secret?

"My dear confreres," Abe started, "I called you to this meeting because we have many things to discuss. Obviously I don't have to talk about what we have been through in the past two years or so. All we have to do is to look at the size of this gathering to know the score. Just the list of the members who are missing is enough to make all of us cry! But unfortunately this is only a small part of what I have to tell you. I hate to be the bearer of bad tidings, but it is in the interest of all of us to be informed. Most of the information I will provide here is top secret and should be kept closely guarded. Other information, bad as it is, the people of the ghetto should know. The reason for the secrecy is twofold: first of all, we do not want the Germans to know that this information had been brought to our attention, and secondly, we do not want to spread panic in the ghetto, since the news is not only bad, but crushing. Be prepared for some horrors which are even worse than what we have been through, and that is saying a lot."

Abe took a sip of water and started pacing up and down. He obviously was trying to figure out how to break the news to us.

"Well, there is no use in procrastinating," he continued, with visible emotion. "I might as well just come right out with it: the Warsaw ghetto no longer exists! It has been liquidated!"

The announcement struck the assembly like a thunderbolt. The deadly silence of a moment ago turned into commotion, with shouting and screaming. "Warsaw ghetto has been liquidated! Warsaw ghetto does not exist anymore!" This was repeated over and over again from all sides.

"How do you know it? How reliable is your information?"

"It is impossible, the Warsaw ghetto had over half a million Jews. How could they kill so many people in so short a time?"

When the clamor calmed down a little, Abe continued. "Let me answer all your questions. First, the information is reliable and don't ask any further question as to the source. There is no doubt about it. The Jews of Warsaw ghetto did not go to their death like sheep. There was an armed uprising and they kept the German army from the ghetto for almost six weeks, longer than the resistance of the entire Polish army. They died like heroes, and with all our grief, we can be proud of them. They fought with small arms against tanks and machine guns, civilians—men, women and children—against a modern army. I suggest we honor the martyrs by a minute of silence."

The assembly rose to its feet and with heads bowed payed homage to the heroes of the ghetto. When everybody was seated again, Abe continued, "This is only part of the horror. It is my duty to tell you much

more. I wish I didn't have to, I wish it were not true, but the information
is accurate and is to be kept to yourself and your families. The ghetto was
destroyed not by shooting, the way we have experienced it here, but the
Germans, in their ingenuity, have invented and built death factories and
death vans! There are several places in Poland where the Germans have
built huge gas chambers, where the Jews are being subjected to lethal gas
until they suffocate. The gas chambers are built like bathhouses with
showers and the Jews are being told that they are being taken to a bath,
except that instead of water, gas comes out of the showerheads and the
people die of asphyxiation."

"That is awful, that's barbaric! How can this be?"

"Brothers, I told you in the beginning that the information is too
horrible even to listen to, but it is true!"

I felt my knees start to buckle and my entire body begin to tremble. My
teeth were rattling and a cold sweat covered my forehead. The other men
didn't look much better. This was the first time we heard about the
crematoria and the gas chambers. So that's what they had in store for us!

Abe took another sip of water and went on. "To the best of our
knowledge, they started the liquidation of the Warsaw ghetto by taking
people out, presumably to work, but the people never returned. They
had been taken to these chambers and gassed. The dead bodies then were
burned in huge crematoria until there was no trace left of them. These gas
chambers and crematoria were working for months until the ghetto
became suspicious and found out the truth. Since they suspected foul play
all along, they started to buy arms, and when the truth was discovered,
they refused to surrender, but rather rebelled."

"Do you know where these death factories are?" asked somebody.

"So far we have heard three names: Auschwitz, Treblinka, and Maid-
anek. Auschwitz is apparently the biggest."

"And you mean to say that half a million Jews have been thus exterminated?"

"No doubt about it. In fact this is not even the whole story. The gas
chambers and the crematoria are only one part of the program. In
addition to the above, they have constructed death vans which Jews are
forced to enter in the belief that they are being deported to another place
in Poland. These vans are hermetically sealed and gas is pumped into them
and the people suffocate."

"What monsters, God, what monsters," one could hear from all over.

"Does the world know about it?" somebody asked.

"Positively. There is no doubt about it. First of all, if we, without radio
or telephone, without mail or any communication with the outside
world, know about it, do you really believe that the governments of

Britain and the United States do not know? They know of every secret weapon factory in German-occupied Europe and bomb them day and night. Besides, hundreds of thousands of Jews are disappearing all over Europe in broad daylight and never surface any place else. Don't you think somebody might be interested in finding out what is going on? Jews are being deported from Germany, Austria, France, the Netherlands, and even from Italy, right under the nose of the Pope, and nobody knows about it? Didn't Hitler repeat over and over again that the Jews of Europe will be annihilated? You know how enthusiastically the German crowds used to greet this statement."

"And apparently nothing is being done about it."

"No. The world just doesn't care. And that is where I have something else to tell you. From the same source I mentioned before we also found out about a top-secret meeting of the top brass of the SS and SD somewhere around Berlin, where the decision was made to implement what they call the Final Solution of the Jewish Question. In other words, the decision was reached to exterminate all the Jews of Europe."

Again a ripple went through those assembled.

"We have an historic account with the German people," he continued. "During the Crusades whole Jewish communities were destroyed. Then during the Black Plague we, the Jews, were accused of having poisoned the wells. Tens of thousands of Jews were murdered. But never in history has there been a government whose official policy was the extermination of all the Jews. And what is even more frightening is that nobody cares. The whole world looks on and goes about its daily routine as if nothing were happening. This is the most earthshaking event in human history!"

There was a short pause in Abe's monologue. We had confirmation of what we had known all along, but tried to ignore: we were doomed, and the world didn't give a damn.

"So what is the solution?"

"Should we also consider revolt, Warsaw-style?"

"Well, this brings me to the real reason for today's meeting," said Abe. "All I have just told you was secret information, but what I will tell you now should be told to everyone you know."

Again the room fell silent.

"For the last month or so, our ghetto council has been wrangling with the problem of what to do. We have considered revolt, as mentioned here before. Under our conditions, however, it is totally impossible. First, the Lithuanians are not ready to cooperate. Second, our ghetto consists mainly of small wooden houses and there is no way to barricade ourselves to launch even a semblance of a fight. We have, therefore, charted a different course, whereby we are trying to get as many Jews as possible working for the Germans. Any German who profits from us will be interested in the status quo and not in our extermination. Any delay or postponement of the Final Solution may ultimately bring us closer to possible redemption. The war has now turned around and is at a point of no return: the Germans have lost it. At this juncture, therefore, our goal is to save as many Jews as we can, so that there will be a tomorrow."

"So what is your solution?" somebody asked from the floor.

"Let me finish and you will know. There are three ways that survival can be achieved. None of them is easy. One, we can join the underground movement. As the front comes closer to us, this underground will be increasing. Anyone willing should join these partisans. The ghetto has connections and there has been a beginning. Our underground is doing everything in its power to assist these youngsters. They even have weapons. Two, if you know a Lithuanian who is a close enough friend of yours and is willing to take a risk to save your life, contact him. There are people in the ghetto who have access to forged papers. This method is good only if you have a reliable Lithuanian, but unfortunately there are very few willing to take that risk. But with the front moving closer, there will be more Lithuanians willing to help. This again shows you the sound logic of our approach. Postponing the Final Solution will ultimately save lives, simply by giving us more time. And finally, all of you should immediately start building hiding places. The better the hiding place, the better chance you have to survive. The war will not last forever. The Nazis will be brought to their knees. Hopefully we can survive long enough to see it. So again, build hiding places, start right away, don't wait. We know not many will survive in the hiding places either, but some will, and one of the survivors could be you. The goal of this meeting is to drive you to action. I can hardly overemphasize the need for it. This is my message to you today!"

Abe had finished his all-important speech. There was another pause. People started to congregate in small groups and discuss the facts. The mood was one of total depression. Everyone thanked Abe for calling the meeting.

"Mishelski, you are an engineer," Abe said to me, "get going! It could be your life and the lives of your dear ones. Shoham, the same applies to you." With that he waved good-bye to us and walked away.

The meeting started to break up. The period of the three options had begun.

I returned from the meeting disturbed, confused, and disoriented. I was still shivering from shock of the disclosures. Before leaving our house for the meeting I mentioned to my family that I was going to meet some of my fraternity friends. I was careful not to mention that it really was a meeting with Abraham. When I walked through the door my face showed the after-effects of the gathering.

"What is wrong, you look bad," my mother said. "Did something happen to you? Max, look at him, he looks as if he is going to faint."

"Don't worry, he is not going to faint," said Max, "Do you want a tranquilizer?"

"I guess you might as well give me one," I answered.

Max went to the medicine cabinet, took out a tranquilizer, and gave it to me. After I had calmed down a little I asked my family to accompany me into Vera's room. Choosing my language carefully, I broke the bad news to my family. I stressed the parts which had to be kept secret, and the last part of Abe's speech regarding our three choices. From the very outset it was apparent that joining the partisans at that time should be kept as a last resort. The partisan movement was still in its infancy in Lithuania, the front was still far away, and the chances of reaching a fighting unit were almost nil. Lithuania was still firmly in the grip of the Nazis and the Lithuanian population was siding with the Germans. Without the cooperation of the local population, it was impossible to execute any plan to reach the woods where the action was. As to the second choice, contacting Lithuanian friends, we were doubtful that we could be successful. We concentrated on the third alternative. We had one hiding place at our home already and mother reminded me that this primitive hide-out had already saved my life. The hiding place was extremely primitive, but for a short-duration emergency it was sufficient. The problem was where and how to build a better and safer bunker. But at the moment this looked as remote and as hopeless as the partisan movement. Thus all three choices existed in theory, but were far removed from any practical application.

14

THE ESTONIAN ACTION

Summer came and went without any major upheavals in the ghetto. As always, however, tension was inescapable. Everybody instinctively felt that the hour of decision for the ghetto was approaching, and the chances were that the Nazi murderers would not let us live to see their humiliation. Logic dictated that one could be lucky once, twice, but eventually our luck was bound to run out. News from the surrounding ghettos was very bad. The ghettos of Riga and Vilna were in the process of being liquidated. Older, weaker, and sick people were being taken to Ponar and massacred, while the healthy ones were steadily being deported to various slave labor camps. But the most devastating news was that the Warsaw ghetto was no more. This meant that over half a million Jews were destroyed in cold blood, a massacre of unknown proportions even in the sad history of the endlessly persecuted Jewish people. No, they were not just killed, they were annihilated by a death machine operating with methodical German precision; with such refinements as gas chambers, death vans, and crematoria, with an entire government apparatus doing nothing other than planning and executing mass murder. The news from the rest of Poland was not much better. It became pretty obvious that there were no Jews left in the towns and villages. Since there had been over three million Jews in prewar Poland, we concluded that by now more than two and one half million Jews had been exterminated there. This was more than all the population of Lithuania!

And the Jews were gassed and burned not as a nation or as a religious group, but as a racial entity. If Jesus, the Holy Family, the apostles, and the early Christians had shown up on earth at that time, they too would have been gassed and burned in Auschwitz on racial grounds. But the Nazis and their Christian followers conveniently overlooked this aspect of their theories. They were too much intoxicated by the smell of Jewish blood. It was naive to believe that we had even a glimmer of a chance to be the chosen ones to survive. This was worse than being on death row. Convicts still had a chance for an appeal, for a commutation of the death sentence. Our death sentence, however, was not subject to any appeals. We were destined not only to die, but to be tortured before a mass grave in the ground or the smoke of a chimney would relieve us from our misery.

With this mental burden we looked to the front for news to cheer us up. And the news was good. On 5 July 1943 the Germans commenced their offensive near the city of Kursk. We were anxiously following this offensive and praying for its ignominious collapse. We were tense and nervous. But this was not 1941. The Russians were ready for them, on 22 July commencing their own counteroffensive and demolishing the Nazis along the entire front. On 4 August Orel was taken and on 23 August, Kharkov.

Closer to home, the extermination of the last ghettos was now getting into full gear. A ferocious fight developed between the SA and the SS over ghetto Kovno: who would have the honor of writing this chapter in the annals of the German master race? The SA was unwilling to relinquish the ghetto. They had too many benefits from it. But even more important, they were sitting in warm offices in the hinterland, dodging the eastern front, which had become a death sentence for every German. It was so much easier to shoot defenseless Jewish men, women, and children than to fight and be destroyed by the hated Slavs. But the fight against the SS was a lost cause: the SS was much more experienced in liquidating Jews and the decision in Berlin was: let the SS do it. The fight between the SA and the SS was out in the open. Little by little the picture started to crystalize: the SS would soon be in charge and the ghetto would be converted into a concentration camp. Like Vilna, we would be split up into smaller units. In the expectation of a final liquidation of the ghetto, it was simpler for the SS to destroy five or six small units rather than one big unit of sixteen thousand or eighteen thousand Jews. Also, in the ghetto the Jews had "too much freedom." They could move around without total control by the Germans, which would be impossible in smaller concentration camp units. With several smaller units the contact between the individual units could be severed at any moment, weakening every individual camp in the process. These camps would lose all contact with the Lithuanians.

In the meantime the Germans demanded workers for several labor camps in the vicinity of Kovno. The camps were set up for draining peat bogs, a backbreaking job. Again the council was saddled with the thankless task of preparing lists and procuring the necessary labor force. As always, single people came first, healthy individuals next, even if married but without children, and finally physically less qualified individuals if the number required could not easily be produced. Rivka was again in trouble. The number of unattached individuals was growing smaller and her chances of slipping by were getting tougher with every Action. Jewish police were hauling people from their homes at night, locking them up in preparation for delivery to the Germans in the morning. I did not know how long I would be able to cover Rivka.

In September 1943 the SS finally won out. The new boss of the ghetto was now SS-Obersturmbannfuehrer Wilhelm Goecke. His assistants were SS Sturmfuehrers Rinck and Berger.

Events on the western front continued to roll. In May of 1943 the Allies conquered Tunisia. On 19 July a successful landing of Anglo-American troops in Sicily had the Italian army in a state of disintegration. On 25 July Il Duce was summoned to the royal palace by the king and arrested. The sudden arrest of Mussolini gave us new hope that the same could happen to Hitler. This probably would not have brought the war to a sudden end, but it might have stopped the mass executions. We were waiting for the Allies to take over all of Italy with one bold stroke. Then the Italians, who outnumbered the Germans in Italy, could clean up the German pockets. The Allied forces had complete command of the seas. With their air superiority plus the help of the Italian troops and the local population, they held all the cards for a devastating blow to the Nazi war machine.

We in the ghetto were eagerly awaiting this bold strike. Even the Germans expected it. But it never came. The hesitation of the Allies to pursue their unlimited advantage gave the Germans enough time to disarm some rebellious Italian troops and to seize control of all strategically important airfields and passes. The great opportunity to land a staggering, possibly mortal blow to the Nazis was lost. Instead, on 3 September 1943, the Allied troops landed on the boot of Southern Italy, freeing the way for the Nazis to take control of all of Italy, since they now knew where the Allies intended to proceed. When on 13 September a daring plan succeeded in freeing Mussolini, we saw in it more than just a successful operation by a few German daredevils.

We in our graphics shop tried to analyze the situation in the west and the latest news of the abduction of Mussolini. Everything pointed to one thing: the Allies were not ready to let Germany break down as yet. It seemed that the hesitancy was deliberate. For one, the Allies wanted to weaken both Germany and Russia and let them bleed each other white. Besides, the Russians had now fifteen or more million men under arms with superior fire training after years of war against a first rate military power. All their troops were concentrated on one front only, on the European theater, while the Allies were fighting a two-front war, one in the east and one in the west, and had no forces on the continent. Should Germany collapse, so this reasoning went, there was nothing to stop the Soviets from overrunning all of Europe all the way to the English channel, leaving the British and the Americans to salvage whatever possible, with the Soviets holding all the cards. The Anglo-Americans needed to present a well-organized force on the European continent as a counter-balance, but putting ten or twelve million men or even more on European soil was a formidable task. The war could easily go on for another year before the Allies reached this goal.

These were depressing thoughts. Everything around us indicated that the Germans had decided to go through with their bloody war against the defenseless Jews. The west was criminally disinterested in our fate, and our armed resistance had proven futile. The Warsaw ghetto had offered a heroic fight with minimal weapons against tanks and planes. They held out against superior German forces longer than Poland did in 1939, but the net effect was the death of fifty thousand to sixty thousand Jews, as compared to a hundred or two hundred Germans. The exact figures were never disclosed. We in ghetto Kovno couldn't come close to anything remotely resembling the uprising of ghetto Warsaw. It would have been totally senseless. The beginning of our end was now under way. We knew we had lost the fight to survive.

Goecke, our new boss, was an awe-inspiring henchman, an experienced mass murderer. His face reminded us of a death mask, with its protruding cheekbones and jaw and piercing eyes set deep in their sockets. He prepared himself with German thoroughness to take over the ghetto, seeking briefings from every source. His first steps were cleverly arranged. To gain our confidence he at first increased the food rations and relaxed the regime at the gates, allowing the Jews to bring in much more food from the working brigades. He personally visited all ghetto institutions. Among the departments he decided to inspect was our graphics department. We were scared stiff in the drafting room just at the sight of his huge frame and military posture. Peter showed him around and explained our work. Surprisingly enough, he already knew everything about our shop. Before leaving our drafting room he ordered three ghetto plans, and he told Peter that he would immediately issue an order for the other tenant to vacate the floor, since he would have more work for us.

Peter was instructed to have the plans ready by the end of the week and to personally bring them to his temporary office. This seemed like a good beginning, but we were puzzled as to why he needed so many ghetto plans. By now we were used to viewing everything the Germans did or ordered with a great deal of suspicion.

Just as we had anticipated, Goecke started to show his real colors quickly. When he took over the ghetto there were over five thousand Jews working in about two hundred outside brigades, which were economically an enormous asset for the ghetto. Little by little he started liquidating the brigades and concentrating them in a smaller number of commandos which were under total supervision of the SS, most of them completely isolated from the Lithuanian workers. This was a serious economic loss, since less and less food was now brought in. It was also a blow psychologically, since the interaction with the Lithuanians meant news from the outside world and, in a few isolated cases, potential contact with the partisan movement.

One day Goecke informed the ghetto administration that Kovno would be converted into a concentration camp. The people were to be divided among the various working places, and the ghetto administration should assign people to those different camps. Following Goecke's instructions, the Jewish administration set up a special committee to prepare the transition from the ghetto to a concentration camp.

In the meantime our ghetto plans were ready, and Peter went to see Goecke. The floor next to our shop was now being vacated and we expected to move in by the end of the next week. When Peter returned from Goecke he had news for us: we could increase our working staff immediately. He also instructed Peter to set up an art studio in which artists would be painting portraits and landscapes for him and his adjutants Rinck and Berger. This was good news for our shop. It meant that for the time being we would continue to work as before. Pipsi was given the task of setting up the art studio. The studio was arranged in the adjacent room from which the tenant had just been evicted, and we rearranged our drafting room to accommodate more people. Pipsi, Nolik, and Dora were transferred from the toy factory to our workshop. Pipsi also found a well-known artist by the name of Ester Lurie who was willing to join us, and finalized the preparations for the studio. Peter kept his office and shared his time as before between the toy and graphic shops. Pipsi was put in charge of the studio, which included him, Ester, and Nolik, and I was left in charge of the newly-enlarged graphics group.

Goecke also gave the go-ahead to the orchestra to continue as before. While the ghetto was trying to adjust to the new reality, Smolensk was stormed and taken by the Russians on 25 September. By the end of September the German armies were forced to a defensive line along the Dnieper and those in the Crimea were in danger of being cut off. They were unable to hold this new line, either.

This was the situation when Rosh-Hashana, or the Jewish New Year, was approaching. The entire ghetto community was on edge, anticipating savage repercussions for the German defeats. Had our final hour struck? Was Goecke to be the liquidator of the ghetto? How fast would he move, and what would he pull on Rosh-Hashana, or on Yom Kippur, the holiest day in the Jewish calendar? We were like a drowning man who sees a ship in the distance and realizes that it will never reach him in time. Smolensk, where our ship was sighted, was just too far from us, and the stormy sea of the SS was too furious for us to endure.

Again, as last Passover, the axe fell not on our heads but on the heads of the Jewry of Vilna. On Rosh-Hashana of 1943 the final liquidation of ghetto Vilna began. The sick, the elderly, the women with children were forceably taken to Ponar, where all were shot and buried in one mass grave. The able-bodied men and women were split up and deported to various concentration camps, with the majority sent to the notorious slave labor camps at Vaivara and Klooga in Estonia, to build fortifications to stem the Russian advance.

The final liquidation of ghetto Vilna struck our ghetto like a bombshell. The next holiday "gift" had to be ours, since there were now only two ghettos left in the entire vast Ostland: Kovno and Siauliai. Bad as life was in the squalor of the ghetto, it was better than resting forever in a mass grave at the Ninth Fort.

Yom Kippur Eve fell on Friday, 8 October 1943. The committee had cleared a room in the hospital for services, since no synagogues were allowed in the ghetto. The services were supposed to be secret and only the members of the committee were informed about them. The reason for this secrecy, of course, was that the committee was afraid of an overflow crowd which could not be managed. But under the nervous tension in the ghetto this secret could hardly be kept, and thousands of Jews found out about it.

I decided to pick up Minnie and to go to the hospital to join in the prayers. The small room in the hospital was jampacked. People were standing from wall to wall and hundreds filled the corridors and spilled out into the street. The Jewish police tried to disperse the crowd, but in vain. The situation was wrought with danger, but no Jewish policeman dared to profane the holiday. All the police asked was that we pray in silence and suppress the weeping, which was coming from all sides and spreading throughout the crowd. There was not one person, no matter how tough in character, who did not weep. Inside the hall people fainted from heat and excitement and had to be removed.

After the prayer Abraham requested total silence. He had something to say to the gathering. With an emotion-filled voice he began to speak.

"Brothers and sisters! For almost two and one half years we have been struggling against overwhelming odds for survival. Never in history has mankind seen such a regime, where mass murder has been elevated to national honor and national duty, where participation in pogroms is considered a heroic act and is rewarded by the state, by the party, and by society, where saving a Jewish life has become a crime agaimst the state and against society, punishable by death. Never in history have peaceful people been whipped into such mass hysteria against another people and never in history have such vicious crimes been committed against the human race. The bloodshed that we have been witnessing during these two and one half years overshadow the worst massacres in history, whether committed by Genghis Kahn and his Mongols or the teutonic barbarians. And this we call the civilized, the twentieth century!

"But history does not care what happens to the Jews. It has never recorded our torment and will try conveniently to forget this most shameful period in human annals. It is therefore that I admonish you. Do not give up, try to survive, hide, escape the ghetto, go to the forests. We must survive to tell this tale of horror to the comfortable world that does not want to hear it. I want you all to understand that this is the last Yom Kippur in the ghetto. There will be no more ghetto by this time next year. It is everyone's responsibility to try to find a way to survive. The story must be told and the world which is unwilling to listen will have to hear it. It is the first time in my life that I cannot even utter the words, I wish you a happy new year, since it is not going to be a happy year for us Jews even with all the victories at the fronts. All I can wish you is a year of survival, just to be alive next year at this time. *Le shana tova tekhathamu,* may you all be inscribed in the book of life next year."

Everybody in the audience was choking and trying to suppress any sound. The sentence, this is our last Yom Kippur in the ghetto, kept coming back over and over again to all. Abe had made a tremendous impression with his very short speech. He had gotten his point across to the assembly that the time was short, the emergency great, and that everyone was now on his own to act.

The crowd dispersed. Fortunately the Germans did not choose to break up our services, they were too much preoccupied with the liquidation of ghetto Vilna. After the services I took Minnie home. We hardly spoke on the way. Our hearts were full and both had a premonition that our happiness inside the eye of the storm could not last long. We kept our hands crossed, as if supporting each other. In the hall we did not chat as usual. We stood for a little while in a silent embrace, then wished each other to be inscribed in the book of life, the traditional Yom Kippur greeting.

It was mid-October now. The second anniversary of the biggest massacre in Jewish history in Lithuania, the day of the Big Action, when ten thousand Jews were slaughtered, was approaching. Again the question arose: would the Nazis send us a reminder on that day, or would they let us breathe? Despite the liquidation of ghetto Vilna and our terrible anxiety, life was still going on more of less as before. The ghetto orchestra was again having a concert, but the conductor this time was supposed to be Dr. Zacharin, one of the best known surgeons in the country and a very gifted musician. This promised to be interesting and Minnie and I decided to go. The concert was well attended as usual, but the program was somewhat unique. It consisted exclusively of Russian composers. It almost looked like a quiet pro-Russian demonstration to celebrate their great victories at the fronts. They played Tschaikovsky, Mussorgsky, Ipolitov-Ivanov, and of course Rimsky-Korsakov's *Scheherezade*, which was now somehow synonymous with Minnie in my mind.

Although the concert was enjoyable, there was some unexplained anxiety in the audience. There was a lot of whispering and it seemed that somebody knew something. When we left the concert I told Minnie that I had a terrible, inexplicable premonition, and I was awfully worried. This whispering had upset me and I promised to check up on what was happening.

The next morning I did not even have to go to the committee. It was already common knowledge. Goecke had demanded three thousand people for work in a little village about thirty miles west of Kovno on the river Nemunas. It sounded like another Action for work in Riga, and although nobody wanted to get caught in it, it at least was not for extermination. The council set up a committee to prepare lists for this latest scourge. Dr. Elkes, who also felt the tension in the ghetto, particularly since it was so close on the heels of the liquidation of the ghetto Vilna, asked for an audience with Goecke. When Dr. Elkes broached the fears and anxieties of the ghetto to Goecke, the latter assured him that the conditions in the camp would be comparable to the ghetto and there was no reason for panic. Reassured, Dr. Elkes came back and informed the council about the latest assurances. Our graphics department, as usual, was given the job of preparing posters and the language of the announcement was designed to reassure the ghetto of the reason for the upcoming action. The date for the departure had been set for 26 October.

But on 25 October things started to go sour. First the ghetto guard was tripled, a very bad omen. Only two years ago, on 28 October, the Action started by strengthening the ghetto guard at the fence. But worse news was still to come. The brigade which worked in the German motor pool informed the ghetto that a fleet of trucks had been readied for tomorrow for some unexplained purpose. Only a fool could believe that this was not meant for us. An hour later we found out that the wood-cutting brigade which worked in Aleksotas did not return to the ghetto but was taken to the Ninth Fort. A further investigation revealed that they had not as yet been shot, only detained. But why at the Ninth Fort of all places? What would happen to the people of this brigade? Would they be shot tomorrow? Was tomorrow to be another Big Action to commemorate the one two years ago?

Later in the evening the announcement came that nobody would be going to work tomorrow, following the script of two years ago to the tee. The SS, who knew the terror in the ghetto, let it be known that people should prepare packages of the most important necessities, since they would need them in the new camp. The people who believed this statement started to pack some bare essentials, but many did not see any point in it. Among the latter was our family. We did not see any reason to pack, since if we were to be shot, the items would go to the murderers, and if we were lucky enough to stay for the time being in the ghetto, packing certainly was of no use. People who had reason to believe that they could be on the lists tried to hide with friends or relatives, as did Rivka. But the majority had no hiding places and were completely exposed to the upcoming danger.

On Wednesday the twenty-sixth, early in the morning, Jewish police accompanied by Germans started to search the ghetto and proceeded with the lists that the committee had prepared. When the first group was taken out of the ghetto, under the normal crying and lamenting, some Lithuanians followed them and found out that the people were being taken to the railway station in Aleksotas, not to the river Nemunas, which was the place to go if one wanted to reach the camp specified by Goecke. This was the first solid indication that the Germans were lying.

We in our household immediately got into a huddle to decide what to do. After some deliberations we decided to split up: Max, Vera, and Ruthie would hide in our hide-out, and mother and I would go to the workshops, where we hoped that the SS would decide not to search. The reason for splitting up was that to enter the workshops one needed a pass, and I was the only person who had one. Obviously I could not persuade the guard to let a whole family in, but a "worker" from the toy shop could be smuggled in. Mother dressed up to look young, to be a veritable worker, and we rushed out. Max gave Ruthie a shot so she would not wake up in the middle of the searches and all of them entered the hide-out.

As I figured, I had no difficulty in getting mother in. Almost all the Jewish policemen knew me from the graphics department and mother looked good and was not checked. In the workshop I found Minnie, who had had the same idea. She had her parents in the shop, too. Minnie was terribly worried, her cheeks were red, and fear was in her eyes. When she saw me come in she rushed to me. She was so troubled that she could hardly speak.

"What happened to you," she finally whispered, "why didn't you come earlier? I was waiting, I thought you would come. I needed to talk to you."

"Minnie, dear, we were not quite sure this was the right place to go. After all, if they are short of people, the workshops are the best reservoir to attack."

"So why did you change your mind?"

"Many things. First, I knew you would be here and I wanted to be with you. Second, this workshop is working for the SS now, maybe they will spare it."

"That was my thought too, so my parents came with me."

Now that she knew that I was here and near her, she relaxed somewhat but remained agitated. Her cheeks were still red and her nervousness showed.

"Is something wrong?" I asked. "You seem restless."

"I have not felt well the last few days. I have not slept and have been waking up in the middle of the night."

"You are worried about the Action and it shows," I interrupted her. "Tomorrow it will be all over and you will be able to relax."

"I hope so," she replied.

With this she went to her working place, and I picked up mother and we went straight to the toy shop. Pipsi arranged a place for both of us, gave us paint, brushes, and aprons, handed us some toys and explained to us the work we were supposed to do, if an inspection should show up.

By noon the Jewish police was woefully short of three thousand people and the committee hastily prepared new lists which were speedily delivered to the police. But even with these lists it was difficult to apprehend the people since many were hiding. At lunchtime Minnie's parents decided to go home to eat and to fetch some things in case they should be deported. Minnie was now in a terrible bind: should she stay with me or follow her parents? Her parents went to the gate and left. Minnie and I followed them at a deliberately slow pace. At the gate we stopped. She gave me one of those looks which always made me melt and asked once more, "What do you say? Should I stay here with you or go with my parents?"

"Minnie, dear, I cannot make this decision for you. If you decide to go with your parents, please don't waste time and come right back. We are not safe here either, but somehow I feel safer here than outside."

"I don't know; I feel wrong to leave my parents alone in such a time," she said, "but at the same time I would like to be with you."

Walking slowly, we reached the gate. Abruptly the Jewish policeman at the gate turned to us and said, "You cannot block the entrance, you must decide whether you stay or go."

This sudden shock forced Minnie to make a quick decision on the spot, and she decided to follow her parents. I kissed her and reminded her not to waste any time and to return immediately. With this, she walked out through the gate. I went back in, but suddenly I was gripped by a terrible fear. I rushed to the gate and wanted to call her back, but the policeman blocked my exit and did not let me go.

"Let me out, only to the street, I want to call her back, I am worried!" I screamed at the Jewish policeman, whom I knew well.

"Mishelski, you are staying, I will not let you out and this is final."

The road from the workshop to the blocks was uphill, and very far in the distance I could see her figure disappearing on the horizon. I still yelled, "Minnie, Minnie, come back," but it was too late, she was too far away and could not hear me.

Meanwhile the rounding up of the required number of Jews was going too slow for the Germans. Shortly after Minnie had left the workshop they decided to do the job themselves. Suddenly, out of nowhere, hundreds of drunk Ukrainian and Lithuanian police appeared in the ghetto. Like animals they rushed the block buildings where Minnie lived. They surrounded the area and with sticks, rifle butts, and clubs attacked the people inside. With unusual ferocity they chased all the people out of the blocks to the yard. Men, women, and children were bloodied by the dozens. In the process furniture was destroyed, windows broken, and doors smashed. The picture was of a real pogrom, with people bleeding and falling to the ground and being kicked all over. At the ghetto gate they were loaded into trucks and taken away. A few steps farther, Jewish police and members of the council tried to save whomever they could from the hands of the Ukrainian hoodlums. When Minnie's family was about to be loaded on to the truck, Minnie's mother noticed Abe among the ghetto officials at the gate. She started screaming, "Abe, save us, save us, save us! Save at least the child."

But Abe either did not hear or was unable to do anything. He let them be loaded and deported from the ghetto.

By nightfall, under a murderous terror, the number of required deportees was reached. All of them were assembled in Aleksotas near the railroad station. Here a selection took place. At first, under heavy beatings, the children were taken away from the parents and literally thrown into waiting trucks. The men were then separated from the women and packed into waiting train wagons, leaving standing room only. The separated children in the meantime were taken away and, as we found out later, taken to Auschwitz and gassed.

At night, when it was all over and the Jewish police told us that it was safe to leave the workshops since the murderers were gone, we rushed first home. Here we found that Max, Vera, and Ruthie were safe. Our house was passed up and not checked. Ruthie was awakened and she started to cry and scream, not knowing what had happened to her and where she was. It was impossible to stop her. Knowing now that my family was safe, I rushed to Minnie's house. On the way I already saw that things were bad. Furniture was strewn on the streets, pillows and feathers were all over, windows were smashed, blood was on the ground. What I saw reminded me of the description of the famous pogrom in Kishinev, also carried out by the Ukrainians. I rushed up the stairs hoping that Minnie was somehow spared. When I reached the floor the door was wide open and broken and in the apartment was a relative of the family, crying her heart out.

"What happened to them?" I managed to yell in anguish.

"They are gone! They are gone!" and she fell into my arms crying bitterly.

"No, don't tell me that. No!" I still managed to say, and I broke down too. It was all over, Minnie was gone! Who knew, maybe forever!

What a terrible end to a tender love story in the midst of a volcano. I had known her for almost two years. My entire life had changed under her soft touch and sweet disposition, her giggle, her innocent laughter, her poised walk. Everything about her was just divine. Her presence had made my life in the ghetto bearable. In her presence I forgot our troubles. It was Minnie when we went to a concert and it was Minnie when we went to play the piano. And now she was gone. Life would never be the same without her in the ghetto, and yet the living had to go on despite all heartbreaks and setbacks.

On the way back home I found hundreds of packages on Varniu Street which people had dropped when they were murderously beaten on the way to the ghetto gate. My God, did my sweet Minnie have to go through this hell? Was she too beaten on the way to the gate? Who knew what this lovely child had to go through on the way from the ghetto. My head started to spin and that damn tune from *Scheherezade* which she loved so much pounded in my head. And amidst it all mother's admonition haunted me: "I know you love Minnie, why don't you go with her to the civil marriage office and marry her?" The sound got louder and louder—go with her and marry her, marry her! The scene at the gate in the workshop came back to me when she was faced with the decision whether to go with her parents or to stay with me. If we had been married she would have stayed with me. She would not have been taken out of the ghetto, maybe to her death.

At home I found Sonja, Rivka, and Eetke. They were safe too, the police never found them. My family did not have to ask me what happened, my face told the entire story. Mother and Vera started to cry. "I told you, Vulia," said mother, "you should have married her. She would have been safe at least for now."

"Don't you ever say this to me again, you understand, never!" I shouted back, completely out of control. I had never screamed at mother before. Everybody was shaken by my reaction.

"I am sorry, mother," I said when I calmed down.

The rest of the evening and the night were one long nightmare of self-accusation. Why didn't I marry her? Why did I let her go with her parents? Why didn't I stop her? Here for the second time in the ghetto the attachment to family proved to be the undoing of a person close to me. First it was Giza during the action in the Small Ghetto, and now again Minnie. But what a difference it was! Minnie was much more than just a girlfriend to me. She was part of my life in the ghetto. Minnie could have been safe, had I only listened to my mother.

In the morning I rushed to Peter to tell him about Minnie. After all, he had access to Goecke, maybe he could do something. But Goecke was not in, he was supervising the SS. By the time he returned the transport was gone. Two days later we found out that the people were taken to Estonia, to Vaivara and Klooga, to join the surviving Jews of Vilna in building fortifications for the German army, now in hasty retreat on all fronts. The gentle, petite Minnie was on her way to save the German barbarians from defeat. And I was left with a deep wound and a bitter self-recrimination for having fatally erred.

15

K. L. KAUEN

The day after the Action the people from the wood-cutting brigade were returned from the Ninth Fort to the ghetto as if returning from a grave. We all were sure, despite assurances by Goecke to the contrary, that the people deported were destined for extermination. Everything pointed to it: the atrocities, the conduct of the Ukrainians, the beatings, the pogromlike atmosphere, the horror scenes at the railroad station, the unreasonably huge guard, and all the lies by the Nazis about being sent to work in a camp near Kovno on the river Nemunas. Instead of going to work people were anxiously running to the homes of friends and relatives to see who had been spared again. There was no consolation, not even the events on the fronts.

In the afternoon, when Goecke returned, he summoned Dr. Elkes and advised him to see to it that all workers were out in full force as usual the next morning. He also ordered the immediate evacuation of the small blocks B. The people were given forty-eight hours to clear out. It didn't matter that there was no place to go: that was our problem. It also did not matter that the people were unable to muster the energy to go through with this new catastrophic decree, as this was the very area which had taken the brunt of the Estonian Action.

The graphics department was ordered to prepare posters to let the people know about the new edict. We could hardly bring ourselves to sit down and to write it out.

Barely had the news reached the ghetto than the affected people started to besiege the committee, demanding to know where they could go. People were running to friends and relatives, but even they were not eager

173

to admit more people, the congestion was stifling as it was. Some forced their way into homes and challenged the owners to evict them. On the streets people carried on their broken backs huge bundles of all kinds of necessities, trying to salvage whatever possible. Some pushed carts or baby carriages stuffed with their meager belongings, necessities for daily use or for bartering with the Lithuanians. God, how lucky we were in our household that we did not have to move! We still had our home, our own beds, and no new lodgers.

From the latest events I became extremely tense. The failure to save Minnie made me obsessed with the idea that our graphics department needed a quick hide-out. People who had enough warning to slip into a hide-out on a moment's notice stood a much better chance of being safe. Max, Vera, and Ruthie were saved this way, and so was I during some of the previous Actions. Nobody knew how fast one might be forced to disappear next time. An Action could be called without prior warning, and we all could be in the graphics department with no time to rush for cover. Had Minnie been in the possession of such a hide-out at home, she would have been safe now. In my opinion it was imperative to have a fast hide-out in our shop proper. Something had to be done about it, and quickly. The next evening, when I took Peter home, I decided to raise this question.

"Peter," I said, "we ought to draw some conclusions from Minnie's tragedy. It is generally known that some people have hide-outs and these people were saved during this latest Action. It can be assumed that if Minnie had had one, she might have been safe."

"Possible, but go on," Peter replied.

"A sudden attack could occur while we are at work in the shop and we may have just seconds to hide. I propose that we build such a hideaway in our shop."

Peter was taken aback by this suggestion: he did not expect it. "I will never allow this," he said, "because if this should be discovered, I would be held responsible for it and my entire family could end up at the Ninth Fort."

Without telling him that I had just such a hide-out in my house, I replied, "You are wrong, Peter. In such a case I would be in a much more vulnerable position, since you are in the toy workshop most of the time but I am always here. Peter, don't write it off with such finality, but remember, time is very short."

With this we reached his house and he retired home.

Right after the news of the liquidation of ghetto Vilna, a group of youngsters had risked leaving our ghetto in search of partisan connections. The first group was caught by Lithuanians and handed over to the

SS. They were badly mauled and then disappeared without trace. All efforts to find out what had happened to them were in vain. The next group, not knowing what had happened to the first, also left the ghetto and was also caught. One of the leaders of this group was a friend of mine, David.

Then, after the Estonian Action, another unexpected event occurred. Abe disappeared from the ghetto and went into hiding with some Lithuanians. Abe was a leading personality and his disappearance could not be kept secret. He had warned on Yom Kippur to consider going into hiding and he practiced what he had preached. Apparently he knew that staying in the ghetto any longer meant mortal danger. This added to the unrest. Construction of hide-outs increased. Hundreds of Jews were now taking this solution seriously. Also, contacts with Lithuanians proliferated. Our first contact with our Christian friends was fruitless. They were afraid to commit themselves. Others, however, were luckier.

Two evenings later Nucia had an assignment from Peter. By the end of the day she was not through with it and insisted on staying to finish the job. Since I had the keys to the shop I had to stay with her. Everybody was gone. It was half-dark in the shop with only the lamp over Nucia's desk burning. I was tired and sat down in Peter's chair waiting for her to finish the task. When she was done she got up, walked towards me, then all of a sudden, without saying a word, she grabbed me, pulled me over to her bosom, embraced me, placed her lips on mine and gave me a long, passionate kiss. Surprised and not expecting this from the usually poised Nucia, I reciprocated her embrace. There was no sexual overtone in it. It was more an overflow of emotions. We both needed an outlet: I was grieving over the loss of Minnie, and Nucia, I figured, was either expressing her feelings of compassion towards me, or perhaps she had something else pressing on her mind and needed some affection. We stood in a silent embrace for a little while, then Nucia pulled me over to the sofa in Peter's office, took my hand, and said, "I am sorry, Vulia, I lost my composure, but my heart is full."

"No need to apologize, my mood is not much better than yours," I replied.

"I realize it, I know what Minnie meant to you. I am not surprised that she was so much in love with you. You are so much fun to be around and despite the fights which we had so often in the shop, I always admired you. These were precious hours we spent here in this shop amidst the ruins coming down all around us. I was always impressed by your warmth, your logic, your love for music. Remember how I used to ask you how does the first piano concerto by Chopin go? and you used to hum or whistle the main theme?"

"Of course I remember, who can forget it? These little episodes are the ones that helped us maintain our sanity. Were it not for moments like these and my relationship with Minnie, I doubt whether I would have had the energy to go on."

"Your energy helped me weather this storm, too. God, who knows where we will be next year at this time, or maybe tomorrow, for that matter . . ." she replied. She grew quiet, and I took her in my embrace without a word. Never before had I embraced or kissed Nucia. My heart had belonged to Minnie, and Nucia was just a good friend, a pal, one of the boys, rather than the desirable woman she really was. I put my hand on her breasts and gave her another kiss. Nucia did not resist. Neither of us was in the mood for sex. All we both needed at the moment was a warm embrace, compassion, consolation, some pure unencumbered love.

"Nucia," I finally said, "you know, you are quite a woman. As you know, I was deeply involved with Minnie and thus never really thought of you in these terms. How strange to discover it now."

The time was getting late and the curfew was approaching. We gave each other one more hug and kiss and got up, ready to go.

"Vulia, this was a wonderful evening. I will never forget it. You are a real gentleman. Too bad it had to come at such a bad time and so late in the game."

I accompanied her to her apartment and returned home in a strange mood. I could not understand why Nucia was so sentimental all of a sudden, something that was totally out of character for her. Did she really need a shoulder to cry on, or was she trying to start a love affair with me now that Minnie was gone?

The next morning, at eight o'clock when the shop opened, the men were already there, but Nucia, who was habitually late, was not in yet. When Nucia did not show up for the rest of the day I got worried. My instincts in the ghetto were completely extraordinary. Her strange behaviour yesterday and her absence from work made me suspect that something unusual must have happened. Never before did her absence for a day bother me, but that day it was different. After work I walked over to her house and to my amazement I found out that Nucia had left the ghetto to go into hiding with a Lithuanian family. Suddenly the entire evening yesterday fell into place. She knew that she was about to leave but did not dare to tell me. Yesterday's episode was a farewell of sorts, a goodbye to me and through me to her years in the shop. I felt strange. Although I was never in love with her, now that she was gone I felt that she indeed meant more to me than I had ever realized. She was part of my past, part of those unique evenings with Minnie in my house when we were trying to put out of our minds the storm outside and to drown it out by the soft, romantic music of the record player. Now she was gone too. The world around me was crumbling.

Under the impact of my tragedy Pipsi and Sarah decided to get married to avoid a similar fate.

A few days later, on 7 November, we got the news that Kiev had been overrun by the Russians and the advance was still proceeding. Normally this news would have been a cause for celebration and enthusiasm, but this time the mood was much too subdued for any kind of joy. Rather than celebrating the victory, we were concerned about what would happen to us as the front moved closer.

As usual, there was cause for concern. On 5 November 1943, the Germans carried out in Siauliai the most inhumane, the most despicable, the most dastardly Action of all: they forceably tore away all the children up to the age of twelve and all the people over fifty-five years of age. They also took out of the ghetto all sick and all the invalids in one gigantic sweep and deported them to an unknown destination, presumably to Auschwitz. The cost to the ghetto was eight hundred people out of a population of four thousand.

On the heels of the Estonian Action, this was a deadly blow. Obviously if such an Action was carried out in Siauliai, it would follow in Kovno, too. Although we could imagine the heartache of the parents who had lost their children to Satan's forces, we could not fully realize what it meant until it struck us later. Parents suddenly became terribly attached and tender to the children. They were constantly kissing and caressing them as if subconsciously feeling that they may not be around too long. The mood was now ripe to take any risk just to get the children out. The cost of this mood was staggering. People gave their children away to Lithuanians who demanded large sums of money, and after receiving the money handed the children over to the Gestapo. Other unscrupulous individuals took the money in advance and then refused to take the children, leaving the Jews with no recourse whatsoever. Other people gave the children away to clergy who later proved to be missionaries and whose goal it was to save Jewish souls. But in many cases the help was genuine, and Lithuanians were ready to take heavy risks to save Jewish children and adults, as was the case with Abe and Nucia. The decent Lithuanians who regretted what was happening to the Jews before, were now ready to help. The German defeats had given them new courage.

A few days after the news from the ghetto in Siauliai had reached us, Peter deliberately stayed longer in the shop. I stayed with him since I had to take him home. When everybody was gone he called me over to his desk and asked me to sit down.

"Vulia," he said, "the events in Siauliai were a shocking revelation to me. To take children from parents by force and to destroy them is a devilish ploy. Since this news has reached the ghetto, Renee is terribly apprehensive. Something has to be done to reassure her that I am doing everything to save Raanan. It has also come to her attention that many people are building hide-outs and she feels I should do it too."

"This is exactly what I said to you the other night."

"I have checked our house, but I don't see where I could do something like that there. Besides, I am not good at things like this and would not know how to go about it. I have therefore decided to let you build one in our shop, which is very close to our home, in the hope that whatever happens, we would have enough time to reach it. Needless to say, nobody is supposed to know about it, not even our workers."

"Don't worry, I have no intention of advertising it. The only one whom I would like to assist me is Nahum. I will also need a good carpenter from the toy shop."

"It is all right with me, as long as this is the entire team."

On the way home my brain was working feverishly, where to make the hide-out, how to conceal the entrance, how to make the entry efficient and how to keep it secret. By now we had added to our staff a few more people and the workshop was quite crowded. Among the new employees was a youngster by the name of Moolik, Nolik's sister Thea, and a boy named Zoondl, who was about fifteen years old but looked more like twelve, due to the hunger in the ghetto.

The next day I deliberately kept Nahum late. When everybody was gone I explained to Nahum my purpose. We immediately set out to take measurements of the workshop and check its physical layout. We discovered that Peter's room was a mansard-type, flanked on both sides by a roof space. In the wall of our drafting room was a small access door to this roof space. The setup was similar to the roof space in my home.

Once the layout was completed we had to contrive a concealed entrance. We decided that the best idea would be to build shelves for our paints and supplies at this wall. The access door consisted of two leaves opening into the room and the clear opening was about three feet square. We had now the clue as to how to proceed. We planned to space all the vertical frames for the shelves three feet on center, placing the first two frames on the seams of the opening, thus concealing the vertical seams. The shelves we laid out at eighteen inches on center with the first shelf in line with the horizontal slot of the door. On the floor we planned to place a baseboard to conceal the opening at the bottom. The shelves would be backed with plywood to cover the entire wall, which would look clean and professional. All the plywood pieces would be nailed tight to the frames except the one covering the door. This three foot by three foot piece would match exactly the lines of the frames and the shelves and would thus be concealed. This removable piece was to be loose and could be pushed to the side behind the plywood wall. The sliding panel would have a handle enabling us to close it from the inside. Stops were planned to ensure that the panel closed properly. The swing of the existing access door would have to be reversed and the entry would thus be unobstructed. We drew up the whole arrangement and detailed every piece to precision measurements. With both of us graduate engineers, the job was exact and professionally done. On the walls we planned to place blankets and insulation for sound attenuation, since the entire space was separated from the street by only thin siding and roof shingles.

When the plans were ready we presented them to Peter. Peter liked the layout and the details and promised to have everything ready by Sunday. The toy workshop had quite a few good carpenters, but the best and most reliable was a man by the name of Marshak. The next evening Peter called Marshak to his office. At first Peter made sure that Marshak could keep a secret that nobody, not even his family, was to be told. Marshak, who was extremely grateful to Peter for his warm job in the ghetto, promised not to divulge it to anybody. During the next day he cut up lumber and plywood to the desired specification and on Sunday we brought it to our shop. Nobody suspected anything. The next morning when our gang came to work they were surprised to find brand new shelves on the wall, but not a single one suspected what was behind it. We now had a hide-out which gave us a little sense of security in case of a sudden Action.

At the same time as we were building our hide-out, many other Jews were doing the same. Unfortunately most of them could not keep the work secret, due to the terribly crowded conditions in the ghetto.

During the first weeks of November our ghetto's name was officially changed to Konzentrations Lager Kauen, German for Concentration Camp Kovno. The change at first was in name only, but the ghetto did not have to wait long. Several days after the Estonian Action, Goecke ordered the blocks which were vacated after the Action to be renovated, and he and his entire staff moved into these neatly remodeled rooms. Once his offices were set up, he summoned Dr. Elkes to his office and informed him of the following: the entire ghetto would be broken up and set up in barracks near their working places. This would eliminate the exhausting, long marches to and from the jobsite, preserving the strength of the people for work. (What concern for the health of the people!) The first camp would be in Aleksotas, where approximately fifteen hundred Jews were still working at the airport. Following this, another fifteen hundred Jews would be set up in barracks in Sanciai. Following these two camps, several other specified locations around Kovno would be prepared. Finally the ghetto would be reorganized to follow the German prescription for concentration camps. The last to remain in the ghetto would be the people working in the ghetto workshops, in the administration, the police, the institutions supplying services to the outside camps, several brigades which were still scattered, but were working in war-related industries, and finally all the weak, old, and other people unable to work. Goecke made it amply clear that in the final setup, all the Jews would be confined to barracks. The committee was now given the task of splitting up the ghetto into these camps.

The feeling grew among us that it was better to voluntarily join some of those newly set up concentration camps than to remain in the ghetto. It appeared that the remaining ghetto inhabitants would be invalids, older people who were unable to work, mothers with children, and other unproductive elements. The next Action would necessarily have to be in the ghetto. This was reinforced by the Action in ghetto Siauliai only a short while ago, where all the children and aged were exterminated. In our household we had sleepless nights. What course should we take? I was emphatic. As long as we could stay in the ghetto we should not even consider moving voluntarily. In view of the fact that it became more and more dangerous not to work, I promised to set everybody up in the workshops. I managed to provide Max with a position in the first aid station of the workshops. I got mother into the toy workshop, where she worked part-time in the evening, thus enabling her to take care of Ruthie in the morning. Vera and Sonja were situated in a workshop where the work was very strenuous, but no other place could be found. There was enormous pressure on the workshops from hundreds of people who did not want to go to the camps. After the Estonian Action the workshops had become a choice working place, since everybody knew that the people in them were protected during the last Action. Only Rivka remained on her job, since she was working in a war-related brigade.

The reasoning that it was dangerous to remain in the ghetto made the work of the committee considerably easier. People who were afraid to stay in the ghetto did not put up any serious resistance and many even volunteered. As the head of the concentration camp in Aleksotas, the Jewish administration assigned a German Jew by the name of Fritz Bernstein (no relation to Bernstein of the kerchiefs) and a friend of Peter's. Bernstein needed signs, posters, and armbands for himself and for the camp and he was often seen at our shop. I accommodated him gladly and we got to know each other rather well. By the end of November the camp was ready and the people were transferred. Among the people to volunteer for the camp were our friends Nathan and Simon with their families. Rumor had it that the area in which they lived would have to be vacated immediately after the first two camps were filled. Only their in-laws remained, since Mr. Saks had a lucrative position in the ghetto at food distribution.

Camp life, however, proved to be terrible. Men and women were separated, everybody was sleeping on two-tier bunks. Beatings were frequent and the food was lousy. Movement was restricted and the guard was unreasonably large. Feeling sick was no longer an excuse to be absent from work and sleeping in the barracks was impossible. Talking to the women was forbidden, even to your own wife. It was not allowed to have any contact with the Lithuanians. But given the logic that life was safer in the camps than in the ghetto, where a crushing Action was expected, life was at least bearable. A few weeks later another fifteen hundred Jews were being readied for transfer to the concentration camp in Sanciai.

The year 1943 was drawing to a close amidst big victories for the Allies. The Russians were closing in on the Polish and Rumanian borders and the Anglo-Americans were seventy-five miles from Rome. But we were going through a conversion from ghetto to concentration camp and expecting even harder times ahead than we had already been through.

I came home from the shop one evening in an anxious frame of mind. Ruthie and Eetke were asleep and the rest of the household was at work, except Rivka, who was home. Rivka was getting ready to go to bed. She undressed her usual way, which for the first time made me nervous. She proceeded to the kitchen in her semi-transparent nighty, entered the kitchen, leaving the sliding door partly open so I could see the proceedings, where she undressed completely to wash up. My eyes were glued to the door and I felt my blood rushing through my veins. I started to lose control of myself. When Rivka was through with her ritual, which deliberately lasted longer than usual, she returned to her bed. I had a sneaky suspicion that the exhibition was meant for me. I thought I was getting a subtle hint from her and I decided to take her up on it. I got up and followed her to bed. Rivka apparently was expecting my move. She had observed me as I was following her with my eyes to the kitchen. But totally unexpectedly she moved away from me, gave me an angry look, and said, "Vulia, don't try too hard, I am not Minnie."

This was a low blow. She had succeeded in hitting me where she wanted and where she knew it would hurt most. "What is the matter, Rivka?" I asked.

"I will be very blunt: where were you all those years when you had Minnie? You did not even honor me with as much as a look. Nobody knows how I wanted you, but you did not take my hints. Now that you don't have Minnie any more, I am suddenly good enough for you. Well, good enough is not acceptable to me."

"Rivka, I am sorry, but I never noticed any hints from you." I was lying! I suspected all along that her morning ritual and nightly baths were no coincidence.

"Of course you didn't, you were madly in love and nobody else mattered. Well, no woman is willing to play second fiddle, you have missed your chance with me."

"But you had almost half a year before I ever met Minnie, where were you then?"

"Don't confuse the issues. None of us was ready for a love affair in those hunger months. We were happy to have an extra bite to survive. As soon as I could, I tried to draw your attention to me, but I failed. I just wonder where did I fail? I believe that I am more attractive than Minnie was, yet I was passed up."

Rivka was right to some extent. She was extremely pretty, but she was too rough, too unpolished, lacking natural intelligence and poise, totally devoid of warmth, all attributes which the gentle Minnie had in such abundance.

"Rivka, I am sorry if I hurt you, I never intended it. You know very well with what devotion I intervened on your behalf in the committee. I never let you believe that you were not pretty; yet, I believe we owe it to ourselves to take advantage of whatever time we still have left before our ultimate end."

"No, Vulia! Your sweet talk is not going to soften my resolve. The past two years just hurt too much. Don't be mistaken, I still admire you for the way you treated Minnie, I only wish it were me. You do have a way with women, but my decision is irreversible, you shall never have me!"

Rivka's voice at times was shaking, but she was tough, and I knew that any attempt was futile. I went back to my bed. For the first time in the ghetto I realized how deep Rivka's feeling were towards me and how seriously I had hurt her. She was a woman who felt rejected and whose pride had been deeply hurt. For a long time I could not fall asleep. I thought I could hear Rivka breathing heavily. Was she crying? No, not Rivka, she was much too tough for that; besides, she now had her victory and her sweet revenge.

In the meantime the second group was ready for the concentration camp in Sanciai. Old friends were saying goodbye to each other. With heavy hearts, the group of fifteen hundred Jews left the ghetto believing deep down that despite the difficulties in the camp, in the long run they had reached the right decision.

Goecke now ordered us to have eight hundred more Jews ready for another camp. They left in short order. Then he evicted the Jews from Old

Slobotke, who had to move to the now even more restricted space in the ghetto.

Vera, unaccustomed to hard work, caught a cold which did not seem to go away. Based on the rules of the ghetto she was not permitted to stay home, and the cold got worse.

In the meantime the Jews who had to vacate Old Slobotke had absolutely no place to go. The committee had no alternative but to force every Jew in the ghetto to accept somebody. When Saks, who lived in that area, came asking to let him and his wife move in with us, we did not hesitate. One more couple, did it really matter? Besides, if the case had been reversed and we had been forced to move out of our home, we certainly would have expected them to give us refuge. The day before the deadline they moved in with us. Rivka, Sonja, and her daughter Eetke were now put together into one bed and the sofa was given to the Sakses.

This was the beginning of K. L. Kauen.

16

VERA

Vera was always a healthy, robust, good-looking blonde, a typical Lithuanian girl. Born and raised in Kovno, she attended a Hebrew gymnasium and was also a student at the Lithuanian National Conservatory of music. Very advanced in music, she was the life of the crowd, playful, talkative, and entertaining at the piano. During her senior year in high school two young Jewish men in their early twenties moved in next door to us across the hall. One of them was an accountant and the other in his last year of medical school. Living on the same floor made it easy for them to get acquainted. The medical student was a tall, handsome, and charming young man. A casual hello quickly turned into prolonged conversation in the hallway. One thing led to another and things became serious. Vera in the meantime graduated from high school and Max Solc, the medical student, became a physician. With his studies completed, Dr. Solc proposed to Vera and they became engaged. That year at Passover both families got together at the traditional Seder in our home. Dvora Solc arrived with her five sons and introduced them to us. It was truly a remarkable family. The year was 1936 and heavy clouds were already gathering over Europe.

Vera's wedding to Max was like that in a storybook. Our family was prominent and well-to-do and mother did not spare any effort to make it impressive. During the inflation in Germany in the mid-twenties, my parents bought many expensive items for our home, among them the gold-plated set of flatware I mentioned earlier, with pure gold handles in the shape of the czarist crown. This set was one of a kind and was only used on very special occasions. It was kept in a steel safe which father had in his study. For the wedding mother took out this set for the dinner.

In addition to all of Vera and Max's friends, some of the most prominent community leaders were invited to the wedding. Max's friends were all young doctors, practicing in the smaller towns and villages. The situation in Lithuania was such that Lithuanian doctors generally didn't go to the smaller, more remote places; they did not have to, as they were offered positions in the university, the military, or in prestigious hospitals and clinics. All doors were open to them. Jewish doctors, however, could not get jobs in the select places and had to start their careers in the less desirable posts.

The festivities lasted until late in the night. Vera and Max left for a short honeymoon in Riga, Latvia. Germany was already off-limits to Jews.

After the honeymoon Max finished his residency in the only Jewish hospital in town. Postgraduate training was a major problem for Jewish doctors. Lithuanian hospitals would not admit any Jewish doctors at all, or at best, severely limited their number. Thus, with only one Jewish hospital, competition for available residency spots was intense.

Upon completing his residency Max moved to Daugai to start his practice, taking his young wife with him. Daugai was a village with no electricity, no movies, no sidewalks, and no running water. There was no hospital or clinic. More serious cases were sent to Alytus, the regional center. The pharmacist was also a Jew, who, like the Jewish doctors, had difficulty settling in bigger towns. The village had a significant Jewish population, mainly craftsmen and storekeepers. While Max was happy, since he was the only doctor for the entire region, Vera was disconsolate. She made friends with the pharmacist and the Lithuanian school-teacher, Yadvyga Bielinski, but otherwise diversions were few.

In 1939, when the war started in Poland, Max and Vera decided to move to Kovno. The situation for Jews in the smaller towns had begun to deteriorate, and since Max could relocate with relative ease, he made his move quickly.

Vera was then much happier. She returned to the conservatory and even got herself a part-time job. Max, however, had to adjust to a slowly-developing practice and after Daugai this was a big reversal. They now decided that it was time to have a baby and on 1 June 1941 Ruthie was born. There was excitement and happiness all around, only to be destroyed three weeks later. The war was on!

By 15 August 1941 all of us were shut off from the outside world with heavy barbed wire surrounding the ghetto. At first Vera did not have to work, since women with children were allowed to stay home. But after the population of the ghetto was decimated by mass shootings, killings, and deportations, this dispensation was rescinded. She was compelled to join the work force, which the Germans demanded remain at the same high level despite the extermination of fifteen to twenty thousand Jews.

Vera started to work, leaving Ruthie with our mother. Her breast-feeding had to be discontinued and she was put on our meager ration. However, by now we had some side income from the workshop I had set up at home, so the hardship was less acutely felt.

The work was arduous. Not being used to it, Vera quickly caught a cold. Under the ghetto regime, instead of staying home and taking care of it she was forced to continue working. Minor and even major colds were not considered reason enough to let a person stay home.

One evening when she came home it was obvious that she was very sick indeed. Her temperature was raging. She felt alternately hot and cold, was coughing profusely, and complained of severe pain in her lungs. Her breathing was labored. At first we suspected pneumonia. Max didn't want to take it upon himself to treat someone so close to him. Thus a colleague of his, Dr. Gerst, was called in and he confirmed the diagnosis. Under ghetto conditions it was difficult to obtain medicine. Fortunately Isaac Srebnitski, the head of the ghetto pharmacy, was a relative of Max's and he provided Vera with some medication, but far from what was needed.

Vera was now too sick to go to work. A ghetto doctor came to our home to check whether or not this was indeed true. After a brief examination, he signed a dispensation for her. For over a week Vera was seriously ill, but the pneumonia was not demonstrating the normal pattern. Specifically, the so-called crisis never came. Max started to monitor Vera much more closely and established that her fever had an undulating pattern. In the morning it was very high, dropping to normal towards the afternoon, only to repeat itself again. He started to suspect a lung abscess instead of pneumonia. All the symptoms were there. He again called on Dr. Gerst, who confirmed the diagnosis. Now the problem was medicine, and a lot of it. Dr. Gerst prescribed a very potent sulfa drug. Max was amazed at the doses he was prescribing and thought he might have been mistaken. He questioned whether or not he had heard him correctly. The doctor was insulted that his knowledge was challenged by a young physician.

"Doctor," he said, "you are still a young man and only starting in the profession. I have seen a great many of these cases and with some as severe as hers, you need very high doses to knock it out. You can rely on me."

Again Max went to Isaac Srebnitski. The medication was expensive but available. Vera was now taking massive doses of this sulfa drug and was showing some signs of improvement. One evening, however, she complained of severe headaches and difficulty moving her legs. Max looked at her legs but did not notice anything. "I hope it will go away by the morning," he said.

In the morning Vera woke up screaming insanely, "Max, Max, I cannot move my legs. I don't feel them, they are totally numb! My God, my God, what got into me? Help me! Help! Help!"

Everbody in the household was awakened by the screams and ran into her room. Then she discovered that she wanted to urinate and was unable to. Everybody was scared stiff. Out of the clear blue sky, Vera was paralyzed from her waist down! Max immediately left to get Dr. Elkes, the head of the Jewish council, one of the most prominent doctors in Lithuania and a close friend of the family. In the ghetto he did not practice medicine as he was too busy with its political affairs. In fact it was not easy to get to him, as the Jewish police rarely admitted anybody to see him. With our connections to the Jewish council and the police, Max gained admittance. Dr. Elkes listened to the information Dr. Solc had regarding Vera and dropped everything and walked over to our house. He checked Vera out, shook his head, and said, "I am surprised that Dr. Gerst prescribed such amounts of a sulfa drug."

"I did question him on it," said Max, "but he insisted he knew what he was doing. But this is immaterial. What shall we do now?"

Dr. Elkes sat down and asked Vera, "You didn't tell me whether or not you had a bowel movement."

"Come to think of it, doctor, no," replied Vera.

"The gastrointestinal tract can wait another day or so, but the bladder must be relieved immediately. Max, run over the the hospital as quickly as you can and get a catheter. Also, get some laxatives. If she doesn't move her bowels with the first dose, repeat it again, maybe in two or three hours. Also get some Vitamin-B Forte in the highest dose available and a concentrated liver preparation. The vitamins she can take orally, but the liver concentrate must be administered by injection. All are to be administered three times a day. If you will not be home, teach somebody to give the injection. In the meantime talk to Dr. Zacharin. He will have to insert a tube into her lungs to drain the pus. If she is lucky it can be accomplished by an incision alone. Otherwise a rib may have to be removed. Report to me in a day or two; I will try to come over and give you further instructions. Good luck to you, you may need it."

With that Dr. Elkes went back to the council building and Max ran to the hospital. Vera was in severe pain both in her lungs and from her inability to relieve herself. Twenty minutes later Max was back with the catheter. But it still had to be sterilized by boiling it for ten minutes.

"Don't boil it," Vera moaned in pain. "Insert it and give me some relief!"

Max didn't listen to her. The job had to be done right. After the catheter was sterilized he inserted it, and Vera felt substantially relieved. But the pain in the lungs was unbearable.

Now that Max had a few minutes to spare, he ran back to the hospital to get the medicine and to talk to Dr. Zacharin. Dr. Zacharin was the head of the so-called hospital and was one of the best surgeons in Lithuania, but he was an extremely difficult man to deal with. The facilities for this kind of an operation were primitive at best, but he promised to contact a few pulmonary specialists to see what instruments and equipment could be rounded up for the operation. Within a day or two Dr. Zacharin promised to be ready. Max's next stop was Isaac Srebnitski. Isaac had enough medicine for only a few days. The rest would have to be ordered from a Lithuanian pharmacy in town, and we had no access to it. But Isaac promised to get a permit from the German command to go to town to order the needed medicine.

Max came back with the small amount of medicine and administered to Vera the first of many injections. Her condition was critical. As if being paraplegic were not enough, she had to fight her primary insult, the lung abscess, which had been sorely mismanaged and permitted to advance almost beyond hope.

Luckily for Vera, Dr. Nakan had all the instruments needed for the operation and Vera was taken to the hospital. With no cars or wagons, Vera was put on a stretcher and carried all the way to the hospital. There everybody was ready. X-rays revealed that her lungs were full of pus. The doctors could barely believe that she was still able to breathe. Dr. Zacharin got ready to remove a rib. Max was frantic. "Doctor, you haven't ascertained whether or not an incision alone can be used."

"You young doctors have a lot of nerve teaching us what to do! Be glad that she got service at such a short notice."

"I appreciate this, but a rib resection, she will never survive that."

Dr. Zacharin stopped for a minute. At that moment Dr. Elkes entered. "What seems to be the problem?" he asked.

When he was apprised of the situation, he agreed with Max and asked Dr. Zacharin to try an incision before moving to the much more drastic method of rib resection. Dr. Zacharin was very upset at being contradicted, but Dr. Elkes was too highly respected as a physician for him to pick a fight. The instruments for a rib resection were put aside and everything was now prepared for the simpler procedure. The operation lasted several hours, but finally the tube was in. The pus drained well and Vera's breathing improved dramatically.

With the operation over, Dr. Zacharin turned to Max and told him, "Vera must lie in a certain position to facilitate drainage. The lungs must be flushed every so often. Either you, or better, a doctor who has experience with it, should do it. The end of the drainage tube must be put into a bottle containing water, into which the pus will drain. Special care must be taken to prevent the bottle from tipping over, allowing air to enter the lungs through the open drainage tube."

"We will do everything you said," answered Max. "We will also keep you apprised of the situation."

After the operation Vera had to be brought back home. There were no facilities for her in the hospital. Accomplishing this was no minor matter. She could not walk, and sticking out of her side was the tube, which was clamped and could not be touched. With the help of a few doctors from the hospital we somehow put her on a stretcher and brought her home. She was placed in bed as instructed, with the drainage tube put into the bottle. Ruthie now had to be warned not to touch the bottle, in fact not even to get too close to her mother.

After two days of laxatives Vera finally had some results. Being paraplegic, she had to be lifted onto the basinette and taken off of it. My mother was now the nurse. She washed her and placed her back into the prescribed position. In the meantime Max contacted every doctor and pharmacist he knew in the ghetto in an effort to get the medicine needed for Vera. He managed to scrape up some supplies, but not nearly enough for her need. In the evening, when Vera finally fell asleep, we sat down with Max to discuss the prognosis.

"Vera," said Max, "is a very healthy individual by nature. Her heart is strong and with proper care I hope we will win the battle against the lung abscess, although even this is not for certain. But I am afraid Vera will never walk again!"

We were stunned. "Are you sure?" we asked.

"I am afraid I cannot give any better prognosis. Once the spinal cord is damaged it does not regenerate itself."

"Does this mean that she is now an invalid for the rest of her life?"

"I am afraid so," said Max.

Gloom overcame all of us upon hearing his words. "Of course we will try everything Dr. Elkes has ordered," Max continued, "but short of a miracle things look bad, very bad."

For the next four or five days the pus drained conspicuously and the water in the bottle got muddier and muddier by the hour. Vera continued to need catheterization to relieve the pressure in her bladder. She begged Max to have the catheter inserted practically every hour, but Max refused since this carried the risk of introducing infection.

Isaac Srebnitski got a permit to go to town to see what he could do about the medicine Vera needed. The news he brought was both good and bad. The medicine was available, but the Lithuanian pharmacist refused to sell it for currency. He insisted on gold, silver, jewelry, or other valuables. This was a major problem. After the Gold Action, we and most of the ghetto had lost all our jewelry. Nevertheless we told Srebnitski that we would try to have gold for him with which to pay for the medicine. We were frantic! Where could we get it? Except for Saks and his sons-in-law, we did not know a soul in the ghetto who may have gold hidden, since information like this was kept secret. But we figured that Saks, particularly after we had accepted them into our apartment, which was no minor sacrifice, and being such a close friend, would not object and would help us out in this dire emergency. But how surprised we were when Max out of nowhere produced the gold watch he had hidden during the Gold Action and about which we had no inkling. This was like manna from heaven.

On the fifth day after the operation Vera as usual was begging Max for the catheter. Max refused again and told her she must wait three hours. Suddenly Vera's face reddened as she started to press hard: "I don't need you any more," she yelled in ecstasy, "I just did it on my own. Keep the catheter and eat it."

She had indeed wet the bed. She was elated. Despite the embarrassment of the wet bed, there was jubilation at home. Perhaps this partial return of function signified a more favorable prognosis. Although, as Max expected, she did get a bladder infection as a result of repeated catheterization, this was now the least of her problems.

That same evening Vera's condition worsened. She was breathing very heavily, her eyes were turned up, and her appearance was moribund. My mother and I walked out of the room to avoid showing her our concern. Once outside we embraced each other, cried on each other's shoulder, and expected that this was indeed the end. But Max didn't give up. He gave her an extra injection and called his colleague, Dr. Friedman, who was a pulmonary specialist. Dr. Friedman clamped the chest tube and took away the bottle. He then irrigated her lung through the tube. This was successful and Vera perked up.

Our supply of medicine was running low and we now decided to approach Saks about the gold we knew he had hidden. He did not deny it and promised to bring some of it, but said that the gold was very well hidden and he could not readily get to it. Our time was running out and we needed the medicine badly. Vera's condition had not changed appreciably. Her pulmonary problem seemed to be improving, albeit slowly, but it was still a hard uphill battle. The legs, however, remained dead. Our need for medicine was staggering. We again approached Saks, but once more we got the excuse that he could not get to it. Through contacts and with great difficulty we sold some of our best suits and Vera's beautiful leather boots and managed to buy some gold and jewelry elsewhere, with which we were able to buy some more medicine. When several more approaches regarding some gold did not produce any results, an argument ensued and Saks got terribly excited, started to scream like a maniac, grabbed a huge kitchen knife, and lunged towards Max. I jumped between them and stopped him from injuring Max. For all it is worth, he could have killed him. After that we did not approach him about gold anymore.

Ruthie was remarkably well-behaved throughout all this. She approached her mother's bed, talked to her, but never came close to or touched the bottle.

One morning about three weeks after the onset of Vera's paralysis, she called Max over to her bed, asked him to take off the blanket and check her large toe. She had the impression that some feeling had returned. Max uncovered the leg, touched it. It was warm. He wiggled her toe and asked her to try to move it. Lo and behold, she was able to move the toe! Mother, Ruthie, and I were all called in to witness this historic event. Not all was lost. Dr. Elkes was immediately apprised of the situation and he expressed amazement. He admitted that even he, when he had ordered the intensive therapy, had very little hope for recovery, but did what had to be done hoping for some miracle. The miracle was now in the making.

Every day Vera moved her toes a little more. One day she was able to weakly move her leg. But now another problem appeared. Her veins were badly bruised and there was no place left to insert the needle for injection. Not only that, but prolonged lying in the same position had produced bedsores that had to be treated. New medicine and treatment were needed. By now we had traded away just about anything of value for jewelry, gold, and other valuables, but at least Vera was now seemingly on the path to recovery. How full a recovery it would be was anybody's guess.

Yet, throughout this immense struggle and our difficulties to obtain gold for the huge amounts of medicine, Saks not once even tried to offer us some of his gold for cash!

17

THE ESCAPE

The year 1943 was now history and 1944 entered amidst conflicting emotions for us. We had encouraging news from the fronts that the defeat of the Nazis was only a matter of time, but so was our existence. One day was filled with elation at the news from the front and the next was full of anxiety about further evacuations from the ghetto to new camps around Kovno. Every evacuation was accompanied by personal tragedies, the separation of family and friends.

Sometime around January the news reached us that the siege of Leningrad had been lifted after nine hundred days of almost total encirclement by the Germans. We were barely able to digest the news and enjoy it, as news reached us that the rest of ghetto Riga, Latvia, was being liquidated. The Jews who were still able to work and had survived were being transferred to Panevezys, a small town in Lithuania, where the Germans were now building a new airport. The sick, infirm, and elderly were brutally liquidated as in all other such cases. Among those brought to Panevezys were the surviving Jews from Kovno who had been deported in 1942. Rumor had it that the Jews from the slave labor camps of Vaivara and Klooga would also be evacuated to Panevezys. This somewhat lifted my spirits and gave me hope that should Minnie be among the people transferred to Panevezys, the Aeltestenrat could do something to bring her back to our ghetto. But this was wishful thinking, and the rumors died down.

The liquidation of the ghetto in Riga again encouraged the construction of bunkers and attempts to leave the ghetto for a safer haven with Lithuanian families where such could be found. Children again were sent outside the ghetto.

Bunkers sprang up everywhere. The huts of the Lithuanians in the ghetto were terribly primitive and no substantial hide-outs could be constructed in them. There were no construction materials available, and the bunkers turned out to be no more than hiding places in a crawl space, or an attic with camouflaged entrances.

The partisan movement was growing stronger and bolder. After initial failures it had orchestrated a few successful escapes to the woods. To facilitate these escapes German uniforms, boots, and other equipment were stolen from the workshops, where dozens of uniforms were brought in daily for mending and cleaning.

With the steady retreats at the Russian fronts, Goecke was more anxious than ever to complete his break-up of the ghetto. Within a few weeks his first stage was completed. There remained in the ghetto only the people Goecke had wished to remain. He then ordered total registration of the ghetto, including children and elderly. It was made clear that only registered people would be entitled to food rations, which presented a terrible dilemma. Because of what had happened at the ghetto Siauliai, we were afraid to register children and older people, but this would have meant a very serious loss of food rations to most families. Also, since everyone was supposed to get an identity card, not having one was dangerous. We were now caught in a vise: to register or not to register the children and the elderly. Under pressure of the food situation, most people registered everybody. We in our household registered mother younger than she was and skipped Ruthie. For us Ruthie's ration, while important, was not critical, since we had a side income from my kerchief production.

The pressure from the people to get work in the workshops now became fierce. But there were physical limits and many frustrated people, particularly elderly, remained without jobs. The number of survivors was now about eight thousand Jews in the ghetto proper and about five thousand in the outside camps, out of more than thirty-five thousand at the beginning of the war. These numbers comprised all the people, including children, elderly, and invalids.

Goecke's next step was to transfer the committee to another building, and in its place, workshops for the Gestapo were established. The fence, which had been taken apart during the firewood riots, was repaired and the workshop enclosed. We in the graphics department, however, had a full view of the yard from our second floor window. In charge of these workshops was a Jew by the name of Grossman. He was an imposing figure, broad-shouldered, at least six feet four inches tall, and muscular.

The liquidation of Old Slobotke brought several thousand Jews to the already restricted area of the ghetto and living conditions became intolerable. Even the orchestra had to be relocated. Its new location was in one room in Block C, next to the building where Minnie used to live. Occasionally I would go to this room and sit down at the piano and try to forget reality. Every tune reminded me of the wonderful evenings I had spent with Minnie that were now gone forever.

In our building we had now at least five or six new families from Old Slobotke. Every household had accepted at least one new family, almost doubling the previous congestion. Among the families that moved in was Max's brother, Wolf, and his wife, and a father with a daughter by the name of Gitta. At first I did not notice her, but since we were constantly running into each other, whether in the morning going to work or in the evening fetching water at the well, I soon got acquainted with her. Gitta was two years younger than I was and was extremely good-looking. She was the complete opposite of Minnie. Whereas Minnie was petite, Gitta was tall, almost my height. She was well-built, light brown hair, big bosom, and possessed a rosy complexion, which was extremely rare in the ghetto. At first our encounters consisted only of a polite hello, or I would help her lift the water up from the well. Occasionally a short conversation would ensue, but I had no desire to get involved. Minnie was constantly on my mind.

The situation in the ghetto was again normalizing. Goecke was trying to pacify the ghetto to prevent panic and to cut down on the escape movement about which he knew all too well. This calm lulled the ghetto into a false sense of security and some of the activities indeed slowed down, particularly the contact with the Lithuanians to give away the children. In fact quite a few children were brought back to the ghetto by yearning parents. As far as Ruthie was concerned, we talked about giving her away, but it was always postponed. In anticipation that one day Ruthie might have to be delivered to some Lithuanians, we started to talk Lithuanian to her so she should hear the language, but Ruthie balked and did not respond. We gave up the idea, a decision to be regretted later.

While the situation in the ghetto was deliberately kept under wraps, life in the outside camps was rough and many people regretted having left. Among these were Simon and Nathan, who were now desperately trying to find a way to get back into the ghetto. But what was impossible for one was not so difficult to a man who was in charge of food distribution in the ghetto. After several tries, Saks succeeded in giving the right bribes to the right people in the ghetto administration and got both families out of the camps. He even got Nathan his position back in the ghetto police. With no place to go, they now forced us to accept them. We had lost control over our own home. I was persuaded to give up my bed in favor of one of the couples. After all, they were married and I was only one person. From then on I slept on the table, which was lined with blankets to make it softer. The table was hardly long enough for me, and I had to curl up not to have my legs hang out over the edge. It was a most miserable existence for me, but there was no space anymore, not even on the floor.

My existence was now so pitiful that I looked forward for the night to end so I should be able to go to work where I had some air to breathe. In the shop we were now receiving orders from the Germans in town, but more important than that, the entire SS-hierarchy became frequent visitors. All three chiefs of our ghetto—Goecke, Rinck, and Berger—had orders in our artists' shop. Rinck and Berger brought photographs of themselves and requested large oil portraits from Pipsi. Occasionally, when their time permitted it, they posed in the evening to ensure a better reproduction. Goecke, on the other hand, brought Pipsi a color print of a landscape from a book and told him to make a large oil reproduction of it.

The relationship with Rinck was very formal. Rinck kept his distance from us Jews. But the dealings with SS-Sturmfuehrer Berger were different. While he, too, was a devoted SS-man and no friend of the Jews, in his dealings with us he acted like a human being. He was talkative and even got into discussions. We felt that his willingness to talk and his friendly attitude towards us could not hurt. Peter and I were only worried they should not discover our hide-out. All three of them were trained SS-bullies. Fortunately during their visits they were in Pipsi's studio and not in our drafting room and nobody had any inkling that there was something behind the wall.

The congestion in our home was now such that I tried to stay away. Occasionally I walked around the house to breathe fresh air, which was now in very short supply. During these walks I often ran into Gitta, and I was glad to spend the evening with her. A new friendship was developing between the two of us.

Some very strange rumors started to reach our graphics shop: we heard that a mass escape of Jews had occurred from the Ninth Fort and some of the escapees had reached the ghetto and were hiding there. If true, this was the most fantastic event imaginable. A mass escape from Alcatraz could not begin to compare with it. These fugitives were witnesses of atrocities on a scale unknown in human history, survivors of massacres of unprecedented cruelty. In this fort, in 1941, Russian prisoners of war were forced to dig ditches, which were later used as mass graves for the Jews and occasionally also for the Russians themselves. Of the thousands of Russian prisoners of war who became the mass grave-diggers, only a handful were still alive. All of them had witnessed the massacres and none were expected to survive to tell the tale.

The news about the escape and the presence of the escapees in the ghetto reached us only to be suppressed. The fear was that the Germans could demand the release of these escapees to the Gestapo, threatening mass reprisals. We in our shop were among the very few who knew about it. But details were sketchy and we were anxious to find out more. I decided to check on the details myself. The best source for these rumors was my friend Labl, who was intimately involved with the underground and had first-hand information about all their activities. When I reached Labl's home I knocked on the door, but there was no reply. When I knocked a second time I noticed Labl look out through the window. When he saw me, he came to the door and opened it. As I entered his room, I saw an older, grey-haired man with face and hands full of blisters and eyes which at first scared me.

"Hello," I said to the man without further comment. Both Labl and the stranger looked at me as if I had missed something.

"Don't you recognize me?" the stranger asked me.

The voice sounded awfully familiar, but I really didn't seem to recognize him. "Hold a minute," I suddenly said, "could you be . . . are you David?"

"Yes, I am," he said with a smile.

"God, how could I miss this? Of course I recognize you, except for this grey hair and this rash. You and a few others were involved in the underground movement and I thought you had left the ghetto; what are you doing here?"

David turned to Labl to glean an indication of whether or not he should talk.

"David, you can talk, Vulia is quite familiar with what is going on and is reliable. In fact I believe you should tell him everything. It is good that he should know. The people in the graphics department are well-informed and are also involved in preserving the facts for posterity."

"Yes, I did leave the ghetto with a group from the underground movement back in the fall of 1943," David began. "The whole group was apprehended by Lithuanian police and delivered to the Gestapo. The Gestapo tortured us, trying to pry information from us, but we held firm. Finally, after days of savage interrogation, we were taken to the Ninth Fort."

"To the Ninth Fort?" I exclaimed, "then you must be one of the fugitives who escaped from the fort?" I broke out in a cold sweat.

A silence ensued after this statement. After a few minutes he replied, "Yes, I am. It is now about a month that I have been hiding here."

This was a shock. I had gone to Labl to try to find out about the escape and stumbled right into one of the fugitives, one who happened to be a friend of mine. I was facing a main actor in this unspeakable drama. I turned to David and said, "Well, tell me the whole story, I will try not to interrupt you."

"After we were brought to the fort, we met a group of Jewish prisoners of war of the Red Army who had spent almost two full years there. They had witnessed all the Actions and had stories to tell which would curl your hair." And David proceeded to tell me what we already knew about the massacres, plus some extraordinary gruesome facts. "About a week later, we were mobilized to build a very tall enclosure around the fort to block the view from the adjacent homes. Hundreds of trucks loaded with firewood, chemicals, gasoline, and tar were brought in and huge excavation equipment showed up on the fort. The next week the excavation started. The excavators removed the topsoil from the entire site and huge mass graves appeared below the surface."

"Jews massacred during all the Actions," I interrupted.

"Exactly. Our job was now to eradicate all traces of the mass executions. Between the prisoners of war and us, we were a group of sixty-four people. Except for several specialists who stayed behind in the barracks, we performed the dirty work. We were divided into three groups. One group was forced to drag the corpses out of the mass grave and put them on the ground alongside the ditch. The second group pulled the corpses across the site to a huge bonfire which could be seen all around the fort. Here the bodies were piled in layers, a layer of wood and a layer of corpses one on top of the other, drenched with gasoline, and ignited. All work was done by hand. At first we revolted, but after several good beatings we had to go on. The stench was terrible and the view was even worse: mothers with children in their arms, people with split-open heads, people naked and fully dressed one on top of the other, layer upon layer, the full depth of the trench. From the documents we found in the pockets of the dressed people, we established that these were the foreign Jews who were brought to the fort. Most of them had documents showing that they had been recruited for "work in the east." These foreign Jews, apparently, resisted and refused to undress. From the expression on their faces, we could tell who was killed by the bullets and who suffocated later when the bullet failed to kill him. Of course, the ones with cracked skulls needed no explanation."

David had to stop for a while. "We workers knew all along," he continued, "that after the job was finished we would be shot and end up in the same ditch we were now cleaning. They could not leave such witnesses alive. We were all in good health since we were given ample food to be able to perform the work. The Russian prisoners of war, most of whom were Jewish, had already investigated all kinds of escape plans. None of them worked. During the investigations they found out about the underground tunnels and also figured out approximately which should lead closest to the fence. Their first trial at building an underground tunnel failed when they hit a concrete abutment.

"When we were brought to the fort, the spirit among the old-timers was raised. Here was a group of youngsters who were determined to join the partisans and were not about to give up easily. We got together and created a secret committee to plan an escape. The committee also attracted the locksmith and the carpenter. These tradesmen had access to tools and made all kinds of gifts for the guards. All participants in the plot were alerted to check the pockets of the dressed corpses and to confiscate anything metal, like keys, combs, or knives. We then discovered a metal door with a padlock at the end of the corridor. The locksmith reviewed the lock and decided that he could make a key to fit, and he did. After a few days of work he succeeded in opening the door. When the door was opened, it led to a dark chamber full of old clothing and uniforms. At the end of this chamber was a heavy steel door which was the last major obstacle before reaching the deep trench. Once the trench was reached, the twenty foot wall would have to be scaled to reach the outside."

"It almost sounds like a detective story. I am almost forgetting that this is the bloody Ninth Fort," I commented.

"The plan, although extremely difficult, was now clear. The carpenter was given the assignment of building two sectional twenty-foot ladders which could be quickly assembled and taken apart. Two were made in case one should fail. The locksmith was ordered to make a few master keys which could open the cells. Without proper tools it was a difficult task, but he finally succeeded. He then manufactured drills from keys found on the corpses. A man was assigned the job of starting to drill the heavy steel door at the end of the chamber. This was a most difficult task. The cook prepared two bottles filled with gasoline and outfitted them with wicks, creating two lamps for the dark corridor. When the fellow who was drilling got tired and his fingers were too bloody to continue, a second man was assigned this task.

"The cook was on the lookout should Germans show up, to warn the man to stop drilling. Several times during this operation the Germans made inspections of the premises, but never went as far as the door at the other end. Just imagine the anxiety of our man at the door, who was petrified lest he be discovered. But the Germans never bothered to check further. No escapes had ever occurred in all those years. Besides, the inspectors themselves were eager to get out of this place which smelled so much of death.

"Shortly before Christmas the job was complete. Nobody except the organizers knew about the conspiracy. A day before Christmas the crew got special rations, including vodka. The people were instructed not to touch the vodka and wherever possible to give it to the guards. The escape was set for 26 December, since most of the guards got an extra day off for the holidays. Christmas Day was used to wash the smell out of our clothing, so everybody should be able to move about on the outside.

"Everything was now set for escape. Several hours in advance, everybody was apprised of the situation and warned to meticulously carry out the command given by the assigned group leaders. In the evening everybody got ready. The air was thick with tension.

"At the predetermined time the group leaders went from cell to cell opening the doors, which had been oiled the day before so that there was no sound to be heard. The wick was lit and everybody was instructed to watch their step, not to stumble. When the group reached the first door the locksmith took the padlock off and the group proceeded unmolested through the chamber to the tunnel. When the end of the tunnel was reached, two reconnoiterers were sent to survey the terrain. When they did not return immediately we were all scared to death. We thought for sure that they had been apprehended.

"Needless to say, we were happy when they came back. The reason for their delay was that they had to clean the path to the wall or people would have stumbled. A blanket was stretched out in front of the door to resemble the snow, which was very heavy outside, and to cover the silhouettes which were moving across the white background into the trench. The snow was now a big help, since it made the sliding much easier and quieter. When everybody was in the trench the ladders were quickly assembled, the barbed wire on top of the wall was snapped, and everybody scaled the wall as quickly as possible. Once across, we split up as previously arranged. Some of us went to the ghetto and some proceeded directly to the partisan hide-outs. I was assigned to the group that went to the ghetto. Entering the ghetto was difficult too, but all the members of my group managed to get in successfully. Of the other groups many were apprehended. The Gestapo were frenzied, to say the least, when they found out about this escape. Gestapo chiefs from Berlin came to Kovno the next day as soon as they found out about it, and many were shot."

"Is somebody writing all of this down?" I asked.

"Yes, we have documented everything," said David.

Meanwhile it got late and curfew was approaching. Nobody at home suspected anything, since I was usually late getting home. A few days later, David was gone. He had joined a group of young men who had left the ghetto to join up with the partisans. They went to fight the German murderers, to avenge our innocently spilled blood.

18

A VISION OF HELL

A week or two after the escape of the Jews from the fort, the Gestapo ordered the replacement of the fugitives with new workers. Under the pretext of various crimes, like a Jew caught away from his working place, or a person discovered bartering with a Lithuanian, these people were arrested, brought to the Gestapo cellar, and from there dispatched to the Ninth Fort. These hapless people were now forced to complete the horrible assignment of destroying the corpses. But aside from this event the situation in the ghetto was rather calm, in fact much too calm. Goecke had completed the disperson and registration of the ghetto on schedule and his job was now to lull the population into a false sense of security. But most of us were not easily deceived and watched this calm with a great deal of skepticism.

In our household Vera had been bedridden for about three months, paralyzed from the waist down with a drain in her lung between her ribs. It was still very much a life and death struggle, although there were some signs of improvement. These signs of improvement, however, seemed to be too little and too late.

It had been close to half a year since I had lost Minnie, but her memory was as vivid as ever. This inner attachment to Minnie stood in my way in developing close relations with Gitta. I was now meeting Gitta every evening and little by little I started to enjoy her company more and more. We took a stroll almost every night and chatted. Without realizing it we became more attached to each other. In the evening before parting I would give her a kiss, which in time became more passionate. Just embracing her and feeling her full bosom near my chest made me excited. But I was not ready yet for a full scale love affair. I was afraid to get too deeply involved only to suffer another tragedy as with Minnie. Inevitably our little conversations turned to music. I had the urge to invite her to a concert of the ghetto orchestra, but was very apprehensive. I did not want to hear the tune from *Scheherezade* and reopen my wounds.

One day when I went to the room where the piano was, I found the orchestra rehearsing a Mozart minuet from Symphony Number 39 in E-flat. I was surprised: Mozart in the ghetto? After the rehearsal I stayed to talk with some of the musicians, who all knew me. I found out that Goecke had removed the ban of playing music by German composers. In fact he had given the orchestra a list of pieces by Mozart and Beethoven which he liked and told them to prepare it for a concert. This meant that the next concert would have a new program. I felt relieved. I could now attend a concert and not have to worry. I took Gitta to the next concert and we enjoyed it immensely. Gitta now realized that there was a piano in the ghetto and felt an urge to practice. The next time we met I took her to Block C and let her do some playing. She was not very advanced, but I let her have the piano to herself. I was reluctant to go to the piano, since every tune would have reminded me of days past with Minnie. Deep down, however, I knew that I could not hold out. One day after letting Gitta play for awhile I got up, went to the piano, and asked her whether she would like to give me a chance.

"Do you play the piano?" she asked, surprised. "Why didn't you tell me about it?"

I was not about to tell her the truth. She did not know my past and there was no reason to reveal it to her. "Well, I did not want to interrupt you. You were as excited as a little kid at the piano and I was reluctant to spoil it for you."

"You are right, I had not heard any music or played the piano for over two years, since I lost my mother in the ghetto. Even when I found out about the orchestra I avoided it. I don't know how to explain it, but since we started to take our short walks in the evening something has changed. Our conversations, the mood associated with those walks have moved something within me. Suddenly I was ready for music."

A short silence followed. "Vulia, why don't you sit down and play," Gitta finally said.

"What would you like to hear, classical or jazz?"

"Let's go with classical," she answered.

I got down to the piano, struck a few chords, and proceeded with a Chopin nocturne. As usual I got deeply involved in my playing. I was almost sorry I did sit down to play. I was afraid it would be Minnie all over again. Deep down I felt that I was falling in love with this beautiful girl.

She was absolutely amazed. "Vulia, I did not expect you to play so well." She looked straight into my eyes, shook her head in disbelief, and said, "Why don't you go on? My God, if I knew you played so well, I would not have dared to play for you."

I turned back to the piano and played for a good half an hour or more, mostly sentimental music by Chopin. Finally it got late. We were both in a romantic mood with passions aroused, and we returned home. The corridor to her apartment was directly below the stairs leading to our home upstairs. The corridor was dark and below the lower flight stood a piece of furniture which somebody had thrown out of one of the apartments for lack of space. We did not feel like parting. We both had some strange feeling that something inside both of us had moved. We sat down and before I knew it, we were indulging in fondling, petting, and caresses; our goodnight kiss was far more passionate than ever before. At night I could not sleep. Was I ready for a new love affair? I did not know the answer. I only knew that I was looking forward to the evenings and the exciting encounters with her, and yet she could not replace Minnie. Something was different. I did not know what.

Passover was approaching and as usual we were worried about what surprises the Gestapo would spring on us this time. The approaching holiday also made me think of the Seder, the holiday dinner, last year at Minnie's home, the wonderful evening we spent together, and my mother's admonition when I returned home. Here it was close to Passover again and I was getting deeper and deeper into a new love affair. I was confused and torn. Should I pursue my relationship with Gitta to its full potential, or look for an honorable retreat? Yet I knew from experience that when emotions reach such an advanced stage as mine were in, it was too late to call it quits.

In March rumors arose that an Action would take place in the ghetto on the fifteenth. The rumors were persistent, but no information was available regarding the details. The tension and fear in the ghetto escalated and the calm of the past months was shattered. Gitta was terribly upset and looked for relief and assurances in my embrace. It was almost a replay of two years ago, when Minnie and I lost our resistance during such an evening of persistent rumors. I was determined not to let it happen now, at least not until I could resolve the inner conflict regarding my deep attachment to the memory of Minnie.

March fifteenth came and went uneventfully. I was glad not to have succumbed under the impact of the now-forgotten rumor. The ghetto again settled into its normal pattern and everything was seemingly back to business as usual. But everything was not entirely the same. With the front coming closer the visits of Russian aircraft got more frequent and we were not at all surprised when, on Sunday 26 March, Goecke called the chief of police into his office. He instructed him to return the next morning at 8 AM with the entire police force. They were to be mobilized on the plaza in front of the SS headquarters in Block B, which was just across Varniu Street and in full view of our shop. Here they were to receive air raid instructions. Special instructions to the police were in order under the circumstances, so everybody went to bed in the evening quickly and unsuspectingly.

On Monday morning all the city brigades left the ghetto as usual. The workers of the workshops and the ghetto institutions, the workers of the night shift, the nonworking elderly, the children, the sick, and of course, the police, gathering in front of the police headquarters, were all who remained in the ghetto. The police lined up in formation and drilled several times in order to be impressive when marching into the yard. The workers of our shop were a few minutes early getting to work, since we all wanted to observe the police exercises as ordered by the SS. Even Peter, who normally used to go to the toy workshop first, came to our graphics shop to witness the goings-on. At eight o'clock sharp the Jewish police marched into the plaza in fine formation and with military precision and then came to a halt. Goecke and several of the SS-officers on his staff came out to the plaza in short order. Simultaneously a few trucks pulled up on Varniu Street. Goecke looked over the police and selected several policemen from the line-up and told them to step aside. On closer observation I recognized the Jewish policemen—all of them were members of the ghetto orchestra. This was extremely strange. Why would they be removed from the line-up? Also the trucks looked rather suspicious, but we still did not suspect a thing. Suddenly Goecke ordered all the Jewish policemen to sit down on the ground and the SS-men of the ghetto guard stepped forward. During the past years in the ghetto I had developed an unusually keen instinct. Like an animal in danger, I could discern a life-threatening situation. Instinctively I sensed peril. A sudden thought struck my brain: this was the Children's Action! Without any reason or proof as yet, I felt that this was it.

"Children!" I suddenly screamed in an unnatural voice, "this is a Children's Action! Don't waste time! Every second is precious! Run home and bring the children to the shop," and without asking Peter I rushed to the hide-out and swung the door open.

Everybody in the shop was stunned. They were speechless. Here they had been working for who knows how long and none of them had ever suspected that behind the wall with the paint and brushes was a hide-out.

"Zoondl," I screamed to our messenger boy, "run as fast as you can to Peter's home and tell his wife and Rosl to bring the children here. Peter, you are much slower, just follow him. There is no time to be lost."

Peter was not as yet convinced, but things looked awfully ominous and he decided on the spur of the moment to follow my advice.

"Nolik," I turned to him, "you rush home and tell your sister Thea to come here with her baby. Don't procrastinate."

I myself rushed home. My decision was to hide everybody in our household in the graphics shop rather than in our hide-out. My intuition told me that our chances in a shop were much better than in a private home. A shop where no people lived could conceivably be overlooked, but a home would be scrutinzed with such thoroughness that escape might have been impossible.

Short of breath, I ran up the stairs. Everybody was home except Rivka, who had left for work. Mother, who only worked part-time, had her day off. Vera was paralyzed and lying in bed. Sonja and Max were scheduled for the night shift, and Simon's wife and their little three-year-old son were all home. The rest were at work, including Nathan, who was on the plaza with the police.

"Mother, grab Ruthie and Sonja, you take the children," I screamed. "Rush across the street to the graphics workshop. Don't ask questions. There is no time. Max, prepare Vera, we are taking her across the street to my shop. Rush and don't waste time with questions."

Everybody was baffled and at first hesitated. What was going on? What did I know that they didn't?

"Rush, I told you!" I screamed again, "you hear me!" and Max and I ran into Vera's room.

"Vera, let Max do whatever is necessary, there is no time," I said.

We had a terrible problem with Vera. She could not walk across the street. She could not even help us to get her dressed and the situation was further complicated by the tube in her chest which drained to a bottle of water on the floor.

"Max, this is the Children's Action, I am sure of it. Please rush. Vera is an invalid and must be hidden quickly."

Max quickly disconnected the pipe extension and put a clamp over the stub to prevent air from entering the chest cavity. There was no time to dress her properly, so we wrapped her in blankets, grabbed some underwear and a warm dress, and tucked them into our pockets. We lifted Vera out of the bed, which was an extremely difficult job with a patient who could not help, and rushed down the stairs as fast as we were physically able. By the time we entered the street the Jewish police were being loaded onto the trucks and the SS-men were rushing down the street to take up their assigned positions. We ran straight into them.

"Hold!" one German yelled.

This was it! We were too late. It had taken us too much time to get Vera ready.

"Where are you going?" he screamed at me.

"We have a sick person here and we are taking her to the hospital," I answered.

"Very good, very good," he replied, "make it quick," and they let us go.

The Germans ran down Vytenio Street to their destination. When we were out of their sight we rushed into the door of our shop. For the moment we were safe. Here we caught our breath and rushed up the stairs. We carried Vera on our hands, which we had crossed to make a chairlike arrangement on which Vera sat, holding us both around the shoulders. When we entered the shop everybody was already in the hide-out. When Peter saw Max, he turned to him quickly and asked, "Doctor, do you think we should give the children some shots to keep them quiet?"

"No," said Max, "as long as they are awake you can reason with them and hopefully keep them quiet. But should one be medicated and suddenly awaken, we would have no control over him. It is better to take our chances this way."

We put Vera on the floor, pulled the underwear and dress over her, and put her on top of the blanket. With Vera on top of it, we dragged the blanket into the hide-out. How everybody fit into the hide-out space was a mystery, but all were in except Peter. Peter decided to remain in the shop, come what may. He felt that his presence would distract the SS-men should they come to search. Obviously if this was a Children's Action he was safe. But if it was more than that he was taking a grave chance. He told me to get in and close the door.

In the meantime trucks with loudspeakers began to roam the streets with an announcement that was repeated over and over again. "Everybody must go into their houses. Anybody caught on the street will be shot."

Dozens of trucks were criss-crossing the ghetto, blaring out the same message. People who were far remote from the SS headquarters and had not witnessed the scene with the police were caught unaware. Disoriented and scared to death, they scampered in every direction, clearing the streets in a hurry. Those who had a hiding place and time to reach it rushed to what they hoped would be a safe haven. The ones who had no place to go were in dire straits. Instinctively, the first thing people tried to do was hide the children, although nobody knew yet that this was indeed a Children's Action. They were pushed into closets, under the bed, into beds covered by blankets that camouflaged the silhouette of the child. Others pushed the children into wardrobes and some even rushed to storage sheds outside the home.

We barely managed to close the sliding door. Outside, Peter removed any trace of dirt from the floor. Inside the hide-out there was barely space for everybody. The mothers took the children into their arms to keep them warm and cozy and to be close to them in case a child should get restless. My mother took Ruthie since Vera was prone on the floor and could not be of any help. The instructions were not to talk, not to sneeze, not to cough, not even to move, assuming there was room to move, and especially, to keep the children under control. The hide-out was, for all practical purposes, almost on the street. Only a thin wall stood between us.

Once the Germans had finished staking out the ghetto, an armed band of Ukrainians entered and dispersed in all directions. We could hear them screaming in Russian.

Meanwhile the Jewish police were forced to enter the trucks. When one policeman refused, he was shot on the spot. The trucks containing the Jewish police were taken to the Ninth Fort.

The tension in the hide-out was growing by the minute. Inside we could clearly hear everything that was going on outside. Obviously, if we could hear what was going on outside, the Germans and the Ukrainians could hear us if we were not careful enough. But how do you explain to a two- or three-year-old not to talk? The gamble was less than fifty-fifty.

After five or ten minutes the bullhorns on the trucks stopped transmitting the message about retreating into the homes and records with all kinds of music were boomed into the ghetto. The philosophy was that children love music and might run out of their homes to hear it more clearly. As long as our children did not react to the music outside, it was an advantage to us. Noise could cover up quiet sounds that we inadvertently might make in our hide-out.

The first indication we had that this was indeed a Children's Action was when a group of Ukrainians broke into a neighboring house and found the children within. The ensuing screams and cries of the mothers and the children was sickening. Under heavy blows the children were separated from the mothers, who were hysterical and resisting fiercely. One German SS-man who apparently was in charge of the group kicked a woman and yelled, "Ihr verfluchten Juden braucht keine Kinder" (you cursed Jews don't need any children).

A cold shiver crawled down the spines of everybody in the hide-out.

The Bacchanalia now got into full swing. The murderers went from house to house, beating everybody and turning everything upside down. Mothers clinging to their children were mercilessly beaten. Where beatings did not work, huge German shepherds trained in violence were incited against the helpless mothers, tearing them apart with the bastards looking on and laughing. When the ferocious dogs could not pry the children loose from the mother, the child was shot and the mother kicked into the gutter. "You, bitch, can still work for us," was the statement that followed.

In some cases the mothers tried to climb into the trucks. When beating did not stop them, they were shot. The children were thrown into the trucks like footballs and when an older child resisted, his head was bashed in with the butt of a rifle. Babies were grabbed by their legs and their heads were smashed against the sides of the trucks.

The fate of the invalids and the elderly was no better. Through the thin walls of the hide-out we could hear elderly people pleading with the monsters, "I am still healthy, I can still work for you. Don't take me to the trucks, don't take me to the trucks," and they showed their working cards.

"Don't worry, you will still work for us," came the cynical reply.

The working certificate was ignored. The selection was made strictly by appearance and not the age given on the pass. The older children too were judged only by looks. When a truck was filled it left the ghetto, accompanied by hysterical outcries both from the people on the trucks and the people left behind, most of whom had been beaten to a pulp or torn apart by the dogs. For hours these scenes repeated themselves in every corner of the ghetto. Since our shop was on the main street, most of the victims were led past our hide-out.

The ghetto police had been taken to the Ninth Fort, where they were all locked up in the cells from which, only three months previously, the prisoners had engineered their escape. One by one the chiefs of police were hauled out for interrogation. Using murderous beatings, the Gestapo would try to force them to disclose facts about the partisan movement and about hide-outs in the ghetto. Despite the most sadistic torture, the chiefs of the Jewish police stood fast and denied their tormentors any victory. No information was divulged by the chiefs. After the interrogations they were shot on the spot and their bodies instantly dragged by the fort commandos to the bonfires.

In the afternoon the searches in the ghetto intensified. From the census the Gestapo knew exactly how many children and elderly were in the ghetto and they saw that the number was still very short of the target. The instructions were to break walls, torture people, shoot on the spot, anything to procure the hidden children. The searches were carried out with even more than the ordered brutality, if such a thing was possible. The hospital was now surrounded and all the patients forced into the trucks and hauled away. (Later in the evening, when I found out about it, it became clear to me why the German guard was so polite to me, so cooperative, and even urged me on to take Vera to the hospital when I told him that she was sick.)

The children were getting hungry, but were so scared that they did not utter a sound. When Peter was certain that no search party was near, he took some water, which was always available in the shop to mix the paint and to wash the brushes, quickly opened the sliding door, and handed it in for the children. He then quickly closed the door. Only the children were given a sip of water. The adults did not even touch it.

Late in the afternoon the SS surrounded the ghetto workshops and sealed them off. A room-to-room search began and dozens of elderly people and children were apprehended. They were again murderously beaten and chased out. The workshops which last time saved the lives of many, were not safe this time.

For hours the sounds of shooting, screaming, barking of dogs, and blaring music from the trucks permeated the air of the ghetto. Every five or ten minutes, another group of crying and pleading victims was dragged past our hide-out. The mothers inside pressed the children to their bosoms, trying to keep them quiet. But under the circumstances we ourselves needed all the fortitude we could muster not to go berserk.

By six in the evening the madness died down. A deadly silence descended on the ghetto. Now the Jewish work brigades started to return to the ghetto. At the gate they discovered the tragedy and raced towards their homes frantic to discover the fate of the children and elderly they had left behind in the morning. When it became certain that the ghetto was clear of the SS and their helpers, the Ukrainians, and that the Action was, at least for now, concluded, Peter opened the door to the hide-out and we crawled out. Our shop had not been checked and our children had passed the test: none of them had cried.

Vera had to be pulled out. We placed her on the sofa in Peter's studio. The day's events had taken their toll on her. Without drainage her lungs had filled up with fluid and she became quite short of breath. Fortunately her condition was better now than a month ago and the amount of effluent was much smaller.

Our problem now was where to go from here. "Peter," I said, "my intuition tells me that the Action is not over. They will continue tomorrow. They could not possibly have found all the children and they know it. Just in our hide-out alone we have successfully hidden six, and how about the dozens of other hiding places? The SS has a complete count of the ghetto and they are not going to let so many children get away from them."

"You have a point," said Peter, "under the circumstances all the children and their mothers will sleep here. The rest can either remain or go home."

"I suggest," I said, "that the adults go home, wash up, eat something, and come back with food for the children."

"Vulia is right," said Peter. "Let us not be too conspicuous and move in small groups."

"One more word of caution. Nobody, but nobody, is to know where you were hiding, not even relatives. We kept the secret of the hide-out for almost five months, so you can hold it too, for as long as it takes."

We started to disperse. Sonja and I went across the street and Max joined us a little later, as if coming from work. We had barely entered the house when Rivka literally broke in. She was completely out of breath and could barely talk. "Where is Eetke? Where is she?" she screamed to Sonja, with fear written all over her face and tears running down her cheeks. Never had I seen Rivka cry. She was as tough as nails, but this was too much even for her. Sonja rushed into Rivka's embrace. "She is safe, Vulia saved her." She was barely able to utter the words.

"What happened? Where is she?" Rivka pleaded.

"She is hidden. Don't worry, I just don't know how to thank Vulia. Were it not for him we all would have been lost," and she and Rivka rushed to me, embracing me and crying over my shoulder. Sonja was stroking my head and my shoulder and kept repeating, "My sweet child is safe, God sent you to save her."

When Sonja calmed down and loosened her grip on me, Rivka rushed over and began kissing me. Forgotten was the feud she had with me, for at this moment I was a saint and not a sinner.

But the jubilation did not last long. When Ester, their sister, returned from work, she rushed to her home and, to her horror, found the house empty: her little son and her mother-in-law were both gone, gone forever. She checked the house, the yard, and any possible nook or corner, but they were gone. Heartbroken, she rushed to our house to see what the situation was here. When she entered the room we immediately saw the catastrophe on her face. Her eyes were swollen as she ran to Sonja. Not seeing Eetke, she exclaimed in pain, "Where is Eetke? Is she safe? Why isn't she here?"

Sonja was now in an awkward situation. Her child was safe and opposite her stood her sister who was not as fortunate. How could she break the news to her without making things worse?

"Why don't you talk?" she admonished Sonja again.

"Eetke is safe," finally Rivka said. "She is hidden."

"Thank God for that," Ester cried, "at least one is safe. God, my little Wolfinke, my little angel, how can I live without you? First my husband, now you. God, why do I deserve this fate?"

Here they were: two sisters, both had lost their husbands in the beginning of the war. All they had left was one child to each mother, a child that was the only link to their beloved husbands. Now suddenly they were worlds apart. One still had her child but the other had lost hers. We all tried to console her, but to no avail. It was nearly three years since the war had started and she had managed to save him through hundreds of traps and perils, through hunger and Actions, only to lose him now.

While Ester, Sonja, and Rivka were wiping their tears in one corner, Nathan's wife returned from work. She was hysterical. She already knew that the entire police was at the Ninth Fort and her husband, who had been a policeman, was there. The scene at home resembled an insane asylum, with people crying, lamenting, screaming, and pacing the floor up and down. And who knew whether tomorrow would bring a sequel to today's drama and whether our luck would still be with us.

Max and I had a drink of water, who could eat at such a time, and Max gathered some food for Vera and Ruthie. He also took the bottle and the rubber hose extension for Vera's drainage. When we returned, Mother and Dvora went home to have something to eat and drink.

The other adults did the same, leaving at intervals and finally all returning to the shop. I took Peter to his house. On the way, we ran into an official of the labor department who worked at the gate. We found out quite a few details from him about what had happened in the ghetto. The best estimate was that approximately one thousand people had been murdered or carried off, about 60% of these children from the ages of one to twelve. In addition to the ghetto proper, the same Action was carried out in all the outside concentration camps, where not one single child was able to hide. The adults had all left the camps for their working places and the SS with the Ukrainians assaulted the barracks. The women taking charge of the children during the day were manhandled and the children were dumped with unsurpassed brutality into the waiting trucks. They were taken to the railroad station, apparently on their way to Auschwitz. It was estimated that in all camps together another five hundred people, mostly children, were rounded up. How ironic that these people volunteered to those camps in order to save the children.

To our complete horror, we found out that this undescribably brutal action was carried out under the command and leadership of none other than SS-Sturmfuehrer Berger! The same Berger for whom we were preparing a large portrait, the same Berger who, in the shop, behaved like a decent human being, the same Berger who, unlike Goecke and Rinck, used to chat with us, totally ignoring that we were Jews and he was an SS-man. We never expected an SS-man to be a gentleman, but to stoop so low, to betray us so completely, was beyond our comprehension.

When we returned to the shop we related the information to Pipsi and Nolik. They too could not get over it. "These are the fruits of two thousand years of Christian doctrine and education. They have raised a generation of animals," said Nolik. "Pagans and cannibals are gentle creatures in comparison with these animals who call themselves Christians."

Whoever wanted to go home was now urged to do so, leaving the mothers with the children in the shop just in case the Action should be continued tomorrow. The instructions were that everybody was to return to the shop between six and seven o'clock in the morning instead of the usual eight o'clock. This was a time when the people of the various working places were filling the streets and we would thus not be so conspicuous.

The following night in the ghetto was the worst we ever experienced. In the houses where children had been brutally abducted the parents and even the neighbors were in a state of shock. In the households where elderly and children had been saved the sense of apprehension was oppressive. Everyone was worried sick about tomorrow. Some elderly people who one way or another had escaped this time were preparing make-up to look younger and decided to try to leave the ghetto in the morning with some brigades. Some young children who were tall for their age also escaped the ghetto in this manner.

Needless to say, nobody slept that night. By seven in the morning everybody was already in the workshop. Since workers were not touched in yesterday's Action, it was decided that all our workers would stay in the shop and continue working as usual, whereas the mothers with the children would hide in the same manner as yesterday. Only Max would stay with them in case Vera needed him. We closed the hide-out door and set up shop. Again the children were not given any injections or sleeping pills, as advised by Max. We were now fearfully anticipating whether the Action would continue. Up until this time no Action had ever lasted two days and it was difficult to predict what would happen.

But the mystery was resolved pretty quickly. At eight o'clock in the morning the trucks loaded with the SS and the Ukrainians were back. Again the record-players started blaring music full blast and policemen from the SS with a substantially increased canine brigade entered the ghetto. The murderers were armed with picks and axes as well as hand grenades. They staked out the area, again rushing the ghetto with uncontrollable zeal. They broke walls, turned over beds, checked wardrobes and even sheds in the yard. Children hidden the previous day were now discovered. But this time everybody, children, parents, and whoever was in the hide-out, was pulled out, murderously beaten, and chased into the trucks. When the slightest resistance was offered, two, three, and more dogs were let loose upon the lot.

We in the shop could hear and see the bloody orgy on the street. From a neighboring house we could hear unearthly shrill sounds, then barking of dogs, screaming Ukrainians, then heavy blows of a rifle butt. Apparently a woman resisted and would not part with the child. Even the dogs failed to pry the child loose. But suddenly it got quiet. Apparently the woman was dead or unconscious and the child was dumped into the truck, probably dead too. We could not see from our window who the woman was. When the Ukrainians left, the woman was dragged into the house by the neighbors. It seemed that despite the beating and dog bites, she was still alive. How many more scenes like these could our nerves endure?

Suddenly, at around eleven o'clock, we heard boots banging on the stairs leading to our shop. We were now the target. Yesterday we had escaped without being checked. Apparently the instructions this time were to cover all workshops. We immediately started working. The job which we had prepared for everybody was armbands, which had to be painted by tapping a hard, almost dry brush over the cloth. The idea was to do as much banging on the table as possible to drown out any possible sound from the hide-out. Two SS-bullies walked in and started checking the shop. Peter got up and said he was in charge here. They checked all the rooms, then stopped in front of Zoondl, looked at him, and asked, "How old are you?"

We were holding our breath.

"Fifteen," said Zoondl.

"Fifteen?" the SS-man repeated, "you don't look it. What are you doing here?"

"I am a painter and prepare armbands," came Zoondl's reply.

They gave him another look and walked away. Zoondl for the moment seemed safe. But our relief did not last long. As if they knew, they suddenly walked straight to the shelves behind which we had the hide-out, tapped the wall, and asked Peter, "What is behind there?"

If we did not turn grey at this moment, it was God's miracle. But Peter displayed an almost supernatural presence of mind. "I don't know," he replied completely casually, "this must be the roof construction, I guess."

His superb aplomb convinced the SS-men. They had a quick look at the other walls, turned around, and left. Peter had to sit down. His legs were shaking. The deceit had worked. Again we were safe, at least temporarily.

From our workshop they crossed the alley and entered the SS-work-shops, which were in the building where the Aeltestenrat was previously located. We quietly got up to go to the window to see what would happen. What followed was unparallelled horror. The Jews of the SS-workshop had gambled that since they were working for the SS their shop would not be checked. Quite a number of children were hidden there. The SS-men who had just left our shop were now followed by a group of Ukrainians. They all entered the workshop and started a search. Unfortunately the SS-workshop did not have a hide-out as we did and the children were hidden in the last room on the upper floor, in the hope that the search party would not go so far into the building. But they searched every room methodically and in the last room they discovered their prey.

The children and their parents were ordered into the yard. The parents were ordered to step aside, leaving the children in the middle of the yard. Among the children was the son of Mr. Grossman, the man in charge of the workshop. Mr. Grossman stepped out of the group of assembled parents and fell to the ground, begging the SS-men not to take the children away. This shop was their shop and the work done here was for the SS. But the SS-man kicked him in the side with his foot. Mr. Grossman winced but again pleaded with the murderer. Under normal conditions one punch delivered by the huge Mr. Grossman could have almost killed that comparatively little Nazi, but here he was surrounded by dozens of armed Ukrainians with rifles pointing at him.

"Abmarschieren!" (march!) the miserable SS-man commanded, and the children, about eight or nine of them, were forced through the gate while the horror-stricken parents fell into each other's arms, crying in agony and despair.

We retreated from the window and had to sit down. We all were thinking how it would have been if our hide-out had been discovered. Time dragged on at a snail's pace. We were in constant fear of what else would still happen this fatal day.

We did not have to wait long. Suddenly we heard a child's cry. At first we thought the sound came from outside, but within a few fateful seconds we realized that the crying came from our hide-out. Peter and I rushed to the door, ripped it open, and in the doorway was Renee with Raanan. He had broken down. For almost two days the children had not issued a sound. They were so scared and the surroundings were so awe-inducing that they were terrified and intimidated. Miraculously, none of them had even coughed for more than thirty hours. But finally Rannan was at the end of his endurance. He began to cry and could not be calmed down. His crying could definitely be heard on the street, but between the cries of the children who were caught and the noise of the music blaring from the trucks, his crying was drowned out.

We pulled him out of the hide-out, closed the door quickly, and put him on the sofa. Peter was as white as a sheet. He quickly threw a few coats over Raanan's head to muffle the sound and tried to calm him down, but to no avail. Every sound produced could have meant our downfall. Max, who was with us in case Vera needed help, suggested an injection to put him to sleep. He was afraid that under the circumstances oral medication would take too long to work and every second was precious. Peter agreed. Max rushed down the stairs. Once on the street, he walked slowly and calmly to avoid suspicion. The moment he was out of sight he broke into a run. At home he had a large assortment of pills and injections which he used for Vera. He grabbed what he needed, hid it under his jacket, and hurriedly returned to the shop. Raanan was given the injection and fell asleep. For five or ten minutes the entire shop was on edge. Did anybody hear the cries? Would anybody return to check our shop again? Fortunately our luck held. We had been spared once more.

While all of this was going on in the ghetto, the Jewish policemen at the Ninth Fort were subjected to the most inhumane torture. The policemen were informed by the SS-men that they knew about the hide-outs in the ghetto and that all would be shot unless they cooperated. One by one the regular policemen were interrogated, but without success. Over forty policemen, including the entire leadership, had already been shot. Finally several policemen broke under the stress. They agreed to cooperate with the SS to save their own skins. Private limousines with shades over the windows started to appear in the ghetto. Behind the shades were the Jewish policemen who had agreed to cooperate. Only their silhouettes could be seen, making it difficult to recognize them. Led by the informants, the limousines pulled up directly in front of specific houses and walked straight up to the hide-outs. There was no way out, they knew the exact house, the very place and the secret entrance. Everybody in any hide-out was in jeopardy. Despite our valiant attempts to keep things secret, even we could not be absolutely sure that nobody knew our hide-out. To our knowledge, however, except for the carpenter Marshak, who was not a policeman, nobody knew about it. The minutes were ticking away and the day just would not end.

It was now five o'clock. It started to get dark outside, but the Action was still going strong. Finally, by six o'clock, the murderers left the ghetto and it got quiet. We waited for another half hour or so before we were finally convinced that the SS and their helpers were gone. We walked out to the street. The streets were empty except for work brigades returning from town. We went back up, opened the hide-out, and let everybody out. Once everybody was outside we carefully closed the door and sat down to take a deep breath. We had managed to save the children for a second day in a row. Raanan was still asleep but was expected to wake up within the hour, at which time he would require special attention to keep him from crying again. As last night, we brought some food for the children, who were quite hungry, and discussed what to do tomorrow. Should we hide for one more day or not? Could the Action really last three days? What else could they discover after playing out their final trump card with the police? The children started to loosen up and to move about. There were six in all. As we were in the midst of our deliberation, we heard steps on the stairs leading to our shop. Who could it be? All workers were still in the shop. Nobody had left and we did not expect anybody to be looking for us at such a time.

Suddenly the door opened. To our complete horror SS-Sturmfuehrer Berger stood before us. Here was the man who only yesterday carried out the bloodiest Children's Action in the outside camps. A deadly silence ensued. With eyes expressing utmost fear, we all looked at Berger. The mothers automatically grabbed their children in a desperate embrace. But just as we were fear-stricken, he was perplexed. The view in front of him caught him totally by surprise. He stopped, looked at us, and said, "Ich habe garnichts gesehen (I have not seen a thing). I came only to let you know that the Action is over."

Without saying another word he turned around and rushed out.

We were utterly confused. What would Berger do? Would he tell his superior, Goecke? Would he send in his SS-men to take the children away? In case our children were ever discovered at a later date, how could he explain that he had seen the children and done nothing? Would he deny ever having been upstairs after the Action? Was he really here only to let us know that the Action was over, to put us at ease? The questions had no answers. After a brief consultation, the decision was made to keep the mothers with the children hidden for one more day. Obviously if Berger wanted to get our children he knew where to find us and we could not do a thing about it. We could not deny that he had seen them. However, if the Action continued tomorrow, the children had to be hidden.

We remained in the shop for several more hours to see what would happen. When nobody showed up we dispersed and went home, leaving the children and their mothers behind.

The next morning we again put the children into the hiding place and waited for the day's events to unfold, but the Action was indeed over and no SS showed up in the ghetto.

We found out from the ghetto adminstration that close to two thousand people had been taken out of the ghetto and the camps, among them more than one thousand children. In the evening we faced the logistic problem of getting the children home, hiding them from even the other Jews. We did not dare go to the homes of friends or relatives for fear of revealing the truth.

We asked about the woman from our neighboring house who had been dragged from the street after that vicious beating. To our horror, we found out that she was Mrs. Davidowitsch, the woman who had her child in the ghetto after twelve years of childlessness. She absolutely refused to part with the child until she and it were beaten senseless. The child was then torn away from her arms, mauled by dogs, and clubbed by rifle butts. She was left on the street, presumed dead, but her neighbors expected her to survive.

Two days later something unbelievable occurred. Rivka, who worked in a war-related brigade outside the ghetto, brought home, under risk of being shot, the local German daily newspaper. Lo and behold, in the paper was a most detailed description of the Children's Action in ghetto Kovno, with all the cruelty, the beatings, the dogs, and the anguish, in detail. There was, however, one small difference. For the Ukrainians, the paper had substituted soldiers of the Red Army, and for the Jews, they had substituted White Russians.

A few days later a Lithuanian engineer who was employed by the Germans came to our shop to pick up some completed signs. When he entered our shop he was rather surprised by our very tense mood. Prior to this we had always been friendly to him. When he noticed it and asked us about it, we told him the whole story. Stunned, he looked at us in disbelief. When we pointed out to him that he could look for himself throughout the ghetto, that no child or older person was present anywhere on the street, he finally spoke.

"I cannot believe it. I just read in the German paper a similar description. I thought the others were doing it."

Without saying another word, the Lithuanian engineer, who was a gentleman, packed up our work and left our shop, totally shocked by the revelation. We never saw him again.

19

RUTHIE

Vera's lung was healing slowly. There was one last frightful moment during one of the flushing therapy sessions, when Dr. Friedman let the tube slip out of his hand and air entered Vera's lung. She got quite cyanotic and almost collapsed. Had it not been for Max's fast reflexes, she might have died. But the day finally arrived when the tube was to be removed from her lung and this was a day of joy and celebration at home.

Her legs too improved gradually and Max began physical therapy. The long bedridden illness had wasted her legs into two thin twigs, devoid of muscle. The physical therapy consisted of standing between two chairs, holding onto them, and moving the legs as much as possible. It took unbelievable patience on the part of Max, to work with her on her recovery. Some months later Vera was able to walk with a cane from one room to the other for the first time. Subsequent improvements were slow in coming, but progress was being made. She would walk again after all!

One day, a Sunday, the orchestra gave a concert in a hall in the workshops and I got tickets for her and Max. I persuaded her to try with our help to go to the concert. She agreed. This was the first time she had been outside the house in more than five months. The big question was now whether or not Vera had enough time left to recover sufficiently to be able to walk should evacuation occur. But as for now, we had survived a major crisis and Vera was alive. Our major concern now was what to do with Ruthie after the impact of the Children's Action.

The Varniu gate was one of two which served the ghetto as a connection to the outside world. Through these gates Jewish brigades used to leave the ghetto, marching to slave labor work in the city. Upon leaving the

219

ghetto a strict count of the number of Jews going out to work was taken and they were accompanied by heavy contingents of Lithuanian guards. Some special brigades were picked up by the Germans and taken to working places serving the German occupation force. These special Jews had contact with the local population. The Lithuanians already knew where the Jews were working and used to come with food, which they traded for whatever the Jews had to offer. The Jews were ready to pay any price for food. The Lithuanians took advantage of this and obtained exorbitant prices for their products. The workers then would hide the food and try to smuggle it into the ghetto where their hungry families were waiting for them. The smuggling was not an easy task. The gate guard frisked every Jew and confiscated everthing. It was heartbreaking for the struggling Jews to carry the little bit of food, obtained at great risk and cost, for miles, only to see it taken away from them under beatings and sometimes even death. It was particularly dangerous to bring in food during German defeats. The defeats made them particularly brutal and ruthless and since shooting a Jew was not a crime, some guards actually shot Jews at the gates when their whim called for it. Dozens of Jews were thus shot at the gates. But this did not deter them from risking their lives to support their hungry families. For a few days the carrying of food to the ghetto would stop, but soon it would start again. The hunger was just too strong.

There were some guards who were known to be murderers and were particularly feared. When these guards were at the gate special messengers went out to meet the homebound brigades to warn them to get rid of the food rather than to risk being murderously beaten or even shot. The streets leading to the gate would then be littered with groceries and loose food items. The hungry people had to step over those precious potatoes which had been carried for miles on their bodies after a ten or twelve hour workday. At home the families waited impatiently for whatever was brought, but the bag was empty. This always meant another day with barely any food at home. But at least that father was safe.

A few Jewish inspectors were also assigned to the gates. Over the long months and years they served there they acquired an enormously keen perception of what could be expected at the gates every day. They knew every guard, and when new guards were assigned to the ghetto they did not need much time to evaluate them. When the brigades left in the morning the workers would check with the Jewish gate inspectors as to what could be expected in the evening, thus knowing whether or not to risk bringing food.

Important also was their fast grasp of a situation. Occasionally some Jews escaped the brigade and did not return to the ghetto. The group leader of the brigade would then tip off the Jewish inspector about the situation and he would arrange the count at the entry without the German official noticing that somebody was missing. This was of utmost importance, as a missing Jew would have initiated severe reprisals. By virtue of their unique position these inspectors wielded enormous power in the ghetto. Since not all working brigades were equal, an assignment to a better brigade often meant the difference between life and death by starvation. The inspectors could easily switch workers from one brigade to the other, thus changing those persons' lives. This power occasionally was abused, but in general the inspectors did their job with great personal sacrifice and sometimes even at personal risk.

In addition to being an outlet for the working brigades, the ghetto gates served as entry ports. Once the working brigades were out, the gates were used by the workers supplying the ghetto with food and other necessities. The food was brought in by horse and wagon. Each wagon was served by a Jewish driver and one helper, and each was checked thoroughly on departure and upon return, to be sure that nothing was smuggled in or out. These exits and entries were handled by the Jewish inspectors, which gave them substantial control over what was going out and coming in. Among these inspectors was a good friend of mine, Jacob Verbovski, who was efficient, honest, and generally trusted by the ghetto. Twenty-four hours a day the gates were open and under extremely heavy guard, and people who had no business at the gate would try to stay away from it. My work in the graphics department was inside the ghetto and I rarely went to the gates.

In the aftermath of the Children's Action panic gripped the parents who had managed to save their children. Since the ghetto officially did not have any children anymore, it was obvious that the surviving children could not remain in the ghetto for long. If they were found they could be destroyed. A mad rush to find some Lithuanian family willing to hide the children began. The problem was extremely difficult. Most Lithuanians were not willing to undertake such an action since it entailed great personal risks. In the rare instances where a Lithuanian family was willing to save a Jewish child, it had to be a girl, unless the boy was not circumcised. The child also had to be light-complected, because dark hair and skin were rare among Lithuanians. A Jewish child could be easily recognized.

Ruthie did not have any of the above problems. She was a beautiful little girl with blonde hair and blue eyes like my sister. The problem was how to persuade Vera to part with Ruthie and how to save her. For weeks Max had been trying to convince Vera that there was no other choice. Some evenings were particularly hectic, the discussion ending with Vera sobbing hysterically. It must have been for the tenth time that Max picked up the subject again.

"Vera," Max said, "I have been trying in vain to convince you that we must find a way to save Ruthie. We have friends among the Lithuanians and somebody hopefully will agree to take her. I don't want to part with Ruthie any more than you do, but here she is doomed for sure. Out there perhaps she can survive. It is tragic, but you have to get used to the idea."

"I know," Vera replied, "but it is so difficult. Max, you know that I am an invalid and who knows whether or not I will ever recover fully. What have I left in life if not my child?"

"But Vera, before the Children's Action I never pressed the issue, although we knew about Siauliai. But until you experience it yourself, you just refuse to believe it. Now we have seen how horrible the Action was. What will you do if Ruthie runs into the street? She is a child, what does she know?"

"I simply refuse to think about it," Vera replied. "Thank God I can now walk a little and I am not confined to bed anymore. I can prevent this."

"But that is not the point, Vera! The child is not safe anymore. The Germans have a complete count of the Jewish population in the ghetto and they know that they did not get all the children. What would you do if they surprised us with another Action?"

"But what sense does life make without Ruthie, tell me," Vera pleaded with Max.

A heavy silence fell over the room. Nobody uttered a word. My mother and I tried to stay away from this discussion. We knew that Max was right, but the decision had to be made by them. It was their child.

"I don't know whether I told you," Max broke the silence, "but our neighbors across the street, the Daitches, gave their child away a few days ago. You know how much they loved little Lubinka."

"Who told you they gave their child away?" Vera asked.

"Everybody knows it," Max answered, "and they are not the only ones."

Vera got up and walked over to Ruthie's bed. Ruthie was sound asleep and had no idea what was being planned for her. Vera stood for a while and stared at her angelic face, her beautiful blonde curls. She then turned around to Max and asked, "Do you really mean you are ready to part with Ruthie?"

"Vera, I don't want to part with her any more than you do, but I want to have a clear conscience that I have tried everything to save her life."

"And if I should agree, to whom would you give the child?"

"First I would try Paplavski, and then, possibly Yadvyga Bielinski."

"I don't believe they will agree to it. Go ahead, prove it to yourself."

The ice was now broken for the first time. The problem now was how to get in touch with Paplavski. There were no telephones in the ghetto and no mail. We were totally isolated from the outside world. Only the workers in the brigades had outside contacts. Since both Max and I were working inside the ghetto, one of us had to try to join a brigade and go to town. Even then it would be difficult to contact our Lithuanian friend, since we could not phone from work.

As workers in the graphics department we also did work for the German authorities and needed supplies and paint. Through our contacts with them and the Jewish council I got a permit to go into town to a graphics supply shop to buy paint and supplies. I joined a small group of Jews who also had to procure materials for their workshops and we left the ghetto accompanied by a guard. Since my stop was the first on the way, the guard left me in the store and told the shopkeeper to watch me. In about two hours he would be back to pick me up. It was the shop-keeper's responsibility that I not escape. He then left with the other men. This was a unique opportunity. Here I was, alone and unguarded, with a telephone in the rear of the store. I had to take advantage of this opportu-nity to contact our good Lithuanian friend. Maybe he could save Ruthie. He was not only a friend of the family but also owed a great deal to my father, who had helped him when he was in serious trouble with the authorities. My father subsequently helped him build up a very successful business and the man became prosperous. We considered each other more than just friends, almost like family. I got into a conversation with the owner of the store. In fact he knew our family, since the store was only one block away from the apartment building we had lived in. After buying all the supplies I needed I persuaded him to let me make a phone call. I took the phone and dialed the number I knew so well.

"Hello," I heard a man's voice at the other end of the line. It was his voice!

"Hello, Mr. Paplavski, I am glad I caught you. You must be surprised to hear my voice. Remember me, we used to live on the third floor of Ugniagesiu Street 19. Remember now?" I purposely avoided giving my name, since anybody listening in could recognize that the name was Jewish. There was no answer for a few seconds. Apparently he had gone into shock. He certainly was not expecting to hear my voice on the other end of the line!

"Mr. Paplavski? Mr. Paplavski?" I said, "what happened?"

"I am still here, where are you?"

I gave him the address and continued, "I would like to see you if you can come over immediately. I will be here only for another hour or so."

"I am coming, wait for me."

I hung up and waited for some anxious moments. Would he really come? Was he still our friend? How many of our friends had turned their backs on us. How sure could I be that he did not turn Nazi?

Fifteen minutes later the door to the store opened and there he was. He looked around carefully, making sure nobody was in the store. When he saw that all was clear he looked at the storekeeper, trying to figure out who he was and what his reaction would be. The storekeeper already knew that I was expecting somebody and was very fair. He led Mr. Paplavski and me into a back room and left us alone.

Paplavski grabbed my hand and said, "I am glad to see you. I know what you people have been through. Don't blame us all. Not all of us have participated in the atrocities against you. Many of us feel very bad about it. How is your family? I know that you lost your father. He was a very fine man. It is a shame that people like him have to fall victims to hooligans. Are the rest of you all right, or have you lost any more members of your family?"

I told him briefly what we had been through, particularly the Children's Action. "Mr. Paplavski," I continued, "I will be very blunt with you. We don't have much time. Can you save Ruthie for us?"

Paplavski was stunned. He did not expect this! "I hate to be ungrateful after everything your father has done for me," he stammered, "but you know things are not that simple here either. We are constantly under surveillance, particularly since I was once in trouble with the authorities, you know. Ruthie would not be safe in my house."

This was a shock to me. I did not expect such a fast rebuff. His troubles with the authorities were long forgotten and it was a very poor excuse indeed. He sort of sensed what I was thinking.

"It is not that I don't want to help you," he continued, "but you know we have many neighbors and suddenly, a child, they would get suspicious. It is not good."

"But you have a farm, maybe there?" I did not give up easily.

"Well, the farm is not much better. True, there are no neighbors nearby, but the helpers cannot be trusted, you know. Maybe I can help you with money?" he asked.

"No, I don't need any," I said curtly. Our conversation was obviously getting nowhere. It was clear that he was unwilling to help. Pursuing the issue any further was useless.

"Well," I said, "then at least you can do one thing for me. In Williampole not far from the rubber factory lives Yadvyga Bielinski, the lady you once met in our house. She used to live in the village of Daugai."

"Yes, I remember her. What about her?"

"Can you find her and ask her to come to the rubber plant next Wednesday? My brother-in-law, Dr. Max Solc, will be there waiting for her. I am reasonably sure that I can get permission for him to go to the factory on that particular day. It is not always easy to arrange such a thing for us, but I hope that with my connections I can manage. Are you willing to try to find her and set up the meeting?"

"Yes, I will try everything in my power to find her and to make sure that she comes." He seemed to be relieved that I did not pursue the previous line of thought and was willing to do anything as long as I would leave him alone. He obviously did not feel right about denying me my request. He owed father too much, but he was not willing to take any chances whatsoever. We talked on for a few minutes more. He then took a package out of his pocket and gave it to me. "This package has some food and cigarettes. I know you need it. Give it to your family and remember me to them." With that we parted. The only thing I hoped was that he would not forget to contact Yadvyga.

About an hour later the guard and the other Jews came back, picked me up, and we returned to the ghetto. I was very disappointed. We had played what we thought was our biggest trump card and lost.

When I came through the door Max and Vera were waiting for me anxiously. I saw in Vera's face that she was hoping I would return with a rejection. "Well, did Paplavski come to see you?"

"Yes, he did."

"He did?" Vera said with obvious disappointment in her voice. "What did he say? Is he willing to do it?"

"Well, he was very apologetic but did not budge. He is not ready to take Ruthie."

"I told you so, you see, I told you so," Vera turned to Max, "nobody will take a Jewish child. It was pointless to even argue with you over it."

"Then how about Yadvyga," asked Max. "I still would like to try her."

"Here is what I did," I replied. "I have asked Paplavski to try to find her. I told him approximately where she lives. If he can find her he will ask her to come to the rubber factory on Wednesday to meet you."

"Very well. I hope he will keep his promise. I will gladly go to the factory to meet her," said Max.

Vera was not very happy with this turn of events. I was not too eager to disappoint Vera, but I said: "He will find her, don't worry. You see, he knows that if he can find her we will stop bothering him. He will do his best to find her and arrange the meeting." Vera did not like the idea but was reasonably sure that Yadvyga would not take Ruthie either and the whole issue would finally be settled. Ruthie would stay with her for better or for worse.

Arranging for Max to join the brigade that was going to the rubber factory was not exactly the easiest thing. The brigade was one of the better ones and people were always eager to join it. It took some pull on my part to arrange a place for him in the brigade, but on Wednesday morning Max was at the gate. One of the gate inspectors with whom I had spoken had seen to it. The big question now was whether Paplavski had kept his bargain and sought out Yadvyga, and if so whether or not she would show up.

Yadvyga was a former patient of Dr. Max Solc. After graduating from medical school Dr. Solc had moved to Daugai, the village in which he was born and raised. He opened his practice there. All the Lithuanian peasants in and around Daugai were his patients since he was the only doctor in the entire county. Being very conscientious, he soon earned the confidence of the people and was highly respected by the Lithuanian population. Even some of the highly anti-Semitic Lithuanians in the area had high regard for his integrity and devotion. Yadvyga was a schoolteacher in Daugai, not married, in her upper thirties, a highly intelligent person. The first winter after Dr. Solc had established his practice in Daugai, Yadvyga became seriously ill. Only the extreme devotion of the doctor, way beyond the call of duty, pulled her through. She had never forgotten it. Even later, when Max had already moved to Kovno and she to Williampole, she would occasionally contact him. With the start of the war and the establishment of the ghetto the contact was severed.

As the brigade was approaching the rubber factory, Max started to look around anxiously. Would she or would she not show up? As the group entered the gate of the shop Max had the impression that he heard somebody say, "Hi, doctor." He turned around in the direction of the voice and just could not believe his eyes. Here she was, Yadvyga Bielinski. Max motioned to her but could not stop. The brigade entered the factory. Yadvyga very skillfully mixed herself into the brigade and got into the shop. Once inside, Dr. Solc took advantage of an opportunity and sneaked out to meet with her.

Yadvyga was visibly shaken to see her doctor dressed like an unskilled laborer, dirty and dusty from the long road from the ghetto to the factory, with two yellow stars on his coat, one on his chest and one on his back. But she was glad to see him alive. She knew everything the Jews had been through in the past two and one-half or three years. The conversation started with a few reminiscences from the years in Daugai and then Max, without hesitation, proceeded to explain the problem to her.

"Yadvyga," he said, "we don't have all day to talk. The foreman will notice that I am not at my working place, so I have to make it fast. I see you know more about what we have been through than I imagined. So let me ask you, would you or somebody else you know be willing to take Ruthie and save her life?"

"Doctor," she said, "there is not a thing in the world I would not do for you. I have not forgotten what you did for me and never will. Bring your daughter. I will take her."

Max was stunned. He did not expect such a fast answer. He was moved to tears. His heart was pounding, his hands shaking, and he stood there speechless.

"Bring your daughter," she repeated, "my home will be her home. How do you intend to proceed? How will you get her out of the ghetto?"

"Let me make all the necessary arrangements," said Max, "and we will meet again next Wednesday, here at the same place. By that time I will know exactly what the game plan will be."

"I will be here, don't worry."

"I don't know how I will ever be able to repay you for this."

"It will not be necessary. You have already done more for me than I can repay, so don't waste time. It is valuable and very short." With that she said good bye and grabbed his hand. Tears welled up in the eyes of both. "Who would have ever thought that we would meet here under such conditions," Max added in parting. But both had missed one very important problem which later proved fatal.

Vera was very unhappy with the news. For several days she was in a severe state of depression, constantly crying. She could not get used to the idea of parting with her only child. During one of these severe states of anxiety Ruthie suddenly disappeared. Vera was frantic. Where could she be? She was not at home and could not be seen on the street. She obviously had run out of the house into the street to play. But where was she? Vera was hysterical. Since we lived just one block away from the SS ghetto administration, there were always Germans around the area. The chances were very real that a German might have noticed her and taken her into custody. Since Vera had difficulty walking, my mother ran out of the house into the street to look for her, but after searching the entire immediate vicinity she returned home without Ruthie. Both my mother and Vera were shaking. Where was the child? What happened to her? God, not the Germans! Hopefully they had not picked her up.

Moments of anxious waiting were ticking away. Both were at a loss as to what to do next, when suddenly somebody knocked at the door. Their hearts stopped! Who could it be? When the door was opened a relative of ours, Mr. Chapelunski, stood at the door with a big bag on his back. "Don't get scared," he said when he saw the agonized faces of Vera and my mother. "I brought back your child."

He lowered the bag from his back and opened it. In it was Ruthie. She had taken advantage of a moment when her mother was not watching very closely and walked out the door. Knowing from before where the Chapelunskis had lived, she just strolled over for a visit. Fortunately the Chapelunskis lived nearby and nobody noticed the child.

"I knew that you would be anxious," he started, "so I rushed back to your house. It took me a little time to find a proper bag. Under normal circumstances we would have played with her a little and then returned, but under the present conditions we knew how frantic you would be. We packed her into this bag so nobody should see that this was a child and brought her home right away. She really is a good child. She did not cry. She let us hide her in the bag and was quiet all the way home."

This episode was the clincher. It changed Vera's mind. She was now ready to let the girl be taken to a new "Lithuanian mother." In the meantime, I went to Jacob Verbovski to ask him how these things were done, as he was experienced at it. Vervobski got straight to the point.

"Mishelski," he used to call me by my second name, "I will do everything I can for you. This thing is not without risk. If it fails and we are caught, it is my head, yours, and everybody's involved in it, including the child. So we have to be very careful. We are doing it because it is our duty to save as many children as we can. We have paid already very dearly in these past years.

"Here are your instructions. Generally it does not make any difference which day you choose, except Friday. Friday they have one Lithuanian guard who is a son of a bitch and we cannot do anything on that day. The best day generally is Thursday, although Tuesday is good, too. The child must be put to sleep with sleeping pills or an injection so she will not wake up and start crying while the exchange is taking place. You or the doctor, whoever goes out to take the child to meet the Lithuanians, must be dressed like a porter, since he will have to carry sacks with potatoes. The child has to be put into a potato bag. She will be taken out in one of the wagons delivering potatoes to the ghetto. The wagon has some straw on it and about a dozen bags. The bag with the child will be at the bottom of the pile and the other bags and the straw will be above. When the Lithuanian guard is at the gate, he always pokes his bayonet into every sack. He could injure or even kill the child. That's why this operation cannot be carried out on Friday. Occasionally the other guards do it too, but so far we have been successful in diverting them from the wagon carrying children. Your doctor has to be at the depot at six in the morning where we keep the wagons.

"The wagon driver involved in this operation will contact your brother-in-law. He will arrange the sacks and both will then proceed to the gate. You wait at the gate. You are sort of an insurance man. Should conditions be unfavorable, the sack containing the child must be removed quickly and inconspicuously. That's where you come in. You must pick up the sack and carry it back through the ghetto to your house. You might also be caught, but that is the chance you take. Your brother-in-law cannot leave the wagon since he has the certificate showing he belongs to the wagon and has permission to leave the ghetto. And secondly, it is advisable that he immediately get in touch with the Lithuanians and apprise them of the situation."

"And where does the Lithuanian pick up the child?" I asked.

"I am coming to that," Jacob continued. "The place where we are picking up the potatoes is half a mile from the rubber plant. There is always activity there. Lithuanians also come to pick up potatoes and therefore a Lithuanian with a bag of potatoes is not conspicuous. You understand? That's where the meeting point is. So far things have gone smoothly, but one never knows. There is always a first time. Caution is advised always."

A few more details were discussed and I rushed home to start the necessary preparation.

Next Wednesday Max again was at the rubber factory where Yadvyga was already waiting for him. The decision was made to proceed with all deliberate speed. The girl would be brought the very next day, as Thursday was supposed to be a good day.

The atmosphere at home that evening was as if a dear one were dying. There was crying, kissing and hugging of the child. Ruthie was confused by all the attention and commotion and did not understand what was going on.

In the morning Max gave her an injection and soon she was sound asleep. The entire project went off as planned, without a hitch. The wagon left on time and Yadvyga was at the other end to receive the child. Max and Yadvyga also decided that, for the foreseeable future, they would meet every Wednesday at the rubber plant. It was also made clear that if for one reason or another one of the two parties should miss a Wednesday, the next Wednesday would still stand.

Max returned to a lonely home, heartsick. This was the first day without Ruthie. For the ensuing two weeks Yadvyga did not show up and Max and the entire family were extremely worried. What had kept her away? What was the trouble? Could she have been discovered? All kinds of thoughts were going through our heads.

The following Wednesday Yadvyga was finally there and Max was very apprehensive. Why hadn't she been there the two preceding weeks? In the course of the conversation the problem became clear: Ruthie barely spoke or understood Lithuanian, a problem which neither Max nor Yadvyga had thought to discuss at their first meeting. As almost all Jews in Lithuania spoke Yiddish at home, Ruthie was raised with that language. After the Children's Action when the problem of placing the children with Lithuanian families outside the ghetto became acute, we and most other families started to speak Lithuanian with our children. But they, being used to Yiddish, resisted the new language. By the time we were ready to give Ruthie away she understood some Lithuanian words, but not enough. That's where Yadvyga's problem came in. She could not leave the child on Wednesday unattended by her. One Jewish word would have given her away. It was a struggle for both Yadvyga and Ruthie, but progress was being made.

Vera was happy that the child was at least safe and that nothing terrible had happened. But two things happened after that meeting which decided the fate of Ruthie. June first was Ruthie's birthday, her third. Vera was inconsolable. A birthday without Ruthie! Where was the child at this moment? How was she being treated? Was she homesick? Was she crying a lot? What kind of birthday did she have? Vera started to demand that Ruthie be brought back to the ghetto.

"I am an invalid," she said, "I certainly will not survive the war. At the next Action I am sure to go. What use is there in Ruthie surviving, even with a good "mother" like Yadvyga? I want her back."

It took all our powers of persuasion to keep her calm. We reminded her of the Children's Action and of Ruthie's disappearance last month, but it got harder and harder to reason with her. The clincher came the following Wednesday.

When Max met with Yadvyga, she disclosed a secret: Ruthie was no longer with her. Ruthie had used some Yiddish words and neighbors had discovered that Ruthie was not a "niece" of Yadvyga's but rather a Jewish child. The word got around and it became too dangerous to keep her in Yadvyga's home any longer. But Yadvyga was determined to save the child. She had given Ruthie to some friends of hers who lived a few blocks from the ghetto. Yadvyga claimed that these people were honest and God-fearing. Ruthie would be safe there, particularly since her speech had improved considerably now and the Yiddish words were gradually disappearing. Of course this Lithuanian couple would have to be reimbursed, but that was a minor problem. The important part was that Ruthie would have a good home.

When Max came home with the bad news, Vera became frantic. Could it be that Yadvyga was lying and something terrible had happened? Could it be just a plot to get money out of us? There was something in the story that aroused her suspicion. "When you told me that Yadvyga would take my child I consented. Yadvyga is someone I know, but this new couple, who knows who they are? I want my child back."

Again all the arguments about being an invalid were raised. But this time Max himself was not sure. Was Yadvyga's story true or not? He still trusted her, but who were these other Lithuanians? And why was he trusting Yadvyga so much? Couldn't she have played an act for him to get the child and to start milking money now? Stranger things had happened lately. For all it was worth, Yadvyga might not be the same as she had been, either. How many Lithuanians became Nazis in those years, turning their backs on their former Jewish friends? Before he was ready to put up a fight with Vera, but now his confidence was shaken. The battle was lost. Ruthie had to be brought back to the ghetto.

Again I went to Jacob Verbovski, this time with the reverse problem. Verbovski was not surprised. This was not the first time children had to be smuggled back in. Here too the method had already been tested. Again I had to be at the gate and Max had to go and pick up Ruthie.

Yadvyga was very upset over the decision to take Ruthie away. She pleaded with Max, but to no avail. Vera was inconsolable and unshakable in her demands. The decision had been made and had to be carried out. Even the other Lithuanian couple came to plead for Ruthie. They did not look too bad, but it was very difficult to know with certainty, so Max stood by the decision. On Tuesday 20 June Ruthie was back in the ghetto.

We barely recognized her. Her golden locks were shorn off to make her look more Lithuanian. Her neat dress was gone. She was dressed like a Lithuanian peasant girl, which in itself was only right. Her language was now more Lithuanian, very abusive, containing four-letter words, something she had never heard in our house. She was cursing and kicking, but worst of all, there were signs that she had been mistreated by the other couple. Thus there was a mixture of joy and sorrow at her return. But the deed had been committed. Exactly two days later, on 22 June, the Russian offensive at Vitebsk started. If we had wanted to get Ruthie back out, it was too late. The ghetto was closed.

20

LAST GASPS

The Children's Action left the ghetto devastated. One of our biggest problems was to maintain sanity. We could no longer be so naive as to assume that the unfavorable events at the fronts would auger well for us. In fact just the opposite seemed to be true. The worse the situations at the fronts became, the more vicious the recriminations against the Jews. In one article Goebbels stated that even if they wanted to stop their war against the Jews, they could not, because the revenge of the survivors would be horrendous. Thus all the Jews had to be annihilated to prevent a vendetta against the "honorable" German people. It seemed clear: the Nazi war against the Jews was now the only war they were winning, and they were worried that time could run out on this victory, too.

Information reached the ghetto that on 19 March the German troops had swept into Hungary and a vicious manhunt had started against the Jews. There were over half a million Jews in Hungary who had been persecuted by the Hungarian government but not exterminated. It almost looked as if the occupation of Hungary had only one objective: to exterminate the last remaining Jewry in the heart of Europe. Hungary had virtually no strategic importance in the German war effort. But the ovens of Auschwitz were going full blast and needed fodder for their fires, and here was an untapped reservoir of Jews. The Action had to be swift since the Russians were closing in on Auschwitz and the "Page of Glory" would soon come to a halt.

The mood in the ghetto was now one of extreme urgency. The most pressing problem was what to do with the children. Officially there were no more children in the ghetto. These three-and four-year-olds had to be kept indoors. They could not cry for fear of being detected, and the parents had to enforce this strict, almost impossible regime on them. Parents were now ready to pay any price. They were even ready to give the children to Lithuanians they had never met, as long as they were willing to accept Jewish children. After all, outside the ghetto they stood a fifty-fifty chance of surviving, whereas in the ghetto their fate was sealed.

Even the adults were ready to leave the ghetto, to go anywhere, anyplace, just to get out. OUT. Max's brother Wolf and his wife hurriedly found some Lithuanian who was willing to hide them for a rather substantial fee and left the ghetto.

The mood was so depressing that the only thing that kept me going was my work and Gitta. My evenings and my life now revolved around her. One evening, several weeks after the Children's Action, I took Gitta for a walk as usual. She barely spoke. It just was not like her. When we returned she asked me to come into her home. Her father was working afternoons this week and was not expected till ten o'clock. He was a very stern man, German-educated, with broad shoulders and a strict military posture. I wondered what was coming. Why did she suddenly call me in? When we walked in we were all alone. I did not wait, took her into my arms and embraced her. I suddenly felt my shoulder getting moist from her tears. I pressed her hard to my chest, stroked her hair, and gave her a kiss. When she relaxed she looked at me, and after a few minutes of hesitation she said, "Vulia, this is the first time that I disobey my father, but I have to tell you something."

Now I was even more surprised than before. What did she have to say? Where did her father come in into this picture? "I am listening, Gitta," I said.

"My father has instructed me not to meet with you today. Promise me that you will keep it a secret."

"Gitta, you are getting rather mysterious. Has something happened?"

"Vulia, you still have not answered my request to keep it a secret."

"Darling, I promise. You can rely on me."

"I know; and this is why I have decided to tell you." She gave me a look expressing deep internal struggle, reached for my hand, and said, "Vulia, I am leaving the ghetto tomorrow."

It struck me like a thunderbolt. Gitta was about to leave the ghetto! Tomorrow night she would no longer be here! There would be no more nightly walks, no more embraces, nobody to kiss, and nobody to calm my tense nerves. Another girlfriend was to disappear from my life. But at least this time she was going of her own free will. Or was it really her own free will? How quickly was this deal made? How thoroughly was this

Lithuanian checked out? What would she do if the Lithuanian demanded sexual favors of her? He could always threaten her with the Gestapo. These thoughts criss-crossed my mind with lightning speed. When I regained my composure, I looked at her. "Gitta," I asked, "how safe a place do you have?"

"To be truthful, I don't know. My father arranged it for me and I have no choice. Father is a very domineering man and has never tolerated dissent, besides, what are my chances here? The ghetto is finished."

Again quiet permeated the room.

"Gitta," I finally said, "I am by nature a pessimist and I often see things in dark colors, but somehow something inside me tells me that I will see you again. I don't know how to explain it. This is totally contrary to my usual way of thinking. Yet despite everything I have that strange, instinctive feeling that I will meet you after the war."

"Vulia, I only wish that this prophecy should come true."

The rest of the evening passed quietly. I held her tight in my arms and caressed her. Gitta was very apprehensive. She knew little about that Lithuanian, except that she would be working on a farm as a farm hand. Leaving the ghetto was very risky and I really did not hold it against her father that he did not want me to know about it. After all, we just had been through the experience of the hide-outs which were betrayed by some of the Jewish policemen. How well did he know me and what I might do to keep Gitta?

The final minutes were ticking away and the time came to say good-bye, perhaps forever. Neither one of us could foresee the future. But at least, off-hand, Gitta's chances seemed to be far better than mine.

Our parting was without tears. We were both too numb and overcome by emotion. When the time finally came to say goodbye, I walked to the door, turned around, looked at her once more, and walked out. Another chapter in my life had run its course.

The ghetto proper in the meantime was rapidly being transformed into a concentration camp. The surviving policemen had now returned from the Ninth Fort, which was like a miracle. When Nathan's wife met her husband there were hysterics amidst embraces and kisses. In our house all eyes were filled with tears. This was indeed a miracle. Here was a survivor of the Ninth Fort, a survivor of the death factory.

But Goecke was only beginning. He dismissed all the policemen and disbanded the entire Jewish police force. A small number of former policemen were recruited to form a new so-called security service. They were to be responsible to the SS, not under the jurisdiction of the ghetto administration, as had been the case with the former Jewish ghetto police. The new security service officers were now looked upon with great suspicion. How was it that they had been spared? There was no doubt in anyone's mind that they must have cooperated with the SS during the Children's Action one way or another, to save their skin. Nobody trusted them anymore. This put a terrible strain on those people as well as on the entire ghetto as a whole, which now saw a traitor in every person.

During the first or second week of April the ghetto received another blow: the ghetto administration and all its institutions were disbanded. The Aeltestenrat was arrested and taken to the Ninth Fort. Here they were tortured in an attempt to extract information about the underground activities in the ghetto. For several days nobody knew what had happened to them. Finally, when they were released, they were instructed to stay home until all external signs of their torture were gone.

Simultaneously the SS doubled the guards around the ghetto and took over all the functions which heretofore were handled by Jewish institutions. The guard at the working places was increased in an attempt to cut down on people trying to leave the ghetto. No one was to escape the Final Solution. The Nazis wanted a perfect job: one hundred percent of all European Jews killed. The page of glory could not tolerate any compromise. German honor was at stake.

It was now a race between the SS to stop the flight from the ghetto and the desperate attempts by the Jews to escape. The SS resorted to some ugly tactics. They engaged Lithuanians who presumably were ready to help the Jews, but in reality were double agents. Thus numerous Jews were tricked from the ghetto into presumably safe hide-outs, only to be betrayed and handed over to the Gestapo. The worst of these cases was a group of youngsters which was misled into believing that it was being taken by truck to join the partisans in the nearby woods, only to be tricked into an ambush and attacked by German SS-men and a group of Lithuanian collaborators. Goecke personally conducted the raid. The Jewish group, however, was armed. They immediately killed the driver of the truck, who was obviously a double agent, and then returned the fire. Grossly outnumbered and fully in the open, however, most of the youngsters were killed.

Even these measures were not capable of stemming the drive of the persecuted and harassed ghetto inhabitants to escape. Even provocations of greedy, unscrupulous Lithuanian agents did not stop the partisan activities or individual attempts. For everyone caught and executed, someone else was lucky enough to contact an honest Lithuanian who was really willing to help. Apparently the number of Lithuanians willing and ready to help the Jews even at great personal risk was on the increase. And every so often we would find out about somebody else who had fled the ghetto. Unfortunately Max's brother, Wolf, was not among the lucky ones. He was trapped by a double agent who, after pressing everything he could out of him, delivered him to the Gestapo. Wolf and his wife were brought to the ghetto prison, which was now also under SS control, and from there to the Ninth Fort. Here he and his wife were executed and burned.

This brought my thoughts back to Gitta. What if her Lithuanian was in the service of the Gestapo, too? Only the future could tell.

Meanwhile our shop was so busy that an expansion was badly needed. We had to make dozens of signs to be placed all around the ghetto announcing that this was now a concentration camp and warning people to avoid coming close to the fence. Shoot to kill without warning was the penalty for disobeying. We also had to make armbands for the newly created security service and prepare new certificates for them. Since in the ghetto there were officially no more children, elderly, or invalids, everybody was theoretically an able-bodied person and had to have a worker's pass. Again our shop was involved.

All this constituted so much work that Goecke ordered the evacuation of the first floor of our building and assigned it to our shop. We now added to our staff Peter's wife and sister-in-law, a certain Dr. Burstein's wife, a girl by the name of Luba, and a few others. The rooms downstairs were quickly cleaned and renovated and we moved in. The only drawback to these enlarged facilities was that in order to go from the first floor to the second we had to use the outside stairs. Peter did not like it and one day when Goecke was in our shop, Peter pointed it out to him and asked for permission to build a wooden spiral stair to create an inside connection within the shop. When Peter finished explaining his plan, Goecke started to laugh. This was the first time we ever had seen him do so. His laughter was just as scary as his entire appearance.

"Peter," he said, "you are crazy. But if you want it, I will let you have it." Goecke immediately authorized lumber for the project.

To some extent Goecke was right. Who in his right mind would ever think of a spiral stair at a time like this? But one thing which Goecke did not think about was that we needed lumber for a more substantial hideout, which we were already planning. Nahum and I again sat down and drew up plans for the stair, figuring out that sufficient lumber should remain for future use.

With a greatly enlarged staff we had no difficulty accommodating Renee and Rosl so that when one was working, the other was home attending the children.

In our household things were not easy. Vera was steadily improving, but the progress was much too slow. If the ghetto were to be liquidated now, she could not walk out of the ghetto and would have been shot on the spot. Every day Max set up a walkway between two rows of chairs and forced her to walk up and down to the point of tears. But Max insisted that no matter how painful, time was short and physical therapy was the only thing that could bring strength back to her legs. However, they could never be perfect again.

Goecke's next step was to liquidate the city brigades, since these provided a convenient outlet for escape from the ghetto. Fortunately Rivka's brigade was scheduled to be liquidated among the last. It was a war-related enterprise and as such the authorities were interested in keeping it going.

Despite the tough measures by Goecke, he was unable to stem the flow of people to the partisans. One day when I came to our shop the youngster Moolik was absent. One day's absence could have been explained by illness. But when he did not show up again, I knew that something was up. I knew all along that Moolik had been in contact with the partisan movement, but we seldom spoke about it. Now that he was absent two days in a row, I became suspicious. A very brief check confirmed my suspicion: Moolik had left the ghetto with a group of youngsters to join the partisans.

The month of May passed and June rolled around. For the past few months there was constant talk about a possible second front, but nothing ever materialized. To our surprise and delight, on 6 June news came over the wires that the invasion had started. Amidst all the troubles in the ghetto this was welcome indeed. We never doubted that the invasion would be successful. We only hoped that it would be quick and overwhelming enough to destroy the Nazi regime before they could close their account with us.

A day or two after the invasion had started Goecke, as so often, came to our shop. He was in a surprisingly good mood. We wondered what caused his happiness. After all, it was already clear that the Allies had taken a firm foothold on the continent and the Nazis faced overwhelming odds to push them back into the channel. This was not 1940 and the Allied airforce was in total control of the skies.

"This is what we have been waiting for all the time!" he turned to Peter.

We were flabbergasted. We, the Jews of the ghetto, were waiting for it, but why would he be so excited? He was an SS Obersturmbannfuehrer, a close associate of Himmler, deeply involved in the Final Solution. He had nothing to gain from a German defeat. As if guessing what we had in mind, he continued, "Peter, the Fuehrer has been waiting for this all along. You just don't know what secret weapons we have ready for this event. I have seen them! They are deadly accurate with devastating power. The Fuehrer is a genius and he did not want to use them until the British and their American stooges became totally involved. This is now the hour. The war will be over in no time."

He walked into Pipsi's room to see the progress of his landscape and was very pleased. While he was in the shop nobody dared to open his mouth. It was as quiet as a morgue. But when he left everybody suddenly got excited. "Do you think there is anything to it?" somebody asked.

"Forget it. Even if they should invent the deadliest weapon, it is too late for them. They cannot destroy the huge Russian front with it, and now Normandy plus Britain and America. Even if they have something really deadly, at most they can cause a lot of damage. It is too late for winning," I replied.

"I hope you are right," came from every side.

"Of course this does not mean that the war is over and freedom is around the corner for us. But Hitler's defeat is now beyond any shadow of a doubt."

We speculated as to the nature of this weapon. Was it gas, bacteria, or something as yet unheard of? Ultimately, however, we dismissed the whole thing as pure fantasy by a deranged, fanatical SS-man.

A week went by. The Allies were consolidating their hold on the coast of Normandy when the news arrived that self-propelled projectiles had hit the heart of London. There was no defense against them. The Germans called it the V-1 weapon, for Vergeltung, or retaliation in English translation. Now we were worried. Was this weapon indeed as powerful as Goecke had described it? He knew something after all! The German paper in Kovno described the damage in London to be as severe or worse than during the height of the London Blitz. If this was true London was in trouble. The outcome of the war, however, could not be reversed by it—but not in the eyes of Goecke. His outlet was our shop. Here he could talk completely freely. Nobody could answer him. He could be even more at ease than with his buddies, where everybody was an agent and could misinterpret his remarks and report him. A day after the first rockets had hit London he was back in our shop boasting. "I told you only one week ago about our secret weapons. Now they are coming. Watch! Britain will now come crawling on their knees asking for peace and then we will destroy the communists! We never doubted the Fuehrer and he came through again with a vengeance."

His confidence in the Fuehrer in the face of overwhelming adversity was truly astounding.

Several days later some bad news came our way. The pharmacist Srebnitski, who actually saved Vera's life by providing her with the much-needed medicine throughout her illness, had left the ghetto only a few weeks earlier. He unfortunately picked one of those ruthless Lithuanians with whom to hide. The unscrupulous Lithuanian reported him to the Gestapo and Srebnitski was taken to the Ninth Fort and shot.

From the fronts the news was encouraging. The Red Army had broken through and the advance of the Russians was quick. We decided to build a more solid bunker in our shop and work started on it in great haste. But the news from the fronts did not stop Goecke from initiating new draconian measures against the ghetto and the camps. First he took away all the civilian clothes from the people of the camps. He then issued them prisoner's garb, making escape virtually impossible. The first time I saw these prisoner's outfits was when Fritz Bernstein from the Aleksotas concentration camp came to our shop to pick up some armbands. We were shocked. This was the way we too would look once Goecke got around to us. With civilian clothing we still felt like human beings, but with this our last semblance of individual dignity and self-respect would be gone.

In the ghetto a block system was now instituted, where every Jew was responsible for the others on the block. If one Jew was missing the chief of the block and his assistants would be shot. In addition these block leaders were to take a count every morning and evening to make sure that nobody had escaped, and had their heads in the noose. All these measures were to ensure that nobody would escape the grip of the Nazis.

Rumors again entered the ghetto that due to the breakthrough at the fronts the camps in Estonia were being liquidated and the Jews were being sent to Panevezys. Indeed, a small transport did arrive there. Again my hopes of seeing Minnie were kindled, but it was too late.

The advance of the Russians was much faster than the Germans had anticipated and panic broke out in Kovno. Lithuanians by the thousands were now abandoning the city. The German civilian administration also packed up and left in a hurry. Only the SS, the Gestapo, and the Sonderkommandos, the groups in charge of exterminating Jews, were left. The guard around the ghetto was now increased even further and large numbers of machine guns were posted around it.

We had one more piece of good news, but it was too late to enjoy it. Russia had entered Rumania, and out of a million Rumanian Jews, they managed to save around three hundred thousand. In our eyes this was a miracle. The German paper in Kovno managed to publish an issue lamenting that three hundred thousand Jews had escaped their deserved fate, since all of them were communists. The proof was that they all had met the Russian troops with songs and flowers! The Rumanian Jews were indeed lucky, only 70% of them had been annihilated. In Lithuania the number already stood at over 90% and was still rising. For us, even the extremely rapid advance by the Russians was too slow.

21

THE BUNKER

A few days after the front broke I went to see Peter and we weighed our options. According to our logic the Germans had three choices with regard to our ghetto: 1. Transport the Jews to the Ninth Fort, shoot and bury us in one mass grave, as they had done in 1941. 2. Retreat in haste ahead of the Russians and leave us to be liberated by the Red Army. 3. Evacuate us to Auschwitz and gas us, as they had done with millions of European Jews.

The first choice didn't make sense in July of 1944. This was no longer 1941; the Germans were retreating rather than advancing. At this point they were trying to cover their tracks. Only half a year ago they were in a rush to exhume all the bodies from the mass graves and have them burned to erase all traces of the mass executions that had taken place there. It was doubtful that they would embark on the same trail again.

As to choice number two, this was totally out of the question. From all we knew, no Jewish ghettos in the East were ever left to be liberated by the advancing enemy forces. We were witnesses to monumental crimes and had to be eliminated. The Germans could not leave people alive who could later produce evidence against them.

This left only alternative 3—evacuation to an extermination camp. The only way to escape this alternative was a bunker, and the only place where we could build something resembling a bunker was in our workshop. The reason was very simple. Not only was it imperative to keep it hidden from the Germans, but it also had to be concealed from the neighbors. Many Jews during the Children's Action had succumbed to pressure and torture by the SS and revealed the locations of some bunkers to the Germans, who then proceeded to clear out the people, sending them to the Ninth Fort to be shot.

We were thus severely limited in our choice. It was better by far to have a poorer hide-out which nobody knew about than the best one which was known to too many. Under conditions where every house was packed with people, it was almost impossible to build a hiding place without being noticed. My house had a primitive setup in the attic, and our graphics shop had a similar concealed space in which we had saved the children of our coworkers during the Children's Action. But these were only good for a short emergency. A much more durable bunker was needed if we were to survive.

The next day we surveyed the building and came to the conclusion that the best place for a bunker was the cold storage cellar below the first floor. The room was reasonably big and could accommodate a fair number of people, depending on who would be going along with us. This earth cellar was located right below the stair. It was deep enough and high enough to move about in and was fairly well insulated from the outside, except for the top, where a hatch served as access to down below. To camouflage the entrance we would have to rebuild the cover, insulating it as well as we could. It seemed that here the children would be safest.

A large amount of carpentry work was required to set up the necessary decoys, accesses, and closures. Fortunately we had two superb craftsmen in the brothers David and Gershon Kahn. They were not only carpenters but also turners and woodcarvers. The job had to be done with the least amount of raw materials, which were almost unavailable. Even if they were available, bringing boards and lumber into the shop would arouse suspicion. We thus decided to approach the Kahn brothers and ask them whether or not they were interested in the project, of course under strictest confidentiality. The Kahns had no bunker of their own and were excited over the project. They moved quickly to implement the job. Only a few workers were informed of the plan and asked to help. Not a single person declined. On the contrary, everybody agreed with us: we were right, there was not much choice but to proceed with all deliberate speed.

We quietly assembled tools and even had lumber left over from the construction of the spiral stair. The trap door to the cellar was removed and a floor installed to cover the hole. An access was created through removable boards in the floor which only we knew existed and only we knew how to open. We started to bring in pillows, blankets, kettles, and bowls. All the latter were filled with water, which had to be fetched from a well in the yard. The amount of water brought in was not excessive, but we hoped that the liberation would come quickly. We estimated that we had enough for about fourteen days, perhaps another day or two. The women prepared bread and crackers and everything was stored in the vegetable cellar. A corner of the cellar containing a few big pails was set aside for human needs. This corner was separated by a bed sheet to give at least some privacy.

When we sat down to figure out who was coming with us, we soon discovered that with all our attempts at secrecy we had twice the number of people that could be accommodated in the vegetable storage. Frantically we prepared space in the crawl space below the first floor. We dug a few pits in remote corners to be used for sanitary purposes. Some of the earth below the floor was moved towards the outside walls for additional sound insulation and leg room, and to provide a little more depth for movement in the tight space below. Within less than a week the whole project was completed.

It was not much of a bunker, but it was better than nothing and, God willing, if the Russians proceeded at their current speed they could be in Kovno within a week to ten days. We could hold out that long.

During the final preparations we decided that the women and the children would be placed in the vegetable cellar. The crawl space was assigned to the men. It was also agreed upon that off and on every man in turn would be allowed to crawl into the cellar to stretch his limbs from the prolonged motionless stay below the floor.

With everything ready, we waited for the signal to move in.

We were not the only ones making preparations. With the breakthrough at the Russian front, the Germans started feverish preparations for our evacuation. The guard around the ghetto was suddenly tripled, with instructions to shoot to kill anybody attempting to escape from the ghetto. All contacts with the outside world were cut off, including the workers brigades who used to work in town. Nobody was allowed to leave the ghetto any more.

Panic broke out among the survivors in the ghetto. Numerous Jews tried to escape through the barbed wire fence, but all of them were gunned down mercilessly while attempting to cross the wires. Some guards offered to let Jews escape in exchange for gold or silver, but after accepting the bribes shot them in cold blood on the other side of the fence. One of the victims was the brother of Dora, who had committed herself to go with us into our bunker.

On 6 July, around noontime, the commander of the ghetto, SS-Obersturmbannfuehrer Goecke, called Dr. Elkes, the head of the council, to inform him about his plans for the ghetto. Since as of 5 July no Jews were allowed to leave the ghetto, hundreds of people had gathered in front of the Jewish council to await events. An air of nervous anticipation was all around us. The tension and anxiety were building steadily. Rumors, mostly planted by the SS-men themselves, were adding to the uncertainty.

After about twenty minutes Dr. Elkes stepped out of the German headquarters and proceeded straight to the council chambers. Bad news was written on his face. Once inside he immediately went into a meeting with the other members of the council. The news was devastating. With a shaking voice he gave the members the following instructions:

"Obersturmbannfuehrer Goecke had just informed me that after three years of existence the ghetto will cease to exist in a few days. On 8 July, a complete evacuation will begin. Since he could not obtain railroad cars for the transport, the Jews will be evacuated by boats and will be brought to the area of Danzig, where they will continue to work as in the ghetto. In fact the workshops will also be transferred, so that many of the Jews will continue working in the same shops. I was advised to inform the ghetto that they are to show up voluntarily on 8 July for deportation. He also stressed that once the deportation is completed, searches will be conducted from house to house and anybody found will be shot on the spot."

Dr. Elkes stopped for a few seconds to catch his breath. The room was quiet. One could hear a leaf drop to the floor.

"My friends," Dr. Elkes continued, "I don't have to tell you that this is no idle threat. We had ample opportunity to see such threats carried out in previous years. We have to send somebody to the graphics department to give them the news, so they may prepare posters to inform the ghetto. As I see it there is not much else we can do. May God help each and every one of us."

A long silence followed this announcement. There were no discussions. This was the end of the road. One by one the members of the council walked over to Dr. Elkes, embraced him, and filed out of the room, depressed and downtrodden.

In the meantime, Peter was called to the council to see Dr. Elkes.

"Peter," he said, "this is the last assignment you will ever do in the ghetto. There will be no ghetto anymore in a few days. All the time we lived in the ghetto we knew that one day it would come to an end. Well, the day is here. On Saturday the eighth, the deportation of the ghetto will start. In three days it is supposed to be completed. There is only one hope; Goecke can not get any railroad cars and intends to evacuate us by boat, which is much slower . . ."

He stopped and did not finish the sentence. An uneasy quiet ensued.

"I only hope," he then continued, "that somebody will live to tell the world the story of the ghetto, the story of one of the finest Jewrys in the

world, whose last chapter we are witnessing now. We have tried everything under the sun to save as many Jews as we could, but this time we
cannot save anybody. Such, apparently, is God's will."

Peter walked straight to the graphics shop with the news. Although we
had expected it all along, when it came it was a shock. Without saying a
word we sat down and prepared the posters announcing the liquidation of
the ghetto. Our final poster!

When the last poster was completed, we took them to the council for
distribution. Outside the people immediately gathered around the poster.
Women started to cry. The men stood petrified and speechless. When the
initial shock had worn off, the people started to comment. "What a lie,
they are going to ship the workers to Germany so we can work there.
They haven't even started to dismantle the workshops. Lies, nothing but
lies! Just to get us to report voluntarily for the so-called deportation."

"They don't even have railroad cars and they want us to believe that
they are going to ship the workshops just for us!"

"Let us not report. They can shoot us here and save us the trip to the
Ninth Fort."

Little by little the crowd started to disperse.

We returned to our shop and instructed all our coworkers who had
committed themselves to hiding with us in our bunker, to show up on 7
July at our workshop and to prepare to go into hiding. No friends or
outside people were to be informed. The people should come one by one,
not in groups, to avoid arousing suspicion.

In Normandy in the meantime D-Day was exactly one month old. But
here in the ghetto our D-Day, D for deportation, had begun.

In my household across from the workshop, everybody was watching
me like a hawk. Would I and my family report for deportation? We could
not hide from them that something was in the works. Although we never
talked about going into hiding, they noticed that we were packing some
things and carrying them out. Often we would hide and whisper in a
corner, so nobody would hear what we were saying. Finally they confronted us with the big question, Were we going into hiding? We could
not conceal the fact any longer. Yes, we were going into hiding. A heated
discussion ensued and it was decided: the Chazans would hide in my
hide-out in the attic space. Rivka would join them; her sister, Sonja, and
Eetke would join me and my family wherever we went. The other families
would go to the attic space in the graphics shop.

Peter did not fare much better. He was being watched by Dr. Burstein
and his wife and when confronted had to accept them into our bunker
too. Similarly the Kahn brothers were blackmailed by a few relatives who

lived with them and they also were admitted to our bunker. Space was rapidly dwindling.

Peter and I decided to enter last, so we could maintain contact with the outside world. The latest news from the fronts was good. Both fronts, the Russian and the Allied, were doing very well. But just as important was the fact that the Germans could not get any railroad cars and evacuation by boat was much slower.

In the evening the SS let ut know that they had enough boats and the evacuation would proceed rapidly, as planned.

Late in the evening we decided to join our families in the bunker.

When we approached the shop we noticed from the distance that a woman was in the backyard not far away from the entrance. This was very disquieting: how could we enter the shop in full view of a stranger? We decided to wait. We turned back and returned ten minutes later, but the mystery woman, like a ghost, was still there. We had to delay our entry again. When after another fifteen minutes the woman was still there, we decided that we had no choice. We could not be seen that late at night on the street without arousing suspicion. We figured that going into our own shop where we had worked for three years should not be suspicious, and we proceeded towards the door. As we approached the house the mysterious woman started to walk towards us. We were startled.

"You are Peter," she said, "and you are Mishelski, aren't you?"

"Yes," we answered, "what seems to be the problem, is there anything you want?"

"Yes," she replied, "I will be very blunt with you. I know that you have a bunker in your shop and I want to join you with my family."

"You must be mistaken," Peter said, "we have no bunker."

"I don't think denying it will help you," she replied, "I have observed you very closely over the last week and your denials won't help."

We still tried to laugh it off.

"But what about the water you carried in, and the lumber, and all the people who entered the workshop today and did not come out. Well, if you continue to deny I will go to the SS in the morning and tell them about your bunker."

The last statement hit us like thunder. There was no use denying any longer. She certainly was capable of going and denouncing our bunker. Then all would be lost. Despite all our precautions we had not been careful enough. This woman knew what she was talking about and her threat was not to be taken lightly. There was too much at stake.

"So what is it that you want?" asked Peter.

"I want a place in your bunker for me and my husband."

"Are you sure that nobody else knows about it?"

"Positively."

"How soon can you make the move?"

"Immediately."

"We will unlock the door and leave it open. Don't go in together and try not to be too conspicuous. Should somebody be watching you, wait for later. We will enter the house after you, wait for us in the hall."

"It is a deal, we will be here right away. Don't try to play any tricks on us. At the first suspicious move we will scream and all will be lost."

"Don't worry, just get going!"

She moved into the dark and we unlocked the door and stepped into the shadow to avoid being noticed. A few minutes later, one by one, they entered our house. We followed them and locked the door behind us.

The dice were thrown.

When we entered the hide-out the Russians were already at the Lithuanian border and only sixty miles from our town. With tanks and motorized divisions this distance could be covered in no time at all. Time was of the essence now. If the SS did not find us our chances were good. However, if we should be discovered, that would be our end.

That night was spent in the workshop. Nobody entered the hiding places as yet. Since the deportation was not due till tomorrow, the eighth, and the ghetto inhabitants were supposed to volunteer, the Germans were not expected to enter the ghetto. Thus for at least this one night we were safe outside. Peter and I whispered some instructions to the group on how to behave and admonished them not to talk, not to sneeze, not to cough. The children were to be kept close, since one sound by them could destroy us all. We explained that the food was extremely scarce, particularly since we had many more people than we had originally expected. Everyone was required to manage with as little as possible. The same was true of the water supply. We had some water, but not nearly enough for everybody. Obviously we would all share what little we had. Should the front move fast enough, God willing, we might be lucky enough to survive. We also explained the arrangements for toilet use and where the holes in the ground were. After satisfying the natural urge, some of the soil next to the holes was to be taken to cover the feces, reducing the amount of stench which might easily be detected by dogs. We concluded the instructions by telling everyone that they would be sleeping on the floor of the shop tonight. Nobody was to get up, for he could be noticed from the street. In the morning hours everyone was to move into his designated place.

For the next hour no one stirred, each deep in thought. What was in store for us and our families? Would anybody survive? Was there hope? I looked at Ruthie. She was so sweet, so smart, as if God had deliberately made her so to deepen our anxiety. She was far more mature than her three years. A normal childhood had been denied her. At three months of age she entered the ghetto with us. Till about a year ago she was still being breastfed. There was no other food available. There were also no children around with whom to play. There was no garden, no swing, and hardly any toys. Poor child! Miraculously she was saved during the Children's Action. But for what? To face deportation and certain extermination? Was God looking down at this child? If so, how could He bring Himself to send her to her destruction? What wrong had she done? How terrible a crime was it to have been born Jewish? She was tired and sound asleep. But would she remain quiet, not to alert the murderers to our hide-out? The lives of all of us depended on the behaviour of these few small children that were saved during the Children's Action.

Peter was equally deep in thought. He was looking at his son, also about three years old. Raanan was a restless child and more difficult to control. He had been born in the ghetto. This restlessness could prove fatal in the hide-out. I could read every thought going through his mind at that moment. A tear showed up on his cheek. He wiped it quickly so Renee, his wife, should not see it.

The mood of the others was no better. Everyone knew that the hour had struck twelve and our fate would be decided within days, if not hours.

After everybody had fallen asleep, I moved to a corner and took a strange contraption out of my pocket. Anybody not knowing what it was would have been hard-pressed to guess. It consisted of several pieces of cardboard clamped together with a thin metal plate in between. Between the cardboard was something resembling a spool of yarn. Tied to it all was a needle and a small crystal. The crystal acted like a radio tube, the piece resembling a spool was a solenoid, and the piece of metal was a membrane. When properly assembled the contraption turned into a radio, capable of receiving the local German station in Kovno. I put the assembly to my ear. The sound was very faint, but sufficiently strong to make out the words. This was the news: The German army was retreating in an orderly fashion. Unnoticed by the enemy, they evacuated a number of towns including Minsk on the eastern front. On the border of Lithuania between Minsk and Vilna, the Lithuanian capital, the resistance was stiffening and the Russians were suffering heavy casualties. Of course, there was no word about German casualties.

I listened to the news and enjoyed every minute of it. For a moment I was not in the ghetto hiding from my would-be executioners; I was on the front with the victorious armies that were smashing the most terrible monster in history. Quietly I told Peter the news. The news was good, but not good enough. If the front should come to a halt we would be lost.

Exhausted from a nerve-wracking day, we fell asleep. But nobody slept well that night. For the first time we had no home, no beds of our own. There were no pillows or blankets, as these were inside the bunker downstairs. Besides, the blankets were used up to insulate the hide-out. There was also no supper. But who wanted to eat anyway?

The night dragged on endlessly, for what seemed like an eternity. Only the children slept. They were exhausted too. They did not know what was going on around them, but instinctively they felt that something was very, very wrong. Fortunately they did not know that these were their last days on earth. At the age of three they were doomed to die at the hands of murderers, who would later deny that it had ever happened. Eetke was only nine, but she had already lived too long according to the German law. These children were the war criminals who had prepared the war against the Reich, the land of Goethe and Schiller.

The sun in the east rose slowly. Golden rays were sneaking into the room as if bringing us good tidings from the outside. The only safe place for standing was far away from the window, along the wall. A few of our coworkers crawled to the interior wall and got up to stretch. Suddenly a smile appeared on their faces.

"Come here," they whispered to us, "come here, fast!"

We crawled to the wall and slowly got up. In the distance we saw a sight which almost made all the suffering of the past three years worthwhile. With smiles on our faces we looked through the window to the road that led up the hill to the Ninth Fort, the fort where at least eighty thousand Jews had been shot and buried in one big mass grave. The last time we looked at the road was a few years ago, when several thousand foreign Jews marched to the fort to be shot. Yes, it was the same road, but what a difference. Long columns of retreating German troops were moving along it. The proud Wehrmacht of the Fuehrer, defeated, hungry, thirsty, dusty, tired, was moving in endless rows away from the Russian front towards Germany. Along with them were thousands of civilian Lithuanians in buggies, on foot, on bicycles, with meager belongings on their shoulders. Where were they going? Well, the Germans were retreating to German soil, but these Lithuanians? Lithuania was their home. Why did they have to run? We could not hide our pleasure and satisfaction. Some of these were the Nazi collaborators who were afraid to be left behind. They knew what they had done and had no desire to get caught by the Russians. They could expect no mercy.

At that moment I was suddenly overwhelmed by one desire: to have a set of binoculars to see the faces of the fleeing murderers. Did they still have those cynical smiles? Were they still as cocky as when they tortured and shot us? Those smiles were probably gone forever. No longer would they have Jews to lead to mass graves, to shoot in cold blood. How trigger-happy they were when it came to shooting defenseless Jews. But now that their own necks were in the noose, they did not want to die!

At the same time, however, I could not get over the feeling that among the people who were running now were also some very decent, God-fearing Lithuanians, possibly even some who had saved Jews. It must have been a deadly blow to them to be forced to leave Lithuania behind. However, their fate was far better than ours. Unless a miracle happened we faced certain death. Theirs was the lot of immigrants in a strange country, Germany, where they were heading now, or any other Western country later.

Despite the transient ambivalence, I just could not hide the overwhelming feeling of revenge when looking at the men on the hill. What a sight! What satisfaction! Even if we should not survive tomorrow, today had brought us fulfillment we never hoped to see with our own eyes.

In the meantime the sun had come out completely from behind the horizon, introducing the Sabbath to the ghetto. There was not a cloud in the sky and a light breeze was playing with our windows. Outside the streets were deserted. Only some Jewish policemen and other functionaries were moving about here and there. Early in the morning the Germans brought some Jews from neighboring slave labor camps to the ghetto. Here they were to join the Jews from the ghetto who were supposed to volunteer to be deported. But the number of volunteers was negligible by any standard. Even the Jews who had no hiding places chose to stay home and await events. When not enough people showed up a contingent of SS men came rushing into the ghetto. Within seconds all of us who were still outside the bunker disappeared from the surface and went into hiding.

One group of SS-men surrounded one large area in the ghetto and went from house to house chasing the Jews who were not hidden into the street. A second group of SS-men split up and scoured the ghetto at random. Scarcely had we closed the doors to our hide-out when we heard two SS-men approaching our house. The door sprung open and they walked in. They stormed through the first floor, ran upstairs, tapped at the walls and the floors, but did not notice anything suspicious. The search took at most ten minutes, but for us in the bunker it seemed like an eternity. Finally they left the house.

With these searches the SS-men managed to clear out a few hundred Jews, but many more were still hidden. On Sunday, the ninth, the SS returned again and cleared out yet another area. Again our hide-out was not detected. On Monday and Tuesday, 10 and 11 July, the searches in the ghetto increased in intensity. The number of SS-men was greatly expanded and their methods became more ruthless. The SS knew exactly how many Jews were still left in the ghetto: half had not shown up for deportation. The orders, therefore, were to use any means necessary and employ any method to get the Jews out.

Again they surrounded an area. While the majority of the SS scoured that area, smaller groups in twos and threes scattered throughout the rest of the ghetto. They used bullhorns to broadcast all kind of messages. At first the messages were merely encouragements to the people to come out, but by 11 July the messages were much more ominous. The most important of these announcements was that tomorrow, 12 July, the Jews who reported for deportation would be taken to Germany to work. The rest would perish. This last message was particularly scary. We all knew about the total destruction of the ghetto in Warsaw and could expect the same here.

The intensified searches coupled with the threats produced some significant results: many Jews were found, and some Jews crawled out of their flimsy hiding places for fear they might be killed during the demolition of the ghetto. When we entered our bunkers we vowed that we would not report voluntarily, come what may. We ignored the warnings, possibly to our own peril.

Once again a team of three SS-men entered our house. Again they knocked and searched without success. All the people in our hide-outs, both upstairs and below the floor, managed to remain calm and kept tight control of the children, who, although terrified, did not produce even one sound.

How many more times would we have to go through this harrowing experience? Where was the front? Why were they so slow? Apparently they had their own timetable which had much more time to spare than ours.

After a much more thorough search than the last time, they left, and we again breathed a little easier.

The sounds from the outside infiltrating our bunker were less than encouraging. By the noise we could judge that the number of discovered bunkers was growing. Suddenly we heard a whole group of marching people. Listening attentively, we realized that this was a large group of Jews apparently from an outside work camp. All the Jews were gathered in the plaza within earshot of our bunker. They were told to sit down on the ground and not to move without permission. All these Jews on the plaza spent the entire night under the open sky, waiting for the morning to come.

I tried to fall asleep but could not. I had barely eaten anything the whole time and had not slept the last several nights. Yet sleep was the last thing that concerned me. The same was true of Peter. It must have been very early in the morning when we both decided to crawl out from below the floor into the cellar at least for a little while. Staying below the floor in the smelly, moist crawl space was getting more difficult by the hour. I took out my homemade radio to check on the news. This was the last I was to listen to the news for a very long time.

The news was mixed. The good news was that Alytus, a town south of Kovno, had just been conquered by the Russians. And if the Germans admitted that over the radio, the town had probably been already in Russian hands for a few days, since the practice of the German Wehrmacht was never to admit a fallen position the same day. That meant that the Germans were still retreating, unable to check the Russian advance. But the bad news was that the Red Army had turned south instead of proceeding in a frontal assault on Kovno. It became clear that the intent of the Russians was to circumvent Kovno and to leave it behind for later, when the front would have bypassed the city. This meant a substantial delay in our timetable, very bad news indeed. After catching a brief stretch, we retreated to the crawl space below.

Wednesday 12 July was supposed to be the last day for the evacuation. It was also the day when the search-and-destroy action of the ghetto was turned over to the notorious Einsatzkommando. This kommando was the group which had exterminated hundreds of thousands of Jews all over the eastern front. They were specialists in their field.

They came with explosives, hand grenades, gasoline, incendiary bombs, picks, axes, hammers, and above all with a large contingent of search dogs, which were trained to attack humans on command and to rip people apart. These were no amateurs. They had done their job in dozens of communities. Human life meant absolutely nothing to them, particularly Jewish lives. This was the army we, the defenseless survivors in the hide-outs, were now to face. All the frustration of their defeat on the fronts would be turned on us.

On the morning of 12 July they entered the ghetto and went to work. We could hear explosions in the distance moving ominously closer. About an hour or so later we started to smell what seemed to be smoke. This was very alarming. Were they setting the ghetto on fire, or was this sporadic fire set up by the explosions? The search party was apparently moving slowly, since the sounds were coming closer to us only at intervals. Nevertheless they were approaching. Suddenly we could hear the barking of dogs and the cries of human voices. Everybody in the bunker was petrified.

Shortly before noon the commandant of the ghetto came to the plaza where the apprehended Jews were sitting and ordered them to get up and to form columns of one hundred each. He took a bullhorn and said, "You are lucky, you were found in time. You will be brought to Germany where you will continue to work. All the others who are still in their hide-outs will perish, they will be destroyed in the bunkers."

We could hear every word he said. The bullhorn carried his voice for quite a distance. Suddenly we heard voices from a house nearby. A door opened and a group of Jews came out. "Don't shoot," they clamored, "we have decided to join the evacuation. We are coming, we are coming!"

Their nerves had collapsed. The speech of the commandant had achieved the desired result. Suddenly another door popped open and a few more Jews came out.

We were hard-pressed to decide what to do. Were the others right to capitulate, or were we in our stubborness to hold out? Nobody moved in either of our hide-outs. The decision had been made.

In the meantime the Jews were set up in columns and started to march towards the gate. There was still a chance for us to surrender. Once they were gone our fate was sealed: no more Jews would be deported, the rest would die in the bunkers.

"They will be destroyed in the bunkers."

"They will be destroyed in the bunkers."

The last phrase of the ghetto commandant kept hammering in our heads. But the die was cast. Life or death—here we stay.

After the last Jew had left the plaza an ominous silence set in. All we heard now was the sound of explosions, the barking of dogs, the yelling of the troops, and the smell of smoke.

Around three in the afternoon the Einsatzkommando was closing in on our house. There were no more Jews on the plaza, and if they were to find us they would shoot.

Twice before the SS had missed us. Would they miss again? The tension was unbearable. Life was at stake. For the past several days our group of men, women, and children had been hidden in a makeshift hide-out below the floor of our workshop, with almost no food, strictly rationed water, and the stench of human excrement in a corner not far away. We were unwashed and unshaven and had not seen daylight in quite a number of days. Most of the time was spent flat on our backs, since the space was too low even to sit up properly. We had to be exceptionally quiet, since every careless move could be heard outside.

The noises from outside kept coming closer. We could not see what was going on but we knew very well who was there. Suddenly somebody in our hide-out coughed. Instantly we threw a blanket over his head. Had they heard us? The tension was growing. No, they had not heard us! Thank God.

Suddenly the door in the building above us opened and the members of the Einsatzkommando entered the room below which we were hidden. We could hear the heavy steps of their boots. We could even faintly hear the conversation. They raced from room to room, but the house was empty.

"Check here," we thought we heard. We could hear the noise of some tools being handled and then the banging of axes, picks, and hammers against a wall. A few partitions were demolished. Studs and plaster came crumbling down, but their search was in vain. Nobody was behind the partitions. For a few minutes the assault on the partitions stopped. They started to walk again.

But their checking was substantially more thorough than the ones we had experienced before. More partitions were demolished, walls checked, and boards in the floor ripped out, but we held still.

We did not worry about the adults. We barely moved. We even tried to keep our breath down. After all, the commandos were equipped with search dogs and could detect even the slightest noise. But children! The children! They were petrified. The mothers took them into their arms, stroked their hair, just to keep them quiet.

So far things were going fine. The search was concentrated primarily in areas which were away from the pit where the children were hidden. But the search did not stop there. Our hearts were beating furiously, pounding almost loudly enough to be heard upstairs. Then the bullies started to walk again.

God, maybe they were leaving the house. They seemed to be heading towards the exit. Could we have been so lucky again? But no! That would have been too easy; once more they moved into the hallway. Here the enclosed spiral stair that led to the floor above, aroused their suspicion. They ran upstairs, searched the premises, did not find anybody, came down, and stopped.

"Break the stair," screamed the commander. Again the hammering and hitting of axes and picks began. Although there was no access by way of the stair to our hide-out, the children were hidden right below it. We had picked this space for them because it was the only place where people could stand upright without having to crawl and crouch. We were concerned that the children, not realizing the seriousness of the situation, might unwittingly bang their heads against the beams above and start crying, producing a sufficiently loud noise to be heard outside.

The banging against the stair increased and the breaking up of boards could be heard below. Suddenly with one big crash the entire stair came down, producing a roar as if a bomb had detonated.

The crash was so devastating that a child began to cry. Its mother immediately threw a blanket over its head, but it was too late. The dogs had discovered the sound and started barking, trying to get to the spot where it originated. Before we knew what happened, hand grenades started raining down into our hide-out. One hand grenade wounded Dvora, Ruthie's grandmother, who instinctively had thrown herself over the child to protect her. Her leg was torn wide open. The grandmother looked at the child and despite the excruciating pain in her leg, managed a smile—the child was not hurt.

"Out with you, damn Jews," yelled a commando. "Out! Out!"

We had lost the battle. Our hide-out had been discovered. But too late. Had we been discovered a few hours earlier, we could have been on our way to Germany with the group that had just left the ghetto. Now our fate was extermination right on the spot. We were doomed.

22

DEPORTATION

The plaza across from the Jewish council was a little over a block square. This plaza was the center of the ghetto. All the news concerning us came here first and was then announced by posters throughout the ghetto. But at the council one had not only the posters but also some first-hand information not available at the other spots. This plaza, although big enough to have served as a playground for children, never had a child on it throughout three years of the ghetto.

In the critical days of 1 to 8 July, the plaza was humming with people. Since the Russian offensive had started on 22 June, people were apprehensive. They came to check whether or not there was any news. When information finally came in on 6 July, the plaza, as usual, was the place where the first announcement was posted. As of 8 July, however, there were no more announcements, nor would there be anymore. The plaza was now simply a place for assembling the Jews and dispatching them to the boats or the trains. On 12 July, noontime, the last contingent of Jews was led out of the ghetto and the plaza was empty.

In the meantime the hand grenades had inflicted total panic in our hideout. Now the women, too, started to cry. Outside the SS were yelling, "Out, get out, or we will throw more grenades at you."

The women had difficulty opening the boards to the entrance, which made the SS-men impatient. "Get the hell out or we will shoot," they screamed.

"Don't shoot! We are coming, we are coming!" cried the women. Finally the boards popped open and the women started to come out. Vera, of course, was slow in moving. This again infuriated the commandos. They started to hit the women mercilessly and incited the dogs to attack. Sonja was manhandled nearly to the point of collapse. Vera was bitten badly in the leg, since she was unable to move fast enough to get out of the way of the beasts. But worst of all was the attack on Dvora. The dogs apparently smelled the blood issuing from the wounded leg. Even the Germans had to restrain them lest they tear her apart completely.

Down in the crawl space I checked with the men. All were ready to get out and surrender except Max and Nolik. We could whisper to each other, since the noise upstairs was so overwhelming that they could hardly hear anything. "I am not moving," said Max. "I will not give them the satisfaction of gassing me. Besides, I am sure that Vera will not come out. She can hardly walk and cannot make it out of the pit."

"But everybody is going out," I whispered.

"So what! We will all die anyway, some in the gas chambers and some here, nobody will remain alive. I prefer to die here with my wife and my child beside me."

"I am staying too," said Nolik, "at least I had the satisfaction of seeing their defeat, something millions of Jews have not lived to see."

This was it. There was no time to get into discussions. Upstairs the women had already left the bunker, but the men were still dragging their feet.

"You men there," one SS-man yelled. "Your bitches are out already. If you are not coming we will greet you with another round of grenades. One, two . . ."

"Hold it," we yelled. "We cannot move that fast down here."

One by one we crawled out of the bunker. After several days below ground we had gotten used to the darkness and the sudden daylight hurt our eyes. Before we had a chance to adjust to the rays of the sun, we received a murderous welcome from the members of the Einsatzkommando and their dogs. "You are finally coming out, you bastards; here is one for you." With that he hit one of the men over the head, opening a big bloody gash. One dog attacked Peter. He then attacked me, caught me by the pants, and tore a big hole near the calf. Fortunately he did not catch any flesh and I escaped injury. The commandos kicked at us with their heavy boots. We were scared stiff. We expected a rough welcome, but this!

The first thing we did once we were out of the bunker and on the street was to search for our dear ones. Where were they? Had they come out? The view was terrifying. Here were our wives, sisters, mothers, bleeding profusely. Their clothes were torn, their faces covered with dust from the cellar, their mouths agape with thirst.

The experienced troopers were watching us with piercing eyes. Their vast knowledge told them that people must be missing. With our looking around and the expressions on our faces, we actually gave it away. But they hardly needed the clues. They knew that in most cases some people tried to remain hidden.

"These are not all, you bastards," the leader of the group yelled. "Who is still missing? Speak up, or we will shoot."

"Nobody is missing. Everybody seems to be here," a voice answered pleadingly.

"You swine," he yelled. "You are lying." He then swung his rifle with all the fury he could muster. The man instinctively ducked and the rifle hit a window, breaking the glass to smithereens. This noise was too much for the children upstairs and they started to cry. Instantly the soldiers rushed upstairs with their guns drawn. They still did not know where the people were hidden, but it was unnecessary. Shots were fired into the air and the people in the hide-out kicked the door open and screamed, "Stop the shooting, stop, stop! We are coming."

All the people from upstairs came out. Nobody tried to hide. The German grabbed one man by his collar and ordered him back in. "Make sure nobody is there. If you lie I will send a bullet straight through your head."

The man stepped in, found nobody, and reported this to the SS-man.

"You had better be right. Your life is at stake." He threw a grenade into the attic. But nobody was there, no sound could be heard. "Get the hell downstairs, you damn Jews. We are not through with you yet."

While this was going on upstairs, my sister noticed that in the confusion we had left Ruthie in the cellar. "Have a look," she whispered to me. "Ruthie is missing."

"You are right. I don't see her," I answered. "How did it happen?"

"Never mind how it happened, I want my child. If we all die, there is no point in her remaining alive. Go and get her."

The SS-men again looked at us and yelled, "This is the last time we are asking. Is anybody else in there? You are all in it together."

"Yes," I yelled. "A child has been forgotten in the bunker."

"Go and get her, you bum. Fast, you hear me!"

I rushed into the cellar, took the girl into my arms, and gave her a kiss. The child was shivering, but her fright was so overwhelming that she did not produce a sound. When I came out with the child in my arms, Vera became hysterical. A push by the butt of the rifle brought her to and she grabbed the child from me.

"Get moving to the plaza, you bastards, and fast," yelled what appeared to be the commander of the group.

We instinctively assembled by families. I joined my sister Vera, Ruthie, and my mother. Next to us were also Sonja and Dvora. The others joined their families and we started to move. Moving was not exactly easy after lying motionless in the crawl space below the floor for so many days. The ones who were too slow were helped along with the butt of the rifle.

"Sit down," we heard the command. "And do not move, or we will shoot."

The statement "or we will shoot" almost stopped scaring us. We got used to it. Of course they will shoot, sooner or later. Maybe it was better sooner, thus sparing us the agony of the additional suffering we were to experience before the end. We sat down and accepted our fate, whatever it might be.

Suddenly my sister turned to me and said, "Where is Max? I don't see him."

"Last I saw him he was behind me. He thought that you both had decided not to come out, because you cannot walk. He thought he would be remaining with you. When did you notice that he was not out?" I asked.

"As soon as we came out."

"Damn! Why did you tell me to go and get Ruthie if you knew he was there?"

"I told you before. If I die I want her to be with me. I am an invalid and I will not survive anyway. Who will take care of her? Besides, he should have come out, too. He must have seen that I was out."

"That he could not do from where we were."

"So he should have checked!"

I could detect a sound of bitterness in her voice. I guess she was right. What would his life be worth if we all perished: his mother, his wife, and his child? How could he do that? But in the confusion of the moment anything was possible. What better proof did we need—we all came out of the bunker and forgot that the child was in there! Wasn't it the height of irrationality? At the spur of the moment he had decided to stay, not knowing who else might do the same, particularly his wife who was partially an invalid. But now it was too late. Revealing himself was risking instant execution. And what about Nolik? His parents and sister all came out and he remained. There was not much sense in his staying either. But in many ways it was more logical than coming out. Wasn't this why we got into the bunker in the first place?

An uneasy quiet ensued. I looked around me and noticed that next to me was Mrs. Burstein, the doctor's wife. Alongside her, on the ground, lay her husband. At first I thought he was asleep, but upon closer observation it seemed to me that he was not moving. No, not only wasn't he moving, he wasn't even breathing! My God, he was dead! Or was he?

Then I looked at Mrs. Burstein. Her eyes were sort of dreamy. She had difficulty sitting up straight and the color of her face was strange. I was afraid that she too was on the verge of death. I grabbed her by the shoulder and shook her a little to wake her up. "Mrs. Burstein, what is the matter, what happened?" I asked.

"They are not going to get us. No way are they going to get us. I am glad we did it, I am glad!"

"What do you mean?"

"They are not going to get us," she repeated again and again. "We both decided to take cyanide. We vowed that we would not be deported no matter what happened. It is better this way."

"You mean to say you both took cyanide?"

"Yes. Anything wrong with that? We both decided it, nobody forced us. I am glad we did it!"

She stopped for a minute, her eyes started to roll, and I thought this was her end. But suddenly a strange feeling came over me. We were all destined to die, too: some today, others tomorrow. How does a person feel when he is dying? Here in front of me was a person possibly taking her last breath. In a few minutes or so she would be gone forever. Why not ask her what it feels like to die? As long as she was still alive, this was first-hand information. I shook her again lightly, turned to her, and asked her point-blank, "Tell me, how do you feel now? Describe it to me."

She turned slightly towards me, a smile appeared on her face, and she said, "I feel so wonderful, so wonderful. It is so good, I am floating in space, my body is so light, it has no weight, and I am so happy, so happy! I could float like this on and on without end. O, God, how good it feels, how good it feels."

I just could not get over it—here her husband was lying dead besides her and she was so happy. Obviously she had lost touch with reality. But what I could not get over was how it was that he was dead and she still alive. He apparently died instantly, yet she was still struggling, albeit with little chance to pull through. Could he have purposely given her a smaller dose or a different pill? He was the doctor and knew what he was doing, she did not. But with his death already a fact and hers imminent, nobody would ever know.

Meanwhile the unending searches were going on. The commandos were satisfied that they had cleaned out our hide-out and proceeded to the next house. It was our former home, where upstairs the Chazans and Rivka Gluck were hidden in my makeshift hide-out. Again they raced upstairs and downstairs, breaking partitions, ripping up boards from the floor. But in this hide-out there were no children, nobody to start crying from all the noise. The search didn't yield any results. About twenty minutes later they left the house. Rivka and the Chazans were safe. Rivka's sister, Sonja, and her daughter were shaking the entire time the search was going on. "God, spare her, spare her," Sonja murmured repeatedly. "Please spare her. At least one member of the family should remain alive."

She was right. Rivka and Sonja had already lost their parents. Sonja had also lost her husband. Here on the plaza she and her daughter were doomed. No wonder she was praying for the last member of the family. When the SS-men came out of the house without having found anybody, tears started to pour down her face.

The family in the next bunker, however, was not as lucky. This bunker was discovered and the people were chased out under a barrage of murderous beatings. They were led to the plaza to join us.

As the day wore on more and more bunkers were discovered and more Jews joined us at the plaza. At the far end of the ghetto we could see some smoke and a few local fires burning. One group was flushed out by the heat and the smoke of the burning building. Some people were covered with soot and ashes, others were bleeding profusely from wounds or bites inflicted by the dogs.

The operation was in full swing, but the Germans were still not happy. They knew exactly how many Jews they had to find and were still far from achieving the goal. New, harsher methods had to be used to get at the rest of the hidden Jews.

Suddenly a junior officer appeared at the plaza. With polished boots and a gun in his hand, he started surveying the area around him.

"You," he pointed at one sitting man, "Come out, you are coming with me."

The man got up, shaking like a leaf. He started to plead, "Don't shoot, please don't shoot, I have a family."

"Shut up, come with me."

The man with the officer disappeared into some of the narrow streets of the ghetto. About fifteen or twenty minutes later a shot was heard. Did he shoot the man? Nobody could answer the question. All we knew was that the man did not return. A few minutes later the officer was back.

"God, don't let him pick me," I thought to myself. I sort of had a funny premonition. Although we knew that we were destined to be executed, I still wanted to live, even if it were just one more day. I avoided his look, thereby hoping to go unnoticed.

"You!" He pointed his finger at somebody.

Nobody moved.

"You," he yelled, "yes, you there. Don't hide your face, I can see you. Get the hell up and come here or I will shoot."

This was it. He was pointing at me. My mother and my sister got hysterical. I got up, walked up to him, and waited for his instructions.

"You follow me," he said.

He turned around and started to walk towards Paneriu Street. On Paneriu Street I had a friend who lived with her family in one of the houses near the fence. I had not seen her and her family since a few days before we went into hiding. I also had not noticed them on the plaza. Had they reported for the evacuation voluntarily, which knowing them did not seem likely, or were they hiding? I did not know. If they had a hiding place she was careful enough not to tell me. We walked along Paneriu Street in the direction of the house which was near the fence. I was trying to figure out what he was up to so close to the fence. Why would he lead me to this place? Suddenly it flashed through my mind: he will tell me to go to the fence and when I am near it, he will shoot me, take a picture, and then claim, as they so often did, that I was shot trying to escape.

Right at the fence he stopped and orderd me to go toward it. I could barely move my legs.

"Now turn right," he commanded.

I turned.

"See the shed? Get into the shed and climb up into the attic space. I want you to check whether or not there are any people hidden, you hear me. Don't try to cheat! It is your head if you tell me a lie. Now move!"

This was a strange coincidence, to be forced to search the very shed occupied by my friends. How did he know to pick exactly this house? There were dozens of houses around, but he, with some unseen knowledge, managed to pick precisely this one.

"Move," he yelled again when I hesitated for a minute. Somewhere in the yard there was a ladder. I fetched it and put it against the wall. I climbed up and crawled into the attic space. It was full of straw, piled rather high for the space, as if purposely put there. Darkness was all around and I could not see anything, but I could not shake the feeling that somebody was hiding in there. The straw seemed to be moving, or was this my imagination? I made no effort to search, but made the appropriate gestures. All I hoped was, God forbid, not to stumble over anybody.

"Mr. Sturmfuehrer, I don't see anybody here," I yelled. "Anywhere else you want me to search?"

"Get down," he screamed. "Get over there," and he pointed to another shed.

Here the case was simple. The shed was definitely empty. I turned everything upside down, pretending to be searching in earnest. "Nobody here, Herr Sturmfuehrer."

"Get going." He pointed away from the fence towards the plaza.

Where was he leading me now? We reached the plaza. He pointed to the plaza and said: "Run, you have had enough."

I could not believe my ears. I was safe. He did not shoot me after all. My mother and sister embraced me with tears in their eyes. But our troubles were far from over. By this time several hundred people had been rounded up and among them were also a few children. The mothers held their children and were caressing and kissing them. Ruthie was exhausted and sleeping and so was Raanan.

Despite all the efforts of the Einsatzkommando the total number of people was still below what they knew existed. Obviously many more were still hidden.

Now Obersturmbannfuehrer Goecke himself decided to get into action. Accompanied by a number of adjutants, he appeared on the plaza in person. Just his appearance alone was enough to send a shudder through the hearts of the people as everybody knew that his presence did not portend any good. Without saying a word he pointed his finger at the plaza, looked at the adjutants, and shook his head. His assistants knew what it meant. They ordered the soldiers to enter the plaza, select all the old and sick people, and take them away. These people knew what this meant for them: they were to be exterminated first. They were no longer useful as a work force and therefore expendable. One of them ran to an adjutant of Goecke's to plead with him. "I am still strong, I can work. I can produce more than some of the young people. Let me stay, let me stay!"

Goecke even did not honor him with an answer. He motioned to one of the soldiers and the man was dragged away.

My sister Vera in the meantime was scared stiff. She was almost an invalid and could only walk with great difficulty. Fortunately, however, her face and body were youthful and unless she had been noticed walking when we were driven from the bunker, no one could know her true physical condition. This was the question tormenting her at the moment: did they notice?

The selection continued. Several times they passed her by. There was hope! Finally the selection was over. The old and the sick were led away from the plaza in the direction of the ghetto hospital.

With this part of the business concluded Goecke now turned to the people sitting on the ground and announced, "All mothers with small children are to take their children and assemble here on my right," and he pointed to the place where they were to go.

This announcement struck like thunder. A few minutes ago he took the old and the sick, and now it was the turn of the mothers with children, again an element which was not able to work to capacity. The entire plaza, not only the women and children, were petrified. Only about four months ago nearly one thousand children were taken out of the ghetto, never to be heard of again. We had a very good idea what had happened to them. The few children now present on the plaza were those saved by pure luck. They had miraculously survived the Children's Action and the recent search by the Germans. Now their time had come. Resistance was useless. There was approximately one armed German for every two or three hungry, tired, unarmed Jews. The women walked over to the place Goecke had just indicated. Fortunately for Vera she did not have far to walk and in the commotion nobody noticed her dragging her feet. The soldiers now combed the plaza to see whether or not all the women and children had complied with the order. All had.

"You will now leave the children here and walk back to your places," commanded Goecke.

"I will not leave my child alone. No, no, I will not. I will stay with my child," one woman screamed in anguish.

"Take care of her," ordered Goecke to one of his adjutants.

The adjutant pulled his gun, ran over to the woman, and fired two shots into the air.

"The third one will go straight into the child, not you, but into the child," he yelled. "You hear me? One, two . . ."

There was no reason to doubt his threat. In the past three years we had seen just about everything. The most vicious crimes had been committed by these barbarians without their blinking an eye. Shooting one more Jewish child would be child's play for him.

The woman clenched her fist and shook it. "God will repay you for it," she screamed. She reached for the child for the last time, gave him a kiss, and fell to the ground. She was dead.

The other women returned to their original places. When some semblance of calm had returned, Goecke turned to them again and said in a cool and calm voice, "Tomorrow morning you will be deported from here to the Danzig area. We know that many Jews are still hidden in bunkers throughout the ghetto. Any mother that will show me to a bunker will get her child back and will be permitted to be evacuated with the child. This is your last chance to have your child back. You have exactly five minutes."

If the removal of the old and sick and the separation of the mothers from the children hit the Jews on the plaza as thunder from a blue sky, this last statement was like the detonation of a hundred bombs. The air over the Jews on the plaza was like a heavy cloud ready to unload a devastating storm. Not all the women knew of hiding places, since all of them were built in the greatest of secrecy, but some did. Among these was my sister Vera, who knew of two, one in which her husband was hiding and the other in the attic space of our house, wherein lay the Chazans and Rivka. Across the plaza was Ruthie, a child like an angel, crying her heart out. Here she was faced with an agonizing decision. Suddenly one woman jumped up, ran to Goecke, and screamed, "I want my child, I want my child. Come with me, I will show you a bunker."

Instantly about ten guards jumped to her side and instructed her to move. Ten minutes later she came back with the guards and a group of Jews, cursing that woman with the wildest maledictions.

"What a bitch," said one woman who was sitting not far from me.

"Shut up," said another one, "you have no children."

Goecke motioned to the woman to go and pick up her child. This doubled the strain on the other women who had children out there. Here was a woman reunited with her child, even if it were for only a short moment. She had her child and there across the plaza were their children crying to high heaven. They were faced with an impossible choice: to trade the lives of other fellow Jews for a few lucky, perhaps fleeting, moments with their children. The minutes were ticking away like hours, but nobody moved.

"Well, if that is what you want," said Goecke, "your grace time is up."

A motion of his hand signalled the guards to take the children away. Vera and the other mothers had their last glimpse of their children. Never again would they see them. In the meantime the children were taken to the building behind the plaza where the ghetto laundry used to be.

The searches were continuing and more and more Jews were brought out to the plaza. Suddenly Goecke was stunned. A group of Jews he never expected to see was brought to the plaza by one of the commanders. At the top of the group was a man by the name of Benno Liptzer. Benno Liptzer was known in the ghetto as the Gestapo Jew. He was the leader of a group that worked for the Gestapo in town and the Gestapo used him for various purposes, not always honorable ones. The man was feared by the Jews in the ghetto since his role was very unclear. The Gestapo considered him their man and expected that he would be the first to volunteer when the deportation was announced. Goecke's sense of honor was hurt. If he, Goecke, promised the Jews that they were being sent to Germany to work, Liptzer should have trusted him and reported for deportation. In fact Goecke had reserved a special role for him in Danzig. He even had a letter prepared for him, introducing him to his new bosses in Germany. This was more than Goecke's honor could take. Liptzer noticed Goecke's face. A short silent confrontation took place. Liptzer knew Goecke only too well and could read his thoughts. "You too, Liptzer? You too?" he yelled.

Liptzer didn't wait. Instantly he slipped a cyanide tablet into his mouth, bit it and swallowed. This infuriated Goecke even more. "You damn Jews are all alike!" He pulled his gun and pumped a few bullets into Liptzer's heart. Liptzer fell to the ground, bleeding profusely. His death was instantaneous. But from what, the bullets or the cyanide? This was now a moot point. He was dead.

The searches continued until dusk, when the search party finally left the ghetto. We remained under heavy guard in the open plaza lit by a bright moon. I could not sleep. Here I was on the plaza, sentenced to die, and right across from me was the place where Rivka was hidden. All I needed was to sneak away to the house and be safe. But how? I thought of crawling towards the house but was afraid of being noticed. In the meantime a group of Jews was permitted to walk over to the well in our yard from which we used to draw water. Quickly I joined the group in the hope of being able to slip away and sneak into the house. But it was impossible. Too many guards followed us to the well. Dejected, I came back to the plaza. I finally dozed off. Suddenly I was awakened by shooting and explosions. The Germans were back to search for more Jews. What tenacity! Columns of smoke started to rise from one corner of the ghetto. The explosions were now no longer grenades but rather sticks of dynamite.

I surveyed the plaza: it looked like a battlefield after defeat. People wounded by grenades were mixed with people bitten by dogs, clothes torn to pieces. Faces were darkened by dust and soot, some reddened and pained by first-degree burns. Many were crying from physical pain, many others from emotional strain and the sheer terror of the moment. All men were unshaven, resembling prisoners of war. A few blocks away lay Moses Rabinowitsch. He had just recently lost a leg trying to escape through the barbed wire fence. The guard had promised to let him through, but when he got entangled in the wires he shot him, shattering his leg. Moses was carried to the hospital where his leg had to be amputated. All in all, it was just one week ago when it happened. Moses was forced to get out of the hospital and join the evacuation. He was in his early twenties, a superb dancer, and one of the most popular fellows in the ghetto. There was hardly anybody who did not know him.

Scattered across the plaza were people dead from exhaustion. A doctor tried to volunteer his help but was rejected by the Germans. Bodies were everywhere, some lying on the ground, others sitting. One had to step over bodies if he wanted to move to the corner where people were allowed to relieve themselves. A short distance away I noticed Mrs. Burstein, whose dead husband was lying alongside her. She had vomited severely but was recovering quickly and looked much better. One woman went berserk and was shot by a German sentry. And the shots and fires in the distance only added to the battleground atmosphere on the plaza.

Around 10:30 AM Goecke came and ordered us to line up in formations of five. The guards started moving us from the plaza. I had a last look at the plaza: Max, Nolik, and Rivka were still safe. My mother and I helped Vera get up and braced her between us. She was able to move, but with difficulty. She was numb with despair. She was particularly sorry that she had told me to go back to the bunker and get Ruthie. The child would have been safe with her father, at least momentarily, but now she was lost forever.

Meanwhile we were led in a direction opposite from the ghetto's exit. As we were walking we suddenly realized where we were heading. At the end of the ghetto was a lumberyard which also had firewood. The yard was under German supervision. From this yard, lumber and firewood were distributed to the ghetto workshops and the general population. A sudden fear overcame everybody. They were taking us to the yard and would then set fire to it, burning us alive, as they had done three years ago with the patients and doctors of the ghetto hospital. People started to panic, but a few shots into the air restored order. We were chased into this yard, the barbed wire gate was locked, and we were awaiting what would follow.

Meanwhile I saw a friend of mine sitting calmly in a corner and shaving. This looked distinctly out of place under the conditions.

"You should shave too," my mother said. "You don't know what may happen. The way you look now you will never be able to escape should an opportunity arise. But if you are shaven, who knows?"

She was right. My friend had no objection. I shaved, combed my hair, fixed my shirt, and started to look a little more decent. Oddly enough, I also started to feel better. But where could there be a chance for escape? The number of guards was far too big.

Around twelve o'clock Goecke appeared again. We were ordered to get up and form columns of hundred each. Off we went, marching towards the gate where only a short while ago I stood watching Ruthie leave and then return to the ghetto.

Everything we had done turned out against us. Here was Vera near the gate, still alive, but without her child. Ruthie could have been safe with the Lithuanian couple. Ruthie could also have been with Max. But instead she was now in the laundry building awaiting tragedy. And we were on the way to leave the ghetto, where we had spent three years of horror and destruction. The chapter known as ghetto Kovno was drawing to a close. We were being deported.

The afternoon of 13 July, when we left the ghetto on our way to the railroad depot, part of the ghetto was already in flames and heavy smoke was rising from the burning buildings. There must have been around eighteen hundred Jews in our group, but another fifteen hundred were still missing according to the German count. These were either Jews hidden in more substantial bunkers which the Germans were unable to detect, or people who refused to come out of hiding and were not caught, like Max and Nolik.

Goecke now surveyed his catch. As he was moving along, he noticed that among the people before him remained some old and sick-looking men and women. He turned to his lieutenants and ordered them to conduct another selection. Everybody old or sick was pulled out of the column and ordered to stand aside. Most people at that point were so resigned that they didn't even beg for their lives.

One of the people selected was Moses Rabinowitsch. He had marched with us from the plaza to the lumberyard and from the lumberyard to the gate on crutches. He was at the end of his physical endurance.

Vera and my mother escaped the selection. Vera was young and healthy-looking and, when standing, nobody could guess that she was barely able to walk. Our column was marching very slowly, which Vera was able to handle, and my mother and I propped her up by her elbows, making the walk easier. Mother also looked much younger than her actual age. She had always appeared youthful and, in better days in Kovno, was never given her real age by anybody. Thus she had no trouble passing the selection.

In the meantime a guard was placed around the people who were selected out. They were then ordered by Goecke to march towards the hospital, where a similar group selected yesterday from the plaza had already assembled. After walking another block or two Moses just could not continue. His physical and moral strength were gone. He stepped out of the column and sat down on the edge of the street and refused to continue. One guard jumped to him, struck him brutally with the butt of the rifle, and yelled, "Get the hell up, you cripple, and keep moving."

When Moses did not answer and did not move, the guard unlocked the rifle, readied it for shooting, pointed it at Moses, and yelled again, "This is it, you damn Jew, if you don't join the group I will shoot."

"Just go ahead," replied Moses calmly, looking defiantly into the eyes of the guard.

Those were his last words. The guard didn't hesitate, he pulled the trigger and shot. Moses' body twisted and fell to the ground, he was dead. Only two years ago he was the life of the party in the home of Lazik, where I first got to know Minnie.

The Jews at the column were appalled. They had witnessed the ease with which a Jew was killed. No court, no trial, no arrest warrant, no justice. And the killer—no accountability, no mercy, no charges for murder, a hero of modern Germany in the twentieth-century.

We in the column actually saw Moses being killed, but it was not just Moses, it was every one of us who was being executed. Every one at this moment saw himself standing and facing the muzzle of the gun. The shot not only killed Moses, but any illusion we might still have harbored that the end of the war was near and the murderers might now think twice, knowing that the day of reckoning was approaching. The shooting had been going on for three years and had not been affected in the least by the losses at the fronts.

Goecke was pleased with what he had just witnessed. He took the bullhorn and let us know the following: "You have just witnessed what happens when you disobey orders by the guards. In a few minutes you will be on your way to the railroad dock. Any attempt by any one of you to escape will end the way you saw. The orders are strict and will be carried out without hesitation. You are being shipped to the Danzig area, as I have repeatedly explained to your Head Jew. You will continue working there as you did here. The fools who are still hiding will be destroyed with the ghetto. In fact you are really lucky. You were not supposed to be evacuated, the last transport was scheduled to leave 11 July, but I did not give up and demanded to be given additional railroad cars for you. Just two hours ago I received the cars I requested. Had they refused you would have been destroyed, as the remaining Jews will be. The ghetto will be totally annihilated. In fact the job has already started, just look around . . ."

With that he motioned toward the ghetto and ordered the guards to start moving. We turned around to have one last look at the ghetto. Parts of the ghetto were burning. The lumberyard was one big inferno. Flames were shooting to the clouds and a heavy black smoke covered the skies which could be seen for miles around. The lumber was dry from the summer heat and fed the flames profusely. I could not get over it. Apparently Goecke was right. We probably had been destined to be burned alive, something that had already been done in the ghetto once. Otherwise why did they take us from the plaza to the opposite end of the ghetto? Then, at the lumberyard, we were kept locked up for hours, apparently waiting for Goecke to return from town where he was trying to get additional railroad cars. If he had been unable to get the cars, it now became clear what our fate would have been. When Goecke finally returned we noticed that something was in the air. There was some whispering between Goecke and his lieutenants. The group leaders were apprised of the new developments and that's when the order was given to start moving toward the gate.

We had escaped death again.

But what was the motive of Goecke to try so desperately to get cars for us? Was he trying to save Jews? Not at all! Goecke had only one interest in mind: it was Goecke himself. Without Jews, Goecke would most likely be sent to the Russian front, and that was the last thing any German wanted. With Jews around he was the great ghetto commander, by saving the Jews he really tried to save himself.

When we started to move, most of the members of the Einsatzkommando left our march and returned to continue the searches and the annihilation of the ghetto. More and more fires shot up from every corner of the ghetto. Shots and explosions could be heard. We could even hear some human voices screaming, but salvos of gun shots silenced them. Things did not look good for the Jews remaining in the bunkers. But how good were our fortunes? Who was better off, we or they? I turned to Vera and said in a whisper, "God only knows who was right, we by going out of the bunker, or Max and Nolik by staying. At least their fate will be decided within days. If the Russians advance fast enough they may be saved. If not, they will be spared a lot of additional agony, which we may have to go through before death will finally free us of all this suffering."

Vera had moist eyes. Her world had crumbled in a mere twenty-four hours. Her husband was in the bunker instead of being alongside her, her child was in the laundry, and she was slowly and with great difficulty moving to a certain death.

But hers was not the only world to crumble—that of Dvora was destroyed too. Not only was she seriously wounded by the hand grenade, but she had lost everything and everybody. Before the war she had borne and raised five sons. They were her pride. In the first week of the war she lost Benjamin and Manny at the hands of some Lithuanian partisans. They were never heard of again. The day the war started Hayim decided to run toward the Russian border in an attempt to escape the Nazis. Whether or not he managed to get across the Russian border we had no idea. She was always sure that he did. But his chances were very slim indeed. Wolf entered the ghetto together with the rest of the family. After the Children's Action he contacted a Lithuanian who agreed to hide him. For several weeks he was hidden in a cellar of this Lithuanian, only to be later betrayed by him to the German Gestapo, who took him and his wife away. They were taken to their cellars for interrogation and were shot in the Ninth Fort. And now it was Max's turn. He was in the hide-out and had refused to come out. She believed in God very deeply and in His mercy and hoped that he would be saved. But at this moment she was all alone: all five sons gone. And to add insult to injury, Ruthie, her only grandchild, had been taken away too. She herself was the only one wounded in the ill-fated attack on our bunker. Her leg was torn apart, red, blue, and black. Without a doctor or medicine it was a question of days before gangrene would set in, if it had not done so already. Her moral and physical pain must have been unbearable, but she did not even cry. Her pride would not let her. She was born a proud Jewish woman and if need be, she would die so. All the way from the plaza to the lumber yard she walked erect despite the pain. During the selection at the plaza the SS had overlooked her. She was again not noticed during the selection at the gate. When the order came to move on, she stayed with us and tried to walk as well as she could on her injured leg.

Suddenly we heard a sustained round of gunfire from the direction of the laundry. Everybody turned automatically.

"Move on," the guards yelled, hitting whomever they caught, "keep going!"

But the people didn't listen. Their eyes were fixed in the direction of the gunfire. Suddenly the shooting stopped and thick clouds started rising from the laundry.

"God, oh God, my Ruthie!" Vera cried out in pain. Renee, too, had to be propped up by Peter. Her son Raanan, was there, and so was Sonja's daughter, and the rest of the children whom we had saved during the Children's Action. The woman who had gotten her child back by betraying the bunker, held her in her arms. She pressed her to her heart, embraced her as if protecting her, and kissed her on the head.

"Move on, move on," the guards screamed, hitting and pushing right and left. Finally the last group cleared the gate.

Our first steps led us through an area of Slobotke which was once part of the ghetto and was now occupied by Lithuanian peasants. Once outside we had a much better view of the ghetto. It was ghastly. The hospital, which could be seen clearly in the distance, was ablaze, with all its patients, the doctors and nurses inside. Some patients were trying to jump through the windows, but were gunned down by the soldiers of the Einsatzkommandos. We could hear from the distance the agonizing cries of people. We didn't even cry anymore at the horrible spectacle. We were too numb from everything we had been through during the last twenty-four hours.

As we moved along the street towards a more densely populated area, large multitudes of Lithuanians were gathered to observe the spectacle of the burning ghetto and to watch the Jews being deported. The reaction of the local population varied from hate to compassion.

"You are still alive? They still didn't get you?"

"They should have shot you before you moved into Williampole and destroyed our homes. See what you did to us, now our homes are being burned to the ground all because of you."

"You had it coming long ago, you Jew-Communists. The Red Army is not going to get Lithuania, the Germans will still teach those godless bandits a lesson."

But not all the comments were so virulent. Some people stood on the sidewalks and wished us well.

"Let us hope that God will not abandon you," said one.

"Don't give up, you will survive," said another.

But the well-wishers were in the minority. Most of the people, and the throng was huge, were just looking on dispassionately.

We tried to ignore all the abuse, but one thing I could not get over was the accusation that it was our fault that their homes were being destroyed. For the three years we were actually forced to live in those houses, we took care of them, as they were our homes during all those years. Now, when the Einsatzkommandos were burning them down in a vicious manhunt to destroy the last remaining Jew, it was our fault that their homes were being burned to the ground. What a twisted logic!

In the meantime we were proceeding towards town. Most of the time we were walking on the hard stone pavement, but occasionally we had to get off the street and move to the sidewalk to permit Lithuanian buggies and wagons to pass by. Most of the wagons were moving westward, towards Germany, fleeing the country. But there were also buggies moving into town, apparently local people who had no intention of leaving. Our neatly arranged columns were disorganized and disrupted by the Lithuanian traffic and we were forced to stop to let them through. As we were standing and watching the endless caravan of Lithuanian wagons, my eye caught a glimpse of one in which a very pretty young girl was sitting. I took a closer look at her and I just could not believe it. Was I dreaming, was this an illusion? The girl in the wagon was none other than my first date in high school, Nina. I rubbed my eyes, looked closer. No, there was no doubt, it was she! She had removed her yellow stars from the chest and her back, had taken off her shoes and socks, and was chatting pleasantly with the Lithuanian peasant holding the reins. How did she get out of the march? How did she get onto the wagon? Did the driver know she was Jewish, or did he assume she was a Lithuanian girl hitching a ride? Nina was blonde, blue-eyed, and very athletic. The question now was whether or not the guards had noticed her. If not, she was safe. The wagon continued to move on and there was no attempt as yet to stop them. I whispered to Vera and my mother in Hebrew to look at the wagon and warned them not to show any surprise, as this would tip off the guards. The wagon continued to move and disappeared into a side street. Nina was safe.

Suddenly my immediate problem became whether or not we too could escape and what do to about mother. Vera and I looked just as Lithuanian as Nina. We were both blonde, blue-eyed, and could easily be mistaken for Lithuanians. I quietly surveyed the area to evaluate our chances. Upon seeing Nina disappear, my mother prodded us to do the same. I told mother that I would not move without her, but she insisted that we not worry about her. It was senseless for all of us to perish. It was far more reasonable for at least one of us to escape the death march. Vera agreed, besides Vera had reached the end of her capacity to walk and could never make it all the way to the train. The decision had to be made quickly. We decided for escape. I told Vera that at the next busy intersection, when there would again be a big jam and the streets would be full of fleeing Lithuanians, we would give it a try.

Our column moved on. We were nearing the banks of the river Nemunas. The street was narrow but widened suddenly at the approach to the river. At this point was the new reinforced concrete bridge leading to Aleksotas. Although we could not as yet see the bridge, we could hear that there was heavy traffic over it. I quickly removed the yellow star from my chest and Vera's back and Vera did the same for me. I was freshly shaven, which proved to be fortunate indeed. Without that, the entire escape could not have been attempted. The biggest problem now was that Vera was weakening fast.

"Vera, you have no choice. You must gather all your resources. It is now or never," I said to her.

"I will try, I will do my utmost," Vera replied.

The column turned around the corner and, as I had expected, there was a big commotion at the bridge.

"Now," I told Vera, "move to the right."

The guards were blocked by a throng of people and our move was successful. We walked aside and mixed in with the Lithuanians. But here, suddenly, Vera's knees started to buckle.

"For heaven's sake, Vera, not now. Hold out!"

But she was finished. Instead of proceeding with the crowd, we were forced to step aside and sit down on the embankment.

"Leave me here," Vera said, "and get back into the crowd."

This was entirely out of the question. Vera would be shot the same as Moses Rabinowitsch was, I could not do it.

"For better or worse, I must take my chances with you," I replied, "and don't try to talk me out of it. If I should survive, assuming that everything goes right, I could never live with my conscience that I had abandoned you."

The column of the Jews was moving slowly ahead and was nearing the end. It seemed that our gamble had succeeded, when the last guard walked straight up to us and ordered us to show him our identification cards.

We had none. We simply were too conspicuous sitting at the bank of the river when all around us everybody was rushing and running for their lives.

I helped Vera to her feet, kneeled down, and told her to climb up on my back. With my assistance she managed to pull herself up and we proceeded in the direction where the column of Jews had just left.

The Lithuanians on the sidewalk were watching this strange spectacle, a man carrying a young woman piggyback and a guard, rifle pointed at us, following behind. We knew the area very well and knew every curve it would make between here and the railroad depot. The road was narrow and winding and with the large crowds rushing excitedly in all directions there still was time for another attempt to escape. Vera was frustrated. Here I was, a young healthy man with a reasonable chance at escape, willing to take the risk and deprived of that last opportunity because of her. She felt terrible, particularly since she had no chance of surviving and would perish anyway, and here she was dragging me down with her. She tried to talk to me. "Tell the guard that you cannot carry me any longer and that you are leaving me. Let him shoot, at least you will have another crack at it."

"Vera, you know that I am not going to do that and your effort is in vain."

"That I will perish we know, so why should you go with me?" Vera insisted.

"Nobody knows what can happen. The train hasn't left yet and the offensive is moving on at full speed. As long as you are alive, we ought to fight on."

By now we had reached about midway to the depot. Suddenly a Lithuanian stepped off the sidewalk and approached us. He walked straight up to the guard and said, "What is the matter with you? Let those people go, they have suffered enough."

"I have my orders and you stay out of it," the guard snapped back.

"Forget your orders! For once be a human being. If they are killed it is not going to help you win the war."

The discussion got a little more heated and a few other Lithuanians joined the unidentified man. The guard became anxious, pulled a whistle, and blew into it mightily. Instantly guards who had already turned the

corner with a group of straggling Jews came running to help their com-
rade. The Lithuanians dispersed in a hurry and we continued on our way.
One more chance lost.

As we trudged forward, I looked into every nook and corner with one
thought in my mind: this could have been a good place to try to escape.
But I had no chance. In the meantime we caught up with the straggling
Jews.

The street to the depot led down hill; and from the top one was
afforded a good view of the railroad, the train, the guards, and the
unhappy lot of humanity, the Jews on their way to the Final Solution. A
huge crowd of Lithuanians were standing and watching the spectacle.
From the high grounds they had an excellent view. Being only casual
bystanders the scene below didn't touch them; for some it was even
entertainment. But to us this was a tragedy. No, what we saw from the
hill was not a tragedy, but a horror show. Here were about eighteen
hundred Jews sitting on the ground, covered with soot and ashes, wearing
clothes threadbare and torn, many bleeding, with pieces of bloodstained
material from their shirts tied around the wounds. Some of them were
seriously wounded and all were totally exhausted from the ordeal they
had been through during the last few days. They had been forced to
march through the entire length of the city of Kovno. Cries of agony and
despair filled the air. There was hardly anyone without bruises or swollen
limbs. Some people were just lying on the ground, unable to sit up. The
Germans were ranting and raving, running around with clubs and whips,
hitting the unlucky lot indiscriminately.

All around the depot were hundreds upon hundreds of guards. Even on
top of the street above, soldiers were guarding the echelon with drawn
rifles. Modern Germany had decided to kill all the Jews of Europe, and
nobody was supposed to get away.

Our group of stragglers was slowly approaching this hell. Where had I
seen pictures like this before? Was it in the movies of the Nazi campaign in
Poland? The picture looked familiar, but with one big exception: this time
I, yes I, was in it!

"Vera," I whispered to her when we approached the depot, "I don't
mind carrying you in, but if you have any strength left in you, you should
walk, the Germans don't have to see you in this shape. Are you ready to
try?"

"I don't know, I have rested a little, maybe I will be able to walk these
few blocks," Vera replied.

I kneeled down and let her get off. Among the straggling people were
also my mother, Sonja, and Dvora. Dvora stayed behind because she
could not move any longer with her wounded leg. My mother and Sonja

stayed behind to help her. Mother was surprised and disappointed to see us back. She was sure we had made it. But she was happy to see us. We could have been shot too. Mother quickly walked over to us and we both grabbed Vera, helping her to walk erect into the depot.

When we reached the depot, we were ordered to sit down. The train was not ready yet. Goecke had received the railroad cars at the last minute. The German army was retreating on all fronts and cars were desperately needed for the evacuation of the troops, but the priority was to ship Jews to extermination camps rather than to save German troops from the advancing enemy.

The locomotive and cars were being assembled as we waited our turn to be loaded on to the cattle cars. The locomotive finally stopped—the train was ready. A big German bully wearing a freshly-pressed uniform, polished boots, and black gloves, took a bullhorn and started to scream out orders. "On your feet, you damn Jews!"

The mass of humanity started to come alive. Even getting up was a chore with all the aching bones and joints.

"Hurry up, you bastards, we don't have all night for you to fiddle around."

Some people had to be helped up. The strain of the ordeal of the last few days was written all over their faces. When the movement was not fast enough, some were helped along by a whip or a club. Finally everybody was up.

The train consisted of approximately thirty-five to forty cattle wagons. Most of the wagons had tiny windows at the top of the car, closed with heavy iron grates, but some were totally without ventilation. Some of the wagons had a little straw on the floor, but most didn't have anything. None was clean or ventilated and the smell in the cars was awful. The door had heavy bars and locks to seal it off so nobody could escape.

The first group of fifty people was counted off and led to the first car. Many people had to be helped into the railroad car by their fellow Jews, others were helped by a good blow from a guard. When a car was full, the Germans didn't care whether or not they had separated members of a family from each other.

"Fifty," announced the guard, "you go to the next car."

Fortunately we all got into the same car. Vera, my mother, Dvora, Sonja, and myself were not separated; small consolation under the inhuman conditions of the deportation. The entire loading process took what seemed to be a few hours. The doors were locked shut. The bar behind was dropped with a heavy bang, and we could hear the click of a key.

Inside we made the best of as inhuman a condition as we had ever experienced. There was not enough space for all of us to lie down. We tried to arrange ourselves so that the head of one got to rest on the body of another. Some curled up their feet to create more space. At least we had a car with grated windows, so the air was half-way tolerable. The window was not big enough to ventilate a car containing fifty people, but there was some relief. I had my head on my mother's chest and Vera doubled up with Sonja. We made a little extra space for Dvora, giving her room to maneuver on account of her now foul-smelling leg. A creaky noise indicated to us that the train had started to move. We were pulling slowly out of the depot. Exhaustion overcame me and I fell asleep as if I were sleeping on a cloud.

When I awoke it was morning. A ray of light was stealing its way into our car. Our train was not moving and we seemed, from all appearances, to be still at the depot. The people in our car who could not sleep said that we had barely moved all night.

A ray of hope, like the ray of light coming through the grate, sneaked into my mind: maybe the road to Germany had already been cut by the Russians.

1. The author at high school graduation, 1936.

2. The author with high school classmates, 1936. Nahum is at far right, the author at far left.

3. Massacre in the Lietukis garage, 27 June 1941.

4. Jews awaiting execution at the seventh Fort, July 1941.

5. Jews moving into ghetto Kovno, July 1941.

6. Barbed wire fence surrounding the ghetto, with a
sign, "Danger to Life," prepared in our shop.

7. Armbands prepared in our graphics shop.

8. Krisciukaicio Street near the corridor.

9. Jews gathering in front of the Aeltestenrat.

10. The ghetto bridge.

11. and 12. The Ninth Fort.

13. Executions of Jews performed by Einsatzkommando A, an official German document.

14. Ghetto Kovno's liquidation by fire,
July 1944.

15. Jews burned to death in the liquidation, July 1944.

16. The burned-out ghetto. Nothing remains but chimneys and crumbling masonry.

17. Corpses of Jews stacked to be burned in Klooga, Estonia, 1944.

18. An American delegation vistis the remains of Dachau camp #1, 1946. The author is second from left; I.F. Stone is third from left.

19. Dachau camp #1, 1946. This underground barracks, here a cow shed, housed 50 prisoners during the war.

20. The author with his mother, left, and his wife, right, at his graduation from NYU, 1952.

BOOK THREE

DACHAU

Dachau, 1933–1945, will stand for all time as one of history's most gruesome symbols of inhumanity. There our troops found sights, sounds and stenches horrible beyond belief, cruelties so enormous as to be incomprehensible to the normal mind. Dachau and death are synonymous.

—Colonel W. Quinn, U.S. Intelligence Officer

23

STUTTHOF

The light sneaking in through the little window at the top of our freight car was getting brighter, indicating that the morning was approaching. Streaks of grey dust showed the path of the light. The air in the car was stale and nauseating. Some people in the car were still sleeping, primarily from exhaustion. I tried to sit up, but could hardly move. All my bones were aching from the night on the hard boards. Every move was painful and strenuous. Come to think of it, I really had not had a decent night's sleep for roughly a week: first I slept in the bunker, then on the ground of the plaza, and now on the hard boards of the cattle car. My mother, more than twice my age, was in worse shape. Vera, not fully recovered from her illness, was not much better off. Sonja was still asleep and Dvora was in severe pain from the deep wound in her leg. Outside, we could hear the tapping of soldiers' boots and some conversation. Somebody in the car could not hold out any longer and urinated in the corner, leaving a bad odor. Little by little, everybody woke up and started to move about. Sounds kept getting closer and we could hear doors opening in cars ahead of us. We heard voices of people getting off the wagon mixed with the yelling of soldiers. We started to worry. Where were they taking the people? Could they have decided to shoot us now? Maybe so, if the road had been cut by the Russians. In this respect the people in the hide-outs were better off than we. They were not under the control of the Germans or Lithuanians and as long as they were not found, they could not be shot. The noise outside came closer to our car. Suddenly a click of a key and a dropped iron bar indicated to us that it was now our turn. The door opened and a breath of fresh air and some daylight entered the stinking wagon. The light momentarily blinded us and we couldn't see anything. But before we had a chance to adjust to the light, we heard the screams of an officer. "Out with you, get the hell out of the car! Move, you lazy pack!"

The people in the car started to move. The younger ones got out first and helped the older ones get off the high platform. When we had adjusted to the light we saw that we were indeed still at the depot in Kovno. Almost every second car held people who had fainted. The rest didn't look much better. The fresh air helped revive us.

The Germans now ordered all the men to cross over to the other side of the train, where they were allowed to relieve themselves in the field. It felt good to be able to do it. I never in my life realized how good it could feel to urinate. When the men were done, they let the women cross the tracks and do the same. The German guards were standing there, watching the strange spectacle and smiling. After we finished, we were told to sit down and wait. High German officers were going in and out of the station, apparently waiting for instructions. To us it meant only one thing: they must be checking whether the road to Germany was still open. Wishful thinking!

This shuffling back and forth from the station took a good half hour. I observed anxiety on the faces of these German soldiers. There was something worrying them. Finally, after long hesitation, the order was given to get back onto the train. The front and rear cars were assigned to the military. The doors of the wagons were left open and two guards took up positions at the doors of each car. Their rifles were ostentatiously loaded and kept in a ready-to-shoot position.

The German border was rather close to Kovno. If we were not intercepted by the Russian advance, we would be in Germany in three hours, a frightening prospect. Our last hopes were rapidly dwindling. The chances of the people in the hide-outs were seemingly improving by the hour. A high German SS-man made a final inspection of the train and was satisfied. He signalled to get ready and jumped onto the first car. A squeaking of wheels indicated that we were on our way. By now, it must have been noontime. The train picked up speed and started to roll as fast as the equipment permitted. It was obvious that they were trying to rush out of Lithuania. As we continued on our way, we heard some artillery exchanges in the distance which kept coming closer. Were these German or Russian guns? As the sounds kept increasing, so did our hopes. We forgot our aching bones, our thirst and hunger. All we could think of was, how close were they?

Suddenly a burst of rifle fire from some cars interrupted our meditation. We looked out. A Jew had jumped from the speeding train through the open door. The guards who noticed him opened fire. The man was hit and remained dead on the embankment. But this didn't stop the jumping. The case was clear: no matter how risky this move was, it was the last chance to save our lives. Obviously, if we were being taken to Auschwitz, then all of us would die. If we were being taken to a slave labor camp, as Goecke had promised, some would survive, but the majority would perish. But jumping did involve great risks. Even if the man were successful in his jump, he still had to escape the guards' murderous fire. Supposing that the guards missed him, now the problem was to evade the Germans and even the Lithuanians, because most of them were anti-Semitic, pro-German, and had in the past denounced many Jews whom they had caught. Absolutely everything had to go off right, before a jump could pay off. But in three hours, even this meager chance would no longer exist: in Germany, the Gestapo was everywhere. These were the thoughts that were now pressuring me. It was now or never!

Before we had a chance to recover from the first incident, a second one occurred. Suddenly a whole group of four or five jumped and rolled over the embankment. Amidst all the shooting, we could see two men get up and run for cover into the heavy brush. This encouraged me. Should I try, too? No one as yet had jumped from our wagon. After the first jump, both of our guards stood with their rifles drawn, watching us and the outside like hawks. Despite the escape attempts, the train did not stop. It kept moving at maximum speed, there was no time to be lost. An hour or so had passed since we had left the depot. The time to make a decision was rapidly running out.

I was still struggling with a host of conflicting thoughts: risk the jump? Leave my family? I was scared to jump, but I was even more scared to stay. My entire life was on the line with this one decision which had to be executed within an hour or less. No second chance! I was gambling; maybe, I hoped, the train would slow down somewhere. At this speed, there was hardly any chance for me, as I was not athletic enough for such a daring move. On the other hand, a slower train could give the guards more time to aim and shoot. My mother suspected what was going through my mind. Silently, with a nod of her head and a look in her eye, she encouraged me to jump. In the meantime, the artillery fire got weaker, indicating that we were moving away from the front. Suddenly the train came to a halt and the guards jumped off the cars. We had reached the German border faster than I had figured. It was all over. We were in Germany, no more jumping, no more hide-outs, no more partisans. We were now totally at their mercy.

We were told to get off, and our feet stepped on the bloody German soil. We were already expected at this station and a meager, but hot, meal was waiting for us. We did not spend much time at this border town and were ordered to continue. Again we boarded the train. When we were all back in, the doors were shut and locked. The guards did not ent·r with us, but rather went to the first and last cars. They were no longer concerned with escape attempts.

The familiar squeaky noise again indicated that we were moving on. The train was moving at a slower pace now. At the next stop, we were again ordered to disembark. It was evening. Once more, the station had expected us and a warm "something" was served. The Germans were in a hasty retreat on all fronts, yet the organization was operating with clocklike precision: the station had been informed about our arrival, the station-master and his workers were ready and functioning as in peace time.

It was night when we re-entered the cars and lay down on the hard boards. When I awoke it was already dawn and the sun was again peering through the grating. It was the same sun, but it was now warming German soil and not Lithuanian. We were miles from our home, far from our Lithuania, where we had seen so many good and so many bad years. An air of fearsome anticipation was in the air. It was exactly a week since we had entered the bunker. What a week! Most people on earth would never in their entire lifetimes experience the anxiety, the fears, the horrors, the degradation, the beating, the frustrations, the humiliation, the destruction, that we had seen in this one fatal week.

The monotonous hum of the locomotive and the regular knock of the wheels added to the depressed atmosphere in the car. We still couldn't get used to the thought that we were now in Germany, the cradle of Nazism, the land where anti-Semitism had been developed into a science and where killing Jews had become an art.

The train slowed down as we neared a station. Abruptly, it came to a halt. Some doors up front opened up and the guards jumped to the platform. We could hear voices in the distance. After fifteen or twenty minutes, the doors of the wagons opened up and the people were told to step out. We were now deep in Germany.

The sign at the station read Tiegenhof, in big letters. Tiegenhof! Where was that? We had never heard of it before. Was it in Prussia?

The platform was spotless and the station, a small masonry building, was clean, with flowers around it. The weather was beautiful, the air fresh and crisp. The guards were chatting and from their conversations we figured out that we were near Danzig, over which the war with Poland had started in 1939. A high German officer entered the station and remained there for a little while. When he came out, we were instructed to line up and to march towards the other end of the platform. Here, a train consisting of open wagonettes from which the seats had been removed was ready for us. We were told to board these wagonettes. When everybody was in, the train started to move. It was clear that within twenty-four hours our fate would be sealed: death, or work camp. By this time, we were so apathetic that we almost no longer cared which one we were destined for.

The trip led through a small village, beautifully located near a picturesque forest. The homes looked like little doll houses, with flowers in front of every home, neat white curtains in front of every window, back yards tidy and orderly. Despite the earliness of the morning, some women were already busy in the gardens and the yards. The peaceful serenity of this place was the most striking contrast to our mood. These were the homes of the SS-men.

As the train turned the corner, the sight changed abruptly: a huge concentration camp, previously hidden from view by the trees, came unexpectedly into full view. Tall, electrified barbed wires surrounded a deep moat, and guard towers with huge spot lights were located every several hundred feet around it. Here were beauty and ugliness, life and death, side by side. My heart started to pound furiously. I was being taken to a concentration camp about which I had heard and read so much. All the gruesome facts about Dachau and Auschwitz sprung forth from my subconscious. This place meant fast or slow death to all its inmates. The first thought I had was to see whether there was a high smokestack somewhere in the camp. This meant the presence of a crematorium. I turned my head and my view suddenly focused on a huge masonry stack: this was it! This was the crematorium! I looked at the other people in our wagonette: everybody's sight without exception was nailed to the chimney. Obviously, everybody knew what we had been told in great secrecy at the meeting. Nobody spoke a word—we were all staring death in the face.

Our train was slowly approaching the camp and in the distance we could see people dressed in prisoner's garb moving about. A few minutes later we were at the gates of the camp, which read in big letters: Stutthof.

We had never heard the name before. That, however, didn't mean much. There were hundreds of camps all over Nazi-occupied Europe that we hadn't heard of. The first thing that caught our eye upon arrival were the guards that were waiting for us at the entrance to the camp. These were highly trained men, all of them were very tall and extremely fierce-looking. Their faces were granite-like, there was no sign of any emotion on them, no smile, not even the twitching of a lip or an eye. They were dressed in black from top to bottom: black helmets, black uniforms, black shirts, and black boots. The insignia on the helmets was a skull and two crossed bones. We had seen many different Nazi uniforms, but this one was new to us. They held their rifles in their hands, ready to shoot at an instant. Everything about them was designed to induce fright in the observer. They fit into the surrounding picture perfectly; the electrified wires, the tall chimney, and their poker-face stares. The train came to a full stop and we were ordered to get off. With knees buckling, we stepped down to the bloody soil of Stutthof. The Austrian soldiers that were guarding us on the last leg of the trip turned us over to the commander of the Waffen-SS, the black animals in human shapes. As the old guard departed, this new guard took possession of us. We expected the worst.

Again we had to line up and march. The gates opened and we were led into the camp, where tens of thousands of innocent prisoners had been gassed and cremated, or worked to death. The world knew about this camp, since any bomber that ever bombed Danzig could not avoid seeing it. Yet, the camp, the railroad to the camp, and the crematoria were never bombed. The world was not interested in stopping the death machine. The world and its leaders simply didn't care.

We were now led to the plaza where the roll call was usually taken every morning and evening. In the camps it was known as the Appell-Platz. Here an initial selection took place. Since we had been through two selections before leaving the ghetto, not too many people were singled out for extermination, but among them were the woman and her child, the same one who had informed on the bunker to get her child back. Among them also was Dvora Solc. We all cried when Dvora was singled out, except her. She proceeded with her head held high, as was her way. Before being taken away, she turned to Vera and said, "Vera, remember this day and tell it to my sons, so they may know when to say Kaddish (prayer in honor of the dead). This is the will of God."

The tears rolled down our cheeks as she was taken away. That was the last we ever saw of this courageous and deeply religious woman, the mother of five sons, and probably the last survivor of her family. She was exterminated that same day in Stutthof. The woman with the child was later taken to Auschwitz with another group of women and children, where they were killed in the gas chambers. How cruel a hoax had been played on her! For the comfort of two extra days with her child, she paid with her own life. The other women in our group, Vera, Sonja, Renee, and many others, had lost their children, but at least they were still alive.

After the selection was over, we were told to move on in the direction leading towards the crematorium. Looking at the stack, many people couldn't help but start to cry. At the end of the camp was a huge warehouse which could be seen from far away because of its size. It was at least four hundred feet long, one hundred twenty to one hundred fifty feet wide, and twenty-four or twenty-five feet high. A huge hangar-type door was wide open and we were led into the warehouse. Upon entering, we were stunned by what we saw! The entire interior, with the exception of one aisle along the entrance, was filled with one huge mountain of thousands and possibly tens of thousands of pairs of shoes. Mixed with the shoes were eyeglasses, wigs, braces, artificial limbs, human hair, dolls, doll dresses, toys, and other items. We almost fainted at the sight of this. It was clear that these were items taken away from Jews who had been exterminated in this peaceful countryside. The crying and moaning increased significantly as more and more people entered that room. When everybody was in, we were told to sit down in the aisle and wait.

My mother sat down next to me, crying bitterly. "Why didn't I send you to Palestine or America when there was still time? So many of your friends left Lithuania in time. Why did I hang onto you for so long?" she cried. "We had enough warning, we knew from the newspapers what was happening in Nazi-occupied Europe. Why did we wait? Why didn't we do something about it? Money was no object."

"Mom, it is too late to think back now. It is all over. That's where our shoes will be tomorrow," I said and pointed to the mountain in the center of the room.

"I cannot help it. I feel that it is my fault, I wanted to have my children near me. How selfish of me," she cried. It tore my heart out. "Don't blame yourself, Mom. You were not the only one. Almost everybody remained in Lithuania, just think how few really left."

"Dr. Elkes sent both his children to London. He warned me. Why didn't I do the same?"

"But Dr. Elkes and his wife stayed in Lithuania. If they had this premonition, why didn't they leave too?"

"Yes, but at least they saved the children and I did not."

My mother asked me to move closer so she could touch me for the last time. Vera was also sitting nearby. She was not talking. Her world had ended with Ruthie and Max. There wasn't much left worth living for.

But my mother refused to be consoled. The load on her chest was too heavy. "I hope that you kids don't hold it against me."

"Mom, what difference does it make now? Why should we hold it against you? You did what thousands of other mothers had done. This was the will of God and who are we to challenge His ways? Tomorrow by this time we will be up there," and I pointed to the sky. "We will be reunited, all of us. I have only one prayer: that death in the gas chamber should be as fast and as painless as possible."

I barely finished my sentence as German SS entered the hall and announced that all men had to gather at the garage doors. We were being taken to the showers.

Panic broke out at this announcement. Some men tried to hide in the mountain of shoes, but were chased out and beaten by the guards. We all said good-bye to our loved ones, lined up where told, and marched out of the warehouse.

It was already late, the evening of 15 July, when we lined up for our march to the showers. We were walking in the direction of the crematorium. The road led through part of the camp, which to an outsider might have looked like a peaceful town. The camp was immaculately clean and most of the inmates were already inside. On the way, we passed the sick quarters, known as the "revier." People who could no longer work were transferred to the revier and from there to the crematorium. They were expendable, of no further use to the Nazis. The Reich needed only healthy slaves, not mouths to feed.

The door to the revier was open and we could look inside. What we saw was unbelievable: live skeletons were standing or walking around inside. These people had only bones and skin on them, no muscles, no fat, no meat. Their heads looked like skulls of the dead, with eyes nested in large sunken holes. Their heads were shaven and every bone projected. Their hands and legs were just two sticks and their hips protruded with a big hole in the back and absolutely no buttocks. We had never seen people like these before. Who were these people? How did they get to be so emaciated? None of us from the ghetto was fat, to say the least, but we looked like giants compared to these creatures.

"These people probably have tuberculosis or cancer," I thought to myself. It did not occur to me that not so long ago these were healthy, normal people, who had been run down to their present miserable condition by overwork, by being underfed and severely mistreated. Little did I know that in the course of the next nine to ten months, I would see hundreds upon hundreds of these miserable, wretched, formerly normal human beings. The old concentration camp inmates already had a name for them: they were called Musselmen. Once a person was debilitated to this point, he was beyond recovery. They were lost: either they expired naturally, or they were taken to the crematorium and burned, sometimes even alive.

The sight of those Musselmen had a devastating effect on me. I was almost glad to be going to the gas chambers rather than to reach a state like that.

After a short march, we were led to a plaza in front of what was supposed to be the bath house. Here we were told to sit down on the ground. Now, for the first time, I was all alone. I had lost my father in the beginning of the war. During the liquidation of the ghetto, Max remained in the hide-out, and now I was separated from my mother and sister. Lost and forlorn, I started to look around. Simon and Nathan were sitting just ahead of me, but they didn't see me. Behind me, not too far back, was Nahum with his father, and way in the back was Peter, also all alone. Many people were sitting and crying quietly, some were praying, but most were staring impassively into space, waiting for the inevitable. The plaza was brightly lit by floodlights, which reinforced my belief that the world knew all along about Stutthof. We were kept on the plaza for what seemed like eternity. Suddenly, an SS man appeared in front of our group and announced through a bullhorn, "In about fifteen minutes you will be taken to the showers. All your clothes and belongings will be taken away from you and you will receive striped prisoner's garb. You cannot carry any articles into the showers. The only thing you are permitted to carry through are your glasses. Leave all you valuables in front of you on the ground. In fifteen minutes I will be back."

A murmur went through those assembled. Maybe we were really going to showers, or was this another way to put us at ease, so we would not resist? We were physically and mentally so destroyed that resistance was the last thing on anyone's mind.

Little by little, people started to take off their watches and put them on the ground in front of them. Some people had some gold rings, gold coins, and other valuables, which were put away as told. Some people swallowed small gold coins in the hope of recovering them later if this was indeed a shower. Others were trying to dig holes in the ground, hoping that if they should ever be back on this plaza they might find these valuables. They tried to memorize where the location was for possible future reference. Since I had nothing, I observed what the others were doing. Suddenly, as if bitten by a snake, I cringed. Simon and Nathan were digging a hole and cleaning out their pockets to hide their jewelry, which they had said they could not get to. God Almighty, I felt such disgust, such revulsion that I was ready to scream. They hadn't come up with that gold for Vera when her life depended on it.

But I barely had a chance to recover from the shock, when the SS-man appeared again and told us to get ready. We were now going to the showers. He counted off a number of people from the front row and told them to line up and move to the gate. The gate opened, the people walked in, the gate closed and they were gone. We had no idea what was happening to them. Soon a second group was led through the gate. Again the gate opened, the people disappeared behind it, the gate closed and the people vanished. Nobody was coming out anywhere, people were only going in and disappearing. After a few hours my turn came. With knees buckling I followed the crowd that was moving ahead of me towards the gate. I was walking like a sleepwalker and I awoke only when the gate slammed behind me. Once inside I found myself in a rather big room, poorly lit and with cold concrete floors. A few Polish prisoners of war were in charge. They had whips in their hands and they were yelling and ranting like maniacs. "You will be entering the showers in a few minutes. If you still have anything in your pockets take it out and drop it on the floor and get undressed and move fast, we don't have all night for you here."

I had nothing in my pockets but a postcard-size photograph of Minnie, which she had given me as a birthday gift. The inscription on the back was a short, two-sentence expression of love for me, written in French. More than anything in the world I wanted to keep this picture. I had treasured it throughout all those years in the ghetto and I always kept it with me. I undressed, but kept the picture in my hand to have another look at this sweet face, at those dark eyes and that friendly smile. I almost could hear her giggle.

"Drop that picture!" I suddenly heard a voice, and a fiery slap in my face made me drop the photo. "Get going, this is not a place for romance."

When I turned around to have a last look at the picture, I got a kick in my behind and I moved in a hurry out of the path of this Polish attendant, or "capo," as these and other men in charge of prisoners were called. The capo now chased us into a second room. This room was brightly lit, with tiled walls as in a shower, but there were no shower heads. Inside the room were a number of gynecological tables. Men were lying on them and screaming bloody murder. A number of capos were holding the men with force on the tables and others with large knives and other utensils were doing something to them. From the screams we thought that they were being castrated. During the last year in the ghetto we had heard a lot about medical experiments on concentration camp inmates and we also had heard that many Jewish men were being sterilized. We were all stunned and petrified.

There was total panic. The capos got irritated and started hitting with their whips right and left whomever they caught. One by one the men who were finished were chased from the table and the next one was forced to climb up under heavy blows. Again the screaming began, and our blood froze in our veins.

Finally my turn came. Once on the table, I realized what was going on: the men were receiving examinations to find whether they had not hidden any gold in their insides. The examination was extremely rough and painful. The capos did not have any patience and could not care less about the lousy Jew on their table. After the examination, the men were shaven all over. The shaving was not any less painful than the examination and cutting and bruising was common. Hardly anybody escaped unhurt.

After the examination and the shaving we were given a small piece of rough, sandy soap and told to proceed to the shower. Here the water was cold and only came in a trickle. But at least it was water and not gas. We barely had time to start washing up when we were told to proceed to the next room. We ran, dripping wet, into what was the storage room. Here we were given new striped uniforms, striped hats, and socks. We barely had a chance to put the uniforms on when we were again chased through a side door to the outside. We were now on the rear side of the bath house and this explained the mystery why nobody ever came out when we were in the yard.

Behind the building were hundreds of pairs of shoes. Another Polish capo told us to select a pair and to move on to the side. Some people were trying to find their own shoes, but they were not in this pile. The shoes were first examined before given to other prisoners. When some of the people took too much time selecting a pair of shoes, they were murderously beaten. Under this pressure many people selected shoes which were either too small or too big, or completely torn. Among the shoes I noticed a pair of high boots in fair condition and nobody seemed to want them. I decided to take them. They fit my feet and I was pleased. "It will be good in rainy weather and during the winter," I thought to myself, but what did not occur to me was, that it was summer now and during the summer they could be a nuisance. I put on the shoes and moved aside.

Little by little, more and more people were gathering on our side. By the time our entire group had cleared the showers, it was already morning. We had passed another night without sleeping. When we started to go back to camp, another group from afar was approaching the road leading to the bath house. Our group was stopped and we waited for the other group to pass us up. When the oncoming group came closer we saw that it was a group of Jewish women. We were not sure whether or not these were from our transport. We were trying to find familiar faces in the crowd, when, suddenly, I heard somebody yell, "Vulia, Vulia, look here! Vera, Vera, here is Vulia, he is alive, they did not send him to the crematorium, he is alive, he is alive!"

In the crowd I noticed my mother waving at me. Vera had also noticed me and she too was waving. "Mom, don't worry," I screamed back, "you are going to a real shower, this is not the crematorium!"

Vera was walking between my mother and Sonja. They were holding her by the arms and helping her to walk. But our reunion was very short-lived. I barely had a chance to wave them good-bye as they were gone. Who could know whether I would ever see them again.

When the column had cleared the road, we were led to the camp. The inmates of the camp were Jews from all over Europe, but there was also a large number of Christians, primarily Polish prisoners of war and resistance fighters. But being gentile and racially Aryans, they had it much better than the Jews. They were capos and in charge of the entire camp inside. We were now assigned by the capos to a barracks and told to grab a bunk. I moved quickly to be together with Nahum and his father. We were looking for Peter in the crowd, but could not find him. By the time we noticed him it was too late to join him. Without giving us a chance to rest, we were chased outside and told to line up. Two capos informed us that we would now be registered and asked whether there was somebody who wanted to do the job. It did not occur to me that this was an opportunity to sneak into a comparatively easier job. A man from the crowd jumped out and reported for the assignment. He was given paper and pencil and put at a table. A long, drawn-out registration began. By noon, the registration was complete. We were then given a spoon and a metal plate and proceeded to the kitchen. The meal was a meager soup which tasted awful. Despite the terrible hunger, Nahum could not swallow the stuff and gave it to me. I was so hungry that I did not care how it tasted, I closed my nose and ate both mine and his portion. For the next several days our activity consisted of marching through the camp, or running, if the capo so decided. The preferred exercise of the capos was keeping us lined up in the field all morning and ordering us to alternatively remove our hats and put them back on.

"Muetzen ab, Muetzen auf," hats off, hats on, was the exercise we had to perform for hours on end. And if somebody was not fast enough, he was mercilessly beaten.

It was then that I realized how clever the man was by volunteering to help to register the inmates. He did not have to march with us, but rather was indoors in the "office" preparing lists of the new inmates. It suddenly dawned on me that being in the office was one way to survive. But it was too late. Since it was not yet clear whether we would remain in Stutthof or be sent on deeper into Germany, I concluded that having a pencil and paper might be advantageous at some future time. One evening, when nobody was looking, I stole a pencil and a few sheets of paper from the office and put them into my pocket.

In the meantime 20 July rolled around and rumors flew around the camp about an attempt on the life of the Fuehrer. The Polish capos were very excited and so were we. But as more news about the assassination attempt started to come in, it became clear that the Fuehrer was not hurt and all the plotters were in custody. Just as our hopes were kindled for a fast end to the nightmare, they were dashed. It was not our luck to be rid of the monster so easily. The next day we were moved out of our barracks and transferred to another one. How surprised we were to find a group of Lithuanian Jews who had been brought here before us! We were glad to see them and to know that other Lithuanian Jews besides us were still alive, among them some Jews from Kovno, who had been deported to Riga.

A day or two later we were informed that we would be leaving Stutthof for an undisclosed place in Germany, where we presumably would continue to work.

In the morning we were brought to a large storage room and told to undress in the middle of the yard. For a while we stood naked and waited. The only thing I did not give away was my pencil and the paper, which I hid in my boots. A few capos came out and told us that before we left the camp we had to return the new uniforms. We were to proceed past the storage and obtain other clothing. The clothing we received was atrocious, torn, dirty, and often infested with lice. A friend of mine, an engineer, received a pair of pants having more holes than fabric and everything was hanging out. If it were not so tragic, the view was really funny. When he asked to exchange the pants, he was murderously beaten. Nahum, his father, and I were relatively lucky, our prisoner's garb was half-way decent, by camp standards. As we passed by the storage we noticed Peter and we quickly joined him. We were finally all together. Peter had contracted an infection in his leg and it was badly swollen. Around noon, when we were told to assemble at the Appellplatz, we had to help him walk. A short while later we were led back to the wagonettes and back to Tiegenhof. In Tiegenhof we were turned over to the regular SS and were once more loaded onto boxcars. In the evening we left Tiegenhof, now on a new journey, to where, only God knew.

24

OUR GAMBLE

The squeaking of the wheels indicated to us that the train had started to move. Only a week ago we were in a similar train, but how different it was this time around. First of all we were now in Germany with absolutely no chance of escape. Secondly, we were separated from our families. Thirdly, we were now real prisoners, with heads shaven, dressed in prisoner's garb. In the ghetto we still had a home, no matter how bad, it was still one's own corner with a member of the family around on whose shoulder one could cry. One still had a bed, a pillow, a blanket, an extra pair of shoes or underwear to change. That no longer existed. If the shoes should fall apart or the shirt rip on your body, there was nobody to mend it, there was nothing into which to change. Should it ever rain, we would still be wearing wet clothes. In the ghetto the opportunity still existed to trade belongings for food with Lithuanian peasants. Now we had no more belongings. But there was one thing which was even worse: we had seen a concentration camp for the first time in our lives. We had seen the tall stack, the mountain of shoes, the murderous capos, the rotten food, and worst of all, we had seen the Musselmen. Was this awaiting us?

A sudden jerk and loud screaming voices ripped me out of my sleep. Where was I? Where were my mother, my sister, Max, and Ruthie? What happened? I could not concentrate. I felt a pain in my back and could barely move. Outside, rumbling noises like locks being unlocked could be discerned. It seemed as if huge doors were being opened. Then screaming could be heard, which was coming closer. Suddenly the door of our boxcar opened. Blinding light entered the space. "Raus! Raus mit euch!" (Out! Get the hell out!) It was easy for them to scream "Raus," as they were able to move. But our bodies were stiff from a seventy-two-hour train ride in a cattle car with hard boards below our aching backs. Blinded by light, aching all over, hungry, and thirsty, we made it out of the car as well as we could. I was so numb that I wasn't sure whether or not I had been hit.

The terrible reality quickly awakened me. Little by little, I started to realize what had happened. Yes, I now recalled, mother and Vera noticed me when I returned from the showers. We were then taken to the train. On the way we passed the bungalow with the Musselmen, which now came back to me in its full horror. We were then thrown into the cattle cars and shipped in an unknown direction. The train moved slowly, occasionally changing direction, even turning back when the roads were impassable due to damage from bombing. For three days we were moved about Germany until we reached this place, in all probability our final destination. Thus reoriented, I quickly scanned the area to see whether or not there were tall chimneys around the place. A tall chimney meant a crematorium and thus possibly Auschwitz or another annihilation camp. The Nazis had plenty of those. When I did not see any chimneys, I felt a little relieved. One, however, could never be totally assured of anything. When we arrived in Tiegenhof, no chimneys were visible either, but as soon as we reached Stutthof, there they were, driving a chill down our spines.

After carefully listening to the station master and the SS-guards, we were able to put together the details. We were in Kaufering, a small town in southern Bavaria, about four miles from Landsberg and about forty miles from Munich. Recalling geography, I had a fair idea where I was. Landsberg, located on the river Lech, was the notorious town in the citadel of which Hitler had written his book *Mein Kampf* in the year 1924. And Munich, of course, was a major town in Bavaria. According to the guards, we were headed from here to a labor camp called camp number two, which was under the jurisdiction of Dachau.

Dachau was the first concentration camp in Germany, established in 1933 for the purpose of eliminating Jews and political opponents of the Reich. This was a notorious camp, famous for its brutality; its medical experiments and had been widely written up in world literature. We were now under the command of Dachau and who knew for what purpose we had been brought here? What dreadful word, Dachau! The name alone was enough to strike fear in the hearts of everyone. As a high-school student I had read a lot about Dachau, but never in my life did I imagine that one day I would be a prisoner here. The prisoners I had read about were always the "other people," far removed from my tranquil life. How quickly had this tranquility changed! Now I was one of those other people, possibly destined for medical experimentation, more terrifying than the gas chambers.

The sound of a whistle and the command of an SS-man woke me from my thoughts. "Move up, form a line, you dirty Jews!"

When one did not move fast enough, he was helped along with a few blows. When the line was formed, we were given some warm soup. When we were finished eating, we were ordered to form columns of one hundred each and to start marching. One hundred per column, wasn't this how the Jews were led to the Ninth Fort to be shot? Were we being led to a forest with ready-made ditches? But if this were true, why did they have to transport us all the way to Bavaria? My only thought was that Max and Nolik were right not to get out of the hide-out. Whatever happened to them, they didn't have to worry about Dachau.

Once the columns were ready, we got the order to start marching. I was not sure what date it was. During all these train rides and the stopover in Stutthof, I had lost count. My best estimate was that it was 26 or 27 July. The day was hot and cloudless, the sun beat down mercilessly. The road was rough and dusty and sweat ran down our backs and foreheads, collecting dust and entering our mouths. Our ragtag army resembled columns of prisoners of war, which we had seen so often in news chronicles of the Polish and French campaigns. About midway, my feet started to hurt. The boots that I had selected in Stutthof with my mind set on fall and winter when they would be useful in the mud, snow and frost, were too big and were rubbing my heel. As the march progressed, the pain got worse and I felt that I had a blister on one heel and the beginning of another on my other foot. I decided to pull down the boots and proceed barefoot. When I got my boots down, I saw that I had indeed rubbed the flesh off my heel, which was hurting fiercely. But barefoot, it was even worse. The road was unpaved and the stones cut into the flesh, making new wounds in the sole of the foot. My feet started to bleed. I decided to put the boots back on. As I looked at our column, I saw quite a few people walking barefoot. We were all wearing shoes that did not belong to us and we all had the same trouble.

Our camp destination was near Landsberg. Finally we turned off the main highway and entered a narrow side road. If it weren't for the fact that this was a slave labor camp belonging to Dachau, the surroundings were beautiful. On one side of the road were fields and small hills, and on the other, a thick forest. The air was clean and far in the distance, barely visible, were the Bavarian Alps. The camp itself was nested in the woods with trees surrounding it on three sides and the road on the remaining. Around the camp was a double row of barbed wire with high observation towers at each corner manned by armed guards. A wide gate separated the road from the camp. Inside the camp was one prefabricated wooden building to the left of the gate, and one on the right. The building on the left was the kitchen and on the right the office. Behind the kitchen was a foundation which apparently had been poured for a basement of a future building. Inside the camp was a large plaza surrounded by Finnish tents, reserved for us. In the center of the camp were a few more prefabricated structures which were washrooms and toilets. On the left of the road was a group of much neater prefabricated houses, around which the guards were milling. These were the houses of the guards and the administration of the camp. A little further was a small valley surrounded by low hills.

We were led into this valley and told to sit down. I was happy to finally be able to rest for a minute and attend to my bleeding feet. In the valley was a mass of humanity, approximately two thousand of us, and on the top of the hills, a large number of SS guards with drawn guns. The view was not very reassuring: too many guns were pointing at us. At first I didn't care about it, as I was preoccupied with my feet. Suddenly a terrible commotion occurred at one end of the valley. People were running towards the road and screaming, "Save yourself! This is a trap! They are getting ready to shoot us!" A terrible panic gripped that entire corner and was rapidly spreading to the other areas. People started to get up with the intention of running.

"Sit down, or we will shoot," the Germans yelled. Several shots were fired over our heads. Most of the people, now really scared, watched in panic what would happen at the corner where the entire commotion had started. A group of SS-guards ran down the hills into the valley, started beating the rebellious group and finally got the mob under control. As it turned out, a few people in the mutinous corner were survivors of a massacre who, a few years before, had managed to escape a mass extermination of Jews. To them, the entire setup was too reminiscent of the massacre: Jews in a valley, unarmed, surrounded by a large contingent of armed SS guards with guns pointing at them. They saw a plan to kill the Jews and they did not want to wait until the actual shooting started. The people around them realized that this, indeed, looked very much like a trap and a preparation for a massacre. They too, started to run. A commotion ensued. The Germans were caught by surprise. They did not expect this. Fortunately nobody was killed and the mob was quickly brought under control. During this commotion, I noticed that one Jew in striped prisoner's garb took charge of the situation and managed to calm the frightened people. He also dealt with some German, who was in charge. On closer observation, I recognized the man. It was Fritz Bernstein, who only recently had been in our shop to pick up some armbands. In fact, he himself still had our armband over his sleeve. This was fortuitous. Should he, indeed, be in charge of the camp, our connection with him could prove valuable.

An hour or so after the mob had quieted down, we were instructed to get up and reassemble in groups of one hundred. We were counted and led into the camp. Here, we were issued a towel, a blanket, a bowl, and a spoon, and led to the tents. Further along, we were given a hot soup which was mostly water and were told to establish ourselves in the tents. Within, there were some straw sacks on the ground, arranged in a circle. Each one of us chose a place and quickly fell to sleep after the exhausting ordeal.

I don't know how long I had slept when a shrill whistle pierced the silence. It was time to get up for roll call, which was to become a daily routine. Bernstein was already on the site directing traffic. Several other people who had been his assistants in the camp in Aleksotas aided him in this task. We stood in our groups of one hundred and awaited the expected registration. I looked around, but did not see anybody writing down the names of those in our group. I did not hesitate. Quickly I stepped out of the line-up, confidently walked up to the front, and started writing down the names of the people. I had nothing to lose. If someone noticed that I was self-appointed, the worst that could happen was that I would get hit and ordered back into the line-up. It was worth the gamble. The pencil and paper I had put in into my boots in Stutthof now came in handy. I moved quickly, efficiently and with a great deal of self-assurance. The people in the line-up did not question my authority. Bernstein and the others were busy lining up the rest of the people and the Germans assumed everything was on the level. I quickly registered my group and quietly proceeded to the next row. By the time I had finished registering two hundred people, Bernstein approached me. He recognized me immediately.

"Mishelski," he said, "how many have you registered?"

"I have two hundred," I replied.

"You know," Bernstein said, "I did not realize you were in this camp."

"Yes, Mr. Bernstein, Peter is here too," and I handed him my two lists.

"Then what are you waiting for?" he snapped, "find him, I can use him!"

I ran to the center of the gathered throng and screamed as loud as I could, "Peter, Peter, come here!" When there was no response, I ran through the other rows. Finally in one of the columns a hand raised slowly. I ran to him and told him, "Peter, Fritz Bernstein wants to see you. He is in charge of this camp!"

Peter stepped out and followed me. When we reached Bernstein, he turned to Peter and said, "I did not know you were here in this camp.

Mishelski told me about you. Go to the office near the gate and copy these lists neatly. The Germans like that. And you," he turned to me, "prepare as many lists for Peter as fast as you can. Hurry."

This was an unexpected development. I ran to the next column and feverishly proceeded with my task. Looking around, I noted that Bernstein's assistants from Aleksotas were also registering groups. Obviously, a relatively protected office job was at stake here and I wanted to make sure my part was done exceptionally well.

After the registration in the field was completed, we returned to the office. There Bernstein had already appointed his assistant from Aleksotas, a man by the name of Joe, to be in charge. It was clear that his position was secure. The important question, however, was whether a camp of two thousand people could be run by one man. Obviously, early on, more than one helper would be needed. Later Bernstein might be able to manage with only one. But excepting the office job, the camp was being organized now and practically all the other positions were still open. At this stage of the game, Bernstein could help us get a desirable brigade, perhaps even as capos within them, or as block elders. Two weeks hence, none of these jobs would be available and we would find ourselves in the miserable position of slave laborers in the various commandos, if we were no longer needed in the office. It was now in our best interest to establish warm and friendly relations with Bernstein and to be as visible in the office as possible.

It was a major gamble. We were not in the same bargaining position as the others who collected lists for Bernstein. They had been associated with him in Aleksotas, a major advantage. But our one inalienable advantage was in the quality of our work. The lists prepared by us were superbly done, unmatched in penmanship by the others. Bernstein was elated, and chose us for the assignment of copying all the lists. He was eager for the job to be as perfect as possible and to have it completed quickly, so he could present it to the German commander and take credit for it. This gave us the opportunity of staying in the office, at least temporarily. When the lists were ready, Bernstein grabbed them and ran to the German commander.

The German command consisted of the Lagerfuehrer (head of camp) SS-Sturmfuehrer Haffner; his assistant, Rapportfuehrer Schreyer, and Schreyer's assistant, Rottenfuehrer Helmanowitsch. In charge of the guard was first sergeant of the Wehrmacht, Otto Haug.

Haffner was a big man with broad shoulders. His face, the broad cheeks, military posture, penetrating eyes, immaculate uniform, complete with polished boots, reminded me of Goecke. They seemed to have been taken out of the same mold.

Schreyer, on the other hand, was a rather devious type, looking for trouble. Smaller than Haffner, with no outstanding features, he was always on the move, snooping around and trying to look important.

But the biggest surprise was Helmanowitsch. He was a Lithuanian of German descent, a so-called Volksdeutsche. On the first day he was recognized by a man by the name of Shalkinski. The latter and Helmanowitsch had been coachmen for a Jewish brewery in Kovno before the war. He even spoke Lithuanian.

On the other hand, Otto Haug, the commander of the camp guard, was never a member of the SS (although he wore an SS uniform) and in peacetime he had been a ballet teacher in Stuttgart. Around forty-five years of age, he was completely grey with a reddish face and a rather pleasant expression, as if asking, what am I doing here?

Bernstein was on the way to the camp commander, Haffner. Haffner accepted the lists and was surprised to see such a professional job. He complimented Bernstein on a job well done and asked for another copy for the headquarters. Bernstein was glad that the camp commander was pleased. We immediately began to prepare a second list. Bernstein decided for the time being to keep both of us in the office and to assign his other assistants to other duties. Joe remained in charge. This initial foothold was what we were looking for, hoping to make ourselves indispensable. I and particularly Peter were never short of ideas of what the camp could use in services which we could provide.

The days passed and the camp was divided into blocks. Each block had a block elder assigned who was in charge of his one hundred inmates. It was his job to account for each inmate every morning and evening. He was in charge of distributing the food ration, of caring for the weak, of keeping his tents clean. But most importantly, he was to see to it that all people in his block reported for work and use force if someone attempted to shirk this responsibility. This was a good job. The block leaders did not have to go to slave labor work outside the camp, which was almost like a death sentence. Besides, by handling the food distribution, there was always something left for them.

Following the division into blocks, the outside commandos were organized, and each commando had a capo assigned to it. They themselves did not have to work, but were required to urge the people to work hard and often would try to prove to their German masters how devoted they were by abusing their own people. While this job was not as good as a block elder, it was a far cry from being a laborer in the field. As the commandos were finally set up, all the jobs as capos were also assigned. For better or worse, Peter and I had to come up with ideas to ensure our presence in the office. Otherwise, our gamble would have misfired and we would end up as workers, a fast shortcut to destruction. The work in the field was worse than anything to which the ghetto had been exposed. Not only was the work itself much harder, but the treatment was worse, and there was no home to return to where one could at least rest up for the next day.

The worst brigade of all was the construction firm Moll. Moll was building a huge underground hall to house the Messerschmitt airplane factory. The work continued around the clock with two twelve-hour shifts, day and night. Completion of this was urgent, since most of the factories had been bombed out by the Allies and the Nazis were under severe pressure to relocate these factories in order to continue the war. This work, seven days a week, week after week, of mixing, delivering, spreading, and finishing the concrete for twelve hours at a time, particularly at night, was beyond the endurance of even the strongest man. Besides, the rations provided for the laborers were ridiculously small. In addition, these slaves had to march three or four miles daily to and from work in shoes that did not fit. They would return totally exhausted, barely able to eat the watery soup that awaited them. But even this was not all. When the Germans needed some workers during the day anywhere in or outside the camp, they would simply wake those poor characters and chase them out to work again. When they came back from this assignment, it was time to go to night shift all over again. Needless to say, this was a death sentence under the most cruel conditions. It was better to be shot than to die under these circumstances. But the owners of Moll and their German foremen could not care less. For them, it was simply a free labor force.

Another notorious brigade was the construction firm Holzmann. This commando, except for a few specialists who worked indoors, was not much better than Moll.

Other commandos worked unloading trainloads of cement and building materials. One commando worked unloading trainloads of potatoes. None of these were easy, but some were better than others, and people lasted there longer.

To stay in the office we now needed ideas. My first suggestion to Peter was to draw a plan of the camp. That was the way our association had started in the ghetto. In the ghetto, of course, a plan was a necessity. Here, in the confined space of the labor camp, of what use was a plan? But we sold the idea to Bernstein. After all, all barracks looked alike and there had to be a way of identifying them. Bernstein agreed. I went into the camp, paced the entire layout, and brought the sketches to Peter. We sat down to draw up the camp without any tools. To make circles to represent the tents, we used the bottom of a round pencil which we carefully traced. A piece of lumber from the incomplete basement was our straight-edge. Meticulously we drew up the plan and Peter lettered it in beautiful script. Bernstein had another field day when he presented it to Haffner. Haffner showed the plan to Haug and now the latter also wanted a plan. Not only did he want a plan of our camp, but he wanted a plan of his army barracks as well. This was a big leap forward in our plans to strengthen our foothold in the office. We convinced Bernstein that we could use one more man to prepare all those plans and Haffner agreed! We immediately called in Nahum and told him that we had succeeded in getting him a temporary job in the office with us. Nahum had already tasted a few days in the field and he was overjoyed. All he could say was, "Thanks! Three weeks of what I had been doing could have spelled the end for me."

This was only the beginning of our ideas. We next suggested to Bernstein that every commando leaving the camp needed a pass certifying who the capo was, where the working place was located, and how many people were leaving the camp. This would serve as a check upon returning. Peter designed a form for such a pass and once again Haffner accepted it. Now we had work galore. Just preparing those forms, which were all made by hand on a daily basis, took all three of us several hours. Next Peter convinced Bernstein that we had superb craftsmen in the camp who could be utilized to make gifts for the Germans, as we had done in the toy workshop. By now Bernstein was ready to listen to anything we had to suggest. Within a few days we had provided the brothers Kahn with a job in a workshop in Landsberg. They began making all kinds of small gifts for the camp commander. Next I helped two former neighbors of mine. The first was an expert in leather works, and he became the shoemaker in the camp. In reality, however, he fixed and made ladies bags for the wives or girlfriends of the German command. The second was a house painter by the name of Sam Kagan, whom I set up as a camp painter. Both jobs were sheltered, which in itself was invaluable under the camp conditions. But occasionally they even earned an extra piece of bread for work which they did for the inmates, which meant the difference between death and survival. Both men were extremely grateful to me. "Mishelski," Sam said once to me, "I hope only that one day I will be able to repay you in kind."

We also tried to set up Pipsi doing some painting, but we did not succeed. The best we could do for him was to give him a brigade, where he became the capo. We now had everybody from the graphics department provided for. The other fellows of our shop were in camp #1, several miles away from our camp.

This then became our routine: in the morning, we got up at five o'clock and the entire camp assembled on the Appellplatz for a roll call. Often this lasted a long time, since the figures had to add up and account for two thousand people. This roll call was repeated in the evening, which was torture for the people who had just returned from the field, exhausted and barely able to stand. But our day did not end there. We had to work until all daytime brigades were back from work and until every night shift group had left the camp. This generally lasted till ten o'clock at night, or even later. This was an extremely long day, but it was far better than working outside in the field brigades.

Our neat penmanship and graphics were noticed by the German command, and the German supply officer requested that Peter be assigned to work for him. The chief of the guard, Otto Haug, first sergeant of the Wehrmacht, requested that I report to him as soon as all working brigades were out of the camp. Haffner agreed to both demands and Peter and I now had double duty to perform, both inside our camp and outside of it. We were set up far better than we could have anticipated when we entered the camp.

Our gamble had paid off.

25

CAMP #2

A dark night descended on the survivors of ghetto Kovno in camp #2. After surviving countless Actions, pogroms, and executions, these last remnants of Lithuanian Jewry were again faced with death through hunger, cold, slave labor, and mistreatment. The ration consisted of three hundred grams of bread, one slice of cheese or terrible-tasting blood sausage, which was supposed to last the whole day. In the evening, upon entering the camp, watery soup devoid of meat or fat was distributed at the gate. This ration was not enough for a child, let alone for a grown man performing hard labor for eight to twelve hours daily under the open sky. After work, the people came "home" to a dirty hut and slept on the moist ground. The apparel was one pair of prisoner's coveralls and a pair of shoes, which were often either too big or too small. On hot days there was no shelter from the sun. On rainy days the clothes got wet and remained so for the next day's work, as there was no place to dry them and nothing else into which to change. At night, even during the summer, it got cool, and the one blanket which every prisoner got was not enough. And when the fall and winter approached, we froze.

On the jobsite the workers were murderously beaten when they slowed down. To make matters even worse, lice suddenly appeared in the camp. The lice were apparently picked up with the dirty clothes received in Stutthof. In the Kovno ghetto, despite the congestion, people desperately tried to maintain cleanliness and personal hygiene and we did not know what lice were. This was a monstrous plague. Once one got infested with lice, one could not get rid of them. There was no laundry or delousing center and the inmates had no change of clothes. These lice tortured the body and created wounds which did not heal.

When we noticed that some people were stricken with lice, we reported it to Bernstein. Since we were working for the Germans, we could not afford to have lice and bring them into the German barracks. The problem was brought to the attention of Haffner and anyone in touch with Germans was transferred to a clean barracks away from the main body of the camp. Cleanliness and body hygiene were just as important as food, and we now became a real elite in the camp. Not only did we have better working places and improved living quarters, but we were even allowed to grow our hair, which set us apart from the rest of the camp. In the new barracks for the select personnel, we were joined by the electrician, the cook, the messenger boy, a youngster by the name of Berl, Joe from the office, and several others. Bernstein did not join us; he had set up quarters for himself in the office bungalow, behind a screen.

The addition of the cook to our barracks was a stroke of luck. We quickly became friendly, and every evening when the food was distributed to the camp inmates, after giving some additional portions to the especially hard-working brigades, he scraped the leftovers from the sides of the kettle before washing it and distributed this to us. This, in fact, was the best food in the camp, because the leftovers on the sides were all solids. Occasionally I would sit in the evening in the barracks and contemplate how strange life was. The last few months in the ghetto, when I slept on a table in a room which I then shared with ten people, I dreamed for a speedy end to this misery. Yet here I was, sleeping on a bunk with hardly any straw under my sides, sharing the bungalow with twenty people, but I was happy. In the ghetto our food situation was difficult, but we managed to scrape together a menu by trading with Lithuanians; here, even with the cook's supplement, we had less than in the ghetto, but I was glad. In the ghetto, when an emergency situation forced us to work late into the night, we grumbled. But here, when we worked from early morning till late at night every day of the week, we were fortunate, the others had it immeasurably worse. God, how lucky we were!

The camp was still in the organizational stages when one day two German prisoners from Dachau proper were sent to our camp to assist us in the registration of all inmates. Under their supervision, we registered the entire camp anew and every prisoner obtained a number for identification. The numbers were not tattooed on the forearm, but were written on a tag attached to the prison garb. I registered as a housepainter and received the number 84490.

The effects of malnutrition were now slowly becoming evident. The first thing I noticed was the unusual swelling. Suddenly dozens of people had the outward appearance of having gained weight, particularly in their faces, which became round and puffy. It did not take long for these people to die from malnutrition. And yet we were still fortunate. The weather was good, there was almost no rain in the early weeks in the camp, and there were no extremes of cold or heat, which made suffering easier. But soon this was to change.

During the early fall several hundred women were brought to our camp. These were Jewish women from Hungary who at first had been transported to Auschwitz, earmarked for annihilation. At Auschwitz, during the summer and fall of 1944, two hundred to three hundred thousand Hungarian Jews were gassed and cremated. But even with the huge capacity of Auschwitz with all crematoria in full swing, when six thousand Jews were murdered daily, the influx of Jews exceeded the capacity to kill. Separated from their families who had been sent to the gas chambers, these women were shipped to Bavaria, to our camp. They looked terrible. Their good dresses had been taken away from them and they were wearing dirty rags. Their heads had been shaven and the fear of Auschwitz was reflected in their eyes. Most of them cried incessantly. Their demise had come so suddenly that they had no time to adjust to the new cruel reality. We, at least, had had three years to "prepare" for our ordeal. All these women could talk about was the families they had seen chased to the gas chambers. Some were lamenting parents, others husbands, brothers, and sisters. Most of them wished they were dead and had no desire to cling to life.

I looked at these women and saw my mother, Vera, or Minnie. Where were they now? How badly abused were they? Were they still alive? If so, did they look as miserable as these creatures in female disguise? My mother, always the perfect lady, immaculately clean, well-groomed, if she was alive, did she wear such rags? My mother in rags, what a thought! Were Minnie and Vera working as maids, or on an airfield, digging ditches? But there were even darker thoughts. How could Vera, an invalid, still be alive? Surely she must have been among the first victims during a selection. And, of course, mother would not leave her alone and probably was destroyed with her.

The weather was getting progressively colder and the Germans decided to replace the Finnish tents with a more "substantial" underground habitat. These new structures consisted of a trench dug in the ground, which was the corridor. The earth on each side of the trench was covered with a thin layer of straw and constituted the beds. The roof consisted of two prefabricated wooden frames assembled like a gable and covered with sod. Bad as these were, they protected the people from the wind, which the Finnish tents had failed to do.

To alleviate the clothing problem, the camp command brought wooden shoes and some "winter" clothing. They were all placed in storage and released daily to us for distribution. Every day Nahum and I picked up some of those clothes and distributed them to the people. I took a pair of wooden shoes for myself and was glad to be rid of the boots, which I thought would be so helpful to me.

The Jewish holidays were now approaching and the mood in the camp became terribly depressed. On this Yom Kippur, everyone fasted. The Germans could not get over this. Here were people dying from lack of food and hard labor, yet they were ready to work, to suffer, and not even to take a drop of water. The evening before the holiday, after work, groups of people assembled in various barracks and prayers were recited from memory. The people who did not remember the prayers repeated them after the announcer, who recalled them by heart. There was not a dry eye in the place. Some people collapsed from exhaustion and nervous tension and had to be carried out to their bungalow.

The number of deaths in the camp increased daily and our ranks were thinned to a point where many brigades were short of people. Several days after Yom Kippur the Germans sent in two hundred Czech Jews, all of them professionals that had been removed from their homes just days or hours before, like the Hungarian Jews. They were all dressed in their Sunday best, looking totally out of place in the camp. Who knew what tale the Germans told them when they were taken out of their homes, to cause them to dress so immaculately. As soon as they entered the camp they were accosted by Schreyer and immediately sent to the night shift at Moll to replenish the ranks of the brigade, which was losing people like flies. Two weeks later half of them were dead, and within three weeks just thirty or forty of them were still alive.

People were rapidly turning into Musselmen. The vision we saw in Stutthof quickly became reality in our own camp. These people were now "useless" in the camp and Schreyer decided to get rid of them. One particularly cold morning in the autumn, he carried out a selection. All Musselmen were separated from the more healthy individuals. When all the commandos had left the camp, he ordered them to undress and climb into the unfinished basement behind the kitchen. In this space, they were kept for hours and hours, waiting naked for what would happen next. The morning was extremely cold and numerous Musselmen simply expired. The rest were given blankets to cover themselves and were marched out of the camp, where a few trucks were waiting for them. These trucks took them to the railroad station in Kaufering, where they were shipped directly to Auschwitz.

As the number of dying was increasing, an order came to extract the gold teeth from the mouths of the victims. The dentist of the camp had the honor of doing the job and Helmanowitsch and I were assigned to witness the proceedings so that no gold would be stolen. The bodies were naked and emaciated and in many instances the jaws were so frozen that the dentist had a hard time prying them apart. Even Helmanowitsch, a hardened SS-man, got sick to his stomach and could not take it. Neither could I.

I only recorded what the dentist told me. The record along with the teeth went to the German command for forwarding to Berlin to Funk's Reichsbank. Ultimately I spoke to Haug about it and asked him not to release me from his office to perform this duty. He obliged, and from then on, somebody else was assigned to witness this sickening outrage.

The weather got colder and rains began. There were days when up to fifteen people perished of cold, illness, and hunger. At this rate, in four months there would be nobody left. After the morning roll call, when all the commandos were out, the block elders had to deliver the corpses to the gate, where they were loaded on carts drawn by other barely alive prisoners and dumped in a ditch behind the camp. The chances were that the prisoners who now pushed the death wagon would soon be on one. One day, on the way to Haug's office, a group of camp inmates were pushing the cart with the corpses to the dump. Suddenly, a barely audible voice came from one of the bodies on the cart, "Please don't bury me, I am still alive, please!"

There was so much fear in this jittery voice, it made me shudder. Helmanowitsch turned to the cart and started laughing. It was comical to him that a corpse should talk. The Jewish inmates stopped and wanted to take the man off the wagon, but he was dead. He died from fear, being fully conscious in his last moment that he was in the process of being buried alive. For weeks this scene persecuted me. I was terribly sorry that I ever witnessed it.

It was one of my more pleasant duties to distribute clothes to the wretched humanity which crowded my window each evening. Among the items we had in stock were towels. Many people used those towels to wrap themselves up to keep their bodies warm. But these towels would not hold and kept slipping down. Since there were numerous tailors in the camp, some people decided to cut up those extra towels and make pants out of them. They paid the tailor with a piece of bread for his work.

I decided to do the same. Word reached Dachau that inmates in all the camps were doing it. One day, a surprise check was made in camps #1 and #2 and five young men were caught with those pants on their bodies. Those from our camp were transferred to camp #1, where they and the other "criminals" were locked up in a bungalow awaiting what the verdict from Dachau would be. The next day the verdict was in. All five were to be hanged in the open square as a reprisal for destroying government property. All five were hanged the next morning and kept twenty-four hours on the gallows to let the rest of us "know what government property meant." That same day I threw my pants into the toilet.

A few days later, Helmanowitsch caught Hirsh Shimens with a pair of such pants. Enraged, Helmanowitsch knocked Shimens to the floor and began kicking him with his boots. Shimens curled up on the ground and covered his head with both hands. "You criminal," Helmanowitsch kept shouting in his rage, "you have no respect for government property. I should report you, too, so you would be hanged as well. Be happy that I have some compassion or you would be hanging now." And as an expression of his unusual compassion, he mercilessly kicked him with his boots. Finally his rage subsided. He gave Shimens one last kick and yelled, "Disappear from my sight as fast as you can, before I kill you." Shimens got up and ran for his life. I will never know how, after such a beating, he was still alive and able to run.

One day in the fall Haffner ordered the guards at the gate to check the workers from the potato brigade when they returned from work. A friend of mine, Misha Tartak, was apprehended with potatoes in his pockets. This was stealing government property. Haffner's sentence was that the entire camp was to assemble at the roll call site, form a circle, and witness Tartak receive twenty-five lashes with a leather belt on his naked seat. The punishment was administered with exceptional ferocity by one of the guards until Misha's behind was one big bloody mess. But Misha would not give Haffner the satisfaction of begging or crying. During the entire ordeal he stood his ground without uttering one sound. The men on the plaza were petrified and winced with every blow, but not Misha.

In the middle of October we received some very bad news: one of the finest, most dignified personalities, one of the most prominent physicians in Lithuania, Dr. Elkes, was dead. The man who had led the ghetto through its most tragic days succumbed to the terrible conditions in camp #1. All the Lithuanian Jews in all camps around Dachau met the news of his tragic death with deep sorrow. But this was not the only bad news. With total disbelief we found out that Bobby from our graphics shop had also died. Bobby was a cheerful, happy, healthy youngster, barely twenty

years old. It was incomprehensible that such a young man should succumb so fast to the rigors of the camp. But this was Dachau. Once one got
into a bad brigade, he was doomed.

On the fronts things were going great. In August the Allied troops
landed in southern France. Rumania, now free, declared war on Germany. By the end of the same month Paris was liberated, Paris, the home
town of Minnie, whose image was always with me. In September Bulgaria
joined Rumania in declaring war on Germany, and Finland signed an
armistice with Russia. By the middle of September the German border
was reached at Aachen and the Moselle. Yet the war was far from over,
especially for us.

My situation was relatively good, but it was always in the back of my
mind that should I ever lose my position, I was doomed. Three weeks
were enough to destroy a much stronger man. Two events almost made
this nightmare come true. One of Helmanowitsch's favorite block elders
had made it a habit to annoy me. To endear himself to Helmanowitsch, he
abused the people of his block fiercely, which I could not stand and I let
him know it. His habit of insulting me got under my skin and one day
when he entered our office and again heaped abuse at me, I made a
threatening motion and hit the inkstand. The walls got splashed and the
office looked like a mess. Bernstein, alerted by the noise, came running
into the office. When he saw the mess, he screamed, "Out, I am through
with you! You are joining the night shift today!"

Everybody was stunned. People tried to calm Bernstein down, but to
no avail. In one second of bad luck, I now stood to lose my life. When I
saw that no amount of cajoling softened his wrath, I ran to Haug. After
hearing me out he calmed me down. "Don't worry," he said, "you are
still working for me and Bernstein is not going to take you from here."

With this he walked over to Helmanowitsch and told him about the
incident. Helmanowitsch immediately went to Bernstein, quickly told
him to take it easy, called in our camp painter, and ordered him to repaint
the office. Within an hour the office was freshly painted and my position
was not only saved, but enhanced. Bernstein now knew that Haug was
behind me and would defend me. I had survived a major crisis and came
out smelling like a rose.

During all the days in camp I carefully guarded my eyeglasses. Without
glasses I could not carry out my job. Every night I was watching them.
One day I was extremely tired and broke the frame. Fortunately the
lenses were intact. I was terribly upset, but it could have been much
worse. The lenses could have been shattered. With no alternative, I found
a wire and twisted it around the frame to allow the glasses to sit securely
on my nose. Of course they looked terrible, but as long as the glasses

served the purpose, no harm was done. This incident registered in my subconscious. One night I had a nightmare that a man broke my glasses. I woke up in a cold sweat, checked my glasses, convinced myself that they were all right, and went to sleep. This nightmare repeated itself three times. Unbelievably, next day a man came to our office. The man had some fingers missing on both hands.

"Mr. Mishelski," he said, "it is unbecoming for a man in your position to wear glasses that are tied together with an unsightly wire. Would you let me fix them?"

This was spooky! I just had these nightmares about my glasses being broken and here he was with his proposition to fix them. What a weird coincidence! I was not about to give him my glasses to fix, especially since his injured hands did not seem to have the needed dexterity to do such a job. Unceremoniously, I dismissed him. The dream was still much too vivid in my mind. Several days later he appeared again. He now even had tools and parts needed for the repair.

"Mr. Mishelski, why are you worried? This is a simple job, nothing can go wrong."

By now my dream was already receding. Indeed, how silly was it to believe in dreams. After some pleading from the man, I took off the glasses and handed them to him. "You better be careful," I said.

He took the glasses, the tools, and the part he needed for repair and tried to loosen the screw, but it would not budge. A little impatiently, he applied more pressure . . . That did it! I thought I would die. The rim cracked and the lenses dropped out.

I was terrified. The thing I dreaded most had now happened. I castigated myself. Why did I ever permit this man to touch my glasses? Couldn't I have foreseen that a man with missing fingers could never do such work? And what about that peculiar dream, wasn't it warning enough? I did not believe in dreams, but the coincidence was frightening. I was so upset I started to shiver. When Nahum walked into the office, he was astounded to see me shivering and without my glasses. When he saw the broken frame in front of me, he realized what had happened. He tried to calm me down and suggested I go to the infirmary. People were dying there by the dozens and some of them must have had glasses which the doctors there must have kept.

This suggestion made good sense. I walked over to the infirmary and explained my predicament to the doctor. From him I found out that they indeed kept all the glasses just for cases like this. He led me into a small room where he had piles and piles of glasses. I checked all of them, but with my complicated prescription I could not find even one pair that would fit my eyes. Without choice I settled on one pair which was half-way passable. With these glasses at least I could see and work. My problem for the moment was partially solved. The next day, when I came to Haug's office, he immediately noticed the different glasses. When he asked me about it, I told him the whole story.

"Don't worry," he said, "Do you have your lenses and the broken frame?"

"Yes, I do," I answered.

"Very well, let me see what I can do for you," and with this he left the office.

Haug immediately went to Haffner and asked for permission to release me for a few hours, to which the latter agreed. Without further ado, Haug called one of his men and instructed him to take me to Kaufering to the local optician.

"Mishelski," he said, when he entered the office, "outside I have an armed guard who will accompany you to Kaufering. Take your broken glasses and go to the local optician. Don't be concerned that the guard will have his gun pointed at you. This is regulation. He has my instruction and knows where the optician is."

With this he gave me a note to the optician and wished me luck. I was speechless. Here was a German in Nazi Germany who was willing to go far beyond the call of duty to help a Jewish prisoner in a concentration camp.

The guard took me to Kaufering, to the local optician. I handed the slip and the broken frame to him. He looked at me, shook his head, and said, "It is not an easy repair, but I will do my best for you."

Finally the glasses were fixed. I thanked the man and apologized that I had nothing to reward him with. "That won't be necessary," he said, "just watch these glasses. They are patched and are fragile. Don't break them again."

I removed the glasses I obtained in the infirmary and put on my own. I was elated. I kept the second pair just in case they would ever be needed again. As happy as a child with a new toy, I returned to the camp. All the way back I just could not believe that this was happening to me. How lucky could one get! God indeed was watching over me and not letting me down.

Haug continued to be extremely friendly and supportive of me. Occasionally he even brought me some leftovers from the German kitchen, which in comparison with our food was truly a gourmet treat.

One day, after I had drawn up a rather important map for his supervisors in Dachau, he was so pleased that he asked me, "Mishelski, what can I do for you to reward you for your excellent work?"

He expected that I would ask him for food, there were so many things I had not eaten for years. But as long as I had enough to eat I was not about to ask him for food. I looked at him and sized up the situation. How trustworthy was he? After all, he was still a German and I a Jewish concentration camp inmate. As if guessing what was going on in my mind, he repeated, "Don't be afraid, I really want to do something for you. The credit for your work all goes to me from my superiors. Be frank, I will try to fulfill your wish." I felt that his words were sincere and I lost my last inhibitions. "Could I have a German newspaper each day?" came my reply.

I saw that he was surprised and slightly shocked. As soon as I noticed his reaction, I regretted having made the request.

"I guess you know that it is illegal for a prisoner to have a newspaper. If we are caught, we could both be in serious trouble, particularly you. Are you ready to take a chance, possibly even with your life?"

A short silence ensued.

"I don't see anything wrong if you forget a newspaper on your desk," I said.

Again there was a short pause.

"I guess I could do that. But right from the beginning it should be clear that I don't know anything about it and the paper was truly left by accident."

"No problem. You will never be involved in it."

That afternoon, for the first time in years, I had a chance to read a German paper from top to bottom. Even with all the camouflage and subterfuge, the paper was unable to conceal the German defeats at the fronts. I became the source of front page news in our elite circle.

Hunger in the camp was getting more severe by the day and death from malnutrition and exposure was constantly on the rise. It was scary to even look at the emaciated figures of my friends and townspeople. Nahum and I kept some extra food we got from the cook and distributed it to our less fortunate friends in camp.

One day during those long stretches of hunger, Nathan showed up in front of our camp office. I was surprised. Since the incident with the kitchen knife and the gold, we had not spoken a word. I did not even want to see him.

"Vulia," Nathan started, "I have to talk to you. Let us forget the past. Let bygones be bygones. How long are you going to keep score with us?" His voice was shaking. He apparently had difficulty coming to me to talk.

"I am not keeping score. I just don't want to have anything to do with you."

"Vulia, you cannot be that heartless. We are going through some very hard times and in times like this we have to help each other."

"How much help did you extend to us when Vera needed it? Have you forgotten?"

"No, but this is different. Here we will die if you will not help us. Be thankful to God that you are in a position where you don't need any help and are able to extend a helping hand to others."

He was trying very hard, but I was not ready to help them. The wound they had inflicted on us was too fresh. I cut the conversation short. But all day long it bothered me. True, they had committed a serious offense against Vera, but I did not want to have it on my conscience if one of them should die. All night I could not sleep. The next morning after work Nathan was at my window again, once more pleading for help. To make his point, he showed me his father-in-law, who was standing in the distance, not daring to come close. He looked terrible. He was not far from becoming a Musselman. I could no longer deny them help. After further pleading by Nathan, I finally conceded. I would try to provide all of them with one extra soup each, possibly daily. Under the circumstances, this meant the difference between life and death. Every day they were now given an extra meal, supplementing considerably their meager ration. I was now at peace with myself. They may have committed a grievous error, but two wrongs did not make one right. They had ignored their call of conscience when the need was on hand, but I did not. I rose above it. I had come through with a helping hand when it counted most.

It was now October 1944 and things had never been worse for our people. I had only to wait at the gate and look at the people returning from work: exhausted, hungry, thirsty, unshaven, full of lice, face and hands covered with cement which had eaten itself into the flesh, legs full of blisters. Now they had to stand in line for the watery soup and then go to the square for the roll call. To protect themselves from the cold, most of the people pulled the blankets off their bunks and wrapped them around their shoulders during roll call. And the winter was still ahead of us. Only a miracle could help these people survive the winter.

As the number of the inmates was rapidly decreasing, the Germans replaced them with new transports. The latest transport was a group of Greek Jews, all survivors of Auschwitz. Most of those survivors were people who had worked at the crematoria and death factories, but the Nazis did not have enough time to finish them off. The gruesome tales they had to tell were too much even for us, already hardened by years of massacres and murder. From them we found out about the dizzying pace of the extermination of the Hungarian Jews. And when the capacity of the gas chambers could not keep up with the transports, they resorted to mass shooting similar to our Ninth Fort. The bodies were then thrown into ditches, burned, and earth was bulldozed over the corpses. These Auschwitz survivors were the most gruesome reminders we had of the vicious Final Solution that the Germans devised for the Jewish people.

At the same time that the Greek Jews were brought to the camp, several German criminals, sentenced to long terms for murder, were sent from Dachau into our camp to take over its internal administration. These murderers were supposed to take over Bernstein's place, our office, and the kitchen. This was a most dangerous development. Had they succeeded, we all would have lost our positions and been assigned to work in the field. We would have lost our food supplement from the cook, which would have meant starvation. A fierce fight developed between us. With Haffner and Haug siding with us, we finally won out and their influence in the camp was highly restricted.

The month of October was drawing to a close. It was now one year since Minnie had been deported to Estonia. This was a very difficult anniversary for me. I still felt that I could have saved her had I only listened to my mother.

Around this time Haffner took a vacation and went home, where he was killed in an Allied air raid. For the camp this made no difference. But for us in the office it did. With Haffner we had already established a good rapport, but with the new camp commander we would have to start all over again. Meanwhile Schreyer and Helmanowitsch were transferred to camp #11. But we were lucky again. The new commander for our camp, sent in from Dachau, was SS-Obersturmfuehrer Lipmann. His assistant was Oberscharfuehrer Bier. Lipmann was an easy-going elderly man and gave the reigns over to Bier, who was a reasonable man with whom we were able to quickly establish very good relations.

But the number of people dying got to a point where they could no longer be replaced by other Jews, who had by now been mostly annihilated. Our population was dwindling. Towards the end of November we were informed that our camp would be liquidated and all the people transferred to other camps. This was very bad news for us. Every other camp had their better positions filled long ago and we would have to lose our hard-won posts. Peter, Nahum, and I were terribly worried. We were well aware of the grim fact that it took only three weeks to destroy a person.

The first groups to go were a few specialists and workers to camps #1 and #10. Next, six hundred men were to be transferred to camp #11 for work at Moll. It was obvious that our office would have to be reduced, since we would have no need of so many people. Bernstein was in charge of preparing the lists for the transfer and it was clear that he would stick

with Joe, who was his right hand man since Aleksotas. The day came
when the transfer had to take place. The entire camp assembled on the
Appellplatz and Bernstein read off the names.

Everyone whose name was mentioned had to step forward and join the
group at the gate. We were waiting for the ax to fall. He had already read
off five hundred names, but we were not among them. Finally he reached
the end of the list. Was none of us on it? We looked at each other. When
the last name had been read off, Bernstein turned to Joe and informed him
that he was assigned to be in charge of this group. Joe turned pale, gave us
a dirty look as if it were our fault, backed away, and joined the people at
the gate. The graphics department was safe once more, except Pipsi, who
had to join his brigade which was transferred in full. For the three of us,
this was a reprieve for an unspecified time.

After a short while the work in the field was stopped and we were set to
wait for the next transport. Again the tension rose. Who from the office
would survive this transport? It was around the second week in December when the order came in. The bulk of the camp was to be sent to a
camp in central Germany. Its name was not disclosed, but we later found
out it was Leitmeritz (or Litomerice in Czech), in Czechoslovakia. This
time no lists were prepared, since all able-bodied men and most of the
women were to be assigned to this transport. In the morning of the day
the transport was to leave, the entire camp was lined up on the Appellplatz and SS-Oberscharfuehrer Bier directed the selection. The
number required was eight hundred, which was pretty close to the entire
camp.

First Bier put aside the entire administration of the camp, including
Peter, Nahum, and me. We were to stay in the camp, since we would be
needed for the final liquidation. He sent us to the gate where we were to
supervise the count of the people. He let the inmates pass him by and only
the weakest were taken out of the line-up. The groups of "healthy" people
passed by us. Nahum was the only one amongst us who was worried. He
had his father in the camp whom we had protected all the time we were
there. In order to save him from this transport, we put him into one of the
sick barracks in anticipation that the sick barracks would not be called out
to the line-up.

But while we were outside the camp at the gate, Bier ordered all the
sick out. Since Nahum's father was still relatively healthy, he was ordered
to join the marchers. When he reached the gate he waved to Nahum.
Nahum turned white. Confused, we did not assess the situation quickly
enough. Before we knew it, he had passed the gate. By now it seemed too
late to do anything. Nahum quickly ran to Bernstein and explained the
situation to him. But Bernstein was only concerned about his own

position and refused to intervene with the chief of the guard, whom he did not know. Nahum was left with no other choice. He could not let his father down and leave him to an uncertain fate all alone. He quickly ran over to me, embraced me, and with tears in our eyes we parted for the first time in our lives. Since our early childhood, we were the best of friends, attended public and high school together, and entered and graduated from the university side by side. This was a terrible blow to me.

The march continued and the count went on. Suddenly the chief of the guard ordered the counting stopped. He checked with another guard and found out that he had about twenty men too many. We rushed to see whether we still could catch Nahum and his father, but they were gone. Twenty strangers were recalled to the camp. I still remember the last words I said to him. "Nahum, don't give up. Fight on! The war is drawing to a close, you are still in fairly good health and young, you will survive!"

Once the group had left, we returned to the camp to await our destiny. For the next week there were no orders from Dachau and Christmas was approaching. A few days before Christmas, a prisoner went berserk during the roll call at night on the Appellplatz. He ran out of the line-up, made strange gestures with his hands, and finally started banging his head against one of the walls of a prefabricated building. He spoke of his wife, his children, and totally ignored everybody around him. The Germans found it hilarious. For some ten minutes the guard let him carry on while the entire camp was lined up on the grounds and shivering in the cold. Finally one of the guards shot the man. What a spectacle: a Jew going berserk from grief, the Germans getting amused, and finally the gunshot that killed him in cold blood.

Finally Christmas Eve came. A light sprinkle of snow covered the ground. There was a strange mood in camp. The Germans were all homesick and depressed. None of them seemed to care about the war anymore. All of them had had enough of it and wanted it over. In the afternoon Haug brought me a big bowl of holiday food from the German kitchen and many guards brought leftovers from their kitchen to the inmates in the camp. At night Bier, Haug, and a few other camp officers called a selected group of inmates, both men and women, which was most unusual, into the office of the SS-woman supervisor. The room was dimly lit; only one electric bulb was burning, which almost felt like candlelight. Here they suddenly became human, reminiscing about Christmases past in their homes. Quietly they began singing Silent Night. Many of the prisoners joined them in a unique expression of peace, totally incompatible with the surroundings. This strange joint meeting broke up late in the night and everyone returned to his bungalow in a nostalgic mood. The next day the entire camp was given an improved ration and was released from the routine of the daily roll calls.

The year was drawing to a close. We subsequently found out about the battle of the Bulge, which was halted a few days before New Year.

About one week after New Year, the Russians started their winter offensive, which proved to be the final one of the war. One day later, we were told to assemble on the Appellplatz, where we were told that the camp would be closed today and that we were being transferred to camp #7.

We had spent half a year in this camp, during which close to a thousand survivors of ghetto Kovno perished from malnutrition, abuse, mistreatment, exhaustion, and deplorable environment. Half a year, which all of us would have much preferred never to experience. It was now 1945, a year which was finally to bring peace, but not before many more would die at the hands of the Nazis.

26

CAMP #7

The announcement on the Appellplatz that the camp was being liquidated came as no surprise to the inmates. We all knew that the camp was in
the process of liquidation. But when the actual announcement came, it
was still a shock to me. This meant an end to my exclusive status and
possibly serious trouble ahead. We were given several hours to bring the
lists of the inmates in order. The kitchen was ordered to prepare a better
meal, since the camp administration was not interested in leaving "our"
food for the new inmates that would be brought to the camp. We were
also given an increased bread ration. In fact, from Christmas to the day of
the liquidation our food ration was markedly improved. Some people
who were not working at the moment, actually started to show some
signs of recovery. At the gate we found out that camp commander
Lipmann, his assistant Bier, and the German mess supply officer, for
whom Peter worked, had been transferred with us to camp #7. Haug and
the guard, however, remained in camp #2 to await the new transport.
Peter was pleasantly surprised by this fact and his hopes of retaining his
current job were raised. I, on the contrary, was very disappointed that
Haug would not accompany us. With him around, my chances of keeping
my job were, of course, much better. In all probability, a similar job in
camp #7 was already filled by someone else, leaving me out. Our cook
was also apprehensive. His job was by far better than mine. He never had
to worry about his next meal, which was the single biggest concern of
everybody in camp. But his problem was also my problem. The additional portion which I received from him at night while cleaning the kettle

was vital for my survival. This would now be lost, and the specter of potential hunger now stared me in the face.

At the gate several German officers were assembled. Among them was Haug. When I reached the gate he waved good-bye. Even in parting he had not forgotten me and my services to him, and he wanted to express this by wishing me farewell. He wore an SS-uniform and insignia, which the Nazis had ordered the entire command to wear. Haug, in a moment of candor, had confessed to me that he was very unhappy about it, but had no choice. The Wehrmacht had procrastinated in fulfilling this demand as long as they could, but finally they were forced to obey. Oddly enough, when I looked at Haug I did not see the hated uniform, I saw the man, who was a decent human being forced into a position he did not choose or cherish.

The march to camp #7 took us about two hours. By the time we arrived it was twilight. We were led into huts which had been prepared for us. We, the elite group, managed to stay together. The hut to which we were assigned was worse than the one we had in camp #2, but at least we did not have to share it with the people who were infested with lice.

The layout of the camp was similar to camp #2, except that this camp was in the process of completing a delousing center which was supposed to be put into operation any day. During the past half a year the camp inmates here had been performing slave labor, but when their number had dwindled to only a pitiful remnant of survivors, the camp was converted into a non-working "recovery" camp. Emaciated people from other camps were being transferred to camp #7 to die here. The food rations were much smaller and long-term survival in this camp was impossible.

In the evening Bier instructed Bernstein to inspect the camp, the office, the kitchen, the huts, and to get acquainted with the people who held the responsible positions in the camp, since he, Bernstein, would subsequently be in charge. Bernstein, a very thorough and efficient person, made it his business to look into everything and to be ready for his new assignment. The next morning, to our surprise, Bier ordered the leadership of both camps to assemble on the Appellplatz. He explained that since there were now two people for every position in the camp, one incumbent from camp #7 and the other from camp #2, he could not justify this surplus of personnel. He wanted to see all the responsible prisoners of both camps in order to be able to select only one for each position. He would call out the position and the people serving in this capacity were required to step forward and present themselves, whereupon he would select one. Bernstein, who already had his position secured, immediately ran over to me and tipped me off on something he had found out yesterday during his inspection of the camp.

"Mishelski," he said, "I want you to be with me in the office and not the other guy from camp #7. So listen. The guy who will report as the "writer" of camp #7, is really a camp policeman. The true writer got sick one day before we were transferred to the camp. He is very ill and is not expected to recover soon. You rush to Bier and tell him this before he has a chance to choose the other man for the job."

It looked again as if God was watching over me. What a strange coincidence, the man in my position getting sick just one day before our arrival! It was up to me now to act. I did not hesitate. I stepped out of the line-up, which was against German regulations, but I felt I could do no wrong. I approached Bier with a surprising amount of confidence. Of course Bier knew me, but my move caught him by surprise, too. I quickly briefed him on the particulars of my job situation. Bier heard me out and told me to go back to the line-up. The process of assigning men to jobs continued. When the turn came for the "writer" to step forward, we both approached Bier. Both of us briefly stated who we were. Bier listened to both and when we finished he assigned the other man back to the duties of camp policeman and I was retained as office writer. This was almost like a dream. I had my job again! All my fears were suddenly gone. I had obtained a new lease on life. What luck!

The rest of the assignments went quickly. Once they were completed, we moved to establish our authority. Bernstein took over the office and the leadership of the camp and I got busy combining the lists of both camps. Peter, of course, had no trouble retaining his job. In fact, camp #7 did not even have a post like his. The doctors from our camp also had no problem. There were so many sick people in this camp that even twice the number of doctors would have been insufficient. From the doctors we found out that we were probably facing an epidemic of some kind. We did not pay too much attention to their discovery, since sick people were nothing new.

The next morning a transport of Musselmen were transferred to our camp from camp #11. With this our camp was filled to capacity.

The news from the fronts was good. The Battle of the Bulge had ended with a complete German collapse. On 11 January the Russians entered Warsaw and their armies were nearing the Hungarian border. From the inmates of camp #11 we found out that Auschwitz had been liberated. This news was greeted with tremendous relief. The worst death factory in the history of mankind, the cruelest monument of man's inhumanity to man, was out of operation, and a serious blow had been dealt to the German extermination machine. They would no longer be able to gas and kill six thousand people a day, as they had been doing for so many months with the Hungarian Jews, with the world looking on without blinking an eye. The liberation of Auschwitz raised some hopes among the healthier inmates that chances of survival had improved.

Our current problem was where to get an extra slice of bread or an extra soup ration to supplement our starvation diet, and, above all, how not to get sick. Several days passed and we found out from the doctors that the sickness, whatever it was, was becoming increasingly worrisome. The Germans also did not like what they were witnessing and blood samples were sent to the nearest laboratory. The results were: we had epidemic typhus. This news exploded like a bombshell. The Germans immediately slapped a quarantine on the camp and we were now totally isolated from the outside world. The gates were padlocked and were only opened twice a day, once to bring in food and once to remove the dead. Even bringing in the food was now accomplished by a special procedure: the food was brought to the gate and the couriers would retreat. People from the camp would then take over, bringing the food in and returning to camp. This procedure was meticulously followed to avoid any contact between the two teams.

People stricken by the illness ran temperatures of more than 104°. They suffered from splitting headaches, skin rashes, and delirium. After several days, the temperature would suddenly drop and the people started to shiver. They could not hold down any food. Having been weakened and emaciated from before with barely any remaining bodily resistance, typhus was almost uniformly a death sentence. Since the disease was transmitted by lice and fleas, the epidemic spread like wildfire. It was now a more deadly enemy than slave labor or starvation. We were facing a threat which could kill a person in a matter of days. With the quarantine imposed on us, we were confined to crowded quarters with people dying by the dozens on all sides and no way of protecting ourselves from being infected.

Although our own bungalow was clean and without lice, there was no way to avoid contact with other people. One flea was enough to carry the infection. I was scared. I had survived three-and-one-half years of the most cruel persecution in history. How ironic to die now from a bite of a flea!

Bernstein, realizing the severity of the epidemic, ordered every able-bodied man to work on the delousing center so he could start getting rid of the lice that swarmed the camp. This was accomplished quickly.

Word got around that camp #7 was quarantined and in the midst of a deadly typhus epidemic. This news reached our former camp #2 and with it, Otto Haug. The next day, when I was in the office, somebody knocked on my window and wanted to see me. When I got to the window, a camp inmate told me that an SS-man was near the gate asking for me.

"An SS-man?" I thought to myself, "at such a time at the gate of a quarantined camp? Who could it be? Why did he need me?" I was really concerned.

I left the office and to my complete surprise it was Haug! What was he doing here? As I approached the gate, Haug greeted me and said, "Mishelski, it has been brought to my attention that your camp is quarantined and there is a typhus epidemic here. Listen to me. We are not allowed near the camp and are forbidden to get into contact with the inmates. We in the army are extremely sensitive to this disease and many on the fronts have died from it. To prevent an epidemic in the hinterland, all of us have been immunized against it. I really care for you and I want to prevent you from getting sick. I have brought with me several batches of this vaccine from our army infirmary for you and some of your friends. Due to the quarantine, I cannot give it to you directly. I have left the vaccine with the medical officer of the camp guard, since he is allowed to enter the camp. I hope this will protect you from the disease."

I was speechless. A German in an SS uniform trying to save my life and willing to go through a lot of red tape to get the vaccine! He probably could not even tell his staff pharmacist for whom it was needed. But here it was! In the lowest depth, here was a ray of light, a man without prejudice, a man with compassion for people, no matter who they were or what race they belonged to. At this moment I did not even think about the importance of this vaccine to my life and the service Haug had done me. All I could think of was the kindness of this man, unaffected by all that hate and evil around him. I was deeply touched by this attentiveness and goodness of heart. I barely was able to express my thanks to him.

"Don't thank me," he said, "I am glad I can do something for you." With this he departed. Never before had I been sorry to see a man in SS uniform leave, but this time I wished I could leave the camp and shake his hand.

Late in the afternoon the German medical officer brought the vaccine into the camp and gave it to the chief of the camp infirmary, a doctor whom I knew from childhood. He had been our family doctor for years. In the morning I checked with the doctor as to whether or not he had received the vaccine for me. He looked at me quizzically. "How do you know about the vaccine?" he asked.

Sergeant Haug brought it specifically for me," I said.

"I did not get it from him. I received it from the medical officer for the hospital."

"Never mind, you can check with the officer. The vaccine was specifically for me and I would like you to give me the injection."

"Mishelski, I want you to understand that nobody will get any injections of this vaccine. First, I don't know whether it is good, and secondly, even if it were good, it is much too late to administer it to anybody."

"What do you mean? What harm can it do?" I asked.

"You see, you are not a doctor. We have all been in contact with these people for more than a week, which is ample time to contract the disease. There are people who have a natural immunity to typhus. These people can even sleep with a sick person and they will not catch it. On the other hand, the ones who do not have this immunity have been exposed long enough to be in the incubation stage."

"But what has this got to do with the vaccine? If I am sick already, the vaccine will be useless, but, if by some stroke of luck I am still healthy, the vaccine would be helpful," I said.

"This is not quite so," he replied. "The vaccine would be an addition to the bacteria you already have and the disease would be that much more severe."

I felt that the doctor was not sincere with me and was desperately trying to talk me out of it. "But if I do agree to take a chance on the vaccine?" I was still not willing to give up.

"I would not administer it. I don't want that responsibility. The disease is a most serious one and the addition of more bacteria would positively turn it deadly."

There was no point in arguing with him. He had made up his mind that nobody would get the vaccine and that was that. My excitement of yesterday, my hope to be protected, suddenly vanished, and gloom and despair gripped me. My worry was now whether or not I had natural immunity. Was the doctor sincere in his explanation about the harm the vaccine could do at this stage, or did he have some other thoughts in the back of his mind? But I had no way to force him. Haug was not here and I could not go out of the confines of the camp.

We were in a race, man against disease. The number of new cases mounted by the hour and the number of deaths reached twenty-five daily. The entire camp was rushed through the now-opened delousing center in an attempt to rid the camp of lice.

A few days after Haug had left the vaccine for me, an assistant of the head doctor needed some information from me about several patients in the infirmary, since I had all the lists of the camp. In the course of the conversation I asked him, "How does it feel to work in an infirmary with all those typhus patients? Aren't you afraid of getting sick?"

"Well, no one is ever one hundred percent sure, but we, the few doctors, have ben vaccinated against typhus," he replied.

For a second I was speechless.

"Who administered the vaccine to you?" I asked.

"The chief doctor himself did it," he replied.

This hit me like a bombshell. So this was it! That scoundrel!

"Where did he get the vaccine in the camp?" I continued my query.

"The German medical officer gave it to him."

What a murderous double-cross by my own family physician! He had sold me a pack of lies. He turned around and used the vaccine which Haug, with so much personal sacrifice, had specifically brought for me and some of my friends and used it for himself and his cronies. I did not tell the truth to the chief doctor's assistant. There was no point. The vaccine had already been used, and I was left with my "natural immunity," which I did or did not have, and they were all vaccinated and protected.

Several days later, to my complete surprise, the group of doctors that had received the shots all came down with severe cases of typhus. I was still relying on my so-called natural immunity.

The epidemic did not show any signs of abating. Every day dozens of new cases were reported and more people died of the malady. Our food situation was growing worse, since our rations were adjusted for non-working people, and our cook was no longer in charge of the kitchen and could not provide us with a food supplement. For the first time in many months I was living exclusively off the ration. Something had to be done about the hunger if we wanted to survive. Since I was alone in the office and the sole person preparing the daily report for the German command, I knew how many people died daily and how many were listed as sick. The numbers were staggering. There was no way on earth that the Germans could check these figures, particularly since none except the medical officer were allowed into the huts to verify the count, and even he never entered the huts. The stench and the dirt in the barracks were horrible. People were lying on top of one another, with dead and dying between the living ones. In some cases one could not even distinguish between the two.

This fact was noticed by some of the block leaders, who contacted me and suggested that some people who had died at night should be listed as sick, not dead. This way we would get their rations, which otherwise would remain in the SS supply depot. Why should they be the beneficiaries of their murderous regime? I agreed to the proposition, and henceforth we received some additional rations to supplement our meager food intake.

In the first month alone the epidemic had claimed over six hundred dead, almost one third of the camp. At the peak several block elders also came down with it. Among them was the man who used to give me all the trouble in camp #2, which almost cost me my life.

January and most of February were behind us now. Then something most unusual happened. Bier informed us that in a few days the camp would be receiving Red Cross packages. This sounded incredible. If true, it meant that somebody finally knew about our existence. I prepared lists of all the inmates and Bernstein handed them to the Germans. For several days nothing happened, and we were sure that the lists we had prepared were for some other purpose. But by the end of the week the distribution of the packages began. Every inmate received a small bag containing sugar, a can of Nestle's sweetened condensed milk, and a small can of sardines. The distribution of the packages was slow, and it was clear that the Germans were keeping the packages of the dead people for themselves.

But as they delayed the distribution, we too had the opportunity of keeping some extra packages. Between the receipt of the packages and the actual distribution, more people died, and we kept their rations. By the end of the distribution I was in the possession of several cans of milk and a few small bags of sugar. I kept this extra food under strict control and ate only a small part of it, stretching the supply and keeping some of it for a day when I would not have any food supplement. This was a self-imposed control which was extremely difficult to maintain.

Meanwhile Budapest had been liberated by the Russians and the Americans had reached the Rhine. The epidemic was slowing down. With the coming of spring, the weather started to improve and our hopes took a turn for the better. But the number of the dying was still extremely high. Towards the end of March, more than half the camp had perished and the survivors were struggling to stay alive.

The month of March was drawing to a close. The group of doctors had survived the epidemic. The epidemic had run its course and no new cases were reported. Peter and I had miraculously survived the epidemic without getting sick.

Rumors circulated in the camp that if no new cases were reported for a certain number of days, the quarantine would be lifted and the camp liquidated. The end of the epidemic was welcome news, but the liquidation of the camp raised all the same old fears. Despite the successes on the fronts, nobody could foresee how long the agonizing war could last. If the Nazis intended to defend every city the way the Russians had defended Moscow, Leningrad, and Stalingrad, the war could drag on for a considerable length of time. With this in mind, the liquidation of camp #7 and a transfer to another well-staffed camp was again a potential threat to my survival.

During the first week of April, the ax fell. We were all told to assemble on the Appellplatz and Bier gave us a few hours to get ready. We would be transferred to camp #1. The only exception was Peter, whose German boss was being transferred back to our former camp #2, which had reopened with new prisoners. He managed to obtain a permit from Dachau to keep Peter, who received a personal transfer.

Although we had expected this development, the sudden announcement caught me by surprise. I still had a can of condensed milk and a small bag of hard sugar. I knew that I could not carry this into camp #1. No prisoner could enter a new camp unless he had gone through the delousing center, where I knew my food would be taken away. It was a shame to lose all those calories which I had so carefully rationed to last me for several weeks. I decided to drink the can of condensed milk and eat some of the sugar, taking a chance that a small amount of sugar could still be carried through the showers safely. I quickly opened the can and finished it within a few minutes. By then I was so full that I couldn't even touch the sugar. About half an hour later I started to feel nauseated. Then a terrible, splitting headache set in, followed by severe cramps in my stomach. I broke into a cold sweat and started to shiver. My face turned chalky white and I thought I would die. At first I was afraid that this was the beginning of typhus. But as my nausea got worse, I realized that it could be the condensed milk. During all those years of hunger, even with the additional food I used to get, my stomach had shrunk and I was unable to digest the rich, extremely sweet mixture.

I dropped everything and ran to the toilets. I barely reached the washroom as I began to vomit. Pieces of undigested food mixed with body juices poured out of my mouth like a fountain. I thought my head would explode. I grabbed my temples with both hands and pressed to reduce the pressure. At last all the food I had in my stomach was out and I felt relieved. How foolish it was of me to eat all that food at once! A weaker person might not have survived this experience.

The camp was ordered to pick up our belongings, assemble on the Appellplatz, and start marching. Peter had already left for camp #2 and we did not even have a chance to say good-bye to each other. The loss of Peter, on top of the loss of Nahum, was terribly upsetting to me. I was now all alone: my family was gone, my friends were mostly dead, and I was on my way to a new camp, where I could no longer expect any breaks. On the way to camp #1 I had plenty of time to think. Where were my mother, sister, and Minnie? Where was Nahum, and how was he coping with the new camp?

I was afraid at a time when I needed all the strength I could muster. But when I looked around me and saw all those miserable creatures who could barely drag their feet, I felt I had no reason to despair. I was still in reasonably good health. Compared to all the Musselmen, I looked like a creature from another world. I suddenly recalled the words I had said to Nahum when we parted: "Nahum, don't give up. Fight on! The war is drawing to a close. You will survive!"

I repeated these words to myself now and tried to strengthen my morale. The more I thought about it, the better I felt. I was ready for camp #1, determined to fight on.

27

CAMP #1

Camp #1 was the first of eleven slave labor camps to be established during the summer of 1944, all part of the notorious concentration camp Dachau. This was the area in which the Nazis had decided to hide their armament industry, in large, underground, bomb-proof shelters, and for which they badly needed slave labor. But by now this labor pool had dwindled. In contrast to us, the Jews, the occupied nations could not easily be mobilized for slave labor work. Most of them were officially allies or collaborators, and the others resisted any attempts by the Nazis to mobilize them. The Nazis now wished they had some of those massacred Jews available for this emergency. They decided to evacuate all the Jewish survivors from Eastern Europe and ship them back to Germany, back to the place from where they had been driven out through discriminatory laws, street violence, and organized government terror. They scraped the bottom of the barrel in desperation and brought them to Dachau. The first group to come to camp #1 was a small group of Hungarian Jews who formed the nucleus of the camp. Next came the Jews from ghetto Kovno who had reported for deportation "voluntarily." Among these were Dr. Elkes, Dr. Zacharin, members of the committee, Jewish policemen, the ghetto orchestra, and many workers from the workshops.

Goecke had assured the group from ghetto Kovno that they would be relocated as family units at a camp near Danzig. The workshops would be evacuated with them, where they would continue to function as in the ghetto. They hoped in vain that maybe this time the Nazis were telling the truth. But most of the people entered bunkers, as we in the graphics shop had done, in the hope that the Russians would advance rapidly and save us. While we were in hiding, the first group was brought to Tiegenhof. Here the women and children were forceably separated from the men. The crying, the hysterics were horrifying. When Dr. Elkes approached the SS-man in charge and told him about Goecke's promise that there would be no separation of men and women, he was murderously beaten by the SS-bully and knocked to the ground. The men were subsequently chased back into the train, the doors padlocked, and the train left in an undisclosed direction. All the men were sure that the destination was Auschwitz and regretted having so foolishly trusted a Nazi. But it was too late. After several days of travelling this group reached Kaufering, and from there camp #1. But not having been through Stutthof, they saved themselves a lot of agony. They avoided spending a day in the huge hall between the mountain of shoes, and being taken to the showers, positive that they were gas chambers. This first group also managed to salvage some personal belongings. The musicians had even managed to bring along their instruments, which were taken away from them at first but later returned.

When this first group of evacuees from ghetto Kovno arrived in camp #1, they found the Hungarian Jews already in charge of the camp. The top leadership was in the hands of two Jews, Grunfeld and Levy. They were so firmly entrenched in their positions that they could not be displaced. Most of the other posts, however, were ultimately taken over by the Jews from Kovno. Thus Dr. Elkes and Dr. Zacharin took over the infirmary. Also the block elders were Jews from Kovno, and the so-called camp capo, a job in charge of all work inside and around the camp, was in the hands of Gitta's father.

The camp itself was the local headquarters of all those peripheral camps of Dachau, and the SS command here was larger and more authoritative. But as to the camp itself, it was as bad as camp #2. The treatment was rough, the food ration just as meager, and the work was in the same construction firms: Moll, Holzmann, and other equally difficult places. The death ratio was just as high and people were dying daily by the dozens. My worst fears were confirmed: all better jobs inside the camp were filled. There was no chance for me to break in anyplace, particularly since the real power was in the hands of two Hungarian Jews who did not know me.

We arrived in the camp late in the afternoon and first thing had to go through the delousing center. My immediate concern was how to carry through the bag of sugar. Leaving it in my coat made no sense, since the intense heat in the ovens would have destroyed it. So my only choice was to carry it in my hand and hope that the capo would not notice it. This was not an easy task, since I had to hide it from the capo and even from the people around me. And being naked, there just was no place for concealment. I also had to make sure it did not get wet in the shower. Somehow I did manage to bring the sugar through the shower. On the clean side it was a little easier to hide this little bag, particularly once we had our clothes back. I put the package into my overcoat pocket and was delighted to have managed to perform this little miracle. We were then taken to our new huts. This time our elite group was dispersed and ended up with the regular inmates. This was a severe blow, but at least the people had no lice after the thorough delousing they had been through in camp #7 before, and now in camp #1.

The first evening in the camp I tried to approach both Grunfeld and Levy, explaining to them that I had been the writer of camp #7 and asking whether there was any work for me. Both declined. I then approached some of the block elders whom I knew well, but also without any luck. Things looked bad.

The next morning we had to get up early to go to work. I was now in the pool of slave laborers like everybody else. Everything pointed to it: my golden era had come to an end and I was about to be thrown into a churn which devoured people mercilessly.

On the first day Gitta's father managed to pull me out of the line-up for work in the camp. I was assigned to a group paving a road in the yard for the SS guard. The work consisted of hauling large stones, fitting them into the pavement, and tapping them tightly into the ground. The work was backbreaking, but had two advantages. I did not have to march four or five miles to the jobsite and thus had two extra hours of rest. Also the supervision was more lax, making it possible to catch your breath on and off. But even with these advantages, a person could not last long with the food we were receiving.

After work I looked up Gitta's father and asked him whether it was possible to get into something better. He explained to me that it was not easy to pull somebody out of the line-up for work in the camp. Tomorrow, however, he would need more people to be sent to commando Sommerkeller, the yard where all the cold storage cellars for food were located. Here we would be loading food onto buggies and returning them to the camp. The work was hard, but the Sommerkeller had a rich garbage dump where people scavenged for clippings and shreds of vegetables, peels of potatoes, and any food that was still edible. This was the best commando in the camp, but for me it was a one-time shot. This was better than going to Moll or Holzmann, even if it was only for one day.

The yard was not too far from the camp. The march was not too strenuous. Our work was managable: we had to load the weekly supply of bread for the entire camp, including the SS guard, onto buggies. This was a lot of bread, and the buggies were loaded to a point where it became quite hard to pull them by hand (horses were too valuable to serve Jews). During the lunch break I went to the famous garbage dump to see what I could salvage. Here the picture resembled a beehive, with people shoving and fighting over a potato peel. I walked over to the dump and stood there looking at the garbage. I was hungry and would have eaten just about anything as long as it was clean, but to pull garbage out of a dump was too much for me. Whereas everybody else was busy pulling pieces of lettuce and peels of carrots out of the garbage bin, I walked away with nothing.

When I returned to camp, Gitta's father asked me what I salvaged from the dump. I admitted that I was at the dump, but I just could not bring myself to rummage through the garbage.

"You are foolish," he said to me. "This is good food. Most of the people in the camp would be glad to have it."

"What do you do with it? How can you eat this?" I asked naively.

"You apparently are not hungry enough yet," he said. "People wash it in the washrooms until it is clean, then they make a fire and cook it. But there is also another angle to it. If you don't want to eat it, you can always trade it for cigarettes in the camp, if you smoke. If you do not smoke, you can always trade these cigarettes for a bowl of soup or a food supplement. There are people in the camp who will die because they need the cigarettes even more than they need food, and these men are trading away everything."

"I guess I made a big mistake," I said. I saw that he was amused by my inexperience.

"You bet you did. There will be no Sommerkeller now for at least one week, and even then I am not sure if I will be able to pull you out of the line-up and assign you to this commando. There are many people begging me for it, and I just do not know whom to help first."

He was right. In my ignorance I was a newcomer to camp life. For the past months God had helped me and shielded me from all that misery around me. I had been lucky, but that was now a thing of the past. My only hope was that the war should end quickly.

The next morning Gitta's father could not pull me out of the line-up and I ended up in one of the commandos going to Holzmann. We were sent to build fortifications and dig anti-tank ditches. First we marched some four miles to the jobsite. Then we were given picks and shovels and all hell broke loose. With German supervisors from the O.T. (Organisation Todt) on our backs, we were driven like the old Hebrews building the pyramids. This slave labor could break anybody in no time, and it did. My only advantage over the others was the sugar which I still had in my pocket. I was still trying to ration it, but with every day it got harder to restrain myself and the sugar was quickly dwindling. In addition, some sugar had been stolen from me by a friend of mine.

At lunchtime I sneaked away from the jobsite (a major offense for which I could have gotten severely punished). I approached a German farmhouse and knocked on the door. A middle-aged German woman opened it. Encouraged to see a person other than an SS guard in front of me, I asked for potato peels, if she had any. I had learned my lesson from the Sommerkeller that potato peels were fine food for inmates. It did not even occur to me to ask for potatoes or bread.

The woman looked at me and complete astonishment was written all over her face. I must have looked to her like some kind of a nut. "But what do you need potato peels for?" she asked in total disbelief.

Now I was the one in utter amazement. What kind of a silly question was this, didn't she know that potato peels were fine food for concentration camp inmates? For a moment we stood facing each other, both flabbergasted. When I recovered from my bewilderment, I looked at her and said, "I need it to eat, gracious lady. This is good food."

I will never forget the expression on her face. She was suddenly hit with the harsh reality of a concentration camp inmate, a man for whom potato peels were a delicacy. Pity replaced the astonishment on her face.

"Wait a minute," she said, "I will be right back."

I was glad. At least I would have potato peels, which I would exchange for cigarettes and the cigarettes for soup. I was daydreaming. In a few minutes the woman was back and handed me six real potatoes. I could not believe my eyes. This was a treasure, enough for two or even three meals. I must have looked awfully silly to her when I accepted the potatoes, because she said, "Don't be so scared, it is all right. Make yourself a good meal tonight."

I expressed my deep appreciation to her and walked back to the jobsite. I hid the potatoes in my pockets and only hoped that I would not be searched at the gate. When we reached the gate I realized that the meal was not yet mine. I still had to pass! But I was lucky, I was not searched.

In the evening I gave one potato to a friend of mine who let me use his fire. I boiled the potatoes in a pot of water, and when they were ready, I ate them and even drank the water, which tasted like delicious soup to me. After the meal I walked out to the yard, and for the first time I noticed that the musicians of the ghetto orchestra were playing for the inmates. These so-called concerts were provided in the evening after the commandos were in, but I felt as if the concert was just for me. I had just had a lavish meal, and it was only fitting to have music to go with it.

The next morning I was again grabbed by the capo for Holzmann and forced to join the group. We were again taken to build fortifications, but in an area where there were no homes, no place to get food as I did the day before. After a few days doing this slave labor I felt that I could no longer take it. The specter of the Czech Jews started to haunt me and I decided to fight back. But what could I do? There were no lenient jobs in this camp. Everything was taken. In desperation, I decided to report sick. Maybe the doctors, most of whom I knew, would give me a few days off. But even the doctors would have a hard time justifying my release from work, when people a hundred times worse off than I were forced to stay with it. But there was nothing to lose. Everything had to be explored. At this stage of the war, every day counted.

In the evening after work I reported to the infirmary. The people around me begging for a day off were so skinny I could not even look at them. They would probably not live to see the end of the war. These people looked at me and thought I was a doctor. What else would a healthy man like me be doing in the infirmary? While sitting and waiting, in came Dr. Zacharin, the doctor who had operated on Vera in the ghetto. He looked the patients over and suddenly noticed me. "Mishelski," he turned to me in surprise, "I did not know you were in this camp. When did you come here?"

"I came here with the transport from camp #7," I replied.

"Mishelski, come in, I want to talk to you," Dr. Zacharin said, "you could not have come at a better time. My infirmary looks like a mess and you are a capable artist, you could improve its appearance."

"I sure can," I replied with complete confidence. "Is there anything specific you have in mind?"

"Yes. I have seen your work in the graphics department. You made a number of signs for my hospital in the ghetto. Could you sneak out of the roll call in the morning and remain in the camp? I will then see to it that you be assigned to the infirmary for a day."

That sounded very much like a possible break. I started to feel confident that I could bargain with him. He needed me, that was the clue. Sneaking out from the roll call was very difficult even if Dr. Zacharin had told the people in charge that he needed me.

"No, Dr. Zacharin," I said with a great deal of nerve, "getting out of the line-up is a very difficult proposition. Why don't you assign me to the recovery barracks, so I will not be faced with the problem of finding a way out of the Appellplatz each morning. I don't think that this should be so difficult for you to arrange."

I really gambled. What if he refused my request? I could lose everything. Dr. Zacharin looked at me, thought for a minute, and said, "I guess you have a point. Go to my assistant and tell him that I have ordered to admit you to the infirmary and report to me tomorrow morning."

Depending on what he had in mind, I could be busy for as little as a day or two, or as much as several weeks. The war was not standing still and who knew what could happen in a matter of a few days? In the meantime I would be rid of the commandos.

I immediately reported to Dr. Zacharin's assistant, who admitted me to the infirmary's recovery area. Here I met quite a few close friends from Kovno. Among these was Mr. Yatkunski, whose brother and entire family were massacred in the pogrom in Slobotke. Mr. Yatkunski and his two sons, both in their early twenties, were first in camp #2, where I used to support them. Later they were transferred to camp #1. Yatkunski was very glad to see me and reminded me of how grateful he was for my help in camp #2. This sustained them during the long months in the camp and was responsible for their survival.

After a good night's sleep I presented myself to Dr. Zacharin. As the first order of business, Dr. Zacharin wanted numbers put on the bunks. He found it impossible to keep track of the patients who were located on the long rows of congested, two-story bunks without a means of differentiating one bunk from the next. Then he wanted a few signs painted, like "infirmary" and "pharmacy," which would cover his immediate needs. This assignment was right up my alley.

But how does one start without any tools and supplies, without paint brushes? There was absolutely nothing in the poor infirmary. Everything had to be found and scratched together. I was worried. I had to succeed if I was to remain in the infirmary. I checked with some friends of mine who had responsible positions, like Mr. Frenkel and the block elders. From Mr. Frenkel I obtained paper, pencils, erasers, a ruler, and cardboard. But the most important thing, paint and brushes, he did not have. He suggested I see an old friend of mine who was working for the SS guard as a painter. This was good news. In the evening, I figured, I would get paint from him and I would be set for the moment.

In the evening, when everybody was back from work, I looked up my friend and explained to him what I needed. He did not seem to be at all enthusiastic about my request and without much ado, he told me that he could not take any paint from the shop and could not help me. I was stunned. My entire shop could collapse even before it started. Dejected, I left his hut, wondering what to do next. I could not give up on this. My life depended on it. On the way to the infirmary I decided to check with some of the block elders whom I knew. One of them suggested I go to the shop which had been operating in the camp. The shop was somewhat similar to the one Peter and I had set up in camp #2. As I walked into the shop, to my surprise I ran into Sam Kagan, the painter for whom I had arranged the job in camp #2. When he noticed me, he ran towards me and grabbed my hand. "Mishelski, how long have you been in camp #1?"

"I came with the last transport from camp #7," I replied.

"Oh, that was the typhus camp, wasn't it? Did you have typhus too?" he asked.

"No, thank God, I was lucky."

"Good for you. I am really glad. You don't know how I appreciated it when you gave me the job in the shop as a painter. I will never forget it."

"I am glad I could help you," I answered, "and what are you doing here?"

"As you remember, I was transferred from camp #2 to camp #1 during the liquidation process. I was immediately assigned to the shop here where I am again working as a painter. And what are you doing here in the camp?"

I told him the entire story with Dr. Zacharin and the infirmary and asked him whether he or somebody else he knew could help me to obtain paint and brushes.

"Mishelski, there isn't a thing in the world I would not do for you. What do you need?" and he took me to the next room where he had his supplies. Before I knew what happened, I had supplies that could last me for months. This was like a dream.

Now I had my own shop. Starting in the morning, I began putting numbers on the bunks. When Dr. Zacharin came to the infirmary, he was pleasantly surprised. The infirmary would finally start to look decent. This was a great beginning. Now I had to come up with ideas and suggestions to make myself indispensable. In the evening I sat down and worked out a list of suggestions for Dr. Zacharin. I thought of all sorts of things to improve the looks and appearance of the infirmary. I presented the list to him the next morning and to my great satisfaction, he accepted them all. I now had enough work for at least six weeks. First I made a sign for Dr. Zacharin and then one for the Aryan capo, Martin, who was in charge of the food distribution in the infirmary. He was as happy as a child with this sign. Every day he came with his helper, Misha Meilup, and ordered him to give me a second bowl of soup from what was left over. This soup was from the bottom of the pot and a most welcome addition to my diet. For the third time, in three camps, I had managed to find a shelter where I was able to survive. I was eager to finish the numbering on the bunks. I had so much work lined up that I was no longer worried.

My careful and clean work was not lost on the SS officer in charge of sanitation in the camp. A day or so later, to my complete surprise, Dr.

Zacharin brought me a list of orders from the SS officer. Dr. Zacharin was very excited. He had received praise from the officer for his initiative and felt that my services were valuable to him and his relationship with the SS officer. These rapid developments were beyond anything I imagined only a few days ago, when I was marching back and forth to Holzmann.

Now that I was relaxed, I found out that the camp had two discussion groups. One group was conducted by a highly respected lawyer, Dr. Gringauz, and the other by a successful engineer named Blumenthal. In both groups the speakers analyzed the current situation at the fronts and provided the latest information. This was obtained by a group of Jewish electronics specialists who worked in a German shop fixing radios. These meetings were extremely interesting and informative. Dr. Gringauz had an excellent grasp of events, but his philosophy was very depressing. His opinion was that even at the very last minute, the Nazis would still have enough time to kill every surviving Jew for fear of leaving witnesses to their murderous deeds. In contrast, the analysis by Mr. Blumenthal was exactly the opposite. He felt that it was too late for mass killings. Too many atrocities had already been revealed and the few survivors did not make much difference. Besides, this was German soil and not Poland or Lithuania. On German soil the Nazis would be much more careful in commiting mass murder.

Occasionally I would even stop to listen to our musicians when they played. Their repertoire was generally the same as in the ghetto. Inevitably, of course, one day it was the tune from *Scheherezade*, the tune that had persecuted me since I lost Minnie. It brought back both good and bad memories. Where was she now? Was she still alive? It was now a year and a half since I had lost her, but I still carried her memory deep in my heart.

On 13 April Vienna fell to the advancing Russians and the Americans appeared on the Dessau-Berlin autobahn. Despite all this encouraging news, rumors about President Roosevelt's death were a shock to us. We were worried that this would harden the German resolve to fight on. We were still in their grip.

I kept myself busy in my shop and hoped that Blumenthal was right. Maybe they wouldn't have time to massacre us. I hoped that we would not have to move again and the Nazi regime would collapse under the heavy blows of the Allied forces while we were still in camp #1. But this was wishful thinking. On 24 April, while the Russians were already at the outskirts of Berlin, the boom fell on us once again: the order to liquidate the camp had come from Dachau, and once more I was faced with an uncertain future.

The final hour had struck.

28

LIBERATION

Once more an order to evacuate! I should have become accustomed to it by now: the uncertainty, the sudden moves, the loss of a hard-won position and extra soup, the constant grappling for a way to survive. Yet the order to evacuate threw me into panic all over again. Why did they have to drag us along all over Germany when the war was lost anyway? This was obviously the nature of the beast: it had its prey in its jaws and would not let it loose until forced to do so. I was not the only one upset by this order. Even the slave laborers who did not have a lenient job like mine were tired of being dragged every few months from camp to camp. They had suffered enough. Most of them were at the very end of their stamina and endurance, hardly possessing enough energy to survive a death march. We were haunted by the words of Dr. Gringauz and Mr. Blumenthal. Which one was right? Were we finally being led to the pit to be shot, or was this an attempt to keep us alive to continue building fortifications for them wherever their last stand would be? People were worried, and much speculation went on among friends.

The SS were not unaware of the mood in the camp. Later in the day a rumor was planted that the intent of the German government was to exchange the concentration camp inmates for German prisoners of war in the hands of the Western powers. The exchange would take place at the Swiss border. This attempt to soften our resistance and to plant false hopes into the minds of the people was hardly successful. Nobody believed this newest lie. They had lied to us much too often. Even before the evacuation from the ghetto, Goecke had promised us that families would not be separated and that the workshops were following the train. Instead, the people were taken to Dachau.

The instruction to evacuate included a statement that only the healthy and strong were to report for the march. This last statement frightened people and reinforced their mistrust. We remembered all too well what had happened to the doctors and the patients in the hospital in the ghetto. Twice the hospital, including all patients and personnel, were burned alive. It seemed clear that they were planning to do the same to our sick.

People from the infirmary who were too weak to walk summoned their last ounce of strength, dressed, and waddled to the Appellplatz for fear of being burned alive. These barely alive creatures made a frightful procession. It was amazing to see what energy the threat of death could produce even in a body which was beyond redemption.

I was scared. Looking at all the people rushing to the Appellplatz, one could easily be gripped by mass hysteria. I had to exert all the self-restraint I could muster to avoid succumbing. I desperately tried to reason logically. According to the hypothesis of Dr. Gringauz, the Nazis would not leave any of us alive. If this assumption were true, it did not make any difference whether one joined the march or stayed in the camp. The only difference would be in the mode of their death: shooting in front of a mass grave or being torched by fire. However, if Mr. Blumenthal was right, neither group would be exterminated. If so, joining the march was a serious mistake.

The march would be strenuous. Hundreds of people would die in it. Was I still strong enough? Could I survive a march like this? I slowly started to lean towards the gamble of staying in the camp and taking my chances with the sick. Simultaneously, another thought entered my mind. How could I explain the fact that just two weeks before the liquidation of the camp, I found myself in the infirmary? I was not sick and not emaciated yet. I had a strange feeling that this was again the hand of God which had consistently shielded me from all the perils throughout the past four years and directed me towards the infirmary, so I might again be saved. This last thought had no logic, no sense, but faith needs no explanation. And I made up my mind. I was staying in the camp with all the sick and the Musselmen, all reason not withstanding.

Suddenly I was awakened from my thoughts. Berl, our messenger boy from camp #2 and camp #7, was standing beside me. "Mishelski," he said, "I want to consult with you."

"What is on your mind?" I asked.

"I would like to know what you intend to do. Are you staying or are you joining the march? The infirmary, I understand, does not have to join."

"Berl," I answered, "I decided to stay."

"Then I am staying too," he replied.

"Are you ready to be separated from your brother, Jacob, who has to join the march? He is the only member of your family who is still alive."

"I will be frank with you," Berl replied after thinking for a few seconds. "I have infinite confidence in your judgment. You may not have noticed it, but I have always followed you. So far your logic has never failed and I have a premonition that your decision will prove to be right this time too."

"Berl, you are mistaken. The logic of everybody here in the camp has been right so far or they wouldn't be alive. Call it logic, I call it luck, it only had to fail you once and you were dead."

"I agree," Berl replied, "but there is a big difference. In addition to luck, one needs also clear thinking, which you have."

"Berl, I cannot take responsibility for your life. What if I am wrong this time?"

"Don't worry," Berl replied, "the decision is mine. Nobody knows who will be right or wrong. Only the future will tell, if we live to see it." With this, we quietly entered the barracks.

Outside, groups of one hundred were formed, the order to march was issued, and the people began moving towards the gate, finally disappearing behind the road.

At this moment I thought of the famous statement by Julius Caesar when he crossed the Rubicon: Alea iacta est. For better or worse, I had made a fateful decision. This was it. The marchers were gone, and even if I changed my mind, it was too late.

Except for people in the infirmary, the camp was empty. I was waiting for future developments with great apprehension. Occasionally I accused myself: why had I not joined the march? But the next moment I was convinced that I had done the right thing. With these conflicting and torturous thoughts, I went to sleep.

When dawn came Berl and I were awakened by a lot of noise in the camp. Voices screaming and yelling struck fear into our hearts. It sounded very bad. This could be it. The final extermination was probably underway. We rushed to the door. The gates to the camp were wide open and hundreds of new inmates, evacuees from other camps, were entering. Once inside, they were ordered to sit down on the ground. There was no explanation of what was happening. Finally, towards noon, they were sent to the various empty barracks. We breathed a sigh of relief. If they were not shot, we would not be shot either.

Suddenly we noticed that not only were we nervous, but the SS and the guards also displayed a great deal of irritability and fear. They knew better than we how close the American troops were to the camp and they had reason to be worried.

On Thursday 26 April the people who had entered the camp the day before were told to assemble on the Appellplatz. The Musselmen were separated from the rest of the crowd and the others were ordered to start moving. They left the camp. If we had wanted, we certainly could have joined this group, but we were steadfast in our decision to stay.

Early in the afternoon a new group of prisoners was brought into our camp, but they were not allowed to stay. They were given soup, the weaker ones were sent into the camp, and the rest continued on their march. Looking at them, I felt that our decision to stay had been justified. These people had been marching for several days from somewhere in central Germany, and none of them could survive another few days on the death march. In our gamble we had conserved energy. The camp was now full of the sick and feeble.

In the evening our mood changed. Late in the day, after the sun had set, a group of SS-men came into the camp, selected the stronger ones from the blocks, and ordered them to follow the guards. A little while later they came back pushing buggies full of firewood. The people were then instructed to unload the firewood and to stack it along the fence. At first we were not concerned, but when the amount of wood became excessive and the work did not stop, we began to suspect that there was foul play in the making. The people in the camp became alarmed, and when several barrels with fuel were brought into the camp, panic gripped us all. It was obvious. In the last minute the final extermination was being prepared. Berl and I had gambled too long.

We sneaked out of our hut and started to investigate the camp layout, the fences, the gate, but everything pointed to one thing: in case of a conflagration there was no place to hide. From the towers, the guards could oversee the entire camp, and their machine guns were trained on us.

Since the inmates were quite weak, the work progressed at a much slower pace than the SS had anticipated. By midnight there were still large stretches around the periphery which had no wood. In case of fire and a favorable wind, this area of the camp would remain intact. But oddly enough, the Germans were in some sort of confusion themselves. There seemed to be some hesitancy on the part of the guards to go through with the plan. In any case, the preparations were stopped late at night and the camp was awaiting the morning.

Our thoughts were now with the American troops. How far from us were they? Could they overrun the camp before the murderers were able to execute their evil design? We had been disappointed in the ghetto when we were hoping for the Russians to overtake the Nazis. Was this a replay of the same scenario: waiting for liberation, but the redemption not coming in time? This was a sleepless night. It seemed that we had gambled and lost.

On Friday 27 April we were awakened early in the morning and again a group was taken out to bring in more firewood. Suddenly, totally unexpectedly, the commander of the camp ran in and ordered everything stopped. We were to evacuate immediately. What was it now? Where were they planning to take us? There was no point in speculating. Only the people who could not move at all and were close to dying were left in the camp. They were all carried to one area and placed in the huts there. This looked terribly ominous. Apparently they did not have enough wood to burn the entire camp down and decided to liquidate only the totally hopeless cases. But what would happen to us? Everybody was ordered to go to their huts, fetch their belongings, and report to the Appellplatz. I returned to my shop to see whether I wanted to take anything along. Here I met the assistant to Dr. Zacharin who had admitted me to the infirmary. He too came back to see whether there was anything he wanted to take with him. He checked the various bottles and finally decided to take vitamin pills, of which he had an ample supply. He took a few bottles for himself and gave me a few. This was a good supplement to our vitamin-deficient food. I thanked him, put a few brushes and other minor supplies into my pocket, and out we walked. Once everybody was ready, the camp commander informed us that we were being taken to Dachau proper. Bad as this was, it was a far cry from being burned alive. I looked at Berl and he at me. A heavy yoke had fallen off our shoulders. We had escaped destruction once more.

Once out of the camp we were chased towards Kaufering, where we had arrived nine months ago. Several people died from exhaustion on this relatively short stretch and their bodies were loaded on carts which followed us. At the station the carts were taken somewhere and the bodies were disposed of. We were then instructed to enter a train which was already waiting for us. The cars had once belonged to passenger trains. They were now damaged, with broken doors, windows, and seats. The guards took their positions at the open doors and we squeezed together inside. Finally the train started to move. If the SS were not lying again, we were supposed to be on our way to Dachau. We proceeded slowly and covered very little ground.

Around noon we reached a small station. The inscription read Schwabhausen. Here the train stopped for some inexplicable reason. Parallel with our train, several other trains stood on the tracks. Suddenly we heard the hum of airplanes. Before we knew what happened, a shower of bombs hit the trains. In scarcely two minutes it was all over and the planes were gone. The locomotive and all the wagons immediately behind it were badly damaged. The quiet was pierced by loud screaming and crying: hundreds of concentration camp inmates were killed and hundreds were wounded during this air attack. Fortunately we were in the rear of the train and were spared.

The moment the planes were gone, the German guards jumped from the train and started yelling to abandon the train and run to the forest, which was near the tracks. Everybody who could still move scrambled out of the train and ran for cover into the woods. Berl and I made our way quickly out of the train and across the tracks. We had barely reached the outskirts of the forest as a second wave of planes approached the station. The guards screamed to us to hit the ground and we fell on our faces, while a second load of bombs was unloaded on the area. Again people were killed and wounded and the site looked like a battlefield, with casualties strewn all across the tracks. A little later we found out from the guards that the locomotive was damaged and a new locomotive was supposed to come from Dachau to pick us up.

This was serious. Here we were in a small forest, surrounded by an army of SS guards. Who would stop them from shooting and killing all of us? We could not put up any resistance. Most of us were too weak to even walk. Time was passing very slowly and no locomotive appeared in sight. The SS guards were also scared, which made them even more vicious and trigger-happy. Berl and I sat down on the ground deeper in the forest to be as far away from the guards as possible. Suddenly we heard several shots. A man cried out in agony, "My child, my child! Oh, no! Why did he shoot him?"

The anguish and the torment in this father's outcry spread to all the bystanders. Berl and I decided to stay away, since this mad guard could start shooting again. A few people returned from the scene of the shooting. "What happened?" I asked the man.

"The younger son of Yatkunski was shot dead!"

"What," I screamed, out of control, "are you sure?"

"Go and look," he said.

"How did it happen? What did the boy do?" I asked.

"You don't have to do much with those bandits. The youngster got too close to the edge of the forest and the guard assumed that he was trying to escape, so he shot him without warning."

"My God, my God! So close to liberation, why, God, why?" I barely managed to whisper. I tried to approach Yatkunski, but during the shooting more guards rushed to the scene and warned everybody to stay away.

Yatkunski's cries filled the air of the peaceful forest. One more Jew shot. Big deal! They had killed millions, so what was one more. But for Yatkunski this was his whole world, his hope. He had already lost the entire family of his brother, his parents, and numerous relatives. This son was his treasure. Now he had only his last son left. He and this son stood in a silent embrace over the fresh grave of an innocent child. It was so close to liberation, but he had not lived to see it.

Meanwhile time was passing and no locomotive was in sight. I remembered that Dr. Zacharin's assistant had given me vitamin tablets and I decided to see what they were like. The tablets looked very much like little colored chocolate candy, their taste was juicy, and I ate one, which seemed to refresh me a bit. I gave one to Berl, who did not like it and spat it out.

We were all so upset by the Yatkunski case that we did not notice that suddenly there were no guards around the forest. Where had they gone? Were they hiding outside the forest? Was this a provocative action for us to start moving out of the woods, giving them a pretext to shoot at us? What was going on? Dr. Cohn, a Jewish physician from Prague with whom I got friendly in the camps, approached me and said, "Mishelski, I think we are free."

"What do you think, we are free?" I asked.

"Watch, there are no guards, they have all disappeared, the Americans must be very close."

"But how do you know where they are hiding? This could be a provocation."

"I don't believe it," Dr. Cohn replied, "they are scared of the Americans and took advantage of the bombing to get lost."

I was not so convinced of his theory. "And what about the retreating German army? If the Americans are in hot pursuit, the retreating army must still pass the area. I am even more afraid of the retreating troops than the SS. A retreating army is like a hunted animal. It will attack without provocation."

"I don't quite see it your way. I believe we are free."

"So what do you propose to do?"

"I believe we should stay here in the forest and hide. Maybe the Americans are closer than you think."

"This is wishful thinking. I have been through this kind of hopefulness before, in the ghetto, when we were waiting for the Russians."

A group of people had gathered around us, some agreeing with me and some with Dr. Cohn. While we were heating up our discussion, we heard the whistle of a locomotive. The promised locomotive from Dachau had arrived. A group of Germans ordered us to enter the train quickly. A decision had to be made instantaneously. We still had a chance to hide. The Germans had not entered the forest and seemingly did not care to do so. Berl and I decided to take the train. Dr. Cohn changed his mind and joined us, but quite a number of Jews decided to follow Dr. Cohn's original idea and stayed in the forest. Meanwhile I was hungry. I was popping those vitamin pills like candy.

The train was filling up quickly. The majority had apparently decided not to gamble at the last minute. The train was dirty and most of the people had lice crawling all over them. I only hoped that these were not typhus-carrying lice. That was the last thing I needed now. Suddenly I became violently ill. From the overdose of vitamins I got horrendous cramps and I thought I would pass out. There was no toilet in the car and I could not hold it. Berl helped me to the platform, where I barely had time to pull my pants down. I had very little food in my stomach, yet I had convulsions and an uncontrollable urge to defecate. It felt as if I was excreting my entire viscera. But after I had cleaned myself out, my pain subsided and I recovered quickly. I threw out the bottle with the remaining vitamins and was furious with the doctor who had neglected to warn me against the effects of an overdose.

Late in the afternoon our train arrived in Dachau. Here, in front of the gate, a rather surprising view revealed itself to us: Red Cross cars and ambulances and Red Cross personnel, unmistakably foreigners, were mingling with the Germans and apparently issuing orders, as if they were in command. This was something we had not seen in four years, and it was somewhat reassuring. First, we were taken to the showers and delousing center. I was glad about this, since I was worried about the lice on the people with whom I had come into contact on the train. If any had attached themselves to my clothing, I was glad to be rid of them before any damage was done. When we came out on the clean side, we waited for our clothes to come through. When my clothes arrived, my coat was missing. During my days in camp #2, when I was in charge of distributing clothing, I had noticed a brand-new double-breasted coat which fit me perfectly. Since I did not have to account to anybody, I took the warm coat for myself. I wore this coat for the rest of my stay in all the camps. But here in Dachau, apparently the delousing center capo noticed the coat and decided it would fit him, so he appropriated it. When I questioned its whereabouts, I was beaten up. It was 27 April, and in Bavaria it was still very cold. Here I was now in this cold weather freezing fiercely and without any coat. But this was Dachau and that said it all.

On Saturday the twenty-eighth when we got up, we noticed to our dismay that quite a few of our friends were missing. They all had decided to hide in the forest. This was very upsetting. There was a good chance that my logic had failed me in the last minute and the reasoning of Dr. Cohn was correct, although he himself was here too.

Dachau itself was an international camp. There were hardly any Jews there except our latest transport and some Jews who had been there long before. Mostly the people were Czech, Polish, French, and other underground activists, some British and other prisoners of war, plus a considerable number of recent Russian prisoners of war. One could hear just about any language here. Their regimen was substantially easier than ours and they were not at all worried that they would be shot, particularly at this stage of the war. The number of prisoners was estimated at thirty-two thousand and it almost looked like a city. There were hundreds of little prefabricated buildings and at the edge of the camp there was a crematorium. Berl and I looked at the huge stack and started to worry.

Around 11 o'clock, an order came through that all the prisoners who were brought in the day before, in other words our transport, had to report to the Appellplatz. No explanation was given. As soon as this order was issued, we decided to skip our barracks. There was no way we would report to the Appellplatz, no matter what the purpose was. We sneaked out quickly and entered another barracks. The number of people in the camp was so huge that we could hardly be recognized. Some other Jewish prisoners did the same and disappeared. The rest of the people were ordered to form columns of one hundred each and were led out of the camp for another death march. We spent the whole day of 28 April in hiding and surfaced only in the evening for food.

The next day was Sunday the twenty-ninth. The day started as every other day, but around noon an exchange of fire could be heard in the distance.

We did not know how to judge how far this shooting was from the camp. We surmised that this was artillery fire and that the Americans were five or ten miles from us. This had to be the battle between the retreating Germans, which I feared so much, and the advancing victorious Americans. We stayed in the barracks, afraid to stick our noses out. But we were greatly mistaken. The shooting was not five or ten miles away but in the town of Dachau itself, on the outskirts of which the camp was located. The sounds came closer until they seemed to be next door rather than miles away. Suddenly the shooting stopped and an eerie silence covered the camp. All barracks doors flew open and people ran from barracks to barracks, yelling and screaming, "The Americans are here! The Americans are here!"

Pandemonium gripped the camp. People were hugging and kissing each other, groups formed to sing songs and to congratulate each other. Berl and I crawled out of our bunks and went outside. We were still not sure that this was really happening. So deep was fear ingrained into our psyches that we were worried about a possible Nazi provocation. But the next thing we knew, we saw American soldiers for the first time in our lives. We wanted to grab them and embrace them, but they were mobbed by so many people that there was no chance to get close to any of them.

All of a sudden we noticed that hundreds of people were streaming in one direction. We decided to join the mob. When we came to the place everybody was eager to get to, we saw a dozen or two German guards on the ground, placed one next to the other in a straight row. These guards had opened fire from their guard towers on the Americans who had entered the camp and the Americans shot them in the ensuing battle. This was the shooting we had heard before. The overwhelming American firepower knocked them out and they were taken down from the towers and placed on the ground. We stood there for a while, looking at these hated faces and uniforms. How easily it could have been the other way around: we being dead on the ground and these murderers standing and looking at our corpses. It was hard to believe how much grief and sorrow these murderers had caused in a once peaceful world: killing and shooting, gassing and cremating innocent people at will. Even in this last stand they were not ready to surrender gracefully and had to kill the American soldiers who were liberating Europe from a scourge the world had never seen before. These SS guards could not kill anybody anymore.

We stood silently meditating, hundreds of thoughts criss-crossing our minds. Was this all real, or was this a dream? We had to pinch ourselves to make sure we were alive. But looking at those guards on the ground there could be no more doubt. This all was true, unbelievable as it looked.

At last we were free.

BOOK FOUR

THE BALANCE SHEET

. . . Who shall live and who shall die;
Who shall perish by fire and who by water;
Who by sword and who by beast;
Who by hunger and who by thirst;
Who by earthquake and who by plague;
Who by strangling and who by stoning. . . .

—*From the Hebrew
High Holiday Liturgy*

HEADQUARTERS
DACHAU CONCENTRATION CAMP
TEMPORARY PASS

Date _22 May 45._

Good from _10-14:00_

Permit _Mischelski, Wolf_ to pass

to compound as he has bene called
for on official business to perform some special
task for the Military Authorities at the Dachau Concent.
Camp.

MARTIN W JOY CHARLES ROSENBLOOM

Security O-4-PA 0185334 Lt., Inf.

29

IN THE AFTERMATH

Although we always hoped that one day we would be liberated, we had known that our actual chances of survival were almost non-existent. The Nazis had built an extermination apparatus unparalleled in the annals of mankind. They had mobilized all the anti-Semites in Europe, who were so confident of the German victory that they voluntarily joined the massacres. They were sure they would never be held accountable. In every country the Nazis occupied, they had no difficulty finding accomplices to compete with the Germans for the honors of who would kill more Jews. The killings were perpetrated by people from every walk of life, from the illiterate peasant all the way to academicians, who willingly and enthusiastically joined in the fray. Even in countries which the Germans had overrun by force and whose people were deadly enemies of the Germans, the Nazis easily found collaborators. Under this bloody hysteria, our chances of survival were nil, and we were very well aware of it. Yet each of us hoped that maybe God would be gracious to him and grant him the gift of life despite all odds. In our minds, whenever we thought about the possibility of surviving we always envisioned liberation at the hands of the Russians. In our dreams, we saw the Red Army overrunning the Nazi hordes and liberating us in the ghetto in Kovno. As free people, we would then resume our lives where we had left off, and despite the heavy bloodletting, start a normal life as before the war.

How different was the reality from our visions! Never in our imaginary scenario were the Americans in the picture. Never in all those long four years did we foresee that liberation would come to us in Dachau. The whole thing was so fantastic that for days we were in a fog. Every couple of minutes, I would instinctively turn around to see whether or not a guard was following me. When there was none, I still could not believe it. For four horrible years, this was the scene I was used to seeing. Realizing that we were rid of that affliction was both relieving and scary.

This state of fantasy, this state of exultation, quickly evaporated, and reality set in. Not only were we wrong on how and where liberation would come to us, but we were wrong on just about every aspect of our first days of freedom. Who could have thought that hundreds of people would still die after liberation? Yet people were dying, and the causes for death were not only physical. Slowly, mental problems started to surface too. Feelings of happiness over our miraculous deliverance got intertwined with feelings of sorrow and guilt, of fear and apathy. We had been torn apart by scenes of death all around us. Daily somebody dear to us succumbed and died before our eyes. Hundreds had been in a life and death struggle, not knowing whether or not they would make it to the next day. Most of our friends had turned into Musselmen and their survival was greatly in question. And although the Americans had established a hospital almost the very first day, very few were admitted. There was just not enough space available. For all practical purposes, almost every Jewish survivor needed hospitalization! The only thing, short of good medical care, that kept many people alive was the enormous inner drive to survive, to spite the Nazis and the whole indifferent world which had allowed us to reach this state. Liberation was such a major event that we had to live. Besides, we wanted to survive just in case anyone of our dear ones was alive somewhere.

But while the drive to live was the dominant feeling, we were also haunted by feelings of guilt. Why did we survive? Why were we chosen to live while millions of Jews had perished? Were the others sinners while we were saints? What wrong had the others done, beyond having been born Jewish? We were born Jewish too, yet the hand of the devil had somehow missed us. This guilt feeling was not easy to bear. Suddenly, fear and apathy would set in.

I tried to draw my balance sheet, and it was frightening. I had lost my father at the Seventh Fort in July 1941. I had left my mother and my sister in Stutthof, my sister an invalid and my mother an elderly lady who would undoubtedly have stayed with Vera, even if it meant death. There was no chance that they were alive. My sweetheart, Minnie, had been taken during the Estonian Action and her fate was greatly in doubt, too. She was much too fragile, much too childish to be able to cope with the rigors that we had all been through. Max, my brother-in-law, had remained in the hide-out. His chances for survival were reasonable, provided the Russians had advanced with utmost speed. Ruthie, Vera's daughter, was burned alive in the laundry building in the ghetto before our very eyes. The family Mishelski, my father's cousins, had been killed during the pogrom in Slobotke. Dvora, Vera's mother-in-law, had been taken out of the line-up when we first arrived at Stutthof.

Sonja had joined Vera and mother during evacuation from the ghetto. If she stayed with Vera, her fate was sealed. Rivka had remained in the ghetto, in our first hide-out in the roof space behind the sheet metal cabinet. Her fate was probably the same as Max's. Gitta, my last girlfriend in the ghetto, and Nucia had escaped to the Aryan side and were hidden by Lithuanian peasants, hopefully decent ones. A great number of these peasants were provocateurs and in many cases delivered the Jews to the Gestapo for a petty reward. This was the case with Wolf, Max's brother, and with the pharmacist Srebnitski. Max's third brother, Hayim, with his wife ran to the Russian border, trying to reach the safety of its deep expanses, but most people who ran were killed on the roads, as was Sonja's husband in Dvinsk.

Max's two younger brothers had been arrested and shot at the Seventh Fort. Mother's sister-in-law and her mother had been massacred at the Ninth Fort during the Big Action. Giza, my first girlfriend, had been butchered at the Ninth Fort during the Small Ghetto Action. And of my friends, Nahum was transferred to Leitmeritz in Czechoslovakia and Nolik remained with Max in the hide-out. Berl's brother had joined the death march during the liquidation of camp #1 and the fate of this march was still unknown to us. And this was only a partial list of my relatives and friends. From our apartment building in Kovno, all men had been arrested, along with me, the first week of the war and all had been shot at the Seventh Fort together with my father.

The list went on and on without end. As I worked out the balance of living to dead, fear and despair quickly began to supplant my feelings of elation over our deliverance. As I looked around, I was all alone, in the heart of an anti-Semitic Germany and an equally anti-Semitic world which was not willing to admit its guilt. Who cared about the Jews anyway? If anything, the world was sorry that there were any survivors at all! My main hope was that perhaps one of my dear ones had survived. This was the best I could make of my liberation.

Forlorn and lonely, I decided to check the barracks where Jews were housed to see whether I could find some friends from my hometown. One of the first I ran into was a friend of mine by the name of Kupritz. He had been through all the same painful years in the ghetto and in Dachau. At the time of liberation, he was a total Musselman. I got scared when I saw him, he was barely recognizable. I greeted him and tried to engage in a conversation, but he could barely speak. His voice was shaky and hardly audible.

"Mishelski," he said, "I have no more strength left in me. I cannot endure this any longer. I feel I will die."

"Don't talk like this," I answered, "you have lived to see our liberation, our troubles are over. It is now a matter of slowly regaining your strength."

"No, Mishelski," he replied, "I will never regain my strength, I am finished. Nothing can help me any more. It is too late for me, it is all over."

I helped him to his barracks and left, not thinking much about it. The next morning when I came to his barracks, I did not find him there. It still did not register with me. He was free and food was now available, why should I have any doubts? When I did not find him in the evening, I checked with people in the barracks, who told me that he had died that same night. This was a terrible shock to me. Here was a man who had survived all Nazi atrocities, yet was beyond redemption. When was a person beyond recovery? At what state of deterioration could a person still be alive but unsalvageable even with the best medical care? Apparently the human body could recover and regenerate after severe hunger and debilitation, but after a certain limit, the capacity to recover was destroyed and no help was possible. Kupritz had exceeded that limit.

There were others who died after liberation. The Americans, having never seen such living skeletons, were deeply touched by these tragic human beings and were extremely generous with food and gifts. They distributed cigarettes, canned meats, chocolate, and other food from their rations which the emaciated concentration camp survivors were only too eager to accept. But not being accustomed to such rich food, many died from overeating. Among the recipients of such gifts and canned foods was a colleague of mine, an engineer by the name of Mintzer. Mintzer was not as rundown as Kupritz and his chances of survival were probably beyond question. But the next day, Mintzer suddenly felt sick and had severe cramps. The pain was excruciating and he fainted. I and a few friends of mine placed him on a blanket and carried him to the infirmary. His long-starved body could not digest the relatively large quantity of rich food. In one day, Mintzer was gone. This reminded me of my episode with the condensed milk in camp #7, and of the vitamin poisoning. In both cases I managed to survive because, fortunately for me, I was still relatively healthy. A less wholesome body would have succumbed and probably died. I was just plain lucky.

But Mintzer was not the only one who died from overeating. Dozens of prisoners shared the same fate. As soon as the problem was diagnosed by the Americans, the food rations were reduced and the G.I.'s were instructed, in our own interest, not to distribute any more food to weak inmates. But for Mintzer it was too late.

There were more deaths. Herman Frenkel, the father of a friend of mine, was still in good condition. He had slept in an elite barracks in camp #1, the way I had been in camps #2 and #7, and was not used to the awful conditions in regular barracks, where living people lay on the same bunk alongside corpses. The experience of being on the same bunk with dying and dead people and the filth and stench around him was just too much. "I will never outlive this," he said, "I cannot survive such horror."

Over and over again, he kept repeating this statement. I could appreciate the man's problem. He had been probably the best-dressed person in the concentration camp. There was never as much as a speck of dust on his clothes. Always neatly shaven, he didn't fit into the environment around him. Yet it never occured to me that these horrible conditions could be a cause of death. We did not take it seriously. But within a week, unbelievable as it was, the man was dead. His son Shlomo was heartbroken. It suddenly dawned on us how easily one of our survivors could die and how much care everyone of us needed not to succumb and turn into one of the unredeemable.

Several days passed. I was still checking the various barracks in search of friends when I accidentally stumbled across a man who knew Pipsi. He told me that Pipsi was alive and in the American hospital in Dachau, but he was a hopeless Musselman and it would take a miracle for him to survive. I was very eager to see him, but at first I was not allowed to enter. When I finally got permission, I could hardly recognize him. He was completely rundown, perhaps not quite as bad as Kupritz, but certainly not far from it. But there was one basic difference between the two of them: Pipsi was full of fight. The possibility of death did not enter his mind. He held on to life by the skin of his teeth and fought valiantly for survival. Was he winning his fight? I wondered whether a person with a weaker personality would have succumbed and died. Was the difference between him and Kupritz only a matter of inner strength, or was that minute distinction in the health of the two the difference between life and death? From the dozens of people around me who were in the throes of death, I could clearly see that attitude was instrumental in the fight for life. Many borderline cases could easily go either way just by the degree of fortitude and determination to survive. Pipsi had this determination and his condition improved with every passing day.

I was concerned about what had happened to the people who had decided to stay in the forest in Schwabhausen. Were they overrun by the retreating German armies and mowed down by them, as I feared, or were they alive? It did not take long to find out. After the SS-guard had fled, everybody in the group was left on his own. Some entered the abandoned wagons of the bombed-out train to find shelter, others hid in the forest, and some decided to seek shelter in some houses of Germans in the village. Misha Meilup, who used to distribute the food in the hospital, at first decided to hide in a wagon in the bombed-out train. But when he and a friend of his got hungry, they entered the house of a local German and demanded food and shelter. The German was in a serious bind, but he knew that the Americans were expected in town very shortly and he did not resist. The entire group was liberated on 28 April, one day ahead of us. This was the first bit of good news we had in a while.

Next I found out about Peter. He was forced to join the march when camp #2 was liquidated and was freed by the advancing Americans in Allach, a camp near Dachau. News also reached us about the death march from camp #1, which I had missed by hiding in the infirmary. Hundreds of people who could not keep up with the pace had been shot on the road. Others broke down from the rigors of the march and died. But not everyone had perished. The advance of the Americans was just too fast. On 1 May one group was overtaken in Buchberg, and the next day another group was liberated in Bad Toelz. As in Dachau, the Americans were most compassionate and generous in their distribution of food and cigarettes. Unfortunately, here as well many inmates, not realizing the dangers involved in overeating, died from the overabundance of food. Among the liberated were Simon, Nathan, and Berl's brother. The Americans immediately set up hospitals for the survivors, where the care, attention, and human treatment were a refreshing relief after all the ugly and inhumane behaviour we had experienced throughout the war.

Most of the stronger survivors were taken to Freimann, near Munich, where German barracks were made available to them. After leaving Dachau, I went to Freimann first. Here I met Gitta's father, who informed me that Gitta was alive. He also had information that Gitta was on her way to Rome. This was good news, indeed. I was quite excited over the prospect of seeing her again. Shortly thereafter, I left Freimann and went to a sanatorium in St. Ottilien, a former monastery which had been set aside by the Americans for care of the survivors. Here I met Meilup, who was in charge of one wing. Here I also found out about Moolik, the youngster of our graphics shop, who had joined the partisans. He had survived the war but had lost an arm in the fight with the Germans. But there was no word yet from all the women whom we had left in Stutthof.

All we knew was that some of them had been liberated by the Russians, but who was alive was unknown.

A community was now in the process of forming in Freimann, and refugees who found out about it started drifting, first in small groups and later in larger streams, to Munich. Among the refugees was a friend of mine by the name of Meryash, a first cousin of Nahum. As soon as I found out about him, I went to Munich to see him. The news he had was grim. At first Nahum managed to establish himself as a capo and was holding his own. But he was much too refined and much too decent to be a capo and eventually was pushed out by an aggressive inmate. Once he had lost his job, it was one long way downhill. First his father died, then he got sick but was not allowed to take shelter in the infirmary. When his strength was gone, he was beaten to death one day by a capo for not performing on the job. Meryash had great difficulty in relating the details of the tragedy to me. Several times he had to stop to steady his voice and stay the flow of tears. I had a lump in my throat and could not talk. Nahum's death was one of the hardest blows I had experienced after liberation. We were like brothers and had gone through so much together. During the liquidation of camp #2 we were separated, and now it was forever. Once again, as in the case of Giza and Minnie, the desire to stay together with the family, in his case to stay with his father, spelled his doom. I was disconsolate.

A partial uplifting in my spirit, however, came during my next visit to Munich. As usual I was looking for friends among the refugees, when I found one who in the first day of the war ran towards Russia, volunteered to the Red Army, and fought against the Nazis almost throughout the entire war. From him I found out that in 1942 the Russians had organized a Lithuanian unit, the so-called 16th Division. The majority among the soldiers as well as the officers, were Jewish refugees from Lithuania. This Division saw serious action in February of 1943 between Kursk and Orel. They were the first to experience the vicious summer offensive of the Germans in the famous battles in that area. But the determination of this group to fight the Nazis was so fierce that they not only stood their ground, but even entered the much celebrated Russian counter-offensive. In the fall of 1943 up to the summer of 1944 they participated in the battles near Vitebsk and Polock, and were the first units to re-enter Lithuania. Among the many towns they helped to liberate was Mariampole, the hometown of Rivka and Sonja. In fact a Jewish officer, as a special honor, marched into town at the head of his unit. Many soldiers of this division had earned military decorations for valor, with twelve officers receiving the highest honor—Hero of the Soviet Union. Four of those were Jews.

But the cost to human life among this division was exceptionally high. To my deep sorrow, I found out that Moshe Gluck, the brother of Sonja and Rivka, was among them.

I spent the entire afternoon listening to his wartime experiences, to stories of heroism and dedication to avenge the innocent blood of their families, who perished at the hands of the Nazis. These lifted my spirit. I also found out from him that many Jewish youngsters did manage to reach Russia in the first days of the war, when they ran away from Lithuania. This raised my hopes that maybe Hayim, Max's brother, did after all reach the safety of Russia.

But unfortunately, he had no information for me about my family or Minnie.

During the ensuing weeks my physical recovery progressed, but my emotional recovery did not. An agonizing period of waiting to find out who survived set in. Sleepless nights and anguish over the fate of my dear ones followed me wherever I went.

This state of mind was not peculiar to me alone. Most survivors like myself, who had lost dozens of members of their families and friends, were worried about the fate of the people they had left behind in the hideouts in the ghetto and in Stutthof. To alleviate our anxieties, an American chaplain by the name of Rabbi Klausner was assigned to assist the victims of the Holocaust in tracing down survivors. Customarily during a war and after a calamity, lists of casualties are posted on church doors and municipal buildings to let the people know about the people who gave their lives for their country. Our case, however, was totally different. Lists of the casualties would have run into the millions. Instead, Rabbi Klausner started to publish lists of survivors. There were so pitifully few of them that the first list fit into a small booklet. Entire communities had been annihilated by the anti-Semitic orgy in a world gone berserk. There were single survivors from a massacre here and a massacre there, lonely survivors from a town and a village. Of Lithuanian Jewry, 95% had been killed by the bloodthirsty animals who had forgotten the elementary tenet of Christian belief: Thou shall not kill. And nobody had the guts to put a stop to it, including the church! But these booklets of the Rabbi covered only the survivors in the American zone of Germany. There was still no word about the survivors of Stutthof and Kovno proper.

As the months passed, Europe slowly dug itself out of the ruins and connections were established even with the countries behind the iron curtain. With the borders opening up little by little, my first instinct was to return to Kovno. It was logical to assume that if any of my dear ones had survived, they would go back to Lithuania. With the postal service not functioning yet and without telephone connection, the only contact to Lithuania was through a cumbersome combination of short train rides and long walks. This was the only way to find out who was alive. An irresistible drive to determine who was alive was drawing me towards Lithuania. Once more I was caught between conflicting emotions. I had a ghastly, empty feeling that there was nothing in Kovno to which to return. Lithuania was one big cemetery for Lithuanian Jews: the Ninth Fort, the Seventh Fort, the dozens of little provincial towns. There was nothing left. The Lithuanian landscape had been inundated with Jewish mass graves. I could never find happiness there. But I had to know what happened to my family, my Minnie, my friends. How would I ever find out about them? These conflicting feelings robbed me of sleep and peace of mind.

Suddenly a brand-new feeling started to overshadow all else. As during the liquidation of camp #1, in my subconscious the voice of God seemed to be talking to me. God had led me to the infirmary so I might be spared the death march; God had arranged my liberation at the hands of the Americans and not the Russians. I had to accept God's will to me: the Americans had liberated me, the Americans had shown a compassion for mankind and a trust in God, which the Germans, the Lithuanians, and the other Christian nations in Europe had forgotten. I stood with my head bowed to the greatness of the American soldier who had not lost his humanity even in battle. I would not trade these wonderful first images for a permanent stay on the bloody soil of Europe. I decided not to return. If anybody had survived, God would help.

This internal struggle tortured most Lithuanian Jews. But the majority of the liberated Jews, driven by anxiety and many by patriotism, decided to return to Lithuania as fast as their health allowed them.

Days and weeks dragged on in agony without any news from behind the iron curtain. When communications started to improve, a trickle of Jewish survivors from Lithuania began to arrive in Munich, in the American zone of Germany. Every time I heard about such a group arriving, I would rush there to talk to them. Their reports were grim. There was no word about my mother, my sister, Max, or my Minnie. Not one of the refugees knew them or had seen them, but they had horrible news about the ghetto. With the exception of two massive hide-outs, where a few dozen people had survived, there were no survivors. From the reports of the various refugees who were now in Munich and whom I had contacted, I pieced together the whole gruesome story of the liquidation of the ghetto.

The SS and the Gestapo knew that hide-outs and bunkers were being built in the ghetto, and on 13 July they also knew how many Jews were still hidden. The Einsatzkommandos that arrived to liquidate the ghetto were thoroughly apprised of all the facts. They were professional killers who had purged all of Eastern Europe of Jews. They were fanatic anti-Semites, beasts in the disguise of human beings. They killed hundreds of thousands of Jews without the slightest hesitation and without blinking an eye, bringing to Europe the New Order of the Fuehrer.

On 13 July the Einsatzkommandos, assisted by Latvians, came to the ghetto to finish the job. They were equipped with machine guns, dynamite, fuel, dogs, and armored cars. There was a tremendous shortage of fuel at the fronts, but not for the Einsatzkommandos. They had as much fuel as they wanted. The results of their zeal could already be seen by us when we left the ghetto on our way to the railroad station. Wooden houses gave them a very easy time. Max, Nolik, Rivka, and the Chazans were still safe when we left. But for how long?

The Einsatzkommandos were very thorough in their work. First they surrounded a home and took up a position with loaded guns. A second group took the fuel containers they had brought with them and drenched the building and torched the house. When the Jews who happened to be in that house tried to run from the flames, a murderous fire from the machine guns greeted them. Some Jews ran back into the flames and perished inside, the others were shot on the spot. Once a house was liquidated, they moved on to the next one. Here the process repeated itself: drenching, torching, and finally shooting. Where the buildings were of more substantial construction, dynamite was used. By the end of the day they had covered a good part of the ghetto. At night they posted a heavy guard around the ghetto to make sure that nobody escaped. Then they went home to their warm houses and families.

The next morning they returned to the ghetto again in full force. Methodically they proceeded from house to house. In many cases, the people who left the hide-outs were burning torches who succumbed before the volley of the machine guns hit them. When they reached the block buildings, burning was impossible. Now the demolition experts came into action. They wired all the blocks with dynamite and detonated the explosives. The buildings came down as if hit by an earthquake, burying everybody inside. The explosion caused bodies to be torn to pieces. Severed hands, legs, and heads flew through the air. With all their expertise, however, the concrete bunker remained intact. The people in it were now buried alive below the debris, but they had not been killed. The explosion destroyed their well-planned ventilation system and they were left to suffocate. But when the adjacent blocks were detonated, a small crack ripped open in the ceiling below the debris, allowing inflow of some air.

The next step were the blocks called B. The two-story masonry buildings were wired and demolished in a similar manner. By the end of the day, all the blocks were destroyed and about 75% of the ghetto was up in flames. A heavy guard was again posted around the ghetto and the experts went home.

That night Max and Nolik decided that staying in the hide-out meant certain death. They left the bunker and started inching towards the river, where thick brush could provide cover for them under the open sky. At first they moved cautiously, crawling on their stomachs, but the entire ghetto along the river front was in flames. Crawling on the hot debris and through the flames was impossible. There was no way back, they had to get through to the brush. Encouraged by their success so far, they threw caution to the winds. They decided to make a run to the brush and drop there to the ground. They stood up and started running, but in the bright light of the flames they were noticed by the heavy guard and the dogs were unleashed on them. There was no way to escape. They were torn to pieces by the bloodthirsty dogs. The guards followed, chased the dogs away, and finished them off by massive fire from the machine guns.

Rivka and the Chazans got out of the attic space and sneaked down into the vegetable cellar in hopes of escaping the fire.

Saturday 15 July the Einsatzkommandos returned. There was not much of the ghetto left to destroy. With the same ruthless tenacity as before, they proceeded from house to house until not a single building remained standing.

When they left the ghetto at the end of that day, the ghetto looked like a battlefield where war had raged for months. All the buildings had been burned to the ground or destroyed by dynamite. On the ground bodies and parts of bodies lay strewn all over. Men, women, and children charred beyond recognition were lying near the houses where they had lived for three years in the ghetto. The blocks were piles of rubble, as after a massive air attack. The struggle for survival could be seen from the expressions of the faces of some of the victims. Near one home, a woman with two children in her arms was dead on the ground. The eyes of the children were still open. Rivka, the beautiful, vivacious Rivka, the Chazans and their sweet teenager, suffocated in the cellar when they refused to come out.

On 16 July the Einsatzkommandos left Lithuania, their job well done.

In the meantime, the people in the bunker in Block C had survived the collapse of the massive blocks and would have suffocated if not for the crack that opened up in the ceiling below the debris. The air, however, was far from sufficient to accommodate all the people below. Besides, the air had a smell of burned flesh from the victims above and throughout the ghetto. Food was rapidly running out and so was the water. Originally the bunker had a water supply tapped to the main line, but the collapse of the building destroyed all the mains and pump. When the detonations and shooting had stopped they realized that the Einsatzkommandos had left, but who was in control up above? As long as the Russians had not entered the city and taken over the administration of it, even if the Germans were gone, the Lithuanian collaborators were just as dangerous as the Germans. Any Jew caught was in mortal danger from them. The people in Block C decided to stay underground until it was safe to surface. They did not dare to start to dig out or to increase the air supply for fear of being apprehended by hostile Lithuanians. At the end of a week or ten days people started to faint from lack or air, food, and water. One man decided he had enough and demanded to be allowed to dig himself out and leave the bunker. He was forceably detained.

Of the other two concrete bunkers, one was quickly discovered by the troopers and the occupants shot. But the other one remained concealed and the people were in a state of exhaustion, similar to those in Block C. Here a similar revolt occurred. Several men demanded to be allowed to escape. After long arguments and even a fight, three of them finally did leave. Of these, two were caught by local collaborators and shot during their attempted escape. The third, however, managed to hide and ultimately to survive. Tragically, only three days later the city was liberated by the Russians.

On 1 August the Russians finally entered the city of Kovno. The survivors left their bunkers. Their first move was to go through the ghetto in search of any survivors or dead friends. The picture they saw was eerie. The found bodies of friends burned beyond recognition, identifiable only by some objects carried on them or their dress. They found Rivka in the basement and Max with Nolik in the field away from their bunkers. Many survivors collapsed at the horror of the carnage. A few days after the Russians occupied Kovno, a mob of Lithuanians descended upon the ghetto with picks and shovels. A rumor had been spread that the Jews had buried their gold and silver in the ground before deportation. Everyone was eager to get rich quickly by finding those treasures. For days on end the Lithuanians dug up the ghetto in search of the loot. They found only bones and burned bodies.

My health had improved sufficiently to leave the sanatorium. About ten or twelve miles from St. Ottilien was Landsberg, where a Jewish D.P.

camp was in the process of forming. I decided to join this effort and at the end of July I moved to Landsberg. I immediately joined the United Nations Relief and Rehabilitation Administration and got involved in the formation of a Trade School for ORT (Organization for Rehabilitation through Training).

Landsberg was quickly transformed into a center of Jewish life and many surviving Jews were attracted to it. Among the people moving to this D.P. camp were numerous Lithuanian Jews, among them Jews already returning from Lithuania. As expected, they had quickly realized that there was no reason to stay in Lithuania: there was no more Jewish life there. Anti-Semitism in the country was rampant and the returning Jews were frowned upon by the gentile population. Not only did the Lithuanians openly show their displeasure, but many of them who had appropriated Jewish property were now unwilling to part with it. Before moving into the ghetto many Jews had entrusted them with jewelry, furniture, clothing, and other valuables which, upon return, they could legitimately claim. In the intervening years, the Lithuanians had written off the Jews as dead and considered themselves the legitimate heirs to the booty. The returning Jews were thus a thorn in their sides and they were made to feel it.

But even more importantly, after the Children's Action numerous Jews had left their children with Lithuanian families to save them from destruction. These families got used to the children and in many cases grew to love them as their own. Many Lithuanians gave those children a warm and loving home and, in some instances, even had them baptized. The children, particularly the smaller ones, got used to their new parents and already started to call them Mommy and Daddy. These cases presented heartbreaking decisions for all involved. The Lithuanian families very reluctantly parted with the children, who often refused to go with the unfamiliar "aunt" who came and took them away. In some cases, the Lithuanian families refused to hand over the children to relatives, unless the parents themselves came and claimed them. But most parents had been destroyed in the crematoria and in the concentration camps and the relatives had a difficult time pressing the issue.

There were many tales, each one a tragedy of its own, but among the worst was the incident with the family N. This family of ghetto Siauliai had managed to hide their two children and their own parents with a Lithuanian family, but were too late in arranging a hiding place for themselves. Both parents, who originally resided in a small Lithuanian town, were taken to the camps. They survived and returned to Lithuania. They had no trouble getting their children back and decided to settle in their former hometown. They reclaimed part of their property and started to rebuild their shattered lives. But the Lithuanian neighbors were very upset that they had to return all those valuables and waited to get even. One day, the parents and the grandmother went to Siauliai to take care of some personal business. When they returned, they found that both children had been murdered. The grandfather had managed to elude the bandits. The murderers, of course, were never apprehended. The news about this terrible murder spread like wildfire among the Jewish refugees and many made up their minds right there and then not to remain in Lithuania. The number of Jews fleeing their former homeland increased dramatically after this incident and many of them landed in Landsberg.

Every time a group came to the camp, the rest of the survivors mobbed them to find out whether they had any news from their loved ones. At first the Jews were mostly men, but shortly thereafter women started to appear. I could hardly wait to talk to them, but to my deep regret there was no news from my mother, Vera, or Minnie. Their description of the fate of the women and the children was frightening and shocking.

After we had left Stutthof, the women went through the showers where they were shaven clean and received some old, dirty, torn clothes. From there they were taken to the women's compound, where the first of a number of selections took place. During the first selection all older women, all sick and invalids, and all mothers with children were separated and sent to the gas chambers. Among these women was the one who had reclaimed her child during the scene on the plaza, on 12 July 1944, when she pointed out a hide-out to the Gestapo. Vera, of course, had lost Ruthie at that time, and ironically was now safe because of it. But she was still an invalid. Was she among the first to go to the gas chambers?

Since the women were separated from the men in Tiegenhof and Stutthof, they were sure that being physically weaker than the men and unable to perform slave labor, they would be destroyed. After the first selection, however, it started to look as if the healthy ones would not be sent to the crematorium.

Several days later a second selection took place and the healthy ones were sent to slave labor camps. About three thousand women were thus sent to camps in the area of Danzig. The work consisted of digging ditches and building fortifications to stem the advance of the Red Army. The work was beyond the strength of most women and was in fact beyond the strength of most men. Here in the field, they worked under every weather condition, were mistreated, beaten, and humiliated. There was inadequate food and clothing. The shelters were delapidated barracks, where the women were piled on top of one another in filth, hunger, and lice. During the winter, when frost set in and their hair had grown, the hair often froze to the boards and had to be cut off or pulled away by force. I hated to think that my mother suffered so. Once these women got too weak to work, they were sent to Stutthof for a "rest," where they forthwith went to the gas chambers and were destroyed. Neither mother, Vera, nor Minnie had anywhere near the physical strength to endure this kind of punishment. From the description of the suffering of the women, it looked more and more as if none of them had a chance. It became increasingly obvious why there was no news from any of them. I was resigned to the worst.

In January 1945 the big Russian offensive had started on the eastern front and their advance was swift. But the Nazis would not retreat and leave the women alone. In the midst of a ghastly winter frost, the women, with hardly any clothing to speak of on their backs, were driven out on the road westward towards Germany. Unlike the men of Dachau who commenced their death march in the spring under somewhat bearable conditions, these women were forced to march in the midst of a harsh winter. Hundreds of these unlucky people froze or starved to death, others were shot on the road. But the Russian advance was too fast and the first group of women was liberated on 23 January 1945 on the way between Thorn and Bromberg. Among the liberated was a good friend of mine, a former student of the art academy in Kovno and a gifted artist. She had lost all her fingers, with only the thumb and a stub of the little finger remaining on both hands.

The other groups were chased further along, always trying to evade the pursuing Russians. By the end of February they reached a little village by the name of Chinow. Here they were dumped into a barn with almost one thousand women in it. The sick, the dying, and the dead were all lying on top of one another and a deadly epidemic of typhus gripped the women who were still alive. The ones who were still healthy were in contact with the sick. Many of them contracted the disease. The dead were pulled out from underneath the living only every two or three days and dumped in a ditch behind the barn. The ditch was kept open until it filled up, whereupon the healthier women had to cover the ditch with earth.

Several days later a second group of women was brought to the barn. This group had been through a harrowing experience. The girls who were too weak to undertake the march were given injections by the guards. The girls were told that the injections were to strengthen them so they could survive until they were liberated. But in reality, these were death shots, from which all were supposed to die. But the guards, not having medical experience, missed the veins and put the shots into the muscles. Some girls managed to survive. Among them was Nahum's girlfriend Dora. But from the injection, a muscle in her arm had to be removed, leaving an unsightly hole there. The group which had received the death shots was left in the camp to die. They were liberated in a day or two, while the others managed to reach Chinow. For a week or so, it looked as if the barn would be set on fire and everybody would perish, but the SS were now on the run. They left the camp hastily, before managing to execute their evil design. On 10 March 1945 the women who were still alive were liberated by the Red Army.

Stutthof in the meantime was still in the hands of the Nazis, and the Red Army bypassed the camp temporarily. In Stutthof, as in Chinow, a typhus epidemic had gripped the camp and most women died there. The survivors were loaded on ships, since all land roads were already blocked and evacuated. The Nazis would not relinquish even these few miserable survivors. For several days these ships floated in the Baltic Sea, headed for the port of Kiel. When women got sick for lack of food or seasickness, they were simply thrown overboard to drown.

On 2 May one ship was bombed by the British. Dozens of women died during this air raid. The ship was finally towed into the port of Kiel, part of the ship on fire. Many women burned alive. To the complete amazement of the survivors, they found the town of Kiel in the hands of the Allied troops. The few surviving women were too sick and too weak even to celebrate their liberation. Almost all surviving women, as soon as they were able to move, started on their way back to Lithuania. A few remained in Kiel, and some even reached Sweden for recuperation.

What they found in Lithuania was most discouraging, but the war was still on and they remained in Lithuania to wait until they knew what had happened to the men.   Once the war was over and they found out about the Jews in the American zone of Germany, they started to drift towards Munich, Landsberg, and St. Ottilien. From them, I found out that Renee and her sister-in-law, Rosl, had survived the war and were on their way to West Germany, and Sarah, Pipsi's wife, had perished.

How cruel fate was to us! Pipsi had survived but his wife did not. Nahum did not make it, but his girlfriend, Dora, lived to see liberation. I was worried. Would my case be the same as Pipsi's, with Minnie gone? I tried to push those thoughts away and not dwell on them.

From the next group of refugees I found out that Nucia had survived and the Lithuanian couple was very decent and helpful during her time in hiding. Also, Reeva had survived and was on her way to the west.

One day in early August, when I was already in Landsberg, a friend of mine told me that a young girl was looking for me. She claimed to be a good friend of mine. Who could it be? Why was she specifically looking for me? Maybe she had some news for me about my loved ones. It certainly was somebody close to me or she would not have singled me out by name. I was terribly nervous and agitated. Was it about mother, Vera, or Minnie? In the next few minutes I would know something I had been waiting for all this time, but was afraid to face.

Nervously I rushed to the camp in search of that mysterious girl. After checking with a few people, I finally was told that she was waiting for me in the UNRRA office. I rushed to the office, and to my astonishment the girl was none but Haya Tarshiss, a school friend and a former neighbor of ours.

Haya looked extremely good. She had matured since I had last seen her, was tall and shapely, with her hair combed straight back. She was now much more beautiful than in the days we were in school together. I embraced her and invited her to come with me to my room. My room was quite plain, but for a D.P. camp it was rather elaborate. I had a bed, a sofa, a chair, a cabinet, a radio, and even a piano which I had appropriated from one of the halls in the block. The piano was an old beat-up instrument, but playable. When we walked in, I asked her to sit down. I pulled up the chair and put it across from her, so I could better observe her.

The conversation, as usual, centered on the ghetto, the concentration camp, a description of what had happened to us during those years of sorrow, and how each one survived. At first I told her a little bit about myself, and then waited for her to talk. She must have had something for me, since she had looked me up specifically by name. For a little while she was quiet, looking at me and trying to figure out what to say and how to start. She apparently was groping for words. To relieve her anxiety I began to ask her questions, giving her a chance to talk.

"Haya, were you liberated in the area of Danzig with some of the other women?" I asked.

"No, I was on the burning ship," came the terse reply.

"This is terrible, I can imagine what you have been through. So you also were in Stutthof and were evacuated from there at the end of April."

"Yes. This ship was the one which was bombed on May second by the British and caught fire on the open sea. I can hardly describe to you the panic on deck."

"I can imagine. But when did you get to Stutthof and with which transport? Were you in the first transport, or were you hauled from a hide-out like me?"

"No, I was in neither. I came to Stutthof in the first week of August, from Estonia."

This last word dropped like a bombshell. Estonia! So that was it. She must have news of Minnie. My head started to spin. Now I was the one who was stuck for words. The word Estonia was like a death sentence to me.

Haya saw my confusion but waited for me to make the first move. I got up from the chair and paced up and down the room.

"What was the camp like?" I asked. I was not yet ready to ask the cardinal question which so heavily weighed on my heart.

"Don't even ask. The winter in Estonia is worse than in Lithuania and we slept practically under the open sky. The barracks were paper thin and the wind howled through the canvas like hungry wolves. The work was in the field, building fortifications against the Russian offensive."

"Were all the women doing the same work?"

"Yes. And people were dying by the hundreds from frost, malnutrition, and mistreatment."

"So how did you make it?" I asked.

"I worked in the infirmary and was in a sort of privileged condition."

"I know there were two camps in Estonia. Which one were you in?"

"I was in Vaivara."

"When did you find out that you were being taken to Estonia and not for extermination?"

"At first when we left Kovno, we were sure that we were being taken to Auschwitz. But when we passed Siauliai, we knew that we were going in the opposite direction. Besides, on the train station in Siauliai, some Jews who were working there told us that we were being shipped either to Riga or to Estonia to join the Jews of ghetto Vilna who were brought there after the liquidation of the ghetto."

"This probably calmed you down a bit," I said.

"Yes, indeed. In Vaivara we found several thousand Jews from the Vilna area who told us about what a hell we were entering. By spring, more than 50% were already dead and people were dying every day. In the summer the big Russian offensive started, and at the end of July there was a very hasty evacuation. In fact, they did not manage to evacuate the second camp in Klooga and everyone there was shot. A few people escaped the execution and were later liberated by the Russians. The murderers piled the corpses on top of firewood, alternating layers of corpses with layers of wood, and were ready to put it on fire, but they were too late. The unlit bonfire was overrun by the Russians. In fact, I saw a picture of the huge pyramid of bodies and firewood the way it looked when the Russians caught it."

"So you were lucky that you were not in Klooga," I said.

"Yes, very lucky indeed."

I had heard enough, and it was getting late. Neither one of us had broached the subject of Minnie. Was she here only to tell me about Estonia? Impossible! She had to know something. I decided to open up.

"Haya, may I ask you a personal question?" I finally asked after a lengthy pause.

"Go ahead," she said.

"Did you ever meet in the camp in Estonia a girl by the name of Minnie Percikowitsch? I know she was in Estonia, but I don't know which camp."

Haya hesitated a few minutes and then said, "I was waiting for this, Vulia. I was wondering whether you had forgotten her and whether you would ask."

"Forgotten?! You must be kidding," I exclaimed, "she was my sweetheart in the ghetto. I can hardly tell you how much I loved her. She was not a girl, she was an angel." I had to stop for a minute. "Well, what do you know about her?"

"May I assume that this is the first you have heard about her?" Haya said.

"Yes, you are the first person I have met who was personally in Estonia. I have heard about the camps, but never about Minnie."

"Vulia, are you strong enough?" she asked.

This was a rather loaded question. I wondered what was coming.

"I guess I can take it. We are hardened enough by now."

"Vulia, she was with me in Vaivara. Would you like to hear all the details, even if it hurts?"

"Absolutely. Go right ahead."

Haya was now a little more confident. She had conditioned me for the worst and felt she could talk without restraint. But what followed was much more than I had ever anticipated. Just the first couple of statements were enough to send shivers down my spine. My head started to spin. Pictures of the not so distant past flashed past my eyes with blinding speed: the party, our evenings at the piano, the concert, her terrible nervousness and apprehension when she finally saw me come to the toy shop, when the Estonian Action was already underway. And finally, our parting at the workshop gate, when she decided to follow her parents, and my unforgiveable blunder in letting her go. Yes, and the admonition of my mother! Everything was getting mixed up in my mind. Reality and dreams past became indistinguishable. I thought I would faint.

Haya saw my confusion and stopped. A painful silence descended on the room.

"Vulia, do you want me to continue?"

"Yes, please," I replied.

Haya resumed her tale of horrors. But I was so upset and agitated, so shaken up, that had an earthquake hit the camp that very moment, I could not have reacted to it. Of Haya's entire narration I remember only that Minnie was sick and in and out of the hospital, where Haya took care of her. Haya also kept repeating how deeply in love Minnie was with me: she never stopped talking about me and always had my picture with her. This was the picture I had given her as a gift on my birthday, when we exchanged pictures. This picture she carried with her all the way to Stutthof, where she was forced to drop it in the showers, probably in the exact same spot where I had dropped hers a little over a year before.

"From Vaivara the survivors were taken to Stutthof," Haya continued. "During the first selection Minnie, who was by then already completely rundown, was picked out from the line-up . . ."

My petite, my sweet little Minnie! And I was not entirely free of blame. Had I only listened to my mother, had I only stopped her at the gate, had I. . ., had I. . . .

When Haya finished her tale, I stood petrified in the corner of the room and stared motionless at her. All the time after liberation I had feared what I might learn of Minnie's fate. I really didn't have any illusions. But when it came, I could hardly take it. The truth was worse than all my anticipation. An era had ended, and I had nobody to blame but myself.

Haya was stunned by my reaction. She knew it would hurt when she asked me whether I was strong enough. But this was more than she had anticipated. Haya had tears streaming down her cheeks and she could not go on. We stared at each other as if hoping that this all would turn out to be only a dream. Silence permeated the room. Neither of us was in the mood to continue the conversation. But when Haya went to leave, I stopped her.

"Haya, don't leave yet. When I look at you I see her, and I want to hold on to this image a little longer."

When Haya finally left, a terrible emptiness overcame me. Once more, one half of the couple had survived while the other had perished. Never would I see my Minnie again.

30

FINALE

It must have been the first week in September, close to the Jewish holidays, when a large group of Jews from Lithuania arrived in our D.P. camp. As usual I went to see who was among the arrivals. I found a large mob of Lithuanian Jews on the soccer field. Every Lithuanian Jew in the camp was there. They all were eager to meet the newcomers, particularly since this last group was the biggest yet to reach our camp in one transport. I mixed in with the crowd and tried to find some familiar faces. The first few people I met had no information. Then I met some people who were friends of our family, and their refusal to talk was ominous and suspicious. Were they reluctant to be the bearers of bad tidings? I got particularly angry at a friend of ours who played dumb. When I demanded of him to spill the news, even if it was bad, he swore that he really did not know.

That did it! If he did not know what had happened to my family, who did? As I turned around in complete despair, I noticed Dr. Ipp, who had been a close friend of Dr. Solc. He noticed me and waved me over. I pushed my way through the crowd, and after a lot of shoving, I finally reached him.

"Welcome, Dr. Ipp," I said and stretched out my hand to him, "I am glad to see you here. Did you come with this latest group of arrivals?"

"Yes, we came just about an hour ago."

"How long has it been since you left Lithuania?" I asked.

"I left Vilna about two weeks ago. I assume you know that your mother and sister are in Vilna."

I thought I would faint. His statement was so nonchalant, so matter-of-

369

fact, that I started to wonder whether he knew about whom he was talking.

He noticed my confusion, but did not understand it.

"Are you sure you are talking about my mother and sister?"

"You must be kidding. Of course I know your sister, the wife of Dr. Solc, one of my best friends. You mean to say that four months after liberation you still did not know that your mother and sister were alive?"

"No, I did not. You are the first to bring me the good news," and I grabbed him and embraced him with tears streaming down my cheeks.

I wanted to know everything he could tell me about them, but other than that they were in Vilna and fairly well established, I could get nothing out of him. Dozens of people from all sides were pulling him in every direction, simultaneously asking him about their families. He could barely move with all the people mobbing him.

I stood in the same spot, not daring to move. I was afraid that if I moved, the whole story might turn out to be a dream. Mother and Vera were alive! My God, how did they ever make it? How did Vera, the invalid, manage to go through all those strains and horrors? But there was no doubt. Dr. Ipp was no stranger, he knew them personally, and there was no reason to doubt.

In the evening, when things quieted down, I looked him up again and found out that Vera had a good job as a secretary in a government office and mother worked in a big business as a manager. They had a nice apartment in Vilna and they knew that I was alive. Whether they were waiting for me to come and join them or were planning to escape to the west, he did not know. Nobody dared to confide such information in anyone, not even a close friend.

This was exciting! This was unbelievable! This was like seeing somebody return from the dead. I could not sleep all night. I would lie down in bed, try to fall asleep, get up and pace up and down the room, then go back to bed, but sleep eluded me.

For a few days I was elated. Then new worries entered my life: what was I to do? If they were as well established as Dr. Ipp said, they would certainly not be willing to give it up easily, particularly after four such horrible years. They were settled with a home of their own, with good jobs, with food and clothing, things we had not seen during the entire war. To trade it now for a life in a D.P. camp was too much to ask. This meant I would have to drop everything and return to Lithuania if I ever wanted to see them. I was terribly distraught. Moving back to Lithuania was a hard choice for me. I consulted with a few friends of mine, some of whom said that I had no other choice but to return. Most, however, advised against it. I could not procrastinate too long if I seriously considered returning. Russia is Russia and one cannot return whenever one pleases. Waiting too long meant that upon return you would be questioned as to why it took you so long to come back to your fatherland. Apparently you were not sure of your decision. You might be an enemy of the state. The secret police would be keeping an eye on you as a possible security risk or even worse, a spy.

I was in this state of mind when a new transport of Lithuanian Jews arrived. I had lost my fear of finding out anything. I knew that they were alive. I was primarily interested in finding someone who knew what their intentions were. Again the search for friends in the crowd began. This group had come via the Jewish underground through Poland to West Berlin, and over Czechoslovakia to Munich, with the last stop in Landsberg.

"Mishelski," I suddenly heard somebody call me.

I turned around. It was a man whom I had helped in camp #2.

"I have regards for you from your mother and sister. They are in West Berlin and on their way to join you. They asked me to make sure to find you and to let you know about it, lest you decided to go back to Lithuania."

The man even had a group picture of Jews in the camp in West Berlin, and my mother and Vera were in it. I was overjoyed! Both looked healthy. I was suddenly a new man. A heavy load had come off my chest. My worries were over. They were on their way to join me! They had dropped everything: the jobs, the apartment, the friends, everything! And all this to get out of the land of our misfortune and to join me. A period of waiting set in until they arrived. But at least they were out from behind the iron curtain, away from the bloody soil of Lithuania which we loved so much in the past. Out of there, never to return.

In the meantime, I got involved with the UNRRA, the United Nations Relief and Rehabilitation Administration, and was in charge of a group of German trade school instructors working with the D.P.'s in the camp. One of them, Keindl, was a mechanic who lived not far from St. Ottilien. He used to commute to work on his motorcycle.

It was a beautiful autumn day when, one afternoon, I was called to the telephone at the local UNRRA office. On the line was a friend of mine from St. Ottilien: my mother and sister had just arrived there and wanted to see me! I had to sit down to catch my breath. Friends in the UNRRA office who had already heard about it rushed to congratulate me. Never in my life had I experienced such excitement and such a feeling. As soon as I calmed down a bit, I rushed to the German instructor Keindl and asked him to grab his motorcycle and take me to St. Ottilien at once. We mounted the motorcycle, he in front and I in the back, and we sped out of the camp.

"Rush!" I commanded him.

"Hold on to your seat," he shot back at me, and he stepped on the gas as if we were police pursuing a suspect.

The ride, which probably took fifteen minutes, felt like an eternity to me. Once in St. Ottilien, I quickly ran up to the friend from whom I had just heard about my family.

"Damn, that quick! How did you make it so fast?" he said to me when he saw me enter the room.

"Never mind, where are they?" I retorted impatiently.

"They are in Geltendorf, visiting Vera's friends. It is about one kilometer from here. Take the main road and it is the third house on the right."

I ran out as if chased by a hundred Nazis. I told Keindl to rush and off we went, leaving a trail of white smoke behind us. We sped along the unpaved road as fast as conditions permitted and in a few minutes we were in front of the house described by my friend. We parked the motorcycle along the road and I rushed into the house with Keindl following me. Mother did not expect me so soon, and when I entered the room she started to scream hysterically, "My Vulik, my Vulik, my dear, you are alive, you are alive!"

That was all she was able to say. She started to cry. We rushed into each other's arms and froze in an embrace.

"When I stood in the field, shoveling the gravel and filling the trucks, I was praying to God that He should watch over you and bring you back to me alive. My God, He heard my prayers, you survived, you are alive! You survived them, those bloody murderers!"

She repeated this last statement over and over again. All this time, Keindl, the German, stood in a corner, petrified before this overwhelming display of emotion. He knew what the word "them" meant, and whom the word "murderers" referred to. He knew what the Germans had done to us. He was now witness to an outburst resulting from their misdeeds.

Mother just did not want to let me out of her embrace. When she finally let me loose I asked her, "And where is Vera?"

"She is with her friend Miriam. She is on her way here. Our friends have already run over to get her."

"I am going out to meet her," I said.

I gave mother a kiss and walked out the door. When I turned the corner, I just could not believe my eyes. About three or four blocks away,

Vera and Miriam were on their way to meet us. Vera was walking! She was walking without the help of Miriam, normally, without a cane! How did this come about? How could she recover without medicine, without care, in a concentration camp? How could she have survived slave labor in her condition? But here it was. She was walking!

I rushed towards her and we fell into each other's arms.

"Vera, I cannot believe it, you are walking!" were my first words to her.

"Hard times demanded it, and you would not believe what tough demands can do to you," she replied.

Chatting back and forth, we reached the house where mother was waiting for us. Our friends prepared something warm to eat and we sat down to share our experiences. I sent Keindl back home and asked him to pick me up the next morning for work.

There was so much to tell and so much to share that weeks would not have been enough. After dinner, our friends departed and left us to spend the evening alone.

This was a memorable evening. We talked all night and barely got a few hours sleep. First they told me how they found out that I was alive. After liberation, 10 March 1945, in Chinow, they returned home to Lithuania. They hoped to find Max, but found the ghetto totally destroyed and the ghastly end of all who had remained in the hide-outs. The fate of our Jewish community in Kovno was crushing; they could not start a new life on the same soil. They decided to leave Kovno, to move to Vilna and try to settle there. At least the surroundings did not remind them of everything we had been through. And although Vilna had been a cemetery for its Jews, it was a new place for them. Mother and Vera, being fluent in Lithuanian, Russian, and German, had no difficulty finding good jobs. Through the connections on their respective jobs, they easily got an apartment and started to furnish it.

In the following months they waited to hear from the men, but when no information was forthcoming, they assumed that we had all been killed. They had written us off for dead. They began life on the assumption that they would never see me again. Towards the end of May, they had their initial surprise when the first male survivors showed up in Lithuania. From then on, they lived with hope. They watched every group that came back and anxiously inquired about me. Sometime in July, the information reached them that I had survived and was recovering in a sanatorium in St. Ottilien, somewhere in Bavaria. They were overjoyed, but, at the same time, this touched off a serious fight between mother and Vera. Mother wanted to drop everything to try to get out of Lithuania and join me. Vera, on the other hand, was not ready to do that. She was now settled, had a home, had a job, and was not going to risk losing all this again. She had suffered enough. She was not ready to start the life of a refugee all over again.

But mother insisted. Her Vulik was alive and nothing in the world could stop her. She threatened to go by herself if Vera decided to stay, and this was final. Vera had to make a decision. She, too, wanted to see me, but parting with what she had earned was a sacrifice. She could not see why I did not return to Lithuania. But to mother this did not make any difference. She could not be sure whether I knew they were alive, and parting with Lithuania after all we had been through there was the last thing she would ever regret. There was too much Jewish blood spilled on that soil. She would much rather have a new start somewhere else in the world, where Jews had not gone through the horrible experience of Nazism.

Mother's insistence finally won out, and they left everything. One day they vanished from Lithuania. In the dark of the night they started their journey to Bavaria. The route was through underground channels arranged by the Zionist organization. After a journey which lasted about a month, they finally arrived in St. Ottilien.

Now it was my turn to tell my tale, which I tried to make as short as possible. I left out many of the gruesome details to avoid upsetting my mother. After all, in the final analysis what counted was that I had survived. There was no need to burden her with details of murder and extermination which she had been through herself. After I finished my story, I wanted to know what they had been through in the camps and how they managed to survive.

"Vera," I asked her, "during all those long days and nights in Dachau, I never thought you, whom I left an invalid, barely able to walk, could ever survive. Mother, of course, would have gone with you. How did you ever make it?"

"Oh, God, that is a long story. Remember when we met you in Stutthof on the way to the showers?"

"Of course I do, we were just returning from the showers ourselves."

"Right. Well, when we left the hall with the mountain of shoes and eyeglasses, we were sure we were being taken to the gas chambers."

"So were we," I interrupted her.

"But when we met you alive, on the way back already, we realized that we were actually going to a bath and not to the gas chambers. On the plaza in front of the showers, all of us were told to sit down."

"Exactly as with us," I mixed in again.

"We were sitting next to Simon's wife. A German SS-man came out and told us that in fifteen minutes we would be going to the showers and we would be given other clothing. We were told to clean out the pockets and to leave all articles, particularly valuables, in front of us."

"Sounds familiar. Go on."

"People started to take gold and jewelry out of their pockets and began digging holes in the ground. They buried their gold in the hope that we would return to the same place, at which time they could get hold of their valuables. But listen to this. I was watching Simon's wife, and imagine! She pulled from her pockets the gold which we begged them to sell to us when my life depended on it. Those scoundrels! I just could not control myself. I admonished them: 'when I needed the gold to buy medicine to save my life, you said you could not get at it. Now you are burying it here in Stutthof. I am glad! Now you won't have it either.' And we took them into our home in the ghetto, when their area had to be cleared by the order of Goecke and they had no place to go!"

"You are talking about taking them in. I saved their lives. For months I was supplying them with additional rations in camp #2. You know what that meant in those terrible days. But I don't regret it. I could never live with it had I let them die, when I could help."

"You are right, Vulia. The fact that they acted as they did should not have affected your behaviour."

"But this still does not tell me how you survived," I said.

"The next day we had our first selection. All the sick, the invalids, and the elderly were taken out of the line-up and sent to the crematorium," Vera continued. "As you remember, I was already able to walk with some help for short stretches. But I looked very good and so did mother. Mother and Sonja helped me walk past the SS-man and he missed me. Dvora Solc, whose leg was already gangrenous, had been taken away on our arrival. She managed to tell me to remember the day and to let Max and her other sons know after the war when to say the prayers for her soul."

Vera had to stop here. It was terribly painful for her to continue. And Vera, certainly, was no softy. Mother, too, had to wipe her tears.

"She was a great lady. What a spirit! To the last minute, she believed in God and that He would shield her boys. The poor woman. May her soul rest in peace."

Another pause set in.

"A few days after that, a second selection took place. A group of women were taken to work, but the SS-man had enough before he had reached us. In the meantime, Dr. Kaplanaite, the surgeon, you remember her, managed to set up an infirmary for the women of our transport. I asked her to take me and mother out of the camp and into the infirmary. She knew my case from the ghetto and managed to do it. Meanwhile,

Sonja left with the next transport for a labor camp. Dr. Kaplanaite managed to keep me out for almost four weeks. But after this, she could not shield us any longer. During the next selection, when I passed the SS murderer, I told him I was sick and could not walk. He looked at me and saw a healthy-looking young woman in front of him. He told me, 'You either go with the group or you go with the smoke, you see that,' and he pointed to the stack and the smoke coming out of it from the crematorium. I left for work. Fortunately we only had to walk to the wagonettes, and somehow I managed. By the time we reached the camp I had rested and was again able to walk a little. The name of the camp was Sophienwald."

"It was fortunate that you had this little rest in between."

"Yes, indeed. A longer walk would have been impossible for me to manage. The next morning we lined up for roll call and were sent out to work. As we passed the camp commander, SS-Sturmfuehrer Schultz, I stepped out of the line-up and approached him. I told him briefly that I could work in the camp where I would not have to walk a lot, but I was unable to walk a longer distance since I had bad legs. If he wanted, he could send me straight back to Stutthof to the crematorium."

"That was one hell of a move. Where did you get the guts?" I asked.

"I had no choice. What should I have done? He looked at me and told me to step aside for a minute."

"He probably looked at you and thought of a typical German girl, blonde, blue-eyed, with rosy cheeks like a farmer's daughter, speaking perfect German. He probably forgot at the moment that you were Jewish," I kidded.

"Could very well be. When everybody was gone, he assigned me to the laundry. I spent six months there until the camp was liquidated. Every so often, he would come to the laundry to say hello to the 'little washwoman.' He even chatted and joked with me. I almost forgot he was an SS-man."

"You were lucky, but you deserve credit for having the guts to speak up. And what about mother?" I continued my query.

Mother started to tell her story, how for six months she worked in the field, loading trucks with gravel for ten hours a day under every weather condition.

"All this time I was praying," mother said, "that you were spared this kind of work. You could have never made it. It was terrible. With hardly any food, I never thought I would survive."

"So how did you make it?" I asked.

"Vera had access in the laundry to hot water. Behind the laundry room was the camp storage room for bread and potatoes. It had an access from the laundry. The Jewish women in the storage often needed hot water for a bath or to drink, or a favor to do some extra laundry. For this they gave Vera some bread or an occasional potato. Vera used to eat the bread she got from the girls and give me her ration and the potato. In the evening Vera would bring hot water, which we drank as if it were coffee. This was envigorating after a long day in the field in the cold. In addition we had this extra bread which helped us survive."

"Thank God, but go on," I said.

"In those six months," Vera continued, "the strength started to return to my legs. The fact that I was forced to walk on my own every day to the laundry and to stand on my feet to do the wash was the best therapy. With every week, I felt the strength returning, but it was a terribly slow process. By January, when the Russian offensive had begun, I was already able to walk substantially better than before. But when the order to evacuate came, I realized I could not manage a long death march. I went back to SS-Sturmfuehrer Schultz and explained to him that I could not manage to keep up with the march and he should send me back to Stutthof. 'You are crazy,' he said, 'do you want to end up in smoke? No way! You are coming along, and I will see to it that when you are tired, you will be allowed to sit down on one of the carts that will follow our march. You are coming along.' "

"That was decent of him," I said, "it reminds me of Otto Haug. I guess your Schultz must have been a fairminded fellow."

"I don't know. He was not so refined to the other girls in the camp, but he took a liking to me, maybe because of my Aryan looks."

"At least he was good to you," I said.

"Yes, he was. During the entire march, and we were on the way for almost two months, he watched over me and helped me. But I did not need much help. My legs had recovered sufficiently by then that I only needed help in the very beginning. We finally ended up in Chinow, where we were liberated by the Red Army."

"And what happened to Sonja and Ester?" I asked, "did you ever hear from them?"

"Sonja, I found out, died in one of the camps. She simply succumbed to the rigors of the slave labor routine and the hunger. I have not heard from Ester but I am sure she perished, probably in Stutthoff during the typhus epidemic. Nobody had seen her in any of the camps. And after we returned to Lithuania, she never came back."

"Terrible. Both were such fine girls, particularly Sonja. She was a real lady, refined, intelligent and compassionate."

"Yes," said mother, "Sonja was the nicest of the three girls. But what is the difference. None of them survived. The entire family perished: the parents in the town of Mariampole at the hands of Lithuanian partisans; Eddie, Sonja's husband, in Dvinsk in Latvia; Sonja's daughter in the laundry building together with Ruthie in the ghetto; and Rivka in the hide-out."

Again they had to stop talking. It was hard for them to recall all this. Then mother continued.

"Next, of course, we decided to return to Lithuania and see whether Max had survived. The news from the ghetto was ravaging. We then decided to move to Vilna. First we contacted Paplavski for help. Paplavski returned everything we had left with him and even offered us some money. 'When you have it, you will repay me. Don't worry,' he said. This gave us a start. We rented a small apartment but did not try to furnish it, since we did not intend to stay in Kovno."

"Did you try to get the piano back from Stasys Kairys?" I asked.

"Gosh, I almost forgot to tell you," said Vera. "One day we hired two workers to help us bring the piano, and we went to Kairys. He was not home, but his wife was. When she saw us, she almost had a heart attack. When we explained to her that we wanted our piano back, she did not object and the workers rolled the piano out. At that moment, Kairys returned home. 'What is this?' he screamed, 'who allowed you to move the piano?' When we told him that we wanted our piano back, he went into tantrums and started to swear. He ordered the workers to disappear and even threatened them. He then ran into the house and brought the slip of paper which we had signed that we had traded our piano for the vegetables in his garden and that the piano was his. We had no right to it. He would call the police, he said, and he would accuse us of robbery!"

"What a bastard! Our piano was worth several thousand dollars and his vegetables could be bought on the market for pennies. Yet he had the nerve to produce this slip of paper, which he himself had asked us to sign to protect him from losing the piano to the Germans, who were checking on Jewish property left behind in town."

"Yes. And if the case had come before court, he would have won, too. No Lithuanian judge would have dared to rule a case like this in favor of a Jew against a Lithuanian, particularly in the face of such overwhelming evidence as this slip of paper. We had no choice. We left him with the piano and let him go to hell."

"You are lucky," I said. "He could have beaten you up, too."

"And maybe even killed us. He was capable of it. Particularly after four years of Nazi rule, where killing Jews had become a sport."

"We still had a lot of clothing which we had left with Verute, our maid, but after the incident with the piano we decided not to bother," Vera continued.

"But with Verute you really did not have to worry. She was an ardent Catholic and a member of a Catholic order."

"Don't rush, listen," Vera continued. "Three days before we were scheduled to leave for Vilna, we walked on the main street of Kovno. Would you believe it, coming towards us was Verute. When she noticed us she crossed her heart and ran across the street, as if she had seen the devil. We let her run. The few pieces of clothing would not have made us any happier."

"This was our Verute," mother said, "a maid who had served us faithfully for many years and who was so dedicated and helpful in the first days of the war. Even she was not willing to part with the loot appropriated from us. This was Lithuania for you after the war. In Vilna we settled very quickly and things started to look up a bit. Then the good news came that you were alive, and two weeks later, believe it or not, guess who returned from Russia."

"From Russia?" I repeated. I looked at Vera and mother. They had big smiles on their faces.

"Well, what do you say? Guess! From Russia," Vera repeated.

"Not Hayim Solc?" I asked.

"How did you ever guess? Would you believe it. One day somebody rang the door bell and when I opened the door, there he was. I thought I would faint," Vera said.

"No, I cannot believe it," I exclaimed. "Hayim Solc!"

"Yes sir, Hayim Solc and his wife Nehama. They had managed to make it deep into Russia, when everybody else was caught and arrested on the roads and shot. There he was mobilized and fought the Germans all the way to Berlin, where he was released and sent home."

"I cannot believe it," I kept repeating. "Hayim and Nehama are alive."

"Yes, they are. Hayim, the one we least expected to survive, is alive. Both are the only survivors of their families."

"Do they plan to come here?" I asked.

"No, they have no intention of leaving Lithuania. They have decided to stay there. You see, they had not been through what we had in Lithuania and it was easier for them to adjust, even though they had lost their entire families there."

Our conversation now turned to other friends and survivors who were in Vilna. Mother mentioned some names of friends of mine, among them Lazik and Abraham, who were saved by Lithuanians, when mother suddenly asked me, "Did you ever hear anything from Minnie? Nobody in Vilna seems to know what happened to her."

Everything came back to me. "Mother, I will tell you all about her, but under one condition. Don't you dare to mention the words, 'You should have married her,' or 'I told you so.' I hope you understand me."

Mother and Vera saw already that things were bad. But they had no inkling how bad. With a trembling voice, with words sticking in my throat, I told them all I knew. When I finished my tale, there was profound silence. Nobody spoke. We were all choking, deep in thought. This was the end of the story. The three of us had survived the war, but each had a deep scar that would never completely heal. Mother had lost her husband, her grandchild, her son-in-law and her sister-in-law. Vera had lost her husband, her father, her daughter, her mother- and brothers-in-law. And I had lost my father, my brother-in-law, and Minnie, whom I would never see again. The Nazis and all the anti-Semites of the world had cause to rejoice. They had lost the war against the Allies, but they had won a tremendous victory over six million unarmed, innocent Jews, including such enemies of the state as my father, Max, Ruthie, and a sweet, adorable, loving girl named Minnie.

APPENDIX A: THE JAEGER REPORT

Einsatzkommando 3   Kovno, December 1, 1941
Secret State Document

Summary of all executions carried out in the sphere of action of
Einsatzkommando 3 up to December 1, 1941.

Einsatzkommando 3 took over its duties as security police in
Lithuania on the 2nd of July 1941.
(The area of Vilna was taken over by EK 3 on Aug. 9, 1941, and the
area of Šiauliai on Oct. 2, 1941; prior to the above dates Vilna was
processed by EK 9 and Šiauliai by EK 2.)
In compliance with my directives and on my order Lithuanian
partisans have carried out the following executions:

July 4	*Kovno, 7th fort*	416 Jewish men, 47 Jewish women	463
July 6	*Kovno, 7th fort*	Jewish men	2,514

After organizing a mobile unit under SS-Obersturmführer Hamann
and 8 to 10 tried men of EK 3 the following actions were carried out in co-
operation with Lithuanian partisans:

July 7	*Marijampole*	Jewish men	32
July 8	*Marijampole*	14 Jewish men, 5 Communist officials	19
July 8	*Girkalnis*	Communist officials	6
July 9	*Vandžiogala*	32 Jewish men, 2 Jewish women, 1 Lith. woman, 2 Lith. Comm., 1 Russian Communist	38
July 9	*Kovno, 7th fort*	21 Jewish men, 3 Jewish women	24
July 14	*Marijampole*	21 Jewish men, 1 Russ. & 9 Lith. Comm.	31
July 17	*Babtai*	8 Communist officials (6 Jews)	8
July 18	*Marijampole*	39 Jewish men, 14 Jewish women	53
July 19	*Kovno, 7th fort*	17 Jewish men, 2 Jewish women, 4 Lith. Comm., 2 Lith. women Comm., 1 German Comm.	26
July 21	*Panevezys*	59 Jewish men, 11 Jewish women, 1 Lith. woman, 1 Pole, 22 Lith. Comm., 9 Russ. Comm.	103
July 22	*Panevezys*	1 Jewish man	1

381

July 23	*Kedainiai* 83 Jewish men, 12 Jewish women, 14 Russian Comm., 1 Lith. Comm., 1 Russ. political instructor	125
July 25	*Marijampole* 90 Jewish men, 13 Jewish women	103
July 28	*Panevezys* 234 Jewish men, 15 Jewish women, 19 Russian Comm., 20 Lithuanian Communists	288
July 29	*Raseiniai* 254 Jewish men, 3 Lithuanian Communists	257
July 30	*Ariogala* 27 Jewish men, 11 Lithuanian Communists	38
July 31	*Utena* 235 Jewish men, 16 Jewish women, 4 Lith. Comm., 1 double murderer/robber	256
July 11 to 31	*Vandziogala* 13 Jewish men, 2 murderers	15

In August

Aug. 1	*Ukmerge* 254 Jewish men, 42 Jewish women, 1 Polish Comm., 2 Lith. NKVD agents, 1 mayor of Jonava who ordered Jonava to be burnt down	300
Aug. 2	*Kovno, 4th fort* 170 Jewish men, 1 US Jewish man, 1 US Jewish woman, 33 Jewish women, 4 Lith. Communists	209
Aug. 4	*Panevezys* 362 Jewish men, 41 Jewish women, 5 Russian Comm., 14 Lith. Communists	422
Aug. 5	*Raseiniai* 213 Jewish men, 66 Jewish women	279
Aug. 7	*Utena* 483 Jewish men, 87 Jewish women, 1 Lithuanian who plundered the remains of German soldiers	571
Aug. 8	*Ukmerge* 620 Jewish men, 82 Jewish women	702
Aug. 9	*Kovno, 4th fort* 484 Jewish men, 50 Jewish women	534
Aug. 11	*Panevezys* 450 Jewish men, 48 Jewish women, 1 Lith. & 1 Russian Comm.	500
Aug. 13	*Alytus* 617 Jewish men, 100 Jewish women, 1 criminal	719

Aug. 14	*Jonava* 497 Jewish men, 55 Jewish women	552
Aug. 15 to 16	*Rokiskis* 3,200 Jewish men, Jewish women & Jewish children, 5 Lith. Comm., 1 Pole, 1 partisan	3,207
Aug. 9 to 16	*Raseiniai* 294 Jewish women, 4 Jewish children	298
June 27 to Aug. 14	*Rokiskis* 493 Jewish men, 432 Russians, 56 Lithuanians (all active Communists)	981
Aug. 18	*Kovno, 4th fort* 698 Jewish men, 402 Jewish women, 1 Polish woman, 711 intellectual Jews from the ghetto as reprisal for an act of sabotage	1,812
Aug. 19	*Ukmerge* 298 Jewish men, 255 Jewish women, 1 political instructor, 88 Jewish children, 1 Russian Communist	645
Aug. 22	*Dvinsk* 3 Russ. Comm., 5 Latvians (incl. 1 murderer), 1 Russ. guardsman, 3 Poles, 3 gipsies, 1 gipsy woman, 1 gipsy child, 1 Jewish man, 1 Jewish woman, 1 Armenian, 2 political instructors (prison revision in Dvinsk)	21
Aug. 22	*Aglona* Lunatics: 269 men, 227 women, 48 children	544
Aug. 23	*Panevezys* 1,312 Jewish men, 4,602 Jewish women, 1,609 Jewish children	7,523
Aug. 18 to 22	*district of Raseiniai* 466 Jewish men, 440 Jewish women, 1,020 Jewish children	1,926
Aug. 25	*Obeliai* 112 Jewish men, 627 Jewish women, 421 Jewish children	1,160
Aug. 25 & 26	*Seduva* 230 Jewish men, 275 Jewish women, 159 Jewish children	664
Aug. 26	*Zarasai* 767 Jewish men, 1,113 Jewish women, 1 Lithuanian Comm., 687 Jewish children, 1 Russian woman Communist	2,569
Aug. 26	*Pasvalys* 402 Jewish men, 738 Jewish women, 209 Jewish children	1,349
Aug. 26	*Kaisiadorys* all Jews: men, women, & children	1,911
Aug. 27	*Prienai* all Jews: men, women, & children	1,078
Aug. 27	*Dagda & Kraslava* 212 Jewish men, 4 Russian POWs	216

Aug. 27	*Joniskis* 47 Jewish men, 165 Jewish women, 143 Jewish children	355
Aug. 28	*Vilkija* 76 Jewish men, 192 Jewish women, 134 Jewish children	402
Aug. 28	*Kedainiai* 710 Jewish men, 767 Jewish women, 599 Jewish children	2,076
Aug. 29	*Rumsiskis & Ziezmariai* 20 Jewish men, 567 Jewish women, 197 Jewish children	784
Aug. 29	*Utena & Moletai* 582 Jewish men, 1,731 Jewish women, 1,469 Jewish children	3,782
Aug. 13 to 31	*Alytus and vicinities* 233 Jewish men	233

In September

| Sept. 1 | *Marijampole* 1,763 Jewish men, 1,812 Jewish women, 1,404 Jewish children, 109 lunatics, 1 German woman who was married to a Jew, 1 Russian woman | 5,090 |

	Jewish Men	Jewish Women	Jewish Children	Total
Aug. 28 to Sept. 2				
Darsuniskis	10	69	20	99
Garliava	73	113	61	247
Jonava	112	1,200	244	1,556
Petrasiunai	30	72	23	125
Jieznas	26	72	46	144
Ariogala	207	260	195	662
Josvainiai	86	110	86	282
Babtai	20	41	22	83
Vandziogala	42	113	97	252
Krakes	448	476	201	1,125
Sept. 4				
Pravieniskes (agitation in labor camp)	247	6		253
Cekiske	22	64	60	146
Seredzius	6	61	126	193
Veliuona	2	71	86	159
Zapiskis	47	118	13	178
Sept. 5				
Ukmerge	1,123	1,849	1,737	4,709

Aug. 25 to
Sept. 6
Mopping up

in *Raseiniai*	16	412	415	843
in *Vilkaviskis*	all	all	all	412
Sept. 9 *Alytus*	287	640	352	1,279
Sept. 9 *Butrimonys*	67	370	303	740
Sept. 10 *Merkine*	223	355	276	854
Sept. 10 *Varena*	541	141	149	831
Sept. 11 *Leipalingis*	60	70	25	155
Sept. 11 *Seirijai*	229	384	340	953
Sept. 12 *Simnas*	68	197	149	414
Sept. 11 & 12 *Uzusaliai*				43

Punitive expedition against the population which gave provisions to
Russian partisans and some of which possessed weapons.

Sept. 26 *Kovno*, 4th fort	412	615	581	1,608

These children were sick and epidemic.

In October

Oct. 2	*Zagare* 633 Jewish men, 1,107 Jewish women, 496 Jewish children (the Jews rebelled but were crushed at once: 150 Jews were killed on the spot, 7 partisans were wounded)	2,236
Oct. 4	*Kovno, 9th fort* 315 Jewish men, 712 Jewish women, 818 Jewish children (punitive action because a German policeman was shot at in the ghetto)	1,845
Oct. 29	*Kovno, 9th fort* 2,007 Jewish men, 2,920 Jewish women, 4,273 Jewish children (removal from the ghetto of surplus Jews)	9,200

In November

Nov. 3	*Lazdijai* 485 Jewish men, 511 Jewish women, 539 Jewish children	1,535

Nov. 15	*Vilkaviskis* 36 Jewish men, 48 Jewish women, 31 Jewish children	115
Nov. 25	*Kovno, 9th fort* 1,159 Jewish men, 1,600 Jewish women, 175 Jewish children (displaced from Berlin, Munich and Frankfurt A.M.)	2,934
Nov. 29	*Kovno, 9th fort* 693 Jewish men, 1,115 Jewish women, 152 Jewish children (displaced from Vienna and Breslau)	2,000
Nov. 29	*Kovno, 9th fort* 17 Jewish men, 1 Jewish woman who had violated the ghetto regulations, 1 German who had embraced the Judaic religion and had attended a school for rabbins, and 15 terrorists of the Kalinin gang	34

A section of EK 3 in Dvinsk

July 13 to Aug. 21	*Dvinsk* 9,012 Jewish men, women and children, 573 active Communists	9,585

A section of EK 3 in Vilna

Aug. 12 to Sept. 1	*Vilna* 425 Jewish men, 19 Jewish women, 8 Communists, 9 women Communists	461
Sept. 2	*Vilna* 864 Jewish men, 2,019 Jewish women, 817 Jewish children (punitive action because German soldiers had been shot at by Jews)	3,700

	Jewish Men	Jewish Women	Jewish Children	Total
Sept. 12 *Vilna*	993	1,670	771	3,334
Sept. 17 *Vilna*	337	687	247	
and 4 Lithuan. Comm.				1,271
Sept. 20 *Nemencine*	128	176	99	403
Sept. 22 *Naujoji Vilnia*	468	495	196	1,159
Sept. 24 *Riese*	512	744	511	1,767
Sept. 25 *Jasiunai*	215	229	131	575
Sept. 27 *Eisiskes*	909	1,636	821	3,446
Sept. 30 *Trakai*	366	483	597	1,446
Oct. 4 *Vilna*	432	1,115	436	1,983

Oct. 6
Semeliskes	213	359	390	962

Oct. 9
Svencionys	1,169	1,840	717	3,726
Oct. 16 *Vilna*	382	507	257	1,146
Oct. 21 *Vilna*	718	1,063	586	2,367
Oct. 25 *Vilna*	—	1,766	812	2,578
Oct. 27 *Vilna*	946	184	73	1,203
Oct. 30 *Vilna*	382	789	362	1,533
Nov. 6 *Vilna*	340	749	252	1,341
Nov. 19 *Vilna*	76	77	18	171
Nov. 19 *Vilna*	6 POWs, 8 Poles			14
Nov. 20 *Vilna*	3 POWs			3
Nov. 25 *Vilna*	9	46	8	

and 1 Pole for possession of arms and other war material   64

A section of EK 3 in Minsk

Sept. 28 to Oct. 17
Pleshtshenitsa, Bicholin, Shatsk, Bober, Usda
620 Jewish men, 1,285 Jewish women, 1,126 Jewish
children, and 10 Communists   3,050
                                                    133,346

Before the EK 3 assumed security duties, the
partisans themselves killed Jews through pogroms and
executions   4,000
                                                    137,346

I can state today that the goal of solving the Jewish problem in Lithuania has been reached by EK 3. There are no Jews in Lithuania anymore except the work-Jews and their families, which total

in Siauliai   some 4,500
in Kovno   some 15,000
in Vilna   some 15,000.

I intended to kill off these work-Jews and their families too, but met with the strongest protest from the civil administration (Reich Commissar) and the Wehrmacht, which culminated in the prohibition: these Jews and their families may not be shot dead!

The goal to clear Lithuania of Jews could be achieved only thanks to the setting up of a flying squad of tried men under SS-Obersturmführer Hamann who adopted my goal without any reservations and managed to secure the co-operation of the Lithuanian partisans and the respective civil offices.

The carrying out of such actions is first of all a problem of adequate organization. The decision to systematically clear each district of Jews required a thorough preparation of each action and an excellent knowledge of the conditions prevailing in the district chosen. The Jews had to be collected at one or at several collecting points. Their number required us to select an adequate place for the trenches, which had also to be dug out. The road of approach from the collecting points to the trenches averaged from 4 to 5 kilometers. The Jews were driven to the place of execution in batches of 500, the distance between the batches being no less than 2 kilometers. The difficulties and the trying work met with during these actions is best illustrated by the following example chosen at random:

In Rokiskis one had to drive 3,208 people 4.5 kilometers before they could be executed. In order to complete the work in 24 hours one had to detach for driving or guarding more than 60 men from the 80 Lithuanian partisans available. The rest, which had to be relieved every now and then, did the work together with my men. One must bear in mind that lorries are available but seldom. Escapes, which happened now and then, were foiled exclusively by my men at the peril of their lives. For instance 3 men of the commando have shot dead all 38 Jews and Communist officials who tried to escape on a woodpath near Marijampole. The distance we had to cover while approaching the place of execution and then returning from it in the course of each action totalled from 160 to 200 kilometers. Only clever timing helped us to carry out 5 actions a week, and to do at the same time the current job in Kovno without endangering the routine service.

The actions in Kovno itself, where a sufficient number of trained partisans was available, can be described as parade shooting, especially if compared with actions in the country where the greatest difficulties had to be overcome time and again.

All commanders and men of my commando in Kovno took part in the large-scale actions in Kovno most actively. Only one Habitual Criminals' Registry official was set free from taking part in the actions because of ill health.

I consider the Jewish actions to be finished for EK 3 in the main. The working Jewish men and Jewish women left alive for the time being are badly needed, and I presume that when winter is over this Jewish labor force will be still needed badly. I am of the opinion that it is imperative to start at once with the sterilization of the male work-Jews to prevent propagation. If in spite of the measures taken a Jewish woman happens to become pregnant she is to be liquidated.

Alongside with the Jewish actions one of the chief tasks of the EK 3 was the revision of mostly overcrowded prisons in the various localities and towns. In each district town the number of Lithuanians imprisoned without the slightest legal grounds averaged 600. They had been arrested by partisans only on a simple denunciation or the like which served to square accounts. Nobody had ever taken the trouble to inquire into their cases. One ought to have visited the prisons and to have stayed for a moment in the overcrowded cells which beggar any description in sanitary respects. For instance at Jonava—which is typical of many—16 men were imprisoned for five weeks in a dark cellar 3 meters long, 3 meters wide and 1.65 meters high. And all these 16 men could be set free for one could not impute anything to them. Girls aged 13 to 16 have been imprisoned solely on the grounds that they had joined the Communist Youth organization to be able to get any work. In this matter one had to resort to drastic measures to drum a clear-cut direction into the heads of appropriate Lithuanian authorities. The prisoners were lined up in the prison yard and checked according to lists and documents in the case. Those who had been imprisoned for minor offenses without sufficient grounds were ordered to line up in a separate group. Those whom we sentenced to 1, to 3, and 6 months' imprisonment were lined up in another group. A third group was constituted of prisoners to be liquidated as criminals, Communist officials, political instructors and other rabble. In addition to the adjudged penalty some prisoners, first of all Communist officials, were lashed on the spot from 10 to 40 times according to the gravity of their offenses. After the check-up the prisoners were returned to the cells. Those who were to be set free marched in procession to the market square where after a short address they were set free in the presence of numerous local people. The address read as follows (it was translated on the spot into Lithuanian and Russian):

"Had we been Bolshevists we would have shot you dead but as we are Germans we set you at liberty."

Then followed an admonition to abstain from all political activity whatsoever, to report without any delay to German officers the least instance of a resistance movement they happened to get to know about, and to take an active part in the rehabilitation of the country, especially by working in agriculture. But if any one of them should commit another offense, he would be shot. Then they were set free.

It is well-nigh impossible to imagine the joy, gratitude, and enthusiasm which this measure of ours caused each time among the prisoners set free and the population at large. One had to use sharp words more often than not to drive off the grateful women, children, and men who with tears of joy in their eyes tried to kiss our hands and feet.

(signed) *Jaeger*
SS-Standartenfuehrer

APPENDIX B: CHRONOLOGY
Historical Notes

1128	First documented Jewish community in Lithuania, in the town of Grodno (Gardinas).
1280	First Jews settle in Kovno (Kaunas).
1386–1387	Lithuania becomes Christian. Anti-Semitism appears.
1386–1430	Grand Duke Vytautas the Great rules Lithuania and gives Jews many privileges.
1495	Lithuania expels its Jews and confiscates their possessions.
1503	The Jews are invited back to Lithuania.
1648–1649	Pogroms in Russia, but Jews in Lithuania are safe.
1881–1882	Pogroms in Russia, but Jews in Lithuania are safe.
1905–1906	Pogroms in Russia, but Jews in Lithuania are safe.
28 July 1914	World War I breaks out and Russia enters the war against Germany.
April, May 1915	Decree issued by the Czarist government, forcing Jews to evacuate into the deep Ukraine.
1918	Jews return home to Lithuania, and the Lithuanian Council of Ministers (Taryba) invites the Jews to participate.
16 February 1918	Lithuania proclaims independence.
1919–1922	Jews enjoy full autonomy in Lithuania. This is the golden age of Lithuanian Jews.
February 1923	All Jewish language signs in stores and institutions are marred with black tar.
December 1926	Antanas Smetona and the nationalist party take over the government by military coup.
30 January 1933	Hitler comes to power in Germany.
September 1939	Germany attacks Poland and World War II is on. The first Jewish refugees arrive in Lithuania.
14 June 1940	The Russian army occupies Lithuania.
22 July 1940	Lithuania is proclaimed a Soviet Republic.
15 June 1941	Deportations of so-called unreliable elements to Siberia are carried out by the Soviet government.
22 June 1941	Germany attacks Russia.

War Chronology

1941

1 June	Ruthie, daughter of Max and Vera, is born.
22 June	Germany attacks Russia.
24 June	My father is hauled off by Lithuanian partisans to an unknown destination.
24 June (night)	First German troops enter Kovno (Kaunas).
25 June	Random mass arrests of Jews begin.
25–26 June (night)	Massive pogrom in Slobotke. Over 1000 Jews are massacred by Lithuanian partisans and students.
26 June	I am arrested by a group of Lithuanian partisans.
27 June	I am released by the same partisan who arrested me.
27 June	Massacre in the garage of Lietukis, where 60 Jews are tortured to death by a Lithuanian mob.
2 July–1 December	137,346 Jews are killed in Lithuania, as reported by SS Standartenfuehrer Jaeger of Einsatzkommando 3 on December 1, 1941.
4–6 July	Three thousand Jews are killed in a mass execution at the Seventh Fort, among them my father.
9–10 July	Massacre of Jews in Dvinsk (Duenaburg), Latvia, among them hundreds of fleeing Lithuanian Jews, including Eddie Glazer, Sonja's husband.
10 July	Orders issued from the German High Command: from 12 July all Jews must wear a yellow star of David on their chests, both front and back; all Jews must move into a ghetto; Jews who fled to Russia are forbidden to return to their homes.
7–8 August	One thousand Jews are arrested and shot at the Fourth Fort.
15 August	The ghetto is closed off from the outer world.
18 August	Intellectuals Action. Over 500 Jewish intellectuals, tricked by promises of clean, intelligent work in the city, are taken to the Fourth Fort and shot.
19 August–4 September	House searches and confiscations accompanied by shootings and murderous beatings.

4–6 September	Gold Action. All gold and jewelry is confiscated from the ghetto under the threat that for every valuable found, 100 Jews would be shot.
8 September	Slave labor begins at aerodrome.
16 September	Life certificates, also called Jordan passes, issued.
17 September, morning	Test Action in the Small Ghetto staged for motion picture crews.
17 September, evening	Aeltestenrat ransacked by mob demanding Jordan passes for their families.
19 September	I meet Peter. The graphics department is born.
26 September	Malicious accusation against the ghetto. One thousand Jews shot at the Ninth Fort.
4 October	Small Ghetto Action. Two thousand Jews massacred at the Ninth Fort.
October, second week	Vegetable gardens raided by hungerstricken Jews of the ghetto.
28 October	The Big Action. In the largest single extermination of Lithuanian Jews, 10,000 Jews are shot at the Ninth Fort.
16 November– mid-December	Tens of thousands of German, Austrian, and French Jews are massacred at the Ninth Fort.
7 December	Pearl Harbor.
December, second week	The ghetto population, tormented by the most severe winter on record, raids all fences for firewood.
27 December	Fur Action. All furs are confiscated.

1942

12 January	Big Ghetto workshops start operation.
13 January	In −30 degree Celsius an order is issued to clear a large area of the ghetto within three hours. The evacuated Jews move into the already overcrowded remaining ghetto.
January, third week	Toy workshop inaugurated.
January, end of month	Dr. Gerber shot by a Lithuanian partisan for not tipping his hat.
6 February	First Riga Action. Five hundred Jews sent from Kovno to Riga for slave labor.

18 February	Book Action.
1 May	Ghetto boundaries reduced. Congestion worsens.
7 May	Termination of all pregnancies ordered.
July, second week	First concert of the ghetto orchestra.
26 August	All synagogues and schools ordered closed.
20–22 October	Second Riga Action. Four hundred more Jews sent to Riga for slave labor.
8 November	Allied forces land in North Africa.
18 November	Mek is executed by hanging.
19 November	Russian offensive at Stalingrad begins.

1943

4 February	Stalingrad Action. Fifty Jews murdered at the Ninth Fort in retaliation for the German defeat at Stalingrad.
30 March	Five thousand Jews from ghetto Vilna massacred in Ponar (Paneriai).
19 April	Warsaw ghetto uprising starts.
16 May	Last resistance in Warsaw ghetto ends.
September, first week	The SS takes over the ghetto under the command of Obersturmbannfuehrer Wilhelm Goecke.
29 September	On Rosh-Hashanah, the Jewish New Year, the liquidation of the Vilna ghetto begins.
8 October	Yom Kippur in the ghetto. In a major speech, we are warned that the liquidation of the ghetto is near.
26 October	The Estonian Action. Three thousand Jews are deported to Estonia, to the notorious extermination camps in Vaivara and Klooga. Among the deported is my sweetheart, Minnie.
1 November	Transformation of the ghetto into a concentration camp begins.
November, first week	Work to exhume and burn approximately 80,000 corpses at the Ninth Fort begins.
5 November	Children's Action in ghetto Siauliai, in northern Lithuania, destroys 800 children and older people.
November, first week	Goecke informs Dr. Elkes that Old Slobotke will have to be cleared in December.

November, second week	We build our first hide-out in the graphics department.
November, third week	Vera gets sick.
27 November	Order issued to clear the Small Blocks, also called Block B.
November, last week	Vera is paralyzed.
22 December	Final clearing of Old Slobotke creates unbearable congestion in ghetto.
26 December	Spectacular escape of Jews from the Ninth Fort.

1944

27–28 March	The Children's Action. Two thousand children, elderly, and sick are destroyed.
4 April	The Aeltestenrat is arrested and the ghetto institutions are liquidated.
May, first week	Ruthie is carried out of the ghetto.
6 June	The Allies' second front opens in Normandy.
20 June	Ruthie is brought back to the ghetto.
22 June	The Russian offensive at Vitebsk begins.
6 July	Goecke informs Dr. Elkes that the ghetto will be evacuated to Germany.
7 July	We get ready to enter our hide-out.
8 July	Deportations begin.
10–11 July	Massive house searches continue for hidden Jews.
12 July	Our hide-out in the graphics department is discovered.
13 July	We are marched to the railroad depot. The ghetto is burning. Ruthie and the other children perish in the flames.
13–16 July	Final liquidation of ghetto Kovno. Max, Nolik, Rivka, the Chazans, and hundreds more Jews perish.
14 July	Our train leaves for Germany.
15 July, noon	We arrive in Stutthof.
15 July, evening	We are chased to the showers. Most of us believe that this is really the gas chambers.

16 July	Mother, Vera, and the rest of the women are led to the showers.
20 July	Assassination attempt on Hitler.
24 July	We leave Stutthof.
27 July	Arrival in Kaufering and Dachau camp #2.
July, third week	First selection of women in Stutthof. First group of healthy women sent to labor camps.
July, last week	Camps in Estonia are being liquidated. Inmates of Vaivara, including Minnie, are sent to Stutthof. Inmates of Klooga are massacred.
1 August	The Red Army enters Kovno. A handful of Jews is liberated in two massive bunkers.
17 October	Dr. Elkes dies in Dachau, camp #1.
December, second week	Liquidation of Dachau, camp #2, is speeded up. Nahum is sent to Leitmeritz in Czechoslovakia.

1945

8 January	Camp #2 is closed and we leave for camp #7.
12 January	Big Russian offensive starts on the eastern front.
13 January	A major typhus epidemic is diagnosed in camp #7, and we are quarantined.
23 January	First group of women is liberated between Thorn and Bromberg in Eastern Prussia.
10 March	A few surviving women are liberated in Chinow, East Prussia by the Red Army. Among them are my mother and Vera.
April, first week	Camp #7 is liquidated and we are transferred to camp #1.
24 April	Order from Dachau to liquidate all the camps in the area, including camp #1.
27 April	I join the evacuation from camp #1. Our train is bombed in Schwabhausen.
27 April, evening	We arrive in Dachau proper.
29 April	American troops liberate Dachau, including a small remnant of Lithuanian Jews, among them me.
April, last week	Stutthof is liquidated. A remnant of women who survived the typhus epidemic are evacuated.

1 May	Part of death march liberated near Buchberg by American troops.
2 May	Last group of Jews on the death march from the Dachau camps is liberated.
2 May	A ship which left Stutthof with a small number of Jewish women aboard is bombed by the British in the open sea.
2 May, evening	The burning ship is towed into the harbor of Kiel, where the women find out that they are in the hands of the British and are free.
September, first week	I find out that my mother and my sister have survived.
September, fourth week	I am reunited with mother and Vera.
28 October	A service is held in the D.P. camp in Landsberg to commemorate the day in 1941 when 10,000 Jews were slaughtered at the Ninth Fort.

I have tried to authenticate all dates, but on some dates I had to depend on my memory, since they are either strictly personal or connected with events which are not significant enough to appear in general literature. Errors, if any, are minor and do not detract from the authenticity of the events connected with them.

APPENDIX C. LOCATIONS

Bad Toelz	Bavarian town where second group of death marchers was liberated by the American army, 2 May 1945.
Buchberg	Bavarian town where first group of death marchers was liberated by the American army, 1 May 1945.
Bromberg	East Prussian town where the first group of Jewish women from work camps near Stutthof was liberated by the Red Army, 23 January 1945.
Chinow	East Prussian town where my mother, my sister, and my future wife, among others, were liberated by the Red Army, 10 March 1945.
Dachau	One of the first concentration camps in Germany, located near Munich.
Dachau, camps 1, 2, 7	Slave labor camps connected with Dachau, where I spent almost one year, and where thousands of inmates died from exhaustion, starvation, frost, and epidemics.
Dvinsk (Duenaburg, Daugavpils)	Latvian town near the Russian border where thousands of Lithuanian and other Jews were slaughtered, including Eddie Glazer, Sonja's husband.
Forts 4, 7, 9	Fortifications of World War I, where over 100,000 Jews from Kovno and Western Europe were slaughtered, including my father.
Kovno (Kaunas)	My hometown, where one of Lithuania's three ghettoes was located.
Kaufering	Our first stop on the way from Stutthof to Dachau.
Kiel	West German town into whose harbor a burning ship carrying women survivors from Stutthof was towed, and where these women were liberated.
Klooga	Slave labor camp in Estonia where thousands of Jews from Kovno were exterminated.
Landsberg	Bavarian town near Dachau.
Mariampole	Lithuanian town where Sonja, Ester, Rivka and their family came from. Here virtually all the Jews were massacred in the first weeks of the war.
Panevezys	Northern Lithuanian town where a concentration camp was planned but never established.
Ponar (Paneriai)	Extermination site for the Jews of Vilna. Here over 70,000 Jews were slaughtered.

Riga   Capital of Latvia, where hundreds of Jews from Kovno died in slave labor.

Schwabhausen   Bavarian town where our train was bombed two days before liberation.

Siauliai   Lithuanian town where one of the country's three ghettoes was located.

Slobotke   Old Jewish suburb of Kovno.

Stalingrad   Site of a critical battle in World War II. The German army's failure to take Stalingrad cost ghetto Kovno over 50 lives.

St. Ottilien   A Bavarian monastery converted to a sanatorium, where I recovered after the war.

Stutthof   A concentration camp in East Prussia, near Danzig. Thousands of Jewish women died here, among them Sonja, her sister Ester, and my sweetheart, Minnie.

Thorn   East Prussian town near which a group of Jewish women was liberated, 23 January 1945.

Vaivara   Slave labor camp in Estonia to which several thousand Jews from Kovno were deported. Most of them died from hard labor and disease. Minnie was among the deportees to this camp.

Vilna   Capital of Lithuania and home of the country's largest
(Vilnius)   ghetto. Most of the Jews of Vilna were exterminated at Ponar.

Vitebsk   Russian town where the offensive began which liberated Kovno.

Williampole   Suburb of Kovno that included the Jewish suburb of Slobotke.